M000232066

EAS`

How to Live, Retire, Work and Buy Property in Belize, the
English Speaking, Frost Free Paradise on the Caribbean Coast

By Lan Sluder

COPYRIGHT

EASY BELIZE How to Live, Retire, Work and Buy Property in Belize, the English Speaking, Frost Free Paradise on the Caribbean Coast.

By Lan Sluder

ISBN-13: 978-0692616062
ISBN-10: 0692616063
Published by Equator, Asheville, NC.
First Edition originally published in 2010.
Revised, fully updated and expanded Second Edition, 2016.

Photographs by Rose Lambert-Sluder, except where noted.

Cover: Belize Barrier Reef seen from Azul Resort on North Ambergris Caye. Photo by Rose Lambert-Sluder.

E-mail: lansluder@gmail.com
Website: www.belizefirst.com

Notice: This work does not purport to give legal, medical, tax or other professional advice. Seek competent professional counsel and perform due diligence before acting on information contained herein.

Table of Contents

Bay of Chetumal as seen from the village of Sarteneja

ABOUT THIS BOOK

EASY BELIZE How to Live, Retire, Work and Buy Property in Belize, the English Speaking, Frost Free Paradise on the Caribbean Coast by Lan Sluder, the **fully updated, revised and expanded Second Edition for 2016,** is the complete guide for anyone considering relocating or retiring to Belize, and for anyone thinking of buying property or building a home in Belize. In more than 40 chapters and appendixes totaling some 170,000 words, with dozens of photographs and maps, it covers everything you need to know: What things cost in Belize, how to find the best deals on real estate, health care in Belize, safety and security, options for residency and how to stretch your dollars in Belize. While it is primarily a guide for those thinking about retiring, relocating or buying property in Belize, and not a tourism guide, it also includes comprehensive information on hotels, restaurants and what to do and see in Belize. For even more detailed information on visiting Belize on a vacation, please also see the current edition of *Fodor's Belize* or the forthcoming *All the Best in Belize*, both by Lan Sluder.

Easy Belize provides detailed information on all the major areas of Belize, whether inland or on the coast and cayes: Corozal Town and Corozal District, the islands of Belize including Ambergris Caye (San Pedro) and Caye Caulker and the small offshore cayes, Belmopan City, San Ignacio/Santa Elena and Benque Viejo in Cayo District, Dangriga, Hopkins and Placencia in Stann Creek District and the Punta Gorda and Maya villages areas in Toledo District.

This Second Edition of *Easy Belize* is fully updated, revised and greatly expanded for 2016. It is the only truly complete guide to living in Belize.

Author Lan Sluder has been banging around Belize since 1991 and has written more books about Belize than any other living author. He has explored every nook and cranny of the country. Besides *Easy Belize*, Sluder is the author of more than a dozen books on Belize, including *Fodor's Belize, San Pedro Cool, Adapter Kit Belize, Belize Islands Guide, Belize First Guide to Mainland Belize* and *Living Abroad in Belize*. He is the founder, publisher and editor of *Belize First*, now an on-line magazine at www.belizefirst.com and has contributed articles on Belize to magazines and newspapers all over the world.

Lan Sluder also is the author of a number of other books on travel and retirement, including *Amazing Asheville, Frommer's Beach Vacations, Moving to the Mountains, Fodor's InFocus: Great Smoky Mountains National Park* and *Asheville Relocation, Retirement and Visitor Guide*. In addition, he has written a book for novice bridge players, *Play Bridge Today*, and one on purchasing a vintage Rolls-Royce or Bentley motorcar, *Buy a Classic Rolls-Royce or Bentley*.

View of the Belize Barrier Reef from North Ambergris

WHY CHOOSE BELIZE?

Over the years, I've interviewed, talked with or heard from via e-mail and letters hundreds, perhaps thousands, of people who have moved to Belize or who plan to do so, and I've asked them this question: "Why did you choose Belize?" I've gotten many answers, but these are the most common:

"I like speaking English." You don't have to learn a new language to live in Belize, because English is the official language. You don't have to struggle with grammar and syntax in an unfamiliar tongue. While Spanish and several other languages are widely spoken in Belize, and many Belizeans are bi- or trilingual, everything from street signs and newspapers to official government documents are in English. From your first day in Belize, you can shop, dine, chat and gossip without having to thumb through a dictionary or cast about for the right verb ending.

"I love the warm, sunny climate." It never frosts or snows in

7

Belize. The climate ranges from sub-tropical to tropical, similar to that of South Florida. As long as you're comfortable with warm to hot temperatures, perhaps tempered by cooling breezes from the sea, you'll like Belize weather. As a bonus, you'll never have to pay for heating oil or natural gas again.

"I feel welcome here." Belize is not a Never-Never Land where everyone loves everybody in perfect harmony, but the fact is, by and large, Belizeans are as friendly a bunch of people as you'll ever find. Belizeans take people one at a time. Whether you're black, white, brown or green, short, fat, ugly or beautiful, rich or poor, you'll find acceptance in Belize. Your neighbors will say hello to you on the street, check on you if you're sick and share a joke with you over a Belikin at the bar. And they may try to hit you up for a loan! For the most part, Belizeans genuinely like Americans (and Canadians and Europeans). At the official level, the Belize government welcomes retirees and others, especially if they bring some resources to the country. The Qualified Retired Persons Incentive Program *(see below)* is administered not by a bureaucratic immigration department but by the Belize Tourism Board, which generally provides approvals within three months.

"I enjoy the lifestyle here, doing things outdoors and on the water." Belize offers relatively little in the way of cultural activities — museums, art galleries, theatre, the arts. But it makes up for it with a wealth of options for those who love the outdoors. You can garden year-round. The saltwater fishing is some of the best in the world. Boating, diving, swimming and snorkeling can be as close as your back yard. For the more adventurous, there are caves and ancient ruins to explore, rivers to canoe and mountains to hike.

"I can live better here for less money than where I came from." Belize is not the cheapest place to live, and in some areas of Belize an American lifestyle will cost U.S. prices or higher. Overall, however, expats in Belize say they can live larger than back home, enjoying some luxuries such as a housekeeper or meals out. Investment income, pensions and Social Security checks seem to stretch a little farther in Belize. While some items such as gasoline, imported foods and electricity cost more in Belize, other things including medical care, housing, insurance and household help are significantly cheaper in Belize than in the U.S., Canada or Western Europe. Although Belize has a few half million dollar

8

houses and condos, you can rent a small house for US$250-$500 a month, set up a made-in-Belize Mennonite cabin for US$20,000, build an attractive new home for US$75,000 to $175,000 and buy a waterfront lot for as little as US$75,000 to $100,000, although you can pay much more.

"I thought I could never afford to live on the beach ... but I can in Belize." If you've seen the prices for beachfront lots in Florida, South Carolina, Massachusetts, Washington or California – often m a n y hundreds of thousands, even millions of dollars – you know that oceanfront living in the U.S. is out of the question for most people. In Belize, beachfront lots aren't as cheap as they used to be, or as cheap as they still are in places like Nicaragua, but you can still buy a buildable lot on the Caribbean for US$75,000 to $100,000. Lots a row or two back from the sea start at US$25,000 to $50,000. And you can put a storm-resistant concrete house on the lot for US$40 to $150 a square foot. So, with a little patience and planning for around US$150,000 to US$250,000, you can own a small new home on or near the water.

"I appreciate the fact that Belize has a stable, democratic government." You don't have to worry about a coup in Belize. Politics in Belize is highly personal and can be rough and tumble, even dirty, but Belizeans take their democracy seriously. The voter turnout in recent national elections was around 75%. Along with Costa Rica, Belize has the most stable political system in the region.

"I'm glad I escaped from America's consumer society." In Belize, you won't find Starbucks, McDonald's or Walmart. Global franchise businesses are almost unknown. That can be frustrating when you're trying to find a cheap home appliance or a quick meal, but on the plus side you don't need to spend your life accumulating stuff.

"I like living on Belize time." Like many sub-tropical and tropical countries, Belize offers a slower way of life than the frenetic pace of life in many more developed countries. If you don't get it done today, there's always tomorrow. Slow down. Be cool. Don't make your blood boil. "I'll be here at 7:30 Monday morning" really means, "I'll try to get there early Monday, but if I decide to go fishing I'll be there sometime Tuesday." Not everyone can adjust to this way of living, but for those who do it has a lot of appeal.

"I feel healthier here." As I discuss in detail later in this book,

Belize does not have the high-tech, state-of-the-art medical care available in the U.S. or even in countries like Costa Rica or Panama. But the Belizean lifestyle can be very healthful. You eat fresh fruit and unprocessed food. You walk more and ride less. You stay outside in the clean, unpolluted air rather than being cooped up in a climate-controlled box all day. You go home for lunch or take a nap at mid-day. In Belize's balmy climate, your arthritis and other aches and pains may fade away. Many people who move to Belize start feeling better within a few weeks. Quite a few lose weight. Blood pressure levels go down. Of course, you can also live an unhealthy life in Belize — watching cable TV all day, drinking all night and eating fried foods and lardy beans and rice.

"I like the people of Belize." If you're a people person, you can't help liking Belizeans. Belizeans come in every shape, background and color, but nearly all are open and friendly. They love to have fun, and there's always an excuse for a party or a celebration. Of course, sometimes Belizeans can be a little too friendly, and if you're not careful you can lend up lending your neighbors, and their families, money that you may never see again. Expats in Belize are also an interesting bunch, usually with an independent streak and sometimes downright eccentric.

"There's always something to do or see here." If you're bored in Belize, it's your own fault. Belize is a natural wonder. You could spend the rest of your life just learning about the flora and fauna of the country. Belize is home to thousands of species of trees and flowers, hundreds of kinds of birds and butterflies. The culture of Belize is wide and deep. The history of the Maya in Belize goes back thousands of years. Modern Belize was settled by Scots and Brits and by slaves and ex-slaves from Jamaica and elsewhere in the Caribbean. Garifuna came to Belize in the early 1800s; immigrants from neighboring Latin American countries have trickled in over the past several hundred years, in increasing numbers since the 1980s; East Indians moved to Belize in the 19th and early 20th centuries; Mennonites came here in the 1950s; most recently, Chinese from Taiwan and mainland China, along with expats and snowbirds from the U.S., Canada and Europe have made Belize home. Every group in Belize has a fascinating history to explore. When you tire of intellectual pursuits, you can take trips to the enchanting corners of the country, to the high hills of the Mountain Pine Ridge, to the endless caves of the Chiquibul wilderness, to the lush rainforest of Toledo, to the many

islands in the Caribbean Sea and to the 190-mile long Belize Barrier Reef.

"I like the wide open spaces of Belize." With around 368,000 people in an area the size of the state of Massachusetts (population almost 7 million), Belize is one of the least densely populated countries in the Western Hemisphere. Outside the cities and towns, you can often drive for miles without seeing another human being. In that regard, Belize is like a little, subtropical Alaska. Or like Florida 75 to 100 years ago.

"I don't have to worry about losing my property here." Property rights are protected in Belize through the traditions of English Common Law. In some countries, if you leave your house or land unoccupied, squatters can move in, and it's almost impossible to get them out. Legal documents may be written in a language you don't understand. Powerful local interests can take your property through tricky legal — or illegal — means. In many parts of Latin America and Europe, the legal system is Civil Law based on the Napoleonic Code, very different from the system in the United States. But Belize shares with America, Canada and the United Kingdom a legal system based on English Common Law. In Belize, private property is respected and protected. Foreigners can own property virtually anywhere in Belize, with exactly the same rights and protections as exist for Belizeans. Squatters cannot take your property. The Belize legal system isn't perfect, and lawyers in Belize are almost as costly as those in the U.S., but it's a far better system than, for example, in Honduras.

"The U.S. dollar is accepted everywhere in Belize." Belize has its own currency, the Belize dollar, so technically the American greenback is not the official monetary unit of the country. As a practical matter, though, the U.S. dollar is accepted anywhere and everywhere in Belize, and the Belize dollar has been pegged for decades at the rate of 2 Belize to 1 U.S. dollar (though the rate may vary slightly if you exchange with money changers.) Anything of substantial value, such as real estate and hotel room rates, is priced in U.S. dollars. This means that prices in Belize are more stable for American dollar holders than they would be if the Belizean currency floated against the dollar. It also means that in periods when the value of the U.S. dollar declines sharply against the euro, yen and many other hard currencies, prices in Belize remained about the same as always for Americans. Of course, during periods of appreciation of the value of the U.S. dollar, prices in Belize do not become

cheaper for U.S. dollar holders.

What Some Do NOT Like About Belize

I've also talked with many people who came to Belize and decided not to stay, or who were unhappy with their life in Belize but couldn't afford to leave. Here are their major gripes and complaints. Keep in mind that some people who are unhappy in Belize would be just as unhappy where they came from. You can move to a new place, but you can't run away from yourself.

"We can't get anybody to do anything here." If you're expecting a Minnesota-style work ethic in Belize, everything prompt and efficient, you're in for a surprise. People have their own ways of doing things and their own time frame for doing them. In remote areas, many Belizeans have never held a regular job. Belizeans have their own methods of work, sometimes developed over hundreds of years. It may take them longer to finish, but they'll get it done. Eventually. Also, decades of "brain drain" with more than 100,000 of the most ambitious Belizeans moving to the U.S. in search of better jobs means that you may run into folks who are a little less motivated or skilled.

"We're tired of getting ripped off." One of the most common subjects of cocktail party conversation among expats in Belize is how to protect their homes and property from petty theft. Tiefin' (as it's said in Creole) is unfortunately common in Belize, as it is in many poor, developing countries. Leave a tool or a bicycle out overnight, and it may be gone the next day. Leave your house unattended for a week or two, and you may come back to a home stripped of everything of value. You have to acclimate yourself to an environment where petty theft is going to happen, and you have to protect your possessions. Hire a dependable caretaker, put up a fence around your property and get a big black dog.

"Things cost more than we thought they would." Belize is a small, inefficient marketplace. Little is manufactured locally, shops are mostly small mom 'n pop places and shipping costs to Belize are expensive. Import duties are high. All this adds up to an economy where most anything imported is likely to cost more than where it was produced: automobiles, wine, cement, cornflakes, books, shoes. Hotel rates and restaurant prices, especially at the upper end, have increased by ridiculous amounts in the past decade. If you come to Belize thinking

everything across the board will be cheaper than back home, you'll be sorely disappointed. To duplicate a Scottsdale lifestyle in Belize, down to the Jack Black in the liquor cabinet, the Carrier turned to frigid and a big SUV in the drive, you'll spend a lot more than in Arizona. To live in Belize on the cheap, you have to live like a Belizean — eat rice and beans, take the bus, go the local clinic for health care. You can move up a bit from the Belizean lifestyle without paying a ton of money, but you have to buy wisely: Dump the dishwasher, use the ceiling fan instead of the A/C, drink rum instead of American whiskey, eat the healthful local foods — cheese, brown eggs and watermelons from Mennonite farms, mangoes and oranges off your backyard trees and tortillas from the corner *taqueria*.

"We hate the telephone company." Few other facts of life in Belize cause more grouching and griping than telcom service. Belize Telemedia Ltd. no longer enjoys a complete legal monopoly in Belize, as Smart Telcom, aka Speednet, has a major part of the mobile phone and cellular internet market, but BTL still controls much of the telephone and internet service in Belize. Unlike some of its U.S. counterparts, it's still a moneymaking machine. Long-distance and internet costs in Belize are higher than in more competitive markets, and internet speeds are comparatively low. BTL's service really isn't bad, and most of BTL's infrastructure is modern, but for those, especially in business, who depend on telephone and email, the high cost of BTL is a real thorn in the side.

"Belizean politicians are corrupt." Belize isn't Mexico. Petty bribery is fairly rare, though hardly unknown. The average Belizean official wants respect, not a few bucks. But corruption certainly exists in Belize, especially at the higher levels of government. The Old Boy network is alive and well in Belize, too. It's accepted, even expected, that senior government officials will do favors for their cronies and family, everything from awarding lucrative contracts for cruise ship shore excursions to selling prime land at bargain basement prices. Not every government official takes advantage of office, but too many do. Some expats in Belize get sick and tired of this aspect of Belize reality (especially since most are non-citizens they benefit not at all from the political corruption.)

"We can't make any money here." If you want to go into business and make a lot of money, do it in the U.S. America is still the land of opportunity for the entrepreneur, with a huge, wealthy market for

any product or service you can imagine. By contrast, the entire country of Belize has the buying power of a small town of 30,000 or 40,000 people in the U.S. There are some opportunities in tourism and agriculture, but the scale is small – for example, Myrtle Beach, S.C., gets 60 or 70 times as many tourists as does the whole country of Belize. As the saying goes, if you want to make a small fortune in Belize, come here with a big fortune. Belize has some very successful homegrown business people, and some expats have built successful businesses in Belize, but it's not an easy country in which to get rich. Best advice: Make your bucks before you come to Belize.

"We don't have the juice and connections we had back home." When you move to Belize, you lose the network of contacts – personal, business and political – you used to have. Unless you become a Belizean citizen, you can't vote in national elections and, in any case, you don't have the political connections that many Belizeans have built up over the course of their lifetimes. In short, nobody cares what you think about local matters. You're not so much at the bottom rung of the ladder as not even close to the ladder.

Fruit stand near Belmopan – pineapples US$1

WHAT YOU NEED TO KNOW: BELIZE A TO Z

I'm not going to bore you with a long narrative on Belize history, or provide a laundry list of trivia about the country. If you want to know more about Belize's past, present and future, (and much of it is fascinating) *see the Recommended Reading section in the Appendix of this book.*

Here are basic facts to get you up to speed on Belize, listed alphabetically:

Acclimatization: How long does it take the typical expat to acclimatize to Belize? The answer varies from immediately to never. In terms of the weather, it usually takes new residents about six months to a year to get used to the warm, humid subtropical climate, assuming they didn't come from a similar climate. Belize is superficially similar to the U.S. in many ways – from the use of English in official documents to the same standards of measurement – miles, feet, gallons and ounces rather than kilometers, meters, liters and milliliters. You drive on the right and cable TV offers HBO, CNN and other U.S. channels. But, below the surface, the differences are more subtle and significant *(see Getting Along in Belize chapter below.)*

Bargaining: In general, prices in Belize stores are fixed, and there is no bargaining. At street markets, you may do some light bargaining, but haggling is not a way of life in Belize as it is some other parts of the world. Hotels and other tourist services may offer discounts – it never hurts to ask. Of course, when buying real estate or other big-ticket items such as a vehicle, bargaining is the order of the day in Belize as most everywhere.

Business Hours: Most businesses open around 8 a.m. and close at 5 or 6 p.m. on weekdays. Some smaller shops close for lunch, usually from 1 to 2 p.m. Many stores are open on Saturday, or at least on Saturday mornings. On Sundays, many stores and other businesses are closed, except in tourist areas like San Pedro. Banks typically now have longer hours than in the past, usually open until 3 p.m. or later Monday to Thursday and until 4 or 5 on Friday.

Capital: Belmopan, a small town (now technically a city) of around 20,000 people in the central part of the country, is Belize's capital and home to many government offices. The capital was moved from Belize City following the terrific destruction and loss of life caused by Hurricane Hattie in 1961. However, while Belmopan is growing fast, Belize City remains the cultural, social and commercial hub of the country, and many government offices remain in Belize's only sizeable city.

Cell Phones: Belize Telemedia Ltd. offers DigiCell, a digital service on the GSM dual band 850/1900 Mhz technology, including 4G. See www.digicell.bz for more information. BTL has more than 50 cell towers around Belize with good coverage in most urbanized areas. As with cell phone service nearly everywhere, cell plans in Belize are complex and change frequently. Currently BTL offers a basic DigiCell package for US$25 a month that includes 250 anytime minutes and text messages. The Premium Platinum plan is US$125 a month with 2,000 minutes a month, plus unlimited texts nights and weekends. You can also purchase pre-paid cell service at a higher minute rate – US30 cents per minute for the first 5 minutes, then US12 ½ cents per minute; pre-paid text messages are US12.5 cents each. BTL also offers a CDMA-based service in some areas. A BTL 4G cellular internet plan with download speeds of *up to* 1 megabyte for instant messaging, web surfing, sending emails and social networking costs around US$25 to $50 per month. The above plans do *not* include a phone.

A non-Belize resident wishing to sign up for regular BTL/DigiCell service must have a valid passport and offer proof that he or she plans to stay in Belize for the next 12 months. A deposit may also be required.

Short-term visitors to Belize can buy a SIM card for any unlocked GSM 1900 cell phone for US$25, which includes US$5 of air time at per-minute rates for pre-paid cellular *(see above)*, or rent a DigiCell phone from BTL for US$5 a day (not including outgoing call usage). With a pre-paid phone card, international calls are around BZ 65 cents a minute during the day and BZ 50 cents a minute off-peak (9 p.m. to 6 a.m.). Domestic outgoing calls within Belize are BZ 60 cents per minute for the first 5 minutes, then BZ 25 cents per minute for the rest of the call; pre-paid text messages are BZ 25 cents each.

Smart, also known as Speednet (www.smart-bz.com), is another digital cell service that began operating in 2005. It's on the CDMA system only, not GSM. It has monthly voice, text and cellular internet plans from US$15 to US$375 a month. The US$15-a-month Flex Jr. plan has a deposit of about US$34 and provides 125 domestic minutes and 750 SMS texts. Excess minutes cost about 28 US cents. The top-end US$375-a-month Enterprise plan includes 4,500 domestic minutes plus 200 SMS texts and 15 gigs of monthly data. This plan requires a deposit of nearly US850. All charges shown are plus 12.5% GST. International calls are extra. Short-term visitors can also get CDMA phone set up with Smart for a fee similar to BTL's so you can use it in Belize with a Belize number. *See also Internet and Telephone entries below.*

Churches and Religion: Although Belize was a British colony, the Catholic Church, not the Anglican Church, is dominant in Belize. About 40% of Belizeans are at least nominally Catholic, while nearly 9% of Belizeans belong to Pentecostal Protestant churches. Anglicans represent about 6% of the population. Other religious groups in Belize include Methodist, Church of Christ, Mennonite, Presbyterian, Jehovah's Witnesses, Assembly of God and Seventh Day Adventist. Belize has one small Muslim mosque. There is no temple, but Jews meet in local homes in Belize City.

Climate: Most of Belize has a sub-tropical climate similar to that of South Florida. Frost-free Belize usually enjoys lows in the 60s to 70s, with highs in the 80s to low 90s. More rain falls as you go south, with average annual rainfall in Corozal Town in the north being about 50 inches, similar to Atlanta, Georgia, but increasing to 160 inches or more in the far south. Generally the rainiest months are June through October, with the driest months being February through April. January sees the coolest temperatures of the year, while May has the hottest. In general, daytime temps are higher inland, due to the influence of prevailing winds from the sea on the cayes and coast. The humidity is high year round in all parts of the country.

Drugs: Despite its reputation as a source of marijuana and, more recently, as a transshipment point for cocaine and other drugs from South America, Belize has strict laws on the use of illegal drugs, with prison terms and fines for offenders. Quite a few Belizeans smoke marijuana, some fairly openly, but it is still illegal. Unfortunately, crack, heroin, meth and other hard drugs are a fact of life in Belize, as they are in many countries. Much of the crime in Belize City and in other parts of the country is related to drugs.

Economy: The country of Belize **Gross Domestic Product** in 2014 was estimated at US$1.7 billion, or around US$4,900 per capita. On a Purchasing Power Parity basis, the Belize GDP in 2014 was US$3 billion and the per-capita GDP US$8,200. The PPP method involves the use of standardized international dollar price weights, which are applied to the quantities of final goods and services produced in a given economy. This method may be better for estimating economic power when comparing countries.

By comparison, U.S. GDP in 2014 was US$17.4 trillion, and per-capita GDP in the U.S. in 2014 was US$54,600. Thus, per-capita GDP in Belize is less than 10% of that in the U.S. Belize's GDP growth averaged nearly 4% annually between 1999 and 2007 but fell to 0% in 2009 and stayed low through the international recession. However, in 2014, GDP grew by 3.4%, about 1 percentage point higher than the U.S. in the same year.

Average income figures in Belize mask a huge income disparity between rich and poor. About 40% of the Belize population is below the poverty line.

Although the estimated population of Belize is now nearing 370,000, the entire Belize national economy is about the size of the economy of a U.S. town of around 30,000 to 40,000 people.

Tourism and agriculture/marine products are the two

major industries, each representing about one-fifth of GDP. In terms of foreign currency earnings, tourism is number one. Due to recent growth, tourism is now the largest segment of the economy in most years. Ambergris Caye, Cayo and Placencia are the major areas developed for tourism, with Hopkins and Caye Caulker also having significant tourism development. Belize got about 321,000 international overnight visitors in 2014, a record, with more than 60% coming from the U.S. About 239,000 of the overnight visitor count arrived by air at Philip S.W. Goldson International Airport in Ladyville near Belize City, and most of the rest by land through Mexico or Guatemala. These figures do not include nearly a million (938,000 in 2014) day visitors on cruise ships, which mostly call on Belize City, coming in on tenders as large ships can't dock at the Belize City port. In February or March 2016, despite construction delays, some cruise ships are supposed to begin calling on the US$100 million **Norwegian Cruise Lines port** at Harvest Caye near Placencia village. How this will impact tourism and daily life in southern Belize is as yet unclear.

The main **agricultural crops** are sugar cane, citrus, cacao, marine products, timber and bananas. Aquaculture, mainly shrimp and tilapia fish farming, has seen some growth in recent years.

Belize has a **labor force** of around 121,000. The official unemployment rate in 2014 was about 12.9%, but in many rural areas of Belize it is much higher. Even so, there is a shortage of skilled workers in some areas.

Inflation in Belize has been low to moderate in recent years. It was 4.5% in 2007 but increased to over 6% in 2008, before dropping to just 0.5% in 2013 and 0.9% in 2014. The government runs a budget deficit most years. The deficit was 3% of GDP in 2014. External debt was about US$1.25 billion in 2014. That is high given the small size of the Belizean economy, but relatively speaking it is better that the debt to GDP ratio of the U.S. In 2006, the government reached agreement with most international creditors to restructure its external debt, issuing new bonds at lower interest rates. Belize again renegotiated its external debt in 2013.

Concerns include a fairly large public debt relative to government income and GDP and a balance-of-trade deficit approach US$300 million a year.

Key Economic Numbers:

(Figures are the latest available, in most cases for 2014):

GDP: US$1.7 billion
GDP Per Capita: US$4,900
GDP Growth: 3.4%
Inflation Rate: 0.9%
Unemployment Rate: 12.9%

Education: Belize's educational system traditionally was based on the English system, where students move through forms, from first form in primary school to sixth form (a sort of post-high school final grade), although now many Belize schools, following U.S. and Caribbean Community practices, use the grade system -- grades K-12. The Catholic Church, through an agreement with the government, operates many of Belize's public schools. About 35% of Belize's population is under age 15, so in every part of Belize you'll see school kids in their khaki, blue or other school uniforms. In Belize City and elsewhere, there are both Catholic and government-run high schools. A few private or parochial schools run by Protestant denominations also exist. The best schools are in Belize City and in larger towns, and many of the worst schools -- with untrained teachers and few books or equipment -- are in the far south.

More than 100,000 students are enrolled in Belize schools at all levels, including 7,500 in preschools, 70,000 in primary schools, and more than 20,000 in high schools. Close to 5,000 students are in post-secondary schools called junior colleges in Belize. Belize has more than 5,000 teachers at all school levels. Around 6,000 students attend the University of Belize and other universities and community colleges in the country.

Primary education is free and compulsory through age 14. However, a sizable minority of Belizean children does not complete primary school. Only about six in 10 of teachers are professionally trained, but the number is growing. Even teachers with four-year college degrees earn around US$1,000 or less per month. Secondary education, consisting of a four-year high school, is competitive, requiring passage of a comprehensive exam. The student's percentile ranking on the admissions test in part determines which school the student can attend. Charges for books and fees at secondary schools, while small by U.S. standards, are beyond the reach of many Belizean families.

The typical tuition and fees for public schools in Belize is around US$25 per month. The Belize government pays this tuition if the student is a child of a citizen or permanent resident and cannot afford the fee.

About 87% of primary school students do go on to secondary schools, though many do not graduate.

Some expats choose to do home schooling. Private schools are available in a few areas. The Island Academy, a primary school for Beginners through Standard 6 (Grade 8) on Ambergris Caye, as an example, charges around US$3,250 a year per student. This school has an excellent reputation. Belize Elementary School in Belize City is one of the best private elementary schools on the mainland. Saint Catherine Academy for girls, St. John's High School for boys and Belize High School, all in Belize City, are recognized as among the best high schools in the country. St. John's in Belize City has educated many of Belize's leaders.

Junior colleges, such as St. John's College Junior College in Belize City, Muffles Junior College near Orange Walk Town, Independence Junior College in Independence (Stann Creek District) and Corozal Junior College in Corozal Town, offer post-high training. In some ways, these junior colleges aren't like two-year colleges in the U.S., some comparing more with the junior and senior years of high school in the U.S.

Until the 1990s, Belize did not have a true four-year university system. However, in 2000, provisions were made for the development of the **University of Belize,** which combined five existing Belize educational facilities.

UB now has campuses in Belmopan, Belize City, Toledo and Cayo. UB offers associate, bachelor degrees, along with one master's degree in biodiversity management and sustainable development in cooperation with universities in Jamaica, Suriname, Guyana and Trinidad and Tobago. The faculty includes a couple of dozen professors with PhD or other tertiary degrees, along with around 80 instructors with master's degrees. The University of Belize has around 4,000 students in about 50 different programs.

A small private college, **Galen University,** is in Cayo District near San Ignacio. It offers bachelor degrees plus master's degrees in four disciplines, including an MBA. In 2014, Galen opened a new campus center in Punta Gorda and offers BA degrees there. The **University of the West Indies** offers extension courses in Belize and works with the University of Belize on its master's degree.

In addition, there are several offshore medical schools in Belize. The

21

best-known, **Central America Health Sciences University Belize Medical College** (www.cahsu.edu), founded in 1996, has a campus near Belize City. Another offshore med school, one that has been controversial at times, is **American Global University School of Medicine** (www.agusm.org). It is in Ladyville near Belize City. **Washington University of Health and Science** (www.wuhs.org) is in San Pedro. These offshore med schools typically are run on a for-profit basis. They accept foreign students who cannot get into med schools in the U.S. or other home country. Most place students in medical rotations in association with hospitals in the U.S., Mexico and elsewhere.

Here is a sampling of education costs in Belize. All figures are in US dollars:

Primary School

Public schools (often run by the Catholic Church): Free except for uniforms, books and fees, which average US$20-$25 a month.

Island Academy, San Pedro -- private school: US$3,375+ a year.

High School

Saint Catherine's Academy, Belize City: US$4,500 a year (tuition and fees).

Mount Carmel High School, Benque Viejo: US$5,450 a year (tuition and fees.

Four-Year College

University of Belize, Belmopan and Belize City: US$1,350 (undergraduate tuition for 30 credit hours) per year for Belizean citizens and permanent residents; US$2,700 for students from developing countries; US$4,050 for students from developed countries such as the U.S.; all plus fees (around US$200 a year) and room and board.

Offshore Medical School

Central America Health Sciences University Belize Medical Colleges charges a US$2,200 "matriculation fee" for new students, then US$8,000 per trimester (US$24,000 a year) for the basic sciences program in Belize and US$9,500 per trimester in the U.S.; monthly expenses for books, food and housing in Belize are estimated at US$700 to $1,000.

Will Your Kids Adapt to Belize?

Belize is a country of young people, so your kids will probably have a lot of friends. Belizeans love kids, and kids are welcome almost everywhere. It's rare to find a restaurant or any other business that doesn't allow kids. In many respects, most of Belize is the way the U.S. was in the 1950s or earlier: Kids play outside all the time, walk or ride bikes to the store or school and hang out with friends. There are very few "soccer moms" in Belize spending their days driving their offspring here and there.

Whether your kids adapt well to Belize, or not, depends on what expectations they -- and you -- have. If their lives have revolved around going to the mall, seeing movies every weekend and eating fast food, they're probably facing a serious adaptation problem, as there are no malls or chain fast-food places in Belize, and only a couple of movie theaters in the country. On the other hand, if they like to be outdoors, and especially if they enjoy activities on the water (no place in Belize is more than a few miles from the sea, a lagoon or bay, or a river) they'll be in heaven.

Young kids do have to be watched, as they may not know the dangers from scorpions, snakes, Africanized bees and other wild creatures. In Belize City, in some neighborhoods, kids are in danger from gangs and drugs. Finding toys, children's books and children's clothes may be a challenge in Belize, especially in rural areas. Libraries are few and far between, and none is large.

Schooling obviously is an issue for expats with children. Schools vary widely in quality of teachers, equipment, and facilities. In rural Toledo, your local school may have few textbooks, no library and perhaps not even electricity or running water. In Belize City, the best schools are quite good indeed, and motivated students will be well prepared for a rigorous college. Most Belizean schools do teach religion as part of their daily curriculum, and that may be an issue for some families. Some expats home school their kids.

Electricity: 110 volts AC/60 cycles, same as in the U.S., and outlets are like those in the U.S. and Canada. However, electricity is at least twice as expensive in Belize as in the U.S. Rates vary slightly by amount of kilowatt hours used, but most residential users pay round 24 U.S. cents per kilowatt-hour. Service is provided by Belize Electricity Ltd. (www.bel.com.bz), with rates regulated by the Belize Public Utilities Commission. New service requires a US$100 connection charge, plus a US$50 deposit in most cases. Commercial and industrial rates and deposits are different from residential rates.

Embassies: The U.S. Embassy in Belize moved from Belize City to Floral Park Road in Belmopan in 2006. The new embassy is a compound constructed at a cost of US$50 million. In 2005, George W. Bush picked Rob Dieter, Bush's former roommate at Yale, as the new ambassador to Belize. Dieter was a professor at the University of Colorado law school. He went to law school at the University of Denver and before that roomed for four years with W as an undergraduate at Yale. President Barrack Obama also picked a former college roommate at Occidental College, Vinai Thummalapally, an Indian-American businessman from Colorado Springs, Colo., as his ambassador. The current U.S. ambassador to Belize, appointed by President Obama in 2014, is Carlos R. Moreno, a retired judge on the California Supreme Court who was once considered as a possible candidate for a U.S. Supreme Court vacancy. He is the son of Mexican immigrants to the U.S.

The embassy's telephone number is 501-822-4011, fax 501-822-4012 and the web site is www.belize.usembassy.gov. The U.K., Mexico, Guatemala, Costa Rica, Taiwan and about a dozen other countries have ambassadors, consuls or other representatives either in Belize City or Belmopan. Canada only has an honorary consul in Belize City; its Guatemala embassy in Guatemala City handles Belize affairs.

Family Life: With so many different ethnic groups in Belize, you can't generalize about family life. However, as in many countries, Belize faces social problems relating to the disintegration of traditional family life. Especially in Belize City and other urbanized areas, a large percentage of babies are born out of wedlock and the traditional nuclear family is becoming less the norm.

Government: Formerly a British colony, and known as British Honduras from 1862 to 1973, Belize became independent from Britain in 1981. It is now a democratic member of the British Commonwealth, with a Westminster-style government system with a prime minister, an elected house of representatives and an appointed senate. The current prime minister is Dean Barrow, a Jamaica- and U.S.-educated lawyer. He heads the United Democratic Party (UDP), which swept national elections in 2008 and retained control of the government in March 2012 elections. The opposition party is the People's United Party (PUP). Both parties are generally centrist. The "George Washington of Belize" was George Cadle Price, an ascetic Creole who helped found the PUP and was Belize's first prime minister. George Price died in 2011. Politics in Belize is a freewheeling affair and often intensely personal. Belize has strong ties

24

with the United States and Britain, but it also has cultivated ties with Taiwan, Cuba, Venezuela, Jamaica, Japan, Mexico and other countries, often out of the need to seek foreign aid or development funding.

History: The human history of Belize can be divided into four broad periods: the ancient Maya period, the Spanish conquest, the British colonial period and modern Belize.

The **ancient Maya,** whose ancestors likely came originally from Asia, settled in what is now Mexico at least 2,000 years before the birth of Christ. The Maya civilization was influenced by and grew out of the Olmec culture farther north. The Maya migrated to what is now Belize about 3,000 years ago. During the height of the Maya empire, called the Classic Period, roughly 300 BC to 900 (CE, or if you prefer, AD), the area that is now Belize had a civilization that included large-scale agriculture, sizeable cities of up to several hundred thousand people, formalized religion and a sophisticated knowledge of architecture, art, science and mathematics. As many as a million people lived in Belize during the late Classic period, compared to less than one-third that number today. Caracol likely was the largest city-state in Belize, with a population perhaps several times larger than that of Belize City today. Then, rather quickly, in a matter of at most a few hundred years, most of the great Maya cities were depopulated and the Maya civilization went into decline. There are many theories as to why this happened, among them that there was a change in weather patterns that disrupted agricultural, that epidemic diseases swept the region, or that social changes – perhaps revolutions – transformed the society. It could have been a combination of reasons. Whatever the reasons, by around 1000 CE most of the major cities in Belize had been at least partially abandoned, though a few settlements, such as Lamanai in northern Belize, lasted for many more centuries.

The **Spanish Conquest** of Mexico and Central America began in the first quarter of the 16th Century. Spanish troops and missionaries destroyed much of what was left of the Maya civilization, including burning nearly all of the Maya books they found. Soldiers killed many, and the European diseases they brought such as smallpox killed even more. Belize offered little to the Spanish in the way of gold or other riches, so Spain never paid much attention to it.

By the early 17th century, Belize drew the attention of a motley

25

group of **British loggers and adventurers.** The original Brits in Belize sought logwood, a valuable hardwood used to make dyes. These Brits also did a little buccaneering on the side. One of the most fearsome was Edward Teach, called Blackbeard for his huge black beard. According to legend, Blackbeard used Ambergris Caye for his hideout, continuing to terrorize ships of all nations, until he was finally killed off the coast of North Carolina. By around 1700, several hundred British loggers and hangers-on had settled around the mouth of the Belize River, near the bay of what is now Belize City. The Brits were known as Baymen. British logging settlements grew over the course of the next 100 years or so. The loggers imported slaves from Jamaica to help cut logwood and mahogany.

There was continuing conflict between the British and the Spanish. Finally, in early September 1798, a Spanish fleet of 32 ships with about 2,000 men came to settle the score and wipe out the British once and for all. But it didn't work out that way. A ragtag band of Baymen assisted by a Royal Navy battleship on September 10, 1798, defeated the larger Spanish force in the Battle of St. George's Caye. That event helped end Spain's claims to Belize once and for all and is now celebrated as National Day. Spain acknowledged British sovereignty in Belize in the Treaty of Amiens in 1802.

Thus began the **British era** in Belize, which lasted until the mid-20th Century. British Honduras, as it was then known, officially became a British colony in 1862, at the time of the U.S. Civil War. Following the Civil War, about 1,500 Confederate supporters came to British Honduras and established the town of New Richmond. Much of the British period was marked by the traditional colonial approach of exploiting the natural resources of the colony. Though slavery was abolished in Belize in 1838, almost three decades before it was abolished in the United States, English and Scottish companies employing hard-working Belizean blacks continued to log the native forests, exporting the timber back to Europe.

During this time, Belize began to become a melting pot of races and ethnic backgrounds. The old Baymen families, with names like Usher and Fairweather, married former slaves, creating a kind of provincial Creole aristocracy in Belize City. Some Mayas, fleeing the Caste Wars of mid-19th century Mexico, intermarried with the Spanish, and were then called Mestizos. Hundreds of Garifuna from Honduras, with African and Caribbean Indian heritage, settled in southern Belize. As the 20th century dawned, British Honduras was a sleepy backwater of the British Empire. But underneath the sleepiness, things were stirring. Jamaican-born Marcus Garvey helped raise racial consciousness in Belize, as he did elsewhere in the Caribbean.

The worldwide Great Depression and a terrible hurricane in 1931, which killed some 2,000 people in and around Belize City, both had a great impact on Belize. The country was only tangentially involved in World War II, though many Belizeans served in British or other armed forces.

The end of World War II sparked anti-colonial feelings and marked the beginning of **modern Belize history.** The first major political movements favoring independence from Britain arose. Of these, the People's United Party (PUP) under George Price, an ascetic Creole educated at St. John's College in Belize City, was the most important. In 1954, a new constitution for the colony was introduced, for the first time giving all literate adults the right to vote (until then only about 3 in 100 Belizeans were allowed to vote.) In 1964, George Price negotiated a new constitution, which granted British Honduras full internal self-government, although it remained a British colony.

In 1973, the country's name officially was changed to Belize. On September 21, 1981, Belize became an independent nation, with George Price as prime minister. Small by international standards, unpopulated and undeveloped, modern Belize has struggled to create a viable economy and infrastructure. The country several times faced off with Guatemala, which had long maintained that Belize was simply a province of Guatemala. It was not until 1991 that Guatemala finally recognized Belize as a sovereign state, although even up until today populist flag-wavers in Guatemala occasionally threaten to invade *Belice* (as it is known in Spanish).

In the 20th century, agriculture, especially citrus, bananas and sugar, replaced logging as the country's main industry. More recently, tourism has supplanted agriculture as the primary industry.

Democracy found fertile roots in Belize, and the little country has a dynamic two-party system. Occasionally, groups attempt to start a third party, but in recent times that's proved unsuccessful. The United Democratic Party (UDP), under the former schoolteacher Manuel Esquivel, first defeated the PUP in the 1984 national elections, and again in 1993, but the PUP under Said Musa regained power in 1998 and held it until 2008. The current UDP prime minister, Dean Barrow, elected in 2008 and reelected in 2012, is the first black to hold the office.

Prime Minister Dean Barrow – photo courtesy Government of Belize

Holidays: The following are legal public holidays in Belize:
New Year's Day - January 1
Baron Bliss Day - March 9 (date of celebration varies)
Good Friday, Holy Saturday, Easter Sunday, Easter Monday
Labour Day - May 1
Commonwealth Day - May 24
St. George's Caye Day - September 10
Independence Day - September 21
Columbus Day (also called Pan-American Day) - October 12
Garifuna Settlement Day - November 19
Christmas Day - December 25
Boxing Day - December 26

Hurricanes and Other Natural Disasters: June through November technically is hurricane season in the Western Caribbean, but the September and October period is the most likely time for tropical storms and hurricanes. The worst hurricane in modern Belize history

28

struck in September 1931, killing as many as 2,000 people in and around Belize City. About two-thirds of all tropical storms that have visited Belize in modern times have struck during the months of September and October.

Since 1889, some 55 tropical storms and hurricanes have made landfall in Belize, an average of about once every 2.3 years. During the last half of the 20th century, only five serious hurricanes struck Belize, with the worst being Hattie in 1961. Hurricane Keith hit Ambergris Caye in late September 2000, killing five and doing some US$150 million in damage, mainly on the backside of the island. Hurricane Iris in early October 2001 devastated the Placencia peninsula and rural Toledo District in southern Belize, killing 21 people, all in a live aboard dive boat. Hurricane Dean, in August 2007 hit Northern Belize, destroying some crops and homes.

Hurricanes can have a serious economic impact on Belize. For example, the Caribbean Development Bank estimates that in 2000 costs associated with hurricane damage were 13% of Gross Domestic Product and in 2001 6% of GDP. Even without hurricanes and tropical storms, flooding does frequently occur in low-lying areas, especially at the beginning of the rainy season, typically in June or July. Heavy rains from June through September in southern Belize can also cause flooding at any time during this period. Happily, Belize is not much subject to that other scourge of Central America – earthquakes. While earthquakes have occurred in Belize, notably in southern Belize – there were several minor tremors felt in Belize from 2009 to 2015 -- no severe *terremotos* have occurred in Belize in modern times. Likewise, there are no active volcanoes in Belize. Forest fires are a risk at the end of the dry season, typically April and May.

Internet: There are about an estimated 91,000 internet users in Belize (2015 estimate), or about one-fourth of the population. Internet access in Belize has been greatly improved over the past few years. Belize Telemedia Ltd. now offers DSL in most of the country, for either PC or Mac. It also offers wireless internet via line-of-sight towers. However, costs are higher than in the U.S. or most other countries, and speeds, while increasing, are lower than in many other countries in the region. In 2014, the fastest rate (download) for BTL DSL was 8 MB per second.

Costs range from US$12.50 a month for 128 kbps to US$350 a

month for 8 MBps. High-speed internet combined with home phone services reduces Internet rates to US$150 per month for 4MB and US$244 for 8 MB. These are download rates, and in practice you may not get these speeds. In addition, there is an installation charge of US$50 (there's a larger deposit for non-residents) and a monthly modem rental fee of US$5 (or you can buy a modem for around US$75.)

DSL is currently available in the Belize City area, San Pedro, Caye Caulker, Corozal Town, Belmopan, San Ignacio, Benque Viejo, Orange Walk Town, Punta Gorda and Placencia areas, plus in a number of outlying areas. Check www.belizetelemedia.net for current DSL coverage.

Internet via digital cable is available in Belize City, San Pedro, Placencia and elsewhere for around US$50 a month and may soon be available in a few other areas.

Smart Telcom Belize, another major cell service provider in Belize, on the CDMA system, offers wi-fi internet access through properly equipped cell phones. Currently, Smart sells Samsung Galaxy S6 Edge phones for US$1,225, and monthly cell plans range from US$15 to US$375, the latter with 15 gigs of data and 4,500 minutes in Belize per month.

Some internet users in Belize, especially those in remote areas, go with a satellite service, mainly HughesNet, StarBand or Galaxy. Setup, installation (usually a larger antenna, such as a 1.2 meter dish, is necessary), deposits and activation fees vary but currently are in the US$1,000 range. Monthly fees for unlimited service are around US$60 to $100. In some cases, you may need a billing address in the U.S. or Canada. You can add satellite TV service, but it is expensive compared with local cable service. Satellite Internet tends to be slower than DSL and there can be a latency issue or service disruptions during heavy rains.

Most businesses and nearly all hotels in Belize have Internet access. In most cases, internet service for hotel guests is now free. Internet access is also available at cybercafés in San Pedro, Caye Caulker, Placencia, San Ignacio, Punta Gorda, Belize City, Corozal Town and elsewhere. BTL also has internet kiosks for public Internet access in several locations around the country, including some BTL offices.

Language: The official language of Belize is English, and English speakers have little or no trouble communicating anywhere in the country. However, Creole, a combination of mostly English vocabulary with West African grammar, syntax and word endings, is used daily by many Belizeans of all backgrounds. Spanish is widely spoken as well, and tends to be the dominant language in areas bordering Mexico and Guatemala. The Belize government has called on all Belizeans to learn both Spanish and English. Garifuna and t h r e e Maya languages also are spoken, and some Mennonites speak a German dialect. As many as two-thirds of Belizeans are bi- or tri-lingual.

Largest Cities and Towns: Populated areas in Belize are officially designated as a city, town or village. The country's urbanized areas, in order of population from largest to smallest, as of the 2015 estimates by the Statistical Institute of Belize (more or less the equivalent of the U.S. Census Bureau), are:

Urbanized Areas Population, Belize 2015 Estimates

From Statistical Institute of Belize:

Belize City	60,963
San Ignacio/Santa Elena	20,582
Belmopan City	19,458
San Pedro Town	16,444
Orange Walk Town	13,687
Corozal Town	11,722
Dangriga Town	10,108
Benque Viejo Town	6,589
Punta Gorda Town	5,910
Country Total:	**368,310**

Belize is divided into six political districts, which function a little like U.S. counties. The six districts, from north to south, are Corozal (population 40,400 in 2010, 45,530 in 2015, a five-year growth rate of 12,7%), Orange Walk (45,400 in 2010, 49,466 in 2014, a five-year growth rate of 9%), Belize (89,200 in 2010, 110,644 in 2015, a five-year growth rate of 24%), Cayo (72,900 in 2010, 87,876 in 2015, a five-year growth rate of 20.5%), Stann Creek (32,200 in 2010, 39,865 in 2015, a five-year growth rate of 23.8%) and Toledo (30,500 in 2010, 34,929 in 2015, a five-year growth rate of 7.3%). According to the Belize Statistical Institute's 2015 estimates about 45% of Belize's population lives in urban areas, so Belize remains predominantly rural.

Location, Size and Population: Belize is on the Caribbean Coast of Central America, bordered by Mexico to the north and Guatemala to the west and south. To the east is the Caribbean Sea. In Belize waters are as many as 400 islands, most unpopulated specks of sand, coral or mangrove. Belize is about the size of the U.S. state of Massachusetts or the country of Wales in the U.K. — 8,866 square miles — with a population estimated at around 368,000 in mid-2015, about as many people as live in metro Savannah, Ga. From north to south Belize is less than 200 miles in length, and at its widest point it is less than 70 miles across.

32

Mail Service: Mail service to and from Belize is reasonably reliable and not too slow. Mail between the U.S. and Belize City usually takes less than a week. To outlying areas, however, it can take much longer – often several weeks. There are post offices in Belize City and in all towns and some villages. Many areas do not have home delivery. Unlike some of its Latin neighbors, Belize's postal service does not usually suffer from theft and lost mail. However, never send cash by mail. To mail an airmail letter from Belize to the U.S. costs US 30 cents and US 15 cents for a postcard. For fast, dependable but expensive international express delivery, DHL Worldwide Express is one choice. Federal Express is another.

Maps: The best maps of Belize are these:

Belize Traveller's Map, ITMB. Scale 1:250,000. The best general map to Belize, but last updated as 6th edition in 2005. US$10.95. Since so many visitors to Belize also visit Tikal in Guatemala, ITMB also produced a new map in 2013 that incorporates the Belize map with the Tikal/Eastern Guatemala part of the ITMB Guatemala map (scale 1:300,000 and 1:470,000, US$12.95) Available from www.itmb.com, www.amazon.com or at larger bookstores. Other general maps of Belize are *Insight Fleximap Belize* (2003); *Laminated Belize Map* by Borch (2012) at 1:500,000 scale and *National Geographic Belize Adventure Map* at 1:400,000 scale (2009).

Driver's Guide to Beautiful Belize, by Emory King. This mile-by-mile guide to most roads in Belize is really handy if you are traveling around the mainland. It's a 40-some-page booklet in 8 1/2" x 11" format. It was updated annually until Emory King's death in late 2007, but as of this writing it is out of print. It also has maps of Belize City and major towns. If you can find an old copy, the price is around US$12 to $15 in Belize.

Belize Topographical Map, British Ordnance Survey, 1:250,000-scale. Beautiful map, in two flat sheets, with Belize City and town maps on reverse sides. Also, there are 44 individual topo maps to most of Belize, at 1:50,000 scale. These are excellent maps but in most cases haven't been up-dated since the early 1980s. Most are now out of print.

Google Earth has satellite images of Belize. Some areas are in high resolution; others, not.

Media: Belize has a half dozen **television stations,** several radio stations and a number of weekly and monthly newspapers. There is no daily newspaper in the country, although there was one in colonial times.

Cable television companies operate in most populated areas, in some cases with pirated content. Most of the **weekly newspapers** in Belize are based in Belize City, but a few other towns have weekly or monthly newspapers. The two best national newspapers in Belize are *Amandala* and *The Reporter*. These two weekly tabloids are independent and outspoken, though coverage runs to strident political and crime news, and since they are based in Belize City both have a Creole, port city orientation that does not fully reflect the views of all of Belize's diverse society. Both have Web editions: www.reporter.bz and www.amandala.com.bz. *The Guardian* and the *Belize Times* are operated by the two leading political parties in Belize. The weekly *Belize Times* (www.belizetimes.bz) is the Peoples United Party paper, and *The Guardian* (www.guardian.bz) is the United Democratic Party's organ.

Ambergris Caye has weekly print and online newspapers. The *San Pedro Sun* (501-226-2070, www.sanpedrosun.net) is operated by expats from the U.S. It has both a print and an online edition. *Ambergris Today* (501-226-3462, www.ambergristoday.com) is now an online daily. There also are small newspapers in several outlying towns and villages: the monthly *Placencia Breeze* in Placencia, *The Star*, a weekly in San Ignacio, the quarterly *Toledo Howler* in Toledo and others. The *Breeze, Star* and *Howler* have both print and on-line editions. None of these newspapers has extensive classified listings for real estate or other items of interest to prospective expats, although the *San Pedro Sun* usually has a page or so of classified items for sale, and *Amandala* usually has some Belize City home rental and homes for sale listings.

Two Belize City **TV stations,** Channel 5 and Channel 7, may also be picked up in a good part of the country and are carried on most cable systems. Channel 5 has an informative text version of its nightly news broadcast on-line at www.channel5belize.com. Channel 7 also has an on-line news summary at www.7newsbelize.com. Streaming video versions of the evening newscasts are now also available, though the quality can be spotty. Channel 3 in Orange Walk Town (www.ctv3belizenews.com), offers some news of Northern Belize and the nation. LOVE-FM radio also has a TV arm. While some of the equipment is primitive, it has some good locally produced programming. Plus TV and Open TV, both in Belmopan, cover capital news.

KREM-FM 96.5 and LOVE-FM 95.1 (frequencies vary around the

country) are the two most popular **radio stations** in Belize. KREM-FM has a morning talk and call-in show from 6 to 8:30 a.m., with host Evan Hyde Jr. During the day it broadcasts an eclectic mix of local music, rap, soul and other music, along with Belize news. LOVE-FM offers "easy listening" music during the day, with a morning call-in and talk show hosted by station owner Rene Villanueva from 6 to 8 a.m. This station has three full newscasts at 6:45 a.m., 12:30 p.m. and 6 p.m., Monday to Saturday, and news updates frequently. Both stations offer internet broadcasts. Website for KREM is www.krem.bz, for LOVE www.lovefm.com. Another station, this one with a UDP slant, is WAVE-FM.

Belize First Magazine, an on-line magazine about Belize founded by Lan Sluder, author of this book, has hundreds of pages of articles and archives at www.belizefirst.com. Among its free offerings are ebooks on Belize and a news archive going back more than ten years.

Most of these media can be accessed through links from www.belizenews.com. *San Pedro Daily* is an on-line "newspaper" that aggregates articles picked up from other media. *Ambergris Daily* is another daily online newsletter/blog on San Pedro. Cable TV, typically with some 50 or 60 channels from the U.S. and Mexico, is available in many areas of Belize, offered by local companies. You pay around US$20 to $40 monthly for cable service. Some Belize residents have satellite TV.

Medical Care: Belize City is the center for medical care in Belize. It was here that the Belize National Insurance health care system was begun, and from Belize City the public health program, funded initially from Social Security funds and more recently from the government's general fund, was rolled out, beginning in 2007, to Southern Belize and to other parts of the country.

A number of private dentists and private medical clinics also are available in Belize City.

Many serious problems can be treated at the country's tertiary care center, **Karl Heusner Memorial Hospital** in Belize City (Princess Margaret Dr., 501-223-1548, www.khmh.bz). It is a modern public hospital albeit one plagued by occasional supply shortages and management issues. The KHMH has 134 beds, three surgical suites and two labor and delivery suits. The hospital has a 24/7 lab, weekend pharmacy services and more than 25 specialists on staff.

It's hard to beat the rates, though – under US$250 per day for a private hospital room, less for semi-private rooms (not including physician fees, lab charges and other fees). There are seven other public hospitals in Belize, including three regional hospitals: the Southern Regional Hospital in Dangriga, the Western Regional Hospital in Belmopan and the Northern Regional Hospital in Orange Walk Town. Altogether, there are about 600 public hospital beds in Belize.

The public hospitals provide the four basic medical specialties: internal medicine, surgery, pediatrics and OB-GYN. Karl Heusner Memorial also provides neuro, ENT, physiotherapy, orthopedic surgery and several other services.

The quality of these hospitals varies considerably. Karl Heusner Memorial -- named after a prominent Belize City physician -- opened in 1997 and has much modern equipment, such as a CAT-scan, though some Belizeans and expats complain that even this hospital has occasional shortage of supplies or certain medications. It has added new facilities and services including ones for neurosurgery and trauma care. The Southern Regional Hospital in Dangriga, which opened in 2000, is another modern facility, with much of the same medical technologies and equipment as you'd find in a small community hospital in an American town. However, other hospitals leave a lot to be desired. The Northern Regional Hospital in Orange Walk, for example, though it is being upgraded, still looks more like a refugee camp than a hospital, with low concrete block buildings and limited equipment.

The National Health System is divided into four regions:

The Central Health Region has the Karl Heusner Memorial Hospital, three polyclinics, 10 health centers and two mental health facilities, Rockview Mental Hospital and the Port Loyola Mental Acute Day Hospital.

The Northern Health Region is composed of two public health institutions (Northern Regional Hospital and Corozal Community Hospital), 11 health centers and 16 health clinics. The Regional Hospital has 57 beds and Corozal Community Hospital has 30 beds.

The Southern Health Region has two public hospitals, 14 health centers and 12 health clinics. The two public hospitals are Southern Regional Hospital (formerly Dangriga Hospital), which has 52 beds, and

Punta Gorda Hospital/Community Hospital, which has 30 beds.

The Western Region has two hospitals (Western Regional in Belmopan and San Ignacio Hospital), four health centers and a number of health clinics.

Although this sounds good on paper, some of these hospitals, health clinics and health centers suffer from inadequate staffing, too many patients for their available resources and lack of equipment and medicines. Doctors may diagnose health problems accurately, but they may not be able to provide the proper medications or treatment modalities.

In addition to these public hospitals, centers and clinics, Belize has **private hospitals** -- **La Loma Luz** (501-824-2087), a not-for-profit Seventh Day Adventist hospital in Santa Elena near San Ignacio with 20 beds, and **Belize Medical Associates** (5791 St. Thomas Street, 501-223-0302, www.belizemedical.com), a 25-bed for-profit facility in Belize City that is affiliated with Baptist Health Systems of South Florida. Altogether these private hospitals have around 50 hospital beds. There also are a number of physicians and dentists in private practice, mostly in Belize City. **Belize Healthcare Partners Ltd.**, (Chancellor and Blue Marlin Avenues, 501-223-7870, fax 501-223-7876, www.belizehealthcare.com) is a health care facility with about 25 physicians on staff. Belize Healthcare Partners offers cardiology, vascular surgery, OB-GYN, radiology, kidney dialysis, laboratory and services for private patients. It also operates Belize Integral Health Centre at Gibnut and Curassow Streets, a primary and secondary care clinic serving about 12,000 patients under the National Health Care program.

Starting in the late 1990s, health care in Belize got a boost, thanks to the arrival of a group of several dozen medical volunteers from Cuba. Currently around 100 Cuban nurses and physicians are in Belize.

Most physicians and dentists in Belize are trained in the U.S., Guatemala, Mexico, Cuba or Great Britain. There are three so-called offshore medical schools in Belize, but their graduates are unlikely to practice in Belize. A nursing school, affiliated with the University of Belize, trains nurses for work in Belize. While many expats do go to Guatemala, or to Chetumal or Mérida, Mexico, for specialized treatment, others who can afford it go to Houston, Miami, New Orleans or elsewhere in the U.S.

In 2013, the Belize Medical Tourism Association was formed by tourism and medical officials, with the goal of increasing medical and dental tourism to Belize. *(Also see the chapter on Health in Belize below.)*

Money: The Belize currency is the Belize dollar, which for many years has been tied to the U.S. dollar at a fixed 2 Belize to 1 U.S. dollar rate. Moneychangers at the borders often give a slightly higher rate, sometimes as much as 2.1 or 2.2 to 1, depending on the current demand for American greenbacks. U.S. dollars (bills, not coins) are accepted everywhere in Belize, although you often will receive change in Belizean money, or in a mix of Belizean and U.S. money. There has been talk for years of dollarizing the Belize economy, but so far that move hasn't gotten traction.

The Belize dollar is difficult if not impossible to exchange anywhere outside of Belize (except at border areas of Guatemala and Mexico). Paper-money Belize denominations are the 100-, 50-, 20-, 10-, 5- and 2-dollar bills. Belize coins come in 1-dollar, 50, 25, 10, 5 and 1 Belizean cent units. The 25-cent piece is called a shilling.

People of Belize: Belize is truly a multicultural society. **Mestizos** make up about 50% of the 368,000 population (population estimated 2015). These are persons of mixed European and Maya heritage, typically speaking Spanish as a first language and having social values more closely associated with Latin America than with the Caribbean. Mestizos are concentrated in northern and western Belize. There is often a distinction made between Mestizos who came to Belize from the Yucatán during the Caste Wars of the mid-19th century and more recent immigrants from Central America. Mestizos are the fastest growing segment of the population.

Creoles, once the dominant ethnic group in the country, now make up only about 21% of the population. These are people usually but not always of African heritage, typically speaking Creole and English and often having a set of social values derived from England and the Caribbean. Creoles are concentrated in Belize City and Belize District, although there are predominantly Creole villages elsewhere, including the village of Placencia.

Mennonite school children near Little Belize in Corozal District

Maya constitute about 10% of the population. There are concentrations of Yucatec Maya in Corozal and Orange Walk districts, Mopan Maya in Toledo and Cayo districts, and Kekchi Maya in about 30 villages in Toledo. **Garifuna** (also known as Garinagu or Black Caribs) make up about 5% of the Belizean population. They are of mixed African and Carib Indian heritage. Most came to then British Honduras from Honduras in 1830s. Dangriga and Punta Gorda are towns with large Garifuna populations, as are the villages of Seine Bight, Hopkins and Barranco.

The "Other" group, making up about 14% of the population, includes about 19,000 people, or 6% of the population, who say they are of mixed ethnic heritage. About 11,000 **Mennonites,** mostly of European original, originally came to Belize from Canada and Mexico in the 1950s. Divided into conservative and progressive groups, they farm large acreages in Belize. Conservatives live mostly in Shipyard, Barton Creek and Little Belize, avoid the use of modern farm equipment and speak German among themselves. Progressives live mostly in Blue Creek, Progresso and Spanish Lookout.

39

Belize also has sizable communities of **East Indians,** who live mainly around Belize City and in Toledo, **Chinese,** mostly from Taiwan, living in Belize City and elsewhere, **Lebanese** and **"Gringos,"** mostly expats from the U.S. and Canada concentrated in San Pedro, Placencia, Cayo and around Corozal Town. According to the 2010 Census, aside from the Mennonites only about 3,000 Europeans, Canadians and Americans considered themselves citizens or permanent residents of Belize. However, many expats in Belize are in the country for only part of the year or are on tourist permits.

Belize predominantly is a country of the young. About 56% of Belizeans are under 25 years of age, and the median average age is 22 years.

Pharmacies: There are drug stores in Belize City and in all towns. Many prescription drugs cost less in Belize than in the U.S., though pharmacies may not stock a wide selection of drugs. In general, in Belize prescriptions usually are not needed for antibiotics and some other drugs that require prescriptions in the U.S., although pharmacies owned by physicians or operated by hospitals (common in Belize) may require or suggest a consultation with the doctor.

Satellite Radio: Yes, satellite radio is available in Belize. Although Sirius and XM Radio have merged, and most of their programming is now shared, the two services use different satellites. Currently, Sirius can be picked up better than XM in most of Belize.

Taxes: The main taxes you'll face in Belize are:

National Goods and Services Tax (GST) of 12.5% on nearly all products and services. The GST of 10% replaced a 9% sales tax in mid-2006 and later was increased from 10% to 12.5%. A few items are exempt: basic foodstuffs such as rice, flour, tortillas, eggs and beans; some medicines; school textbooks; transportation on buses and airplanes; items being exported and hotel stays taxed under the hotel tax system. Like a value-added tax, the GST is supposed to be included in the final purchase price, rather than added on like a sales tax, but many businesses quote prices without the GST and just add it on at the cash register. Very small businesses, such as street vendors, don't have to register for the GST and don't charge the tax. There are additional taxes on alcohol, cigarettes and a few other items. More than one-half the cost of gasoline is due to government tax.

Import duties of up to 80% on imported items, with some items such as computers and books having no duty (though you pay the GST) and most having 25% or less duty. The average duty on imported items is around 20%.

Personal income tax ranges from 25% to up to 45%, with those making about US$10,000 or less per year effectively paying no tax. The 45% rate kicks in on an income of about US$47,500. Personal income tax is only on income derived in Belize; there is no Belize income tax on income generated outside Belize.

Corporate or business tax on gross revenues (without any deductions) rather than earnings, with the percentage tax depending on the category of business. The rate for what is actually a turnover tax ranges from 0.75% to 25%. For most businesses it is 1.5% of gross revenue; for most professions it is 3% of gross revenue. Revenue taxes for several types of businesses change from time to time.

Property taxes vary but are about 1% to 1 1/2% of the value of the undeveloped land, payable annually on April 1. Property taxes on homes and other developed land are very low. For example, the property tax on a nice four-bedroom U.S.-style home would likely be in the range of US$100 to $200. Many people with simple homes pay only US$10 or $20 property tax annually. There is a 5% speculation tax on land of 300 acres or more, payable annually on April 1 based on the value of the land. In the last decades or so there has been a move to make property taxes based on the market value of the property, but politicians argue that many Belizeans would not be able to pay higher real estate taxes. There has been some implementation of the law that when a property is sold, if the sales price does not accurately reflect the market value, the price can be adjusted by the government and the tax increased according.

Property transfer tax (sometimes called "stamp duty") of 5% of property value payable at time of closing. This 5% tax applies to existing homes, most lots and land, whether purchased by a Belizean or a foreigner. If you are buying a newly built, or substantially renovated (typically about 60% renovated, or more) home or condo, in addition to the 5% transfer tax you will also owe the 12.5% GST, for a total of 17.5% due on closing. This GST also applies, in some cases, to the first sale of lots in a subdivision, but not to their resale. In practice, most new home and condo sellers and residential develops fold these taxes into the price of the property, so the buyer may not even realize there is a tax charge.

Other taxes: There is **no inheritance tax.** Significantly, there also is no **capital gains tax.** The **hotel tax** on hotel stays remains at 9%. An attempt to increase it 12.5% failed.

Belize has signed **double taxation agreements** with many countries, including the United Kingdom, Bahamas, Barbados, St. Vincent and the Grenadines, Dominica, Grenada, St. Kitts and Nevis, Suriname, Guyana, Jamaica, Trinidad and Tobago and St. Lucia. There is no such agreement with the U.S.

Note: This very brief overview of Belize taxation should not be relied on for your actual situation, for which professional tax advice is recommended.

Telecommunications: Belize has one of the best telephone systems in the region, with a combination of fiber optic cable and microwave, plus cell service in most of the country. Mobile or cellular service now dominates telecom in Belize. There are some 173,000 cell phone users and only 23,000 landlines. You can dial to or from even remote areas of Belize and usually get a clear, clean line. That's the good news. The bad news is that telephone service in Belize is expensive, both for users and for Belizean taxpayers who are the footing part of the bill.

Belize Telemedia, Ltd. (BTL) is a company with a checkered history dating back to 1956, when a British firm, Cable & Wireless, set up the first telecommunications system in what was then British Honduras. After several changes, it became Belize Telecommunications, Ltd. in 1987. In 2001, majority ownership in BTL was purchased from the Belize government by Carlisle Holdings, Ltd., a U.K. company under the control of Michael Ashcroft, a British lord and Conservative politician. BTL retained a legal monopoly on all types of telecommunications services in Belize until the end of 2002, when its license to operate all forms of telecommunications in Belize expired.

BTL is no longer the monopoly it once was. Now it has competition, mainly from Smart Telcom, but it's still the 800-pound gorilla of Belize telecommunications. Lord Ashcroft's Carlisle Holdings sold its interest in BTL back to the Belize government in 2004. Later that same year, the Belize government sold BTL to Innovative Communications Corporation (ICC), an American company based in the U.S. Virgin Islands. ICC added 5,000 new landlines and claims to have brought on thousands of new cell users. Then, BTL/ICC and the Belize government got into a row, culminating in a lawsuit in Miami.

In 2006, Lord Ashcroft, long a friend of some top Belizean officials, moved to repurchase some of BTL. However, in 2009 the Belize government under Prime Minister Dean Barrow renationalized Belize Telemedia Ltd. The government has taken over the operations of BTL, with a 90% ownership stake. The balance of the stock is owned by some 900 small investors.

In spring 2005, a new wireless company, Smart, also known as Speednet, began offering digital cell service in Belize, with an interconnect to BTL. Smart offers wireless voice and Internet service in most of Belize on the CDMA platform only. It later was disclosed that Michael Ashcroft also had an interest in Smart. Today, Smart/Speednet claims it has 110,000 customers in Belize.

It costs about US$50 for BTL to install a landline telephone in your home, plus a US$100 refundable deposit. If you are not a citizen or official resident, the deposit jumps to US$500. Monthly residential service fees range from US$18 to $50. At the top tier, calls (up to one hour in length) to another landline within Belize are free. Otherwise calls in Belize are charged by the minute and vary depending on your service plan. Calls to cell phones are US7 ½ cents to 22 cents per minute, plus a US$5 a month add-on fee. Costs of direct-dialed long-distance calls to the U.S. currently are US21 ½ cents a minute for the first 5 minutes, then US17 ½ cents per minute, plus a monthly US$5 add-on fee for international calls. International calls are less at off-peak hours (6 pm to 6 am weekday and on weekends), and also less if you use BTL's 10-10-199 service.

A seven-digit dialing system was introduced in 2002. Formerly, telephone numbers in Belize had five digits, plus a two-digit local exchange. Now to reach any number in Belize you must dial all seven digits. All numbers begin with a district area code: 2 for Belize District, which includes Ambergris Caye and Caye Caulker, 3 for Orange Walk District, 4 for Corozal District, 5 for Stann Creek District, 6 for mobile phones, 7 for Toledo District and 8 for Cayo District. The second digit of the phone number is a service provider code: 0 for prepaid services, 1 for mobile services and 2 for regular telephone service. So a number like 22x-xxxx indicates that it is in Belize District and is a regular telephone, not a cell phone and not a prepaid service.

When dialing from outside Belize, you must also dial the country code and international calling prefix. **The country code for Belize is 501.** When dialing from the U.S., first dial 011, then the country code and then the seven-digit number in Belize.

Pay phones in Belize now operate only with a prepaid BTL calling card. These cards are sold in many shops in denominations from US$1 to $37.50.

BTL provides a single **telephone directory** for Belize, published annually in the spring. Most numbers can be looked up on the online directory on BTL's web sites, www.belizetelemedia.net or www.belizeweb.com. *(See also Internet above.)*

Time: Local time is GMT-6 year-round, the same as U.S. Central Standard Time. Belize does not observe daylight savings time.

Big, modern service station and convenience store near Belmopan

DRIVING IN BELIZE: ROAD UPDATE

The roads in Belize are getting better and better. Sure, there still are sections of wash-boarded dirt that will shake your fillings out, but more roads are now paved and even the gravel or limestone byways seem to be scraped more frequently.

A few roads, such as the Southern Highway, are very good indeed, among the best in all of Central America and the equal of many rural roads in the U.S. or Canada. Not too many years ago the Western Highway, now renamed the George Price Highway, was unpaved, the Hummingbird was a nightmare of potholes, the Old Northern Highway was a jungle of tire-stabbing asphalt chunks, the Southern Highway was a mud trap and not even Belize City had stop lights.

Signage, too, is improving, being better than in most of Mexico or the rest of Central America. Most critical turns and junctions are marked. Many roads have mile markers — although some markers on the Southern Highway and elsewhere are missing. Around Belize City, San Ignacio and elsewhere, new signage helps visitors and newcomers navigate to key destinations such as the international airport or the Mountain Pine Ridge.

Main Roads

PHILIP GOLDSON HIGHWAY (formerly Northern Highway). This 85-mile route is a good two-lane surfaced from Belize City to Corozal Town and then a few miles to the border with Mexico at Chetumal. The worst section is in the northern "suburbs" of Belize City. The only thing that will slow you down are a few "sleeping policemen" in villages and slow-moving trucks when the sugar cane harvest is going on in late winter through late spring, and a tollbooth at the bridge over New River (BZ75 cents). There is a handy paved by-pass around Orange Walk Town, which eliminates the need to fight clogged traffic through town. Your first glimpse of the azure waters of Corozal Bay is a highlight of the end of this route.

Overall Road Condition: Very Good (except some sections near Belize City)

Paved Section: 100%

Gas Availability: Excellent — there are many gas stations including a few open 24 hours

GEORGE PRICE HIGHWAY (formerly Western Highway). The 78-mile road takes you from Belize City quickly past Hattieville, the Belize Zoo, the capital of Belmopan, the "twin towns" of San Ignacio and Santa Elena and then on the Benque Road to the Guatemala border. The George Price Highway is being rerouted at Santa Elena. Just past San Ignacio, you hit "cottage country," where a number of excellent lodges offer cold beer and a soft bed under quiet Central American skies. The George Price – usually the section from San Ignacio to Benque Viejo is called the Benque Road -- is still in pretty good condition, and some sections have been resurfaced. More topes (speed bumps) are popping up as the road passes villages. However, the shoulders are narrow, and the surfacing used on parts of this road can be very slick and dangerous after rains. There used to be a big sign warning of the number of deaths on this road in the past 10 years -- "240 killed and 1,478 injured."

Overall Road Condition: Good (but some sections very slick after rains)

Paved Section: 100%

Gas Availability: Good to Excellent

HUMMINGBIRD HIGHWAY This 56-mile highway stretches from the George Price Highway at Belmopan to Dangriga. The Hummingbird dips and swoops through some of the most beautiful territory in Belize. This was once a very bad road. Now it is in very good condition, with only a couple of bridges that are still one-lane. Take a break at the Blue Hole, where a swim in the truly blue water is refreshing. Technically, the road is called the Hummingbird for only about 33 miles from the George Price Highway to the village of Middlesex, and then it is known as the Stann Creek Valley Road, but everybody calls it the Hummingbird all the way.

Overall Road Condition: Very Good

Paved Section: 100%

Gas Availability: Poor — best to gas up at Belmopan or near Dangriga

SOUTHERN HIGHWAY The Southern Highway, long known as the worst major road in Belize, is now the best major road in Belize. The 100-mile road is all paved. The scenery, save for views of the Maya Mountains at about the halfway point, is mostly unexceptional.

Overall Road Condition: Excellent

Paved Section: 100%

Gas Availability: Fair — best to gas up in Dangriga or near PG; in a pinch, there's gas in Independence and on the Placencia peninsula.

BELIZE CITY The roads and streets of Belize City confuse many visitors. Some streets are not signed, and some are little more than narrow, one-way alleys. Streets abruptly terminate at Haulover Creek, and you have to find a bridge to get from one side to the other. Taxis, bicycles and pedestrians dart in and out of traffic. However, things are getting better. New roundabouts on the Philip Goldson Highway have improved traffic flow, though the section of the Goldson Highway near Belize City is still in need of resurfacing, and new signage has popped up on main routes. Most streets are paved. Since 2012 Belize City has had a major road building program, and many roads have been rebuilt or resurfaced. Belize City is so up-to-date these days it even has a rush hour and traffic jams.

Overall Road Condition: Fair to Good

Paved Section: 95%

Gas Availability: Excellent — modern gas stations have everything that

U.S. stations have including convenience stores, except that you don't have to pump your own gas.

Other Important Roads

OLD NORTHERN HIGHWAY If you want to see Altun Ha ruins, you'll have to drive at least part of this 41-mile arc to the east of the Philip Goldson Highway. Under the British, this highway was paved, and at last the Belize government patched some of the remaining blacktop. The section south of Maskall village is better than the section north. Most sections are narrow and some are dirt. The 2-mile access road to Altun Ha is paved.

Overall Road Condition: Fair

Paved Section: 70% (but paved section is narrow, and some is badly potholed)

Gas Availability: Poor – gas up before leaving the Philip Goldson Highway

COASTAL HIGHWAY This 36-mile gravel road, connecting Democracia near Mile 30 of the George Price Highway with the Stann Creek Valley Road near Melinda, is also known as the Manatee Highway or the "Shortcut." Despite the name, you get no views of the water or of manatees from the road. It does save a little time on trips to Dangriga or Placencia from Belize City. However, the road is washboarded in places and is dusty in dry weather. During heavy rains, bridges occasionally wash out. It is far less scenic than the Hummingbird. It's easy to lose control of your vehicle on the gravel. In fact, some car rental companies forbid renters to drive the road, and others increase the amount you're liable for if you do have an accident. Visitors and even experienced residents are often advised to avoid this road and take the Hummingbird Highway instead.

Overall Road Condition: Fair to Poor

Paved Section: 0%

Gas Availability: Poor — gas up in Dangriga or on the George Price Highway

ROAD TO CONSEJO This level 8-mile stretch takes you from Corozal Town to the Chetumal Bay, where there is a Belize customs station (boats only).

Overall Road Condition: Fair

Paved Section: 0%
Gas Availability: Poor

ROAD TO SARTENEJA FROM ORANGE WALK TOWN Once past the paved section near Orange Walk Town, this road just goes on and on, over rough, wash-boarded limestone. It's about 40 miles to Sarteneja village and Shipstern, but it will seem like twice that. A redeeming feature of this road is Progresso Lagoon, the quintessential tropical lagoon. The Belize government has upgraded and paved part of this road, from near Orange Walk to San Estevan and then to Progresso. If you want to go to Cerros instead of Shipstern, you start the same way, but about 12 1/2 miles from Orange Walk Town, and 6 1/2 miles past the village of San Estevan, you go straight instead of turning right; this takes you to Progresso, Copper Bank and Cerros. The road can be tricky after heavy rains. From Corozal Town, take the hand-pulled ferry across the New River, and then a second ferry across Laguna Seca, saving you several hours of driving time.

Overall Road Condition: Fair to Poor (Poor after heavy rains)
Paved Section: 15%
Gas Availability: Fair – best gas up in Orange Walk or in Sarteneja

ROAD TO SARTENEJA FROM COROZAL TOWN From Corozal Town, take the Philip Goldson Highway south toward Orange Walk Town to just south of town (look for signs to the ferry). Turn east, and follow the road (and the power lines) for 2 1/2 miles to the ferry landing. The 90-foot-long, hand-pulled ferry, made from an old sugar barge, carries pedestrians and up to four vehicles on a nine-minute trip across the river. It operates from around 6 a.m. to 9 p.m. daily; there's no charge. When you disembark the ferry, you're about 2½ miles from Copper Bank village, and about 5½ miles from Progresso. Turn left and follow signs to Sarteneja. You'll have to take second ferry across the mouth of Laguna Seca. The road is unpaved and can be muddy after heavy rains.

Overall Road Condition: Fair to Poor (Poor after heavy rains)
Paved Section: 0%
Gas Availability: Fair – best gas up in Corozal Town or in Sarteneja

ROAD TO CHAN CHICH AND GALLON JUG From Orange Walk Town, it's about a three-hour, 68-mile drive to Chan Chich, the stupendous lodge built by the late Sir Barry Bowen. Along the way, on a road that varies from a poor rubble road to an excellent paved road at Gallon Jug, you'll pass a number of villages, some farms, the progressive Mennonite settlement of Blue Creek and plenty of jungle. As you cross the Programme for Belize preserve and Bowen land (you'll have to stop at two guard houses), you'll almost certainly see a variety of wildlife, including Belize's two species of deer and the oscellated turkeys. At San Felipe village, about 23 miles from Orange Walk Town, you can turn on a dirt road to the Lamanai ruins and Lamanai Outpost Lodge, about 13 miles from San Felipe. This road is now passable year-round. An alternate route for the first part of the road to Lamanai and Chan Chich is the unpaved road from just south of Orange Walk Town through the Shipyard area.

Overall Road Condition: Mostly Fair to Poor, with a few Good to Very Good sections

Paved Section: 15%

Gas Availability: Fair (gas up at the Linda Vista "shopping center" at Blue Creek, run by Mennonites; closed Sunday)

BURRELL BOOM You have two choices to get to Boom, Bermudian Landing and the Baboon (Black Howler Monkey) Sanctuary: Either turn off the Philip Goldson Highway at about Mile 13, or off the George Price Highway at Mile 15½, at the roundabout. The road to the Boom also functions as a shortcut if going between points on the Philip Goldson and George Price highways, eliminating the need to drive through Belize City. The road is beautifully paved.

Overall Road Condition: Excellent

Paved Section: 100%

Gas Availability: Fair

ROUTE 30 ROAD TO SPANISH LOOKOUT AREA FROM NEAR GEORGEVILLE This part of Cayo will remind you a bit of the Midwest, with well-kept Mennonite farms and modern stores. The road from the George Price Highway near Georgeville to Spanish Lookout, signed as "Route 30" and sometimes called Iguana Creek Road, is a good paved road. Other roads are mostly gravel and better maintained than average, with a few paved sections, especially around Spanish Lookout. Baking Pot Road from Central Farm to Spanish Lookout is unpaved and requires crossing the Belize River on a hand-pulled ferry.

Overall Road Condition: Good (Central Farm route Fair)

Paved Section: 70%

Gas Availability: Good (modern stores and gas stations in Spanish Lookout, and gas often is cheaper here than elsewhere in Cayo)

MOUNTAIN PINE RIDGE ROAD TO CARACOL By the route from Georgeville, it is about 46 miles from the George Price Highway to the ruins of Caracol. From San Ignacio, via the Cristo Rey Road, the trip is a few miles longer — this route connects with the Mountain Pine Ridge Road near the village of San Antonio. Even in good weather in a good vehicle, don't expect to average more than about 25 mph on this road — it's a two-and-a-half hour rough ride to Caracol, even with recent improvements to the road in connection with the Chalillo Dam, including some paving near Caracol. Currently you will be much better off going to the entrance to the Pine Ridge on the Cristo Rey Road, rather than the Georgeville Road, as the Georgeville Road is extremely rough. A reward: the scenery in many spots is lovely. After a heavy rain, the limestone marl or red clay can be very slick and dangerous. En route, stop for a cold drink or a hot gourmet pizza at Francis Ford Copolla's lodge, Blancaneaux, about 15 miles in from Georgeville, or at the former Five Sisters Lodge, now Gaia Riverlodge.

Overall Road Condition: Good to Poor

Paved Section: 15%

Gas Availability: None – gas up on the George Price Highway

ROAD TO PLACENCIA This used to be the road people loved to hate. It was a 25-mile mostly dirt and gravel road from the Southern Highway to the tip of the Placencia peninsula, passing Maya Beach and Seine Bight. After heavy rains, the road was occasionally impassable, even with four-wheel drive. Now, however, the road is completely paved and in excellent condition, although it's heavy with speed bumps. Except for the speed bumps (and some huge speed "humps") this road is a joy.

Overall Road Condition: Excellent

Paved Section: 100%

Gas Availability: Fair (stations in Placencia village)

ROAD TO MAYA VILLAGES IN TOLEDO A series of connected

roads take you from the Southern Highway near PG to the Mayan villages of San Antonio, Santa Cruz and Pueblo Viejo villages, or to San Pedro Columbia village, Lubaantun ruins, San Miguel village, and then back to the Southern Highway near the Nim Li Punit ruins.

SAN ANTONIO ROAD from the "Dump" about 14 miles north of PG at the Southern Highway to the Guatemala border near Jalacte, plus a new border crossing, are under construction now. Much of the road has already been paved, and completion is likely in 2016, although the legal border crossing may take longer.

Overall Road Condition: Good to Poor

Paved Section: 60% (Mostly San Antonio Road)

Gas Availability: Poor (gas up at the junction to the road to San Antonio)

AMBERGRIS CAYE You can't rent a car on the island, although residents seem to be stocking up on pickups and cars, crowding out golf carts, bikes and pedestrians on the caye's roads. Front Street (Barrier Reef Drive), Middle Street (Pescador) and Coconut Drive south to Victoria House and sections of other streets, are now paved, mostly with concrete cobblestones.

The bridge over the river channel, now called the Sir Barry Bowen Bridge, takes golf carts, bikes and pedestrians, plus taxis and other vehicles.

In 2014-2015 part of the former dirt/gravel golf path north of the bridge was paved. Plans are to surface it at least 8 miles north of the bridge to around La Beliza Resort (formerly Blue Reef.) You can rent a golf cart and putt south to near the tip of the island, and also north 7 or 8 miles, and even farther, from the bridge at San Pedro, if you have the time and bug juice. After rains, the unpaved parts of these cart paths are rough and muddy.

Overall Road Condition (island wide): Good to Poor

Paved Section (island wide): +/- 40%

Gas Availability: Fair – there are now several gas stations in San Pedro

CAYE CAULKER The streets in Caye Caulker village are still hard-packed sand. The primary means of transportation are shank's mare, bicycles and golf carts, though a few cars have made their way to the island.

Overall Road Condition: Fair to Good

Paved Section: 0%
Gas Availability: Fair

PRACTICAL TIPS

Maps. The best general road map to Belize is from ITMB. A 6th edition was released in 2005. The color, 1:250,000-scale map retails for US$10.95. There is also a National Geographic Adventure Map to Belize (2012, US$11.95) and other maps, most available from Amazon.com. Also useful for most travelers is the mile-by-mile *Driver's Guide to Beautiful Belize,* formerly published annually by the famous Emory King but now out of print; you can occasionally find an old copy. Some car rental companies provide basic maps.

Gas Stations. Belize has Shell and Esso service stations, along with several private brands, including UNO (a Honduras-based brand with locations around Central America that took over 10 Texaco stations in Belize in 2012) and Jaguar. There are a total of around 65 stations in the country. Unleaded gas averages around US$5 to $6 a gallon, with ups and downs depending on world oil prices. Diesel is a little less. Skilled mechanics are available, though like mechanics everywhere not always trustworthy, although you can get a tire changed almost anywhere. Someone will come out and pump gas for you, and there's no need to tip, although tips are appreciated. Belize gas stations accept Belize or U.S. dollars, and sometimes credit cards.

Miles or Kilometers? Like the U.S., Belize has been slow to accept the metric system. Distances are given in miles, and gas is sold by the U.S. gallon. However, some Japanese-made rental cars have speed and distance shown in kilometers only, a source of slight confusion on Belize's mile-denominated roads.

Speed Limits. You occasionally see a speed limit sign in Belize, and technically the speed limit on highways is 55 mph, but there is little traffic law enforcement. Belize drivers, to be charitable, are not always the best in the world. Speeding is common, and road accidents are the leading cause for deaths in Belize.

Sleeping Policemen. Speed-breaker bumps are used to slow traffic coming into residential areas. In many cases, you'll get no advance warning about the bumps, but expect them as you enter any town or village and occasionally elsewhere.

Check Points. Check points are fairly common, but almost always in the same place, so everybody knows where they are. Unlike in some other countries in the region where shaking down gringos in rental cars is a small industry, in Belize you will not be pulled over for phony traffic offenses, and if you are stopped at a checkpoint, which often happens, no one will promote a bribe. Just answer the questions, if any, and you'll be on your way, perhaps with a smile and wave from the police officer. All cars must have insurance. If you don't have insurance, you'll face the consequences, including possibly some time in jail.

Safety. As noted, traffic accidents are the number one cause of death in Belize. Belize drivers are often not well trained, and driving after drinking is unfortunately common. Seatbelts are required, but many people don't use them. Watch carefully when passing stopped buses — people may suddenly dart around the bus to cross the road. Outside of settled areas, you may drive for a half hour or more and never see another car. Be prepared: Bring water, a flashlight and other basic supplies, and a cell phone, just in case. In a poor country like Belize, anyone driving a car is, *ipso facto*, wealthy. Don't leave valuables in your car, locked or unlocked. In Belize City and elsewhere, including in larger towns it's best to park in a secured lot, or at least in a well-lit area. Cars left overnight on deserted rural roads are ripe for the picking. Do not pick up hitchhikers, unless you know them or are sure they're okay.

Driving at Night. Driving at night in developing countries is seldom a good idea, but in Belize night driving is a little easier than elsewhere because there are fewer people on the roads after dark. Foxes, cattle, goats and snakes, yes; people, not so many. Still, after dark it's hard to see potholes and topes, and there are people in the streets in Belize City and on roads in the towns and villages. Animals such as goats and cow may wander on or sleep on rural roads.

Best Vehicles for Belize. Do you really need four-wheel drive in Belize? On the main thoroughfares such as the George Price and Philip Goldson highways, no. In the dry season, even back roads generally are passable without four-wheel drive if you have sufficient road clearance. But four-wheel drive is good insurance, just in case you hit a stretch of soft muck or sand. On long trips in Belize, usually there are a couple of occasions when four-wheel power comes in handy. After a period of heavy rains, some back roads become quagmires.

The vehicle of choice in Belize is a four-wheel drive diesel truck with crew cab. A lot of people swear by Toyota Hilux diesels, although for visitors these are not commonly available as rentals. Larger vehicles such as the Toyota Prado offer a smoother ride on washboard roads, and the large petrol tank cuts down on the need to stop for gas so frequently. However, these are very expensive cars to buy, and rental rates on these large vehicles are high — US$80 to $110 day or more in most cases, plus taxes — and they drink fuel. Get a diesel if possible, as mileage is usually good and diesel fuel costs less than gas.

Tips on Rental Cars in Belize

When visiting Belize on a scouting trip or just for vacation, having a rental car is a real plus. You can go places not easily visited by bus, and while rental prices are not cheap, you may more than pay for the cost of the rental by avoiding high-priced tours. Here are questions to ask and things to check BEFORE driving off in your rental. Keep in mind that a breakdown on a deserted road in Belize is not like a breakdown in Suburbia, USA.

• **Check the mileage on the vehicle you've been assigned.** Even "name brand" renters often have high-mileage cars in their fleet, and local companies more often than not will provide a car with 50,000 to 100,000 miles on it, or more, (but usually in good mechanical condition.) If the mileage seems high, ask for another vehicle.

• **Check the tires.** High-quality radials or six-ply truck tires are best for Belize roads. At the very least, tires should have plenty of tread. Also, check the spare, and be sure you know how to locate and use the jack.

• **Agree on pre-existing dents and scratches.** Most car rental agencies will point out existing dents and mark them on your rental agreement form. Walk around the car with the agent to be sure major problems, such as a cracked windshield, is noted on the form. You might consider taking a photo of the vehicle. But don't stress about this, as the rental companies are almost always fair about this and in most cases aren't trying to rip you off.

• **Ask what will happen if you have a breakdown somewhere in the boondocks.** Major companies, such as Crystal, will send a mechanic out to repair the problem. Others may not.

• **Don't be shy about asking for discounts off published rates.** During busy times, discounts are probably not available, but in the off-season or during slow periods you may be able to negotiate a little on rates.

• **Determine in advance whether you need to accept Collision Damage Waiver/Loss Damage Waiver coverage.** CDW/LDW, which is a waiver, not an insurance product, runs about US$14 to $20+ per day in Belize, and often the basic plan does not cover the first US$500 to $1,000 in damage — so you have to cough up for a windshield broken by a flying rock, for example. American Express and some other credit cards DO provide primary CDW coverage in Belize, but you probably need to pay for a premium credit card plan to get coverage for off-road travel and for larger SUVs and trucks. Call your card issuer to confirm. Note that liability insurance, required in Belize, is provided on rental cars, but liability insurance does not cover damage to your rental vehicle.

Sun, fun and swimming at the Split, Caye Caulker -- free

WHAT THINGS COST IN BELIZE

Belize doesn't have a cost of living. It has several costs of living. The traditional view is that Belize is the most expensive country in Central America, yet one of the least expensive in the Caribbean.

While there's truth to that, it really doesn't take into account that the actual cost of living in Belize can vary from almost nothing to very high. You can live in a luxury four-bedroom house on Ambergris Caye, with air conditioning, telephones, a dishwasher, microwave and cable TV, U.S. food in your pantry and imported booze in your glass, and you can spend thousands a month. Or you can live in a small Belizean-style house in Cayo, around Corozal Town or in rural Toledo, eat beans and rice and rice and beans, ride buses and drink local rum for a few hundred U.S. dollars a month.

Most expats in Belize choose somewhere in between. Some condos and houses in Belize go for more than US$1 million, but I know one expat who built and equipped his small house, using his own labor, with thatch from nature and scrounged lumber, for around US$4,000, and that included furniture and kitchen equipment.

After all, per capita income in Belize is a fraction of that in the U.S. A weekly wage of US$150 to $200 for six days of work is considered pretty good. Tens of thousands of Belizeans live, and in many cases live comfortably, on a few thousand dollars a year. You can, too.

Or you can compromise, forsaking those high-cost icons of civilization such as 80,000 BTU air conditioners, while keeping the family car, boat or other toys that you enjoy. Live partly on the Belizean style, partly in the U.S. style, and enjoy the benefits of both, and you'll get more for less. One American expat, who returned to Colorado after living in Belize for five years, said he was surprised at how much the cost of living in the U.S. had increased since he left. "Compared to Colorado Springs, ANYTHING in Belize is cheap. And I can't wait to get back — I just don't have enough money to live here in Colorado in anything but poverty!"

Price Sampler: What Things Cost in Belize

Here's a sampler of costs for common items in Belize, as of 2015-2016. *All prices are shown here in U.S. dollars.* As in other countries, prices for many items vary depending on where and when you buy them.

Transportation

Gallon of unleaded gas: $4.80 (the pump price varies slightly by area, and fluctuates frequently reflecting the international price of oil and government price controls)

Gallon of diesel fuel: $3.80

Note about fuel costs: The gas and diesel prices shown are in late 2015, when the international cost of oil was at or near record lows. These Belize prices have been considerably higher in the past, with unleaded gas as high as about US$6 and diesel US$5 a gallon, and likely will rise again.

Bus fare from Belize City to San Ignacio: $4

Bus fare from Belize City to Corozal Town: $6

Water taxi from Belize City to San Pedro, Ambergris Caye: $12-$24

Water taxi from Corozal Town to San Pedro, Ambergris Caye: $25

One-way adult airfare from Belize City municipal airport to Placencia: $99

One-way adult airfare from Belize City international airport to San Pedro: $90

One-way adult airfare from Belize City municipal airport to San Pedro: $55

Taxi from Belize international airport to Belize City: $25

Taxi fare within Belize City: $3-$6

Utilities/Telecommunications

1-kilowatt hour of electricity: $0.24

"Current" (electrical service) for 1000 kW hours monthly: $240

Monthly charge for residential telephone: $50 for landline with unlimited calls to other landlines in Belize

DSL internet access: $150 a month for 4 MB (download speed)

Digital cellular service: $25 a month for 250 minutes/texts to $125 per month for 2,000 minutes/texts

Butane, 100-pound tank, delivered: $65 (varies by area)

Bottled water, delivered: $2.50/gallon

Pipe water and sewerage (where available): $25 a month, higher on Ambergris Caye

"Dirt" (trash) pick-up: Free to $10 a month (varies by area)

Staples in Grocery Stores (Prices Vary by Store)

Red beans: $1 per pound

Milk: $1.70 (quart)

Ground steak (lean ground beef): $1.50 per pound

Pork chops: $2--$3 per pound

Chicken (whole): $1.25 per pound

Loaf of white bread: $1.50 (whole wheat $2.50--$3)

Corn tortillas, freshly made: $0.02--$0.04 each

Bananas: 10 to 20 for $1

Avocados: 6 for $1 (varies seasonally)

Valencia oranges: 10 for $1 (in season)

Flour, bulk, 1 lb.: $1

Morton salt: $1.50

Bottle of imported moderate-quality Chilean wine: $16-$18

Case of 24 Belikin beers (pick up from Bowen & Bowen distributor): $24 plus $6 bottle deposit

Case of 24 Coca-Cola, Sprite or Fanta soft drinks (pick up from Bowen & Bowen distributor): $9 plus $6 bottle deposit

Soft drink, Coca-Cola, 12 oz. (at grocery): $0.75 each
Local Mennonite cheese, 1 lb.: $4.50
Kraft pepperjack cheese, 8 oz.: $4.50
Philadelphia brand 8 oz. cream cheese: $4.50
Onions: $0.60 per pound (varies seasonally)
Local rum, liter: $7 - $14
Sugar: $0.30 per pound
Crackers (Premium Saltines): $4.89
Cigarettes, Independence local brand: $4 a pack
Cigarettes, Marlboro: $5.75 a pack
Canned soup (Campbell's Chicken Noodle): $1.80
Cereal (Raisin Bran): $5
Cooking oil (1-2-3 brand from Mexico), 1/2 liter: $1.75

Household Items
Mennonite-made wood dining table: $175
Music CD (pirated): $5
Whirlpool 12,000 BTU air-conditioner: $700
Mabe (Mexican-made) frost-free 16 cubic foot refrigerator: $675
Small home appliances at Mirab, Courts, Brodies, Hofius or other stores: about 25% to 50% more than prices in the U.S.

Entertainment
Fish and beans and rice at local restaurant, Hopkins: $5
Fish, French fries and cole slaw dinner, San Pedro: $14
Lobster dinner at nice restaurant, Placencia: $25--$35
Movie theater ticket, Ramada Princess, Belize City: $8.50
Rum drink at bar, Placencia: $2--$4
Belikin beer at bar in Cayo: $2--$3.50

Shelter Costs
Rent for simple two-bedroom house in Corozal Town: $250--$400
Rent for modern two-bedroom apartment/condo unit in San Pedro: $800--$2,000
Cost to build a reinforced concrete home: $50 to $190 per sq. ft., finished out in basic to high-moderate level
Small concrete house and lot in Belmopan, Corozal Town or Cayo:

$40,000--$100,000
> Modern three-bedroom house and beachview lot in Consejo:
> $145,000--$400,000
> Two-bedroom condo on Ambergris Caye: $200,000--$750,000

Medical Care
Office visit, private physician: $25--$70
Teeth cleaning, private dentist: $40
Root canal and crown, private dentist: $300--$500

Building Supplies
50# bag of cement: $6--$7
"Prefab" Mennonite House, 800 sq. ft., set up on your lot, $20,000+

Family Budgets in Belize
As noted, the cost of living varies greatly in Belize, depending on your lifestyle, preferences and place of residence. Here are several different budgets. All of these budgets assume home/apartment rentals – those who own their own home would have lower costs, though there would be additional charges for insurance and maintenance. **All amounts are in U.S. dollars.**

Monthly Budget for Affluent Couple in San Pedro
This budget reflects the cost of living for a 50-year-old affluent expat couple that rent a two-bedroom condo on Ambergris Caye. Assumption: The couple owns a golf cart for transportation, owns a small boat and spends freely for entertainment and personal expenses.

Rent	$1,500
Electricity (1200 KW)	288
Telephone (including long distance)	150
Water	100
Bottled water	80
Butane	65
Groceries	500
DSL internet	100
Entertainment and dining out	400
Cable TV	30

Golf cart maintenance	100
Boat expenses	350
Health insurance	400
Out-of-pocket medical/dental care	150
Flights to Belize City (monthly)	140
Other travel expenses	300
Clothing	100
Household help	450
Other personal expenses	250
Total	**$5,453**

Monthly Budget for Expat Couple in Placencia

This budget reflects the cost of living for a 60-year-old expat couple who a rent a small home on the Placencia peninsula. Also assumed: Their several-year-old SUV is paid for, and they choose to purchase health insurance.

Rent	$800
Electricity (750 KW)	188
Telephone (including long distance)	100
Butane	65
Groceries	350
Cable TV	30
Internet	50
Entertainment and dining out	200
Auto insurance	25
Health insurance	300
Medical expenses	150
Gasoline	240
Auto maintenance	100
Clothing	75
Other personal expenses	150
Household help/caretaker	300
Other	125
Total	**$3,248**

Monthly Barebones Budget

This budget is for a single 65-year-old permanent resident in a Belizean-style rented house near San Ignacio. Assumptions: The individual uses public transportation and takes advantage of the local public health care system.

Rent	$300
Transportation (bus/taxi)	40
Telephone	40
Groceries	175
Entertainment	75
Butane	40
Water, trash pick-up	40
Electricity (400 KW)	96
Local healthcare/medicines	95
Cable TV	25
Clothing	20
Other personal expenses	50
Total	**$996**

Belize City harbour is scenic, but the city is the crime capital of Belize

CRIME AND SAFETY IN BELIZE

We don't want to scare you, because things aren't as bad as they sound when you read about them from afar, but you need to know: The dark underbelly of life in Belize (and indeed in most developing countries) is crime, especially property crime. As a cautionary tale, I'm presenting some of the most negative reports, so you'll be prepared for the worst.

On the positive side, most expats in Belize say that while they have to be mindful of the possibility of thefts and burglaries that they don't spend much time worrying about it. More positive news: Major crime (murders, robbery, rape, etc.) declined 11% in 2015 from 2014.

An American who owns a home on Ambergris Caye posted this plaintive note on one of the message boards on www.ambergriscaye.com.

"I'd like to know why the [San Pedro] town council or town board can't do anything about getting the thieves and thugs off the island. I just received a call today saying our house had been broken into again. This time they broke into a locked closet, then broke into a large metal lock box with heavy duty locks on it. Took everything of value again. The same thing had happened in July. That time they didn't get into the lock box. Sometimes they break in just to put graffiti on the walls. They also broke into our little guesthouse, with nothing of value in it, (just painted and fixed up) punctured the waterbed and destroyed the inside. We've tried the caretaker thing and have gone thru six caretakers in five years. We pay them good money to live there free, but the only thing they did was steal from us, too. My neighbor was also robbed every time we were. All of his stuff was also locked up, but they have all the time in the world to go thru your things and break into everything. These thieves live in the dump, have no job and live to rob people. After a couple of months with no proof of a job can't they deport them? These are the same ones who have robbed tourists (even at gun point) on the beach. There have been three within the last few months. I'm about ready to sell my place and start talking ... about this terrible (true) situation. When the tourists or people planning to vacation in San Pedro, or buy houses or property, find out the reality of what's really happening, maybe they'll decide to go elsewhere."

This kind of comment, unfortunately, is common among those who own vacation or second homes in Belize. And it's not unheard of among ex-pats who live full-time in Belize, either. One small hotel and dive shop operator on North Ambergris, said: "My house has been broken into four times and if I were to reveal the whole story it ... would make your hair curl. One guy got caught in the house and still got away with it, God knows how."

Another resort owner on the south end of Ambergris Caye said her house was broken into while she was sleeping, and her wallet was stolen. These accounts are from Ambergris Caye, but the situation is similar in most parts of Belize. When I meet homeowners in Placencia, Cayo or Corozal Town often the talk turns to the latest break-in at a neighbor's home. Residents and tourism operators in Placencia village, Caye Caulker and Corozal are reporting increased problems with burglaries and thefts, a trend that mirrors a similar situation taking place in San Pedro.

One tourism operator in Placencia said that of the last five guest parties the operator had booked in Placencia village, all five had been hit with thefts, usually in the daytime. On Caye Caulker, several small hotel owners reported that break-ins at hotels, businesses and homes were occurring almost nightly. "In Corozal, I conducted an informal survey of expat residents and found ... 84% of those living in Corozal Town had experienced at least major burglaries or worse, some victimized more than once [over the past four years]," noted Margaret Briggs, who formerly operated a web site for expats in Corozal, but who, in part because of the crime rate, sold her home in Corozal and moved to New Mexico.

A few years ago, the San Pedro Chamber of Commerce, following a series of high-profile robberies, burglaries and homicides, developed a list of 20 steps -- including screening new arrivals to the island coming from the mainland, registering street vendors and strengthening community watch programs – that it recommends to help stop the crime wave.

Burglaries and petty theft in Belize are disturbingly common. Of course, this isn't unique to Belize. There are about 2.2 million burglaries reported in the United States annually. When you add together burglaries, auto thefts and larcenies/thefts, the total for the U.S. is around 10.5 million. That's one theft-related crime for every 10 households. So, in the U.S., in a decade the chance of your household being a victim of theft or burglary is statistically 100%.

But the situation is perhaps more acute in Belize, in part because often the police do little about the problem. This can be because they are incompetent, or lack the necessary training or, in some cases, they know the culprits or are related to them and decline to arrest them. Most often probably it is due to lack of resources. In many cases constables don't even have the basic tools to do their jobs. There have been a number of reports about police cars that simply sat at the police station because there wasn't money to buy gas for them.

In many cases, the local authorities do have a good idea who is responsible, but in a society such as Belize where most people in a village are at least distantly related, police have to go along to get along, and this may mean turning their eye if they think a cousin is doing the teifin' or drug dealing. One American expat in Placencia had to briefly leave the peninsula because drug dealers thought this person had found and kept a shipment of cocaine. Local constables probably knew who the drug dealers were but were reluctant to take any action. They felt powerless to offer protection, so they recommended this American go away on vacation until things cooled down.

What can you do to avoid being a burglary victim in Belize? Several things can help:

Put burglar bars on your windows and doors. These are available from local hardware stores and cost around US$75 per window. If your house is in a remote area, the bad guys may just attach a chain to the burglar bars and pull them off with a truck, but in most areas they offer a good first line of defense.

Get a dog. A dog is THE most effective deterrent to break-ins in Belize. It doesn't have to be a vicious dog, but it should sound vicious. A big, black dog is considered the best deterrent. Note, however, that bad guys have been known to poison guard dogs to gain entrance to the property.

Put a fence or wall around your property. This won't deter serious thieves, but it may slow them down.

Get to know your neighbors. Community watch programs (there are a few formal watch programs on Ambergris Caye and elsewhere) can be highly effective in deterring crime. But even if you just get on good terms with your neighbors, they will help keep an eye on your property.

Be sure the exterior areas are well lit. Nightlights supplemented by motion-detector lights can help. Using LED bulbs can help reduce your electric power cost.

Hire a caretaker you can trust. Though there are irresponsible or crooked caretakers, there also are many who are dependable and will look out for your property when you are away. Ask around, especially among fellow expats and at local churches, for an honest individual or family. Remember, the mango doesn't fall far from the tree. You will usually have to provide free living quarters and a monthly stipend, typically about US$100 to $400 a month, depending on what you require of the caretaker. There can also be issues related to your role as an employer, including the requirement to provide social security payments, severance pay, vacation time and other employment issues.

Install an alarm system with motion detectors. Belize has several security companies that install and monitor residential security systems. Check the Belize telephone directory for security companies, or ask neighbors about their expensive. Note, however, that security companies don't operate in all areas of Belize, and even if you have a system there is no guarantee that the local police will respond. You are probably best off with a system that uses loud air horns and flashing lights – these may alert your neighbors to a break-in and perhaps even scare off the intruders.

Personal Safety

The homicide and violent crime rate in Belize is higher than in most large urban areas of the United States. Typically, there are 90 to 120 murders a year in Belize. That's a murder rate about five to six times higher than the average in the U.S., which has an annual rate in the range of 6 murders per 100,000 population, which itself is very high compared to Canada (about 2 homicides per 100,000) or Western Europe. However, most of the murders are concentrated in Belize City, and much of the other violent crime involves a farm worker getting drunk on Saturday night and knifing or machete chop- ping somebody in a cool spot (bar.)

To put the Belize crime rate in perspective, Guatemala City sees about 100 murders a WEEK. Also, although there are gangs in Belize City, Belize does not have the severe youth gang problems that plague Guatemala, Honduras and El Salvador. In Central America alone, it is estimated there are 250,000 members of *maras,* Spanish slang for local gangs (*maras* are a species of swarming, aggressive ants.) The situation in Belize is nothing like that in Honduras, where the number of gang members is higher than the total population of Belize City.

A recent report by non-governmental organizations in Central America puts the murder rate for Guatemala, Honduras and El Salvador as follows: El Salvador 55.5 homicides per 100,000 inhabitants; Honduras, 40.6; and Guatemala, 37.5. In 2013, Belize's rate was around 33 per 100,000 and has declined some since then.

While most expats are concerned about burglaries and thefts, most retirees and foreign residents in Belize express little concern about their personal safety. Certainly, it's wise to use common sense: Don't walk on in unlit areas at night; don't pick up strangers in your car; put up exterior lighting around your home driveway and entrance.

Colonial-era buildings in the Fort George area of Belize City

GETTING ALONG IN BELIZE

If you're looking for a place to live or to retire that's just like back home, only better, for a United States or a Canada on the cheap, for Florida with ruins, reefs and rum, you may get a rude awakening when you move to Belize. Because Belize isn't just like the U.S. or Canada. It does have cheap rum, awe-inspiring ruins, beautiful Caribbean seas and much more. But the rules are different. The people who make and enforce the rules are different. Sometimes there are no rules. Sometimes there is a set of rules for you, and a different one for everyone else. Just about every expat resident of Belize has some story to tell about problems he or she faced in adjusting to life in Belize -- or, in not adjusting. Let's look at some of the differences, and what they mean to you as a potential resident or retiree.

Population of a Small City

First, Belize is a country with a population hardly bigger than a small city in the U.S. Even including recent illegal and uncounted immigrants from El Salvador, Guatemala and Honduras, the population of the entire country is only about 368,000. Imagine the difficulties your hometown would have if it suddenly became a country. Belize has to maintain embassies, establish social, educational and medical systems, raise a little army, and conduct affairs of state and international diplomacy, all with the resources of a small city. You can see the difficulties Belize faces in just getting by in a world of mega states. It lacks the people resources, not to mention the tax base and financial resources, to get things done in the way North Americans expect. If you're a snap-to-it, get-it-done-right kind of person, you're going to wrestle with a lot of crocodiles in Belize.

No More Juice

Most expats seeking retirement or residency in Belize are white middle-class North Americans, from a society still run by white middle-class North Americans. Belize, on the other hand, is a truly multi-cultural society, with Creoles, Mestizos, Maya, Garifuna, Asians, and what in the rest of Latin America would be called Gringos, living together in complex and changing relationships, living together in probably more harmony than anyone has a right to expect. In several areas, such as Belize City, Creoles dominate; increasingly, in other areas Spanish-speaking Belizeans and immigrants dominate. One thing is for certain, though: In this mix, North Americans, Europeans and Asians have very limited power. Money talks in Belize, of course, as it does everywhere. Most of Belize's tourism industry is owned by foreign interests. Much of its industry and agriculture is controlled by multinational companies or by a few wealthy, well-connected Belizean families. Thus, to some extent, these wealthy foreigners do have some access to power and some actual power.

Politically, however, the typical North American resident of Belize is powerless. He or she has no vote and is truly outside the political process. That's the fate of expats everywhere, but some who come to Belize, seeing a country that is superficially much like back home, are shocked that they no longer have a power base and are, in a political sense at least, truly powerless. The North American or European is not so much at the bottom rung of Belizean society, as off the ladder completely. If you like to pick up the phone and give your congressional representative a piece of your mind, you're going to miss this opportunity in Belize.

Culture Shock

Culture shock is what happens when everything looks about 20 degrees off kilter, when all the ways you learned were the right ways to deal with people turn out to be wrong. It is a state, someone said, of temporary madness. Usually it happens after about six months to a year in a new situation. At first, you're excited and thrilled by the new things you're seeing. Then, one day, you just can't stand one more dish of stew chicken and rice and beans.

In Belize, culture shock is sometimes masked by the surface familiarity. Most Belizeans speak English, albeit a different English. They watch -- such a shame -- American television. They drive big, old Buicks and Chevrolets or Japanese cars. They even accept U.S. currency. But, underneath the surface sameness, Belize is different, a collection of differences. Cases in point: The ancient Mayan view of time, cyclical and recurring, and even the Mayan view today, are grossly different from the linear way urban North Americans view time. The emerging Hispanic majority in Belize has social, religious and political views that are quite different from the views of the average North American, or, even of the typical Belizean Creole. A Belize Creole saying is "If crab no walk 'e get fat, if 'e walk too much 'e lose claw." Is that a cultural concept your community shares?

In many cases, family connections and relationships are more important in Belize than they are in the U.S. or Canada. Time is less important. Not wanting to disappoint, Belizeans may say "maybe" when "no" would be more accurate. Otherwise honest men may take money under the table for getting things moving. Values North Americans take for granted, such as "work hard and get ahead," may not apply in Belize in the same way. Physical labor, especially agricultural work and service work, because of the heritage of slavery and colonialism, is sometimes viewed as demeaning among some Belize groups. A Belizean may work long hours for himself or herself but be reluctant to do so for an employer.

Respect, Not Money

Respect is important in Belize. If you make a pass at a friend's girl, you may end up on the wrong end of a knife or machete. If you diss one of your employees or neighbors, you may find yourself in a bad situation on a dark night. Just when you least expect it, you may get jumped on a back street and beat nearly to death. If you say something bad about a politician or a business owner, it may come back and bite you years later. Belizeans have long memories, and they don't take well to criticism, especially not from outsiders.

On the other hand, Belizeans can be surprisingly rough and tumble in their personal relationships. They'll say the nastiest things to each other, just run the other guy down for being stupid and a total fool, and then the next day both parties forget about it and act like they've been friends or cousins all their lives, which they have been.

The best advice is to make as many friends in Belize as you can. Sooner or later, you'll need them.

No Walmarts in Belize

Belize has no Walmarts. No K-Marts. No Home Depots. No Circuit Cities. No McDonald's. While this lack of homogenization and consumerism is a big plus for Belize, it also means that you can't go down to your neighborhood hyperstore and select from 40 kinds of dish soap, or 18 brands of underwear. Rum may be US$7 or $8 a bottle, but Cheetos may be US$5 a bag. Every computer, nearly every piece of plumbing and electrical equipment, every car and truck, every pair of scissors, is imported, and often transshipped thousands of miles from one port to another before it gets to the final destination in Belize. Then it's carried by truck or on a bus or in the luggage area of a Cessna somewhere else.

Some items simply aren't available in Belize, or supplies may be spotty. Bags of cement, for example, sometimes are in short supply, and the cost, around US$7 for a 50-pound bag, is higher than you'd pay back home. To get ordinary items such as building nails or a certain kind of auto part, you may have to call several different suppliers. Belize's small population is spread out over a relatively large area, served by a network of bad roads (though they are getting better), well-used planes and sometimes leaky boats. Although the government is shifting its focus from excise and import taxes more to income and consumption taxes, much of government revenue still comes from import taxes, so the prices you pay may reflect a tax of 20% and possibly as high as 80%.

In short, Belize is an inefficient market of low-paid consumers, a country of middlemen and mom 'n pop stores, few of which could last more than a month or two in a highly competitive marketplace like the U.S. This is what gives Belize its unique flavor in an age of franchised sameness. But, you better Belize it, it also provides a lot of frustration and higher prices.

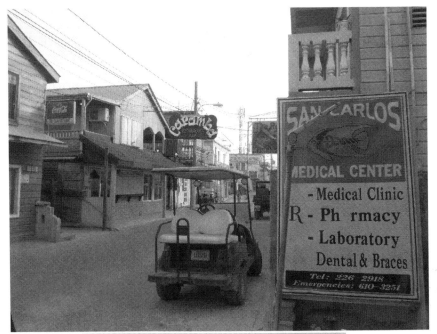

Medical center in San Pedro, Ambergris Caye

YOUR HEALTH IN BELIZE

A major issue for expats, especially retirees, is health care. Health care in Belize is a mixed picture. On the positive side, health and hygiene standards in Belize are considerably higher than in most other countries in Central America or in Mexico. However, as a developing country Belize's medical resources are in no way comparable to those offered in the United States, Canada and Western Europe. If you are older and especially if you face chronic health problems, you will have to look closely at the health care tradeoffs — a healthier way of living, lower medical costs and more personalized care in Belize versus the high-tech, low-touch, high cost of health care and health insurance back home. Plus, programs such as U.S. Medicare and Medicaid, and national health programs in Europe and Canada, generally are not available in Belize.

Hospitals and Other Health Care Facilities in Belize

Belize has a mixed public and private health care system. The vast majority of Belizeans get medical care through a system of government-run hospitals and clinics.

Public Hospitals in Belize

There are eight public hospitals in Belize. **Karl Heusner Memorial Hospital** in Belize City functions as the main public hospital in the country and as a national referral center. Also, there are three regional hospitals: the **Southern Regional Hospital** in Dangriga, the **Western Regional Hospital** in Belmopan City and the **Northern Regional Hospital** in Orange Walk Town. In addition, there are district public hospitals in San Ignacio, Punta Gorda and Corozal Town. Rockview Hospital in Belize City is a psychiatric center. Altogether, there are about 600 public hospital beds in Belize. The public hospitals provide the basic medical specialties: internal medicine, surgery, pediatrics and OB-GYN. Karl Heusner Memorial also provides neuro, ENT, physiotherapy, orthopedic surgery and several other services. The quality of these hospitals varies considerably.

Karl Heusner Memorial Hospital -- named after a prominent Belize City physician -- opened in 1997 and has much modern equipment, such as a CAT-scan, though some Belizeans and expats complain that even this hospital is sometimes short of supplies. In 2004-2005, it added new facilities including ones for neurosurgery and trauma care.

The **Southern Regional Hospital** in Dangriga, which opened in 2000, is another modern facility, with much of the same medical technologies and equipment as you'd find in a community hospital in an American town. For example, the hospital's printed materials and web site boast that its surgical operating rooms have "Narkomed anesthesia and Bovie electrosurgical units with laryngoscope sets, ECG monitoring spacelabs, Vilatert monitoring systems, resuscitators and 'Shampaine' surgical tables." However, other hospitals leave a lot to be desired. Some other hospitals, however, still look more like refugee camps than hospitals, with basic buildings and limited equipment. Several clinics are in San Pedro, but the island, the number one area for expats in Belize, still lacks a hospital.

Besides these hospitals and larger clinics, Belize has a network of more than 60 public health clinics and rural health posts in many towns and villages around the country, providing primary medical and dental care. Most of these suffer from inadequate staffing, too many patients for their available resources and lack of equipment and medicine. Doctors may diagnose health problems accurately, but they may not be able to provide the proper medications to cure them.

Medical Personnel

Government figures show Belize has fewer than one physician per 1,000 population, less than one-half the rate in the U.S. Belize has about 500 nurses, or one nurse per 735 population. Altogether there are perhaps 800 trained medical personnel in Belize. They are not distributed evenly around the country, however. More than one-half are in Belize City are, which has only about one-fourth of the population. About three-fourths of trained medical people work in the public sector, and the rest in the private sector.

Starting in the late 1990s, health care in Belize got a boost, thanks to the arrival of a group of several dozen medical volunteers from Cuba. Currently almost 100 Cuban nurses and physicians are in Belize. These doctors and nurses were assigned to clinics in areas of Belize, which, until then, did not have full-time medical personnel available to the local people. These hardworking Cubans, who exist on stipends of only a few dollars a month, have won many new friends for Fidel and Raul in Belize, regardless of what Belizeans may think of Castro politics. Medical and dental volunteer teams from the U.S. and Canada also regularly visit Belize to provide short-term care. Also, Nigeria and Venezuela have been helping provide medical care for Belize.

Medical care professionals in Belize earn very modest incomes compared with those in the U.S. Physicians employed by the government start at around US$15,000 to $20,000 a year, though they may supplement their income in private practice. Nursing salaries start at around US$8,000.

Most physicians and dentists in Belize are trained in the U.S., Guatemala, Mexico or Great Britain. There are several so-called offshore medical schools in Belize, but their graduates are unlikely to practice in Belize. A nursing school, affiliated with the University of Belize, trains nurses for work in Belize. Belize medical professionals, like Belizean society, come in every shape and flavor. "My dentist is Garifuna, my ear doc is Mayan, my eye doc Mestizo and my OB-GYN is Spanish," says one expat, a former New Yorker who now lives in Belize City.

The following regulatory bodies are established under the laws of

Belize: The Medical Board responsible for the registration of medical practitioners, dentists, opticians and nursing homes. The Nurses and Midwives Council, responsible for the registration and regulation of nurses and midwives; and the Board of Examiners of Chemist and Druggists, responsible for the examining and registration of Chemist and Druggists and for carrying out other matters provided for in this Ordinance. The Nursing School participates in an accreditation program within the CARICOM countries.

What you won't find in Belize is topnotch emergency care, although Karl Heusner Memorial Hospital in Belize City has added a trauma care center. While there are ambulances, a helicopter transfer surface using Astrum Helicopters near Belize City and an emergency air transport service operated by Wings of Hope, a U.S.-based charitable organization with an operations center in Belize City, Belize's spread-out population means it could take hours to get you to a hospital. In specialist care, such as for heart disease or cancer, Belize is behind the U.S. and Canada and even its larger Latin neighbors such as Mexico, Guatemala and Honduras.

"The big minus in Belize is that there is not adequate medical care for chronically ill people who need regular visits to specialists," said Judy duPlooy, who owns a lodge near San Ignacio. She said that for people in Western Belize, Guatemala has "excellent care and is the quickest place to get to in an emergency." While many expats do go to Guatemala, or to Chetumal or Mérida, Mexico, for specialized treatment, others who can afford it go to Houston, Miami, New Orleans or elsewhere in the U.S. For example, both Prime Minister Dean Barrow and his wife, First Lady Kim Simplis-Barrow, have journeyed to the U.S. for medical treatment during the PM's terms in office. Simplis-Barrow was treated for cancer in Miami, and Dean Barrow had surgery for chronic back pain in Newport, Calif.

Private Hospitals and Private Care

In addition to the public hospitals, Belize has two private hospitals -- La Loma Luz, a not-for-profit hospital in Santa Elena near San Ignacio, and Belize Medical Associates, a for-profit facility in Belize City. Altogether these hospitals have fewer than 50 hospital beds.

La Loma Luz Medical Center, Santa Elena, Cayo; 501-824-2087. La Loma Luz is a not-for-profit hospital operated by the Seventh Day Adventists. It has 17 hospital beds, a primary care clinic and 24-hour emergency services.

Belize Healthcare Partners Ltd., Corner Chancellor and Blue Marlin Ave., 501-22307870; www.belizehealthcare.com is a health care facility with about 25 physicians on staff. Belize Healthcare Partners offers radiology, kidney dialysis and laboratory services for private patients. It also operates Belize Integral Health Centre at Gibnut and Curassow streets, a primary and secondary care clinic serving patients under the National Health Care program.

Belize Medical Associates, 5791 St. Thomas St., Kings Park, Belize City; 501-223-0302; www.belizemedical.com. Established in 1989, Belize Medical Associates has a 25-bed hospital, along with two surgical suites, X-ray and ultrasound machines, a clinical lab, emergency services and pharmacy. It is affiliated with Baptist Health Systems of Miami.

Owned by a group of Belizean physicians and businesspeople, a third private hospital, Universal Health Services, ran into financial difficulties and was merged into Karl Heusner Memorial Hospital.

Pharmacies and Prescriptions

There are drug stores in Belize City, in all towns, and in some villages. Many prescription drugs cost less in Belize than in the U.S., though pharmacies may not stock a wide selection of drugs and some drugs cost more in Belize than in the U.S. or Canada. In general, in Belize prescriptions usually are not needed for antibiotics and some other drugs that require prescriptions in the U.S., even some painkillers containing codeine.

However, pharmacies owned by physicians or operated by hospitals, a common situation in Belize, may require or suggest a consultation with the doctor. Among the larger drug stores in Belize are Community Drug Stores, which has three locations in Belize City; Val-U-Med, Family Health Pharmacy and First Choice Pharmacy, all in Belize City; and The Pharmacy in San Ignacio. Also, Brodies supermarkets in Belize City and Belmopan have pharmacies. In addition, especially if you are in Northern Belize, crossing the border to Chetumal is an option. Chetumal has large *farmacias* that have most medications at prices significantly lower than in the U.S., and often lower than in Belize.

If you are taking prescription medications, when you come to Belize you should be sure you have the generic name of the drug, as local pharmacies may not have the same brand names as back home.

Medical Records

If you have preexisting health conditions, you should bring a copy of your medical records with you when you move to Belize or come for an extended stay. It is also a good idea to have a letter from your physician outlining your conditions and past treatments.

Cost of Medical Care

Even if medical care isn't always up to snuff in Belize, at least it is cheap. The majority of health care is provided at little or no charge. Belizeans who can't afford to pay are treated in about the same way as those with more means. Only a tiny percentage of Belizeans have medical insurance. Private medical insurance coverage in Belize begins at US$150 to $200 a month, above what the average Belizean can pay. Rarely in the public health system in Belize will anyone be turned away for lack of cash or insurance, as thousands routinely are in the U.S. every day. Public hospitals and clinics may bill nominal amounts for tests and procedures -- for example, a woman's clinic in northern Belize charges US$10 to $20 for a Pap smear, cervical exam and breast exam and under US$15 for an ultrasound -- or they may ask for a donation. In some waiting rooms you will see a box where you can leave a donation. But even visitors are routinely treated for free. A British friend was injured in a boating accident off Dangriga. In great pain, he was taken to the hospital in Dangriga where he was he was diagnosed as having broken ribs. He was then transported by air to Belize City where he was hospitalized for several days. His total bill, including X-rays, hospital stay, transport and medications: Zero.

If you can accept long waits and less than state-of-the-art medical technology, you won't have to spend all of your pension income to afford care. "Medical, dental and eye care is a fraction of the cost of the U.S. I have my teeth checked and cleaned for US$40, pay U.S. $10 to $20 for an office visit to my physician, and medications are cheap," says one Californian who now lives in Belize full-time. Even if you opt for private care, office visits to a physician generally are just US$20 to $50, though in San Pedro, where docs cater to a lot of visitors and expats, it can be more. In 2013, I paid about US$90 for an office visit after a bad fall, but that included a couple of meds. A root canal with crown might cost US$300 to $500, although some Belize dentists charge more. Hospitalization runs under US$250 per day for a private room, a considerably less for a semi-private or ward room. Belize providers are trying to jump-start medical tourism in Belize, but so far such efforts have had but modest success, in part because of the lower costs and higher skill levels of providers in India, Thailand, Costa Rica and elsewhere.

Prescription drug costs vary but generally are less expensive than in the U.S. A few years ago, I paid just US$5 for a course of antibiotics. Pharmacies are in Belize City and in all towns. By the way, prescription drugs in Belize are usually dispensed in plastic baggies or envelopes rather than in bottles. While it is difficult to compare costs between Belize and the U.S., since the quality of care is different and the amount of medical tests done in Belize pales beside those routinely ordered in America, it's probably fair to say that even in the private sector overall costs for health care in Belize are one-fourth to one-third that in the U.S. and may be even less.

National Health Insurance

The medical care system in Belize is in a transitional period. A National Health Insurance scheme, proposed in the 1990s, is gradually being implemented. Under the scheme, through the Belize Social Security system, all Belizeans and permanent residents would get medical care through a system somewhat similar to that in Britain. The scheme calls for individuals and businesses to pay into Social Security system for health care. The benefit, with the individual's Social Security card the identity card, would be comprehensive universal medical care. The system would pay for care, or at least part of it, at either public or private hospitals and clinics. Initially, a pilot project in Belize City, which started in the early 2000s, was funded by the government and was free to all residents of the Belize City South Side. Later, residents of the North Side were added. Then, in 2006-2007, the NHI was expanded to parts of southern Belize. It provided for care at a group of clinics, free drugs from participating pharmacies and free lab tests at participating clinics. Funding initially was through the Social Security system and then from the government general fund. Unfortunately, the Social Security system in Belize has been troubled for years, with charges flying back and forth about management and financial accountability of the system. The Belize government also usually runs a budget deficit. Together, these factors are hampering and delaying expansion of the NHI.

Private Health Insurance

For routine primary care, most foreign residents in Belize make do with the low-cost public system, or they go to a private physician, dentist or clinic. Mostly they pay cash. They "self-insure," taking a calculated risk that what they save in medical insurance premiums will more than pay for their actual medical costs in Belize.

Health insurance policies for care in Belize are available on a referral basis through a few insurance companies in Belize, as agents for international health insurance companies and brokers, but these companies do not offer health insurance plans themselves:

RF&G Insurance, 81 N. Front Street, Belize City; 501-227-3744;; www.rfginsurancebelize.com. RF&G, the largest firm in Belize, the result of a 2005 merger of Regent Insurance and F&G Insurance, is based in Belize City and has other offices around Belize, including branches in Corozal Town, Belmopan, San Pedro, Punta Gorda, Dangriga, Placencia and Orange Walk Town. It is part of the Roe Group, a diversified local company also with interests in tourism, tobacco and vehicle sales.

Belize Insurance Center. 212 North Front Street, Belize City; 501-227-7310; www.belizeinsurance.com. This group offers a variety of insurance products.

International Insurance Companies

Several international insurance companies and insurance brokers write health care policies for expatriates, with the premiums sometimes covering medical transportation back to the home country along with actual health care.

What rate you will pay for health care coverage as a resident of Belize depends on several factors. The most important factor is your age. Most insurers price their insurance coverage on age bands – for example, under 35, 35-39, 40-44, 45-49, 50-54 and so on. Typically, the biggest jumps in cost occur for those over 50, especially those over age 60 or age 65. Those over 60 likely will pay four to 10 times as much as those under 30.

Other factors that impact the cost of insurance are your health condition including pre-existing illnesses, occupation, gender and lifestyle factors such as Body Mass Index and smoking. Also very important is the deductible level you choose, which might range from zero per year to US$10,000 a year. A zero deductible plan typically is about three times as expensive as a US$10,000 per year deductible. (A deductible is the amount of health costs you pay out of pocket before the insurance kicks in.)

Here are representative annual costs for a basic international major medical plan. A standard plan would include hospitalization, day-patient status at a hospital or clinic and emergency care. A more comprehensive plan that covers out-patient care, medical evacuation, maternity care and other extras could have annual costs twice as high as the figures shown. Most companies offer three or four, or more, levels of coverage, each with different co-pays, maximum lifetime limits and various extra features.

Keep in mind that these plans likely would include coverage not just in Belize but also in other countries, excepting the United States.

This is just an example to show how rates increase with age and is not meant to reflect actual costs for any particular individual in Belize. As a general rule, however, coverage outside the U.S. is much less expensive than in the U.S., under either the Affordable Care Act ("Obamacare") or other private insurance. In great part this is because the cost of hospitalization and other medical services in the U.S. is the highest in the world. Rates are per person and are in U.S. dollars.

Age	Annual Cost
30-34	US$1,800
35-39	US$1,900
40-44	US$2,200
45-49	US$2,400
50-54	US$3,000
55-60	US$3,900
61-65	US$5,400
65-69	US$8,000
70-74	US$9,000
75-79	US$11,500

Online quotes for healthcare plans are available from most of these companies. You will have to provide some information about you and others that you want to be covered, such as name, contact information, country of citizenship, country where you plan to live and whether or not you want coverage in the U.S. Most plans allow you to choose the country where you wish to have medical care. For example, residents in Belize might choose Mexico or Guatemala. Some plans provide coverage on a short-term basis in the U.S., if you are visiting the U.S. and experience a medical emergency. Note that countries served by the companies below change from time to time, so Belize coverage may not be offered by all companies.

Cigna Global Health, 877-539-6295 in the U.S., www.cignaglobal.com. Provides three basic levels of core coverage international and expat: Silver, Gold and Platinum. Cigna's core insurance policies provide you protection for hospital stays and treatment. Surgeon and consultation fees as well as hospital accommodation are covered. In-patient, outpatient and cancer treatments are also covered. A major difference among the plans are the total maximum coverage, ranging from US$1 million to $3 million.

Bupa Global (Victory House, Trafalgar Place, Brighton, BN1 4FY, United Kingdom; +44 (0) 1273 322074, www.bupa-intl.com). This company says it has more than 10 million policyholders around the world. It usually works through medical insurance brokers. Bupa took over Amedex, which had more than 1 million policyholders in Latin America. The Latin American Bupa website is www.bupalatinamerica.com. Most policies cover direct payment to hospitals, reimbursement for outpatient care and medical evacuation. Premium costs vary based on age, but an individual $1 million (annual limit) major medical policy with a US$500 to $1,000 deductible for a middle-aged individual could be around US$2,000-$8,000 annually, depending on the details of the policy, and assuming that you live most of the year outside the U.S. Most but not all policies exclude coverage in the U.S. Coverage in the U.S. typically doubles the premium cost. Bupa Global members have access to some 7,500 hospitals worldwide.

Aetna International (www.aetnainternational.com) is the international health care division of U.S.-based Aetna. Aetna has about 44 million participants in the U.S. and around 500,000 expat members internationally. Aetna International currently offers four levels of plans, from Basic to Exclusive. The Basic plan pays 100% of medical costs after US$2,500 coinsurance limit is reached, a maximum annual benefit of US$250,000 and medical evacuation.

Cigna International (www.cigna.com/international), a division of the U.S. insurance company, offers private international health insurance through a network of network of some 8,700 hospitals, 540,000 physicians and 167,000 dental offices.

Healthcare International (www.healthcareinternational.com) is a U.K-based provider that provides expat coverage worldwide with access to about 7,000 medical centers and 350,000 physicians. It currently has five levels of plans with varying costs and benefits.

My Matchmaker (www.mymatchmaker.com) is an international insurance broker that lets you compare plans from several different companies. To get an online quote for your particular situation, you have to put in your date of birth, gender, nationality and foreign place of residence, along with an indication of what kind of insurance coverage you desire.

Medicare

Medicare and Medicaid do not pay for medical care outside the U.S., except for some limited situations in Canada and Mexico. The U.S. Department of Veterans Affairs will pay for coverage outside the U.S. only if you are a veteran with a service-related disability.

For Americans, this is a major drawback of expat life in Belize, or indeed anywhere else outside the U.S. and its territories. For visitors and short-term residents, some private insurance policies including some Blue Cross policies do cover you regardless of where you become ill or have an accident. Also, some credit cards such as American Express Platinum pay for medical evacuations back to the cardholder's home country.

Health Issues in Belize

Bad water and poor sanitation are major causes of illness in much of the Third World. In Belize, happily these are less of a problem than in Belize's larger neighbors, Mexico and Guatemala. All residents of Belize City and nearly all towns have access to safe and adequate water supplies — "pipe water" as it's called in Belize — and close to 70% of rural residents do, according to the Pan American Health Care Organization.

Thanks to the plentiful rain in Belize — from 50 to 200 inches or more per year — drinking water literally falls from the sky, so even if you decide to live in an area without a community water system you can collect drinking water in a cistern. Concrete or plastic cisterns, with accompanying pipes and drains to gather rain from your roof, are sold in building supply stores or can be constructed by local workers, if your home does not already have one. To be safe, rain- water should be treated by filtering or with a disinfectant such as chlorine bleach. Overall, according to the Statistical Institute of Belize, about 85% of Belizeans have access to potable water. In short, in most areas of Belize, including nearly all areas of interest to expats, you can drink the water and not worry about getting sick. Increasingly, municipal water supplies in Belize are being privatized. In San Pedro, for example, the water system is run by a company based in the Cayman Islands.

In many areas, sewage disposal is less adequate. The Belize Water and Sewerage Authority (WASA), which was privatized in the early 2000s, with majority ownership by a European consortium called CASCAL, operates sewerage systems in Belize City, Belmopan and a few other areas. There is still a lack of facilities in rural areas, and even in urban areas more than one-third of houses do not have adequate sanitation, according to Belize government figures. In rural parts of Belize, refuse disposal is not organized at the community level; households are responsible for the disposal of their own solid wastes. While many homes have reasonably effective septic systems, or at least well-maintained pit latrines, in poorer areas Belizeans dump their household wastes into rivers or the Caribbean Sea. Life expectancy at birth in Belize is about 70 years, only a little lower than that in the U.S. Heart disease is the leading cause of death from illness for both males and females, but Belizeans, as are Americans, are paying more attention to the causes of heart disease, such as smoking, lack of exercise and a diet high in saturated fats, and the incidence of death from heart disease is declining.

There are no reliable statistics on how many Belizeans smoke. Certainly, the antismoking crusade hasn't progressed as far as it has in the U.S. Few businesses, public buildings or restaurants are smoke free, and many Belizeans feel it is their right to light up anytime and anywhere. My own very unscientific survey of foreigners resident in Belize suggests that a large number, maybe as many as one-half, smoke. Perhaps some of these came to Belize just to be able to smoke without being harassed by the lifestyle police? However, with local brands of cigarettes costing US$25+ a carton and imported brands US$40 or more, the vast majority of Belizeans can't afford the habit.

The leading cause of death in Belize is not illness but traffic accidents. About one-fourth of all deaths in Belize are now due to traffic accidents, even though the vast majority of Belizeans don't own cars.

Often the cause of accidents is alcohol-related. Such speed limits as there are in Belize, and most roads have no posted speed limit, don't mean much because Belize has very few traffic enforcement officers. The use of seat belts is now required in Belize, but this rule, too, is rarely enforced. Finally, many Belizeans simply aren't good drivers. Driver's education programs are virtually unknown. Normally you must pass a short written test to get a driver's license and have a medical exam. However, some residents say they have gotten one simply by showing up at your local Transport Department office with the necessary forms, including a certificate from a doctor that you are in good health and two passport-size photos, and paying US$10.

AIDS has become a serious epidemic in Belize, according to health officials. Although government figures are lower, AIDS workers estimate that as many as 7,000 people in Belize are HIV positive. Given Belize's small population of a little over 368,000, this estimate means that about one in 52 Belizeans is HIV positive, thought to be the highest infection rate in Central America. Worldwide, about one in 120 persons is believed to be HIV positive. In Belize, nearly three-fourths of HIV infection is spread by heterosexual contact. The highest number of reported AIDS cases is in Belize and Stann Creek districts. All blood for transfusion in Belize is screened for HIV, with the cost absorbed by the government.

At one time, Belize had on a per capita basis one of the highest incidences of malaria in the world, and the highest in Central America. Thanks to a widespread program of spraying for mosquitoes, the incidence of malaria in Belize has been declining from its peak of more than 10,000 reported cases in 1994. In recent years, the number of reported cases has fallen to under 1,000 annually, mostly in remote bush areas and typically among recent immigrants from Guatemala or elsewhere in Central America. Another good thing is that more than 95% of the malaria cases in Belize are the *Plasmodium vivax* strain, which is less dangerous than *Plasmodium falciparum* and can be prevented with the use of chloroquine, a time-tested and fairly inexpensive drug.

Dengue fever is transmitted by another type of mosquito. It causes flu-like symptoms that are unpleasant but which in most cases are not life threatening. Dengue has become epidemic at the end of the rainy season in many countries of Central America, including Costa Rica and

Honduras. Dengue exists in Belize, especially during the rainy season, but happily it is not very common. However, in 2009 there was an outbreak of dengue in western Belize. There is at present no widely available preventative medication for dengue fever, although a vaccine is under development, but dengue symptoms can be treated effectively with Tylenol or its generic equivalent. Avoid taking aspirin if you think you have dengue, as aspirin can exacerbate internal bleeding sometimes associated with dengue.

Both cholera and typhoid fever are occasionally present in Belize, but only a handful of cases have been reported in recent years.

The Healthy Belize Lifestyle

Belize could be good for your health. A positive side to the typical Belize lifestyle, especially outside urban areas, is that compared to the usual way of living in developed countries you tend to walk and exercise more, get more fresh air and eat simpler, healthier meals of complex carbohydrates and fresh fruits. One Canadian said that after a year in Belize he went for a health check-up. He found his blood pressure was down 15 points and his weight down 15 pounds. "But what do you expect?" he asks, smiling. "I live on the beach, walk 25 feet to work and eat almost nothing but fresh fish and fruit."

The use of herbal remedies also is common in Belize. Bush doctors or snake doctors often have an extensive knowledge of plants with healing properties. Don Elijio Panti was one of the best known of the herbal healers. He was a Guatemalan by birth but a long-time resident of Cayo in western Belize who died in 1996 at over 100 years of age. His work was popularized by Rosita Arvigo (with Nadine Epstein and Marilyn Yaquinto) in the 1993 book, *Sastun, My Apprenticeship with a Maya Healer* and in other books. Dr. Arvigo today operates a herbal healing facility near San Ignacio. Many other herbal or snake doctors operate in Belize.

Enjoying the 80 degree Caribbean Sea in San Pedro

OPTIONS FOR RESIDENCY IN BELIZE

There are three basic options for those wishing to live or retire in Belize or to spend extended periods of time in the country. Each has advantages and disadvantages.

TOURIST PERMIT

This is the easiest, cheapest way to live in the country for a while, and it requires no long-term commitment. The procedure is simple: You get a 30-day entry free (via a passport stamp) when you arrive in the country by air, land or sea. After 30 days, you can go to an immigration office (or police station in remote areas) and renew the tourist card monthly for US$25 a month for up to six months, and then US$50 a month after that. After six months, generally you also must register as an alien. Citizens of the U.S., European Community, the U.K., Canada, Australia, New Zealand, Mexico, Costa Rica, Guatemala, Colombia, Venezuela, Surinam, Brazil, Fiji, Hungary, Iceland, Kenya, Latvia, Lithuania,

Seychelles, South Africa, Singapore, Japan, South Korea. Slovakia, Solomon Islands, Malawi, Malaysia, Maldives, Mauritius, Czech Republic, Namibia, Papua New Guinea, Chile, Norway, Sierra Leone, Sweden, Tanzania, Turkey, Uganda, Uruguay, Zambia, Western Samoa, Zimbabwe, Tuvalu, Hong Kong, CARICOM member states and some other countries get a tourist card without having to apply in advance for a tourist visa. Nationals of more than 75 other countries must apply in advance for a tourist visa, and there is a fee. See the Belize Tourism Board web site, www.travelbelize.org for details.

As a tourist permit holder, you can enjoy Belize without a long-term commitment. You can buy or rent property, but you cannot work for pay. In theory, when you renew your tourist permit, you are supposed to be able to prove that you have sufficient resources, set at US$60 a day (a credit card usually suffices), to stay in Belize, but this requirement is not usually enforced. Of course, there is no guarantee that you will be able to renew your tourist status indefinitely, as rules and conditions can change, as you have no official residency status. If you fail to renew your permit in a timely way, or if you overstay your allotted time, technically you are in violation of Belize law and can be deported. As a practical matter, if you can offer a good reason why you failed to follow the law, and are very friendly to Immigration officers, you'll probably be let off with a short lecture from the official, and perhaps a fine. However, some people who overstay their tourist cards *are* sent packing.

QUALIFIED RETIRED PERSON STATUS

The Qualified Retired Persons Incentive Act passed by the Belize legislature in 1999 is managed by the Belize Tourism Board. The program is designed to attract more retirees to Belize. In the first years of operation, the program attracted considerable interest and a number of applications. But the Belize Tourism Board hasn't publicly said how many applications it has received and how many have been approved. However, we understand that accepted participants in the program number only in the hundreds or low four figures. Interest in the program appears to be fairly high, but because of the income requirement, inability to work for pay in Belize, lack of official true residency status and other factors, the actual number of retirees under the program in Belize is as yet relatively small and far fewer than are in programs in Costa Rica,

Panama, Mexico and elsewhere. For several years, the BTB has said it was reviewing the program to see how it can be improved, but so far no significant changes have been made.

For those who can show the required monthly income from investments or pensions, this program offers benefits of official residency and tax-free entry of the retiree's household goods and a car, boat and even an airplane. This program also eliminates some of the bureaucratic delays built into other programs. The BTB guarantees action on an application in no more than three months, but we have heard of qualified retirees getting approval for this program in only a few weeks.

Who qualifies? Anyone at least 45 years old from anywhere in the world can qualify for the program. A person who qualifies can also include his or her dependents in the program. Dependents include spouses and children under the age of 18. However, it also can include children under the age of 23 if enrolled in a university.

Main benefits: Besides prompt approval of residency for qualifying applicants, import duties and fees for household goods and a late-model vehicle, airplane and boat are waived.

Duty-free import of personal household effects: Qualified Retired Persons under the program can qualify for duty and tax exemptions on new and used personal and household effects admitted as such by the Belize Tourism Board. A list of all items with corresponding values that will be imported must be submitted with the application. A one-year period is granted for the importation of personal and household effects.

Duty-free import of a vehicle, aircraft and boat:

Motor Vehicle: Applicants are encouraged to import new motor vehicles under the program, but the vehicle must be no more than three years old. (Occasional exceptions may be made in the case of an older vehicle with low mileage, but this would be decided on a case-by-case basis.) A Qualified Retired Person may also buy a vehicle duty-free in country.

Light Aircraft: A Qualified Retired Person is entitled to import a light aircraft less than 17,000 kg. A Qualified Retired Person is required to have a valid Private Pilot license to fly in Belize. This license can be obtained by passing the requirements set by the Civil Aviation. However, if the participant has a valid pilot's license, that license only has to be validated by Civil Aviation Department in Belize.

Boat: Any vessel that is used for personal purposes and for pleasure will be accepted under this program. If for whatever reason a Qualified Retired Person decides to sell, give away, lease, or otherwise dispose of the approved means of transportation or personal effects to any person or entity within Belize, all duties and taxes must be paid to the proper authorities. The Belize Tourism Board states: "Qualified Retired Persons must note that only after three years and upon proof that the transportation that was previously imported to Belize was adequately disposed off, will another concession be granted to import another mode of transportation."

Income requirement: To be designated a Qualified Retired Person under the program, the applicant must have a monthly income of at least US$2,000. A couple does not need to show US$4,000 a month – just US$2,000, as the applicant is normally an individual and the applicant's spouse is a dependent under the program. The income rules for Qualified Retired Persons are, like many things in Belize, a little confusing. On first reading, it looks like the income must derive from a pension or annuity that has been generated outside of Belize. The rules do not specifically say so, but according to Belize Tourism Board officials U.S. Social Security income can be included as part of this pension requirement. This pension and annuity information then has to be substantiated by a Certified Public Accountant, along with two bank references from the company providing the pension or annuity. These substantiations may not be required if your pension and/or annuity is from a Fortune 500 company. Several retirees have said that they were able to include other forms of income, including investment income, in the US$2,000 figure, if supported by a CPA's statement that the income would continue indefinitely. In this latter case, the US$2,000 a month income (US$24,000 a year) can be substantiated by showing records from a bank or other financial institution in Belize that the retiree has deposited the necessary money.

Other Documents and Procedures:

Background check: All applications are subject to a background check by the Ministry of National Security.

Application: Applications for the program must be made to the Belize Tourism Board in Belize City and include the following:

Birth certificate: A certified copy of a certificate for the applicant and each dependent.

Marriage certificate, if applicable.

Passport: Color copies of complete passport (including all blank pages) of applicant and all dependents that have been certified by a Notary Public. The copies must have the passport number, name of principal, number of pages and the seal or stamp of the Notary Public.

Proof of income: The current QRP information states that there are two ways to prove that your income is sufficient:

1) An official statement from a bank or financial institution certifying that the applicant is the recipient of a pension or annuity of a minimum of US$2,000 per month.

2) A financial statement from a financial institution, bank, credit union, or building society in Belize certifying that the applicant's investment will generate the sum of a minimum of US$2,000 per month or the equivalent of US$24,000 per year.

Medical examination: Applicant and all dependents should undergo a complete medical examination including an AIDS test. A copy of the medical certificate(s) must be attached to the application.

Photos: Four front and four-side passport size photographs that have been taken recently of applicant and dependents.

The application form for the Qualified Retired Persons Program is available for download on the Beltraide site at www.belizeinvest.org.bz. Beltraide is a quasi-governmental organization whose role is to attract investment to Belize. Application fees and costs for the QRP program total US$1,350 for an individual or US$2,100 for a couple. There is an additional fee of US$750 for each qualifying dependent child.

For information on the program, contact: Belize Tourism Board, P.O. Box 325, 64 Regent St., Belize City, Belize, Central America, 501-227-2420 or toll-free 800-624-0686; www.travelbelize.org. If you have questions or problems, try contacting the Program Officer for QRP. A QRP application form can be downloaded from the Beltraide site at www.belizeinvest.org.bz/.

OFFICIAL PERMANENT RESIDENT

Application requirements and most benefits are similar to those of the Retired Persons Incentive Act, but there are some important differences.

The application process itself and the supporting documents needed are similar to those for the QRP, although the applications are processed by different governmental departments.

Here are the main differences: As a regular Official Permanent Resident, you have two major advantages over a participant in the QRP program. First, you do not have to deposit annually any particular sum in a bank in Belize. However, you do have to show financial resources sufficient to obtain residency status. Second, as a Permanent Resident, you can work for pay in Belize. You also enjoy some advantages as a resident rather than a "long-term visitor" as you are considered in QRP status. As a permanent resident, you can vote in some local (not national) Belize elections.

You must live in Belize for one full year before you can apply for regular Permanent Residency. During this period, you cannot leave the country for more than 14 days. Even a short, two-hour visit to Chetumal counts as one day's absence. Note, however, that the Immigration and Nationality Department sometimes interprets this requirement only as meaning that you cannot leave the country for 14 or more CONSECUTIVE days.

Documents Needed for Permanent Residency Application

Here are the documents you must have to apply for Permanent Residency (photocopies of original documents must be submitted along with the original documents). The exact forms required may vary depending on the official with whom you deal and are subject to change:

Application form.

Passport.

Evidence, such as passport pages with immigration stamps, that you have been in the country for one year.

Recent police record for yourself and all members of your family over the age of 16.

Evidence you have acquired property in Belize if you are claiming that you have – but owning property in Belize is NOT required to obtain permanent residency.

Alien registration for yourself and all members of your family if you have resided in Belize for six months or longer.

Certificate of health including HIV and venereal disease tests for you and all members of your family – these tests must be conducted in

Belize.

Three passport-size photos of yourself and all members of your family,
Birth certificates of all applicants.

Marriage certificate (if applicable).

Income tax form.

After approval, you have up to one year to bring in household effects duty-free, on a one-time basis. However, the duty-free exemption does not apply to a vehicle, boat and airplane, as it does for the Qualified Retired Persons program.

It is somewhat expensive to apply for regular permanent residency.

Application fees for Permanent Residency vary by nationality, ranging from US$250 to $5,000. For Americans, the fee is US$1,000 per person. There is also, upon approval, a fee of US$150. In addition, if you use an "expediter" in Belize to help you with the paperwork, which is NOT required, you'll likely pay a fee of around US$1,500, plus several hundred dollars in travel and photocopying fees and taxes. Note that these fees are per-person, not per-application, as is the case for the Qualified Retired Persons program. For example, an American married couple applying for Permanent Residency would pay US$2,000 with the application and US$300 for residency stamps after approval. Some applicants also have been required to post a bond, supposedly to guarantee the cost of repatriation to their home country, should that ever be required. The bond amount varies, ranging from several hundred dollars to as much as US$2,000. Other applicants say they have not been required to post the bond. Residency cards are no longer provided -- instead, your passport is stamped.

You apply to the Belize Immigration and Nationality Department rather than through the Belize Tourism Board. For information and application form, contact: Immigration and Nationality Department Ministry of National Security and Immigration, Belmopan City, Belize, Central America; 501-222-4620, fax: 501-222-4056.

It is wise, perhaps necessary, to go in person to Immigration in Belmopan to apply for Permanent Residency. Applicants usually find that several trips are necessary, to check on the progress of the application and to keep it moving. Again, being friendly and showing respect to Belizean officials is vital. Getting angry about any delays will probably be counter-productive.

Time for approval of a Permanent Residency application varies. Some find that the process goes fairly quickly, taking only a few months. Others say it took up to a year, or longer, for approval.

Pros and Cons

Each option has pluses and minuses. The main advantages and disadvantages are as follows:

Tourist Permit

Pros: No commitment, no financial requirement, flexibility, little red tape.

Cons: No tax advantages, no official status, inconvenience of having to go in person to extend, possibility rules may change, can't work for pay in Belize.

Qualified Retired Persons Incentive Program

Pros: Quick approval, application through Belize Tourism Board rather than Immigration Department, some residency-style rights (except voting), tax-free entry of household effects, car, boat and airplane, only have to live in country for one month a year.

Cons: Must deposit US$24,000 a year in a Belize bank, somewhat costly application process, can't work for pay in Belize, must be 45 or over.

Official Permanent Residency

Pros: Full residency rights (except voting in national elections), can work, open to anyone regardless of age, tax-free entry of household effects.

Cons: Year-long residency in Belize before applying, more red tape, costly application process, and some people are turned down for minor details; you can bring in household goods but NOT a car, boat or airplane free of duty.

For more information, try Beltraide (www.belizeinvest.org.bz) or the Belize Immigration Department (www.belize-immigration.org).

Other Programs

The controversial **Economic Citizenship** program, under which foreigners were able to buy a Belize passport and residency rights for a fee of US$25,000 to $50,000, was discontinued in 2002. Some dated information on the internet still suggests this program is in effect. If you need a second passport, you might looks at investment/passport programs in St. Kitts at some other Caribbean countries.

Belize Citizenship

In addition to the programs discussed above, regular **citizenship** in Belize is a possibility for those living in Belize over a long period. To acquire citizenship, applicants must have residency status for a minimum of five years. Applicants for citizenship need to provide essentially the same supporting documentation as those applying for Permanent Residency. Applicants also must demonstrate a knowledge of Belizean history. Note that for citizenship residency purposes, stays in the Belize under the Qualified Retired Persons program currently do NOT qualify, although there have been discussions about changing this. To become a citizen, you would have to give up QRP status (perhaps having to pay back the duties you escaped under QRP), apply for Permanent Residency and begin the five-year residency from scratch.

Caution: Rules and regulations and the interpretation of them change frequently in Belize. Do NOT assume that this information is the last word on any matter pertaining to entering or staying in Belize.

This is worth repeating: CAUTION: RULES IN BELIZE CHANGE FREQUENTLY. What is true today may not be true tomorrow. Do not assume that everything you are told will apply for you.

Quiet street in the village of Sarteneja

HOMES AND LAND IN BELIZE

The good news is that real estate costs less in Belize than it does in the U.S., Canada or Western Europe. To be sure, in a few prime areas you can spend hundreds of thousands of dollars, even millions, on a U.S.-style luxury home, or several hundred thousand dollars on a prime beachfront lot, but you can also buy raw land at prices not seen in the U.S. since the 1970s and in some areas find a simple but pleasant rental house near the sea for under US$400 a month. More good news: There are few restrictions on the purchase or use of real estate by foreigners, legal documents are in English and follow English common law traditions.

Shopping for Housing

Except for occasional ads in the *San Pedro Sun* on Ambergris Caye and in Belize City newspapers, and listings from real estate brokers on the internet, few properties are advertised for sale. Real estate agencies do maintain on-line listings. Most real estate brokers use the internet as the primary way of presenting listings and of getting prospective f o r e i g n buyers. See the real estate agent listings below for addresses of real estate web sites in Belize.

Even with the internet, however, you'll miss one-half or more of available properties. To find out what's really for sale, you'll have to spend time on the ground in Belize. Many properties are for sale by owner, rather than being listed with a broker. In many cases, you will see no sign or other indication that a property is for sale. Just start asking around, and before long you'll have more deals being offered you than you can even begin to consider. This goes double for rentals. It is rare to see a house advertised for rent in a newspaper, except in San Pedro or Belize City, and brokers handle only the most expensive rentals.

About the only way to find a house or apartment to rent is to spend some time in the area where you wish to rent. Drive around and look for vacant homes, or ask foreign residents or Belizeans for tips on what's available. Note: Several web sites not affiliated with a real estate company have Belize real estate listings. Belize First maintains a section of free listings of Belize real estate for sale, wanted and trades. Visit www.belizefirst.com/indexrealestate.html. Also on the site are some rental listings.

Real Estate Brokers

In Belize, despite rumblings about changing this, it is still the case that anyone can be a real estate broker. No license needed. No schooling, no bonding, no continuing education. All you need is enough money to print business cards, and, presto, you're a broker. Selling real estate is a popular first job for expats in Belize, and some do it on the side, illegally, without a work permit. Quite a few hoteliers, dive shop operators and taxi drivers peddle real estate to tourists on the side. One of the best-known real estate guys in Placencia, until he left to sail his boat around the Caribbean, was also the proprietor and barkeep of one of the most popular bars on the peninsula.

Efforts have been made to require some basic licensing of real estate brokers, but as of this writing this is still a work in progress. The Belize National Association of REALTORS® has been established – the group's web site is www.belizenar.org. Agent members, of which there are more than 100 in Belize, subscribe to a code of ethics and are supposed to follow other professional guidelines. Another group, the Association of Real Estate Brokers in Belize (www.arebb.com), was established in 2006 and has more than 80 agent members.

Not surprisingly, the quality of agents varies. Some are professional and honest. A few are out for a fast buck. Some are just not very knowledgeable. The ones we've listed here are among the best we know about, but even so your mileage may vary. Real estate commissions in Belize are similar to those in the U.S. Agents typically charge the seller 7% commission on residential property, and around 10% on raw land. Of course, rates are negotiable. Because many properties are in remote areas, brokers often charge prospective buyers expenses for travel and transportation incurred in connection with showing properties.

Selected Agents

These are some of the more frequently recommended real estate agents and companies in Belize:

Belize Land Consultants/Consejo Shores, P.O. Box 35, Corozal Town, 501-423-1005, www.consejoshores.com. Bill Wildman, a land surveyor, developed Consejo Shores near Corozal Town. His family is now involved with the company.

Belize North Real Estate, P.O. Box 226, Corozal Town, 501-422-0284, www.belizenorthrealestate.bz.

Caribbean Properties Consultants/CPC Real Estate Solutions, P.O. Box 149, Dangriga, 501-523-7299 or 669-9000, www.belizeproperty.com.

Ceiba Realty, 119A George Price Highway, Santa Elena Town, Cayo, 501-824-4050 or cell 501-610-4458, www.ceibarealtybelize.com.

Coldwell Banker Southern Belize, Point Placencia, Placencia, 501-523-3500 or 855-723-5493, www.coldwellbankerbelize.com.

Emerald Futures Real Estate, Mile 3½, George Price Highway, Belize City, 501-670-6818, www.emeraldfutures.com.

Pelican Properties, San Pedro, Ambergris Caye, 501-226-3234, www.pelicanbelize.com.

Rainforest Realty, P.O. Box 195, San Ignacio, Cayo, 501-670-4045, www.rainforestrealty.com. Macarena Rose is the founding president of the Belize National Association of REALTORS®.

REMAX Isla Bonita, 10 Coconut Drive, San Pedro, 501-226-4400, www.remaxbz.com.

REMAX San Ignacio, 30 Burns Avenue, San Ignacio, 501-678-2000, www.realestatepropertiesinbelize.com.

Sunrise Realty, 1 Barrier Reef Drive (P.O. Box 236), San Pedro; 501-226-3737, www.sunriserealty.bz. Brokers Chris Berlin and Amanda Syme are San Pedro residents. They focus on properties on Ambergris Caye.

Tropic Real Estate, P.O. Box 453, Belmopan, Cayo, 501-824-3475, www.realestatebelize.com. This is one of the oldest real estate agencies in Cayo. The owner is originally from Texas.

Other Real Estate Agents

For other real estate agents in Belize, check out the websites of the Association of Real Estate Brokers of Belize (AREBB) at www.arebb.com or the Belize National Association of REALTORS (BNAR) at www.belizenational.point2agent.com.

Few Restrictions on Ownership

Belize imposes few restrictions on ownership of land by non-nationals. Unlike Mexico, which prohibits the direct ownership of land by foreigners on or near the coast (though this can be gotten around through certain legal procedures), in Belize foreigners can buy and hold real estate, including beachfront property, in exactly the same way as Belizeans. Formerly an alien landholder's license was needed for purchases of 10 acres or more (or more than 1/2 acre within a town or city.) However, such a license is no longer needed.

The only limitations on ownership by foreign nationals are these: Government approval is required from the Ministry of Natural Resources before the purchase of any island, regardless of size. In a few coastal and caye areas such as Caye Caulker there are rules limiting purchases by non-locals, and approval by the local village council or board must be obtained in advance.

Real Estate Prices

Property prices vary greatly in Belize from one area to another. They generally are highest in Belize City, on Ambergris Caye and in

Placencia, and lowest in remote rural areas.

In large tracts, raw land is available in Belize for under US$300 an acre, but for this price access may be poor and surveying costs may exceed the cost of the land itself. Agricultural land might range from US$500 to $3,000 an acre, or more, depending on quality and access.

Home prices range from under US$25,000 for a basic Belizean-style home in a small village to US$1 million or more for a luxury home on the beach in San Pedro. Finished, newer homes typically sell for from US$75 to $200 per square foot, though of course the location of the lot or land also is a major factor.

The condominium type of ownership is new to Belize, and most condos are on Ambergris Caye. There are a few condos in Placencia and Belize City and on Caye Caulker, and a handful in Corozal Town. Prices start at around US$125,000 for a one-bedroom unit and go up to well over half a million dollars. On a square foot basis, you can expect to pay US$200 to $300 per square foot for a two-bedroom condo with sea views.

Belize has a few timeshares and "fractional ownership" properties, mostly on Ambergris Caye. These are generally not a good investment, and are a high-risk way to use your money, in our opinion.

Property in Belize has appreciated over the past two decades, but by exactly how much is more difficult to say. Real estate agents say that some beachfront property in Placencia, San Pedro and elsewhere that was selling for a few hundred dollars a front foot in 1980 is now going for US$3,000 to $5,000 or more a front foot. Real estate agents naturally talk up the appreciation potential. Keep in mind that the Belize economy is closely tied to the economy in the U.S., and appreciation, or lack of it, in Belize tracks the economy in the U.S.

When the U.S. and world economies went into a tailspin in 2008-2009, real estate sales in Belize slowed. Condo sales in particular stalled. A few condo developments in Placencia and on Ambergris shut down, at least temporarily. Most have been resurrected, typically under new ownership. Former condo owners may have lost at least some of their investment. Several projects and hotels went into receivership. Others stopped or postponed construction. Lot sales also slowed significantly. "Very little is selling in Placencia," one agent said during the height of what has been called the Great Recession. However, even during that downtown interest in small tracts of rural land in inland areas such as Cayo continued.

Despite the slowdown, price levels seem to have held up in most areas. The only big cuts in asking prices are on properties that were overpriced to begin with, real estate agents say.

As of this writing (late 2015/early 2016), some new condo and new home construction is going on again in formerly "hot" areas of Ambergris Caye and Placencia and elsewhere.

Even with appreciation, real estate prices in Belize are still generally inexpensive by the standards of the U.S. or most of Western Europe. That's especially true of beachfront prices, on a relative basis. Waterfront lot prices on the Eastern seaboard of the U.S. or in Florida rarely are less than US$400,000 to $750,000, and in places like Hilton Head, S.C., or Ft. Lauderdale, Fla., can easily reach US$1 million or more, whereas beachfront building lots on Belize's Caribbean are still available for US$100,000 to $250,000, though in prime areas you can pay much more.

Precautions and Pitfalls

Most of the same rules of thumb that apply when looking for a home, land or apartment in the United States or Canada also apply in Belize. But Belize also has its own special situations:

Be prepared to get out and hunt. You're not going to get a deal if you only go to a real estate agent. Many properties in Belize aren't listed with brokers, and the broker listings tend to be priced higher than those that are privately sold (though of course there are exceptions.) You'll need to go out and look for available properties. Just start asking around, and you'll soon have plenty of choices. In Belize, money talks, and if you have the cash some people who have never considered selling may decide it's time to cash in.

Understand that the Belize real estate market is small and inefficient. Someone asked me why a piece of property near Placencia was still on the market three years after he had first seen it advertised. "Is there something wrong with the property?" he asked. No, I told him, nothing wrong with the property. It's just Belize. The real estate marketplace in Belize is even more inefficient than it is elsewhere.

The pool of financially capable real estate buyers in Belize is small, leaving most sellers dependent on foreign buyers. There is little real estate classified advertising, and most properties are sold or rented by word of mouth. Multiple listing services are just in their infancy in Belize. There is no comprehensive computerized database of real estate sales with prices. Thus, it's not easy to find out exactly what is on the market or what the prices are. There are relatively few well-trained real estate agents, appraisers and surveyors. Mortgage financing is not easily available for foreign buyers, further reducing the size of the buying pool and requiring cash sales or owner financing.

All this means that prices for similar properties can be all over the board. The time to sell a property may be measured in YEARS rather months. Which is something to think about as you buy real estate, which you may someday want to sell.

Negotiate. If you're a good horse trader, you'll likely get a better deal in Belize than the guy who isn't. Keep in mind that in most parts of Belize there is far more available real estate than buyers with cold cash, so don't jump at the first deal that comes your way. Remember, too, that in real estate you almost always make your money when you buy, not when you sell. The more you know, the better price you'll get. A common saying among expats in Belize is that the second house you buy or rent is twice as large as the first and costs one-half as much. The real estate market in Belize is so thin that many sellers just pull an asking price out of the air -- similar properties can vary widely in asking price. Unscrupulous real estate agents also sometimes change the asking price in mid-negotiation, in many cases without telling the owner. Spend as much time in Belize as you can before you put any money in real estate.

If at all possible, rent for a while before you buy. That's worth saying again: RENT BEFORE YOU BUY.

Caveat emptor. Buyer beware applies as much in Belize as anywhere else. Real estate agents in Belize still aren't licensed, although licensing efforts are under way, and a couple of real estate associations have been formed (see above). That beachfront lot that looks wonderful in the dry season may be under two feet of water in the rainy season, and there are no laws in Belize that provide for you to get your money back if the real estate agent or seller didn't provide full disclosure. In addition, as soon as the word gets out that you're in the market for a place to live, everybody and his brother will tell you about this little piece of property owned by a cousin of theirs. It may be a good deal, but look before you leap.

In Belize, especially outside resort areas, there are sometimes two prices: one price for locals and another price for foreigners. The difference may be relatively small, but sometimes the Belizean price may be one-half or less of the "rich foreigner" price. From the expat buyers' point of view, this is unfair. From the Belizean point of view, this is perfectly kosher and reflects the reality that Americans (or Canadians or Europeans) make far more money for the same work as Belizeans and can well afford to pay more. One way around this problem is to get a trusted Belizean friend to find out the "local price" for you. Another is spend enough time in the country to get a feel for the difference between the Belizean price and the non-Belizean price, so that at least you can bargain with your eyes open.

What You Get for Your Real Estate Dollar in Belize

Here's a sampler of what you can expect to get for your money in Belize in 2016:

Under US$10,000
Small building lot in some areas of Corozal Town or Toledo or Cayo districts

Under US$15,000
5 acres of land in Orange Walk District or other rural area

Under US$40,000
Back lot on far North Ambergris Caye (no utilities, boat access)
15-acre farm with small very basic dwelling in rural area
Belizean-style house in rural village

Under $60,000
Small cinderblock house in Belmopan
Lagoon side lot on North Ambergris
Lot on Caye Caulker north of the Split

Under US$100,000
Small beachfront lot on far North Ambergris Caye with boat access

only

Riverfront or seaview lot in some areas of Stann Creek, Corozal or Toledo districts

Small but modern concrete home in Belmopan, Corozal or Cayo

Mennonite "prefab" small house on lagoon or riverfront lot on southern coast (including lot)

Under US$150,000

50-acre farm with small dwelling and outbuildings in northern Belize, Cayo or Toledo

Modern 1,000 square-foot home, possibly with waterview in Corozal or Hopkins area

One-bedroom condo on Ambergris Caye or Caye Caulker

Under US$250,000

Two-bedroom condo with sea view on Ambergris Caye

Deluxe 2,000 square-foot home on nice lot in San Ignacio or Corozal

150-acre farm with nice home, outbuildings and equipment in rural

Under US$500,000

4,000 square-foot home on small estate in Cayo

3,000 square-foot home with sea view on Ambergris Caye

400-acre farm with home, outbuildings and equipment in rural area

Small private island

Fees and Costs of Purchase

Besides the cost of the property, you are likely to incur charges associated with the purchase that total 6% to 20% of the purchase price. These include the following:

Stamp Duty: This real estate transfer tax formerly was 15% for most foreign nationals. In 2006, however, it was reduced to 5% across the board, regardless of the nationality or residency status of the buyer. This tax is due at closing and is calculated on the gross sales price of the property, or, in the case of property being transferred at less than market value, of the actual value of the property. There is no stamp duty due on the first US$10,000 of the sale – so if a property is sold for US$50,000 there would be a transfer tax of 5% of US$40,000 or

US$2,000.

GST: The GST of 12.5% applies to the FIRST-TIME sale of new or substantially renovated property. This applies, for example, to newly constructed condos and houses. Substantially renovated usually means that 60% or more of the property was renovated. It also applies in some cases to residential lots selling for the first time in a subdivision. It does NOT apply to the sale of other land or previously occupied homes. Note: In many cases, the GST is rolled into the sales price so that the buyer may not even realize it is being paid.

Attorneys' fee: For around 1% to 2% (usually 2%) of the purchase price, the attorney will draw up sales agreements, transfer documents and ascertain that the title is sound.

Thus, if you are buying a new condominium for US$200,000 at the time of closing you will pay the 5% stamp duty, 12.5% GST and 2% attorney's fee, for a total of 19.5% of the sales price, or US$39,000. Again, the GST is likely included in the sales price and the buyer doesn't see it as a separate charge. Clearly, though, the GST has the impact of increasing the cost of buying new homes, condos or lots in a subdivision. On the purchase of an existing home or tract of land, the total would be around 7% of the selling price.

In addition, there usually are nominal other fees and charges associated with transferring a title, such as for photocopying or filing.

Property taxes: Property taxes vary but are about 1.5% of the as- signed value (NOT market value) of the undeveloped land, payable annually on April 1. In Belize, property taxes outside cities are based on land value rather than the developed value of the property, to encourage development. Property taxes on homes and other developed land even in cities are low, although the government has been increasing them in some areas. For example, the property tax on a nice four-bedroom North American-style home on a large lot would likely be in the range of US$200 to $400, but in some areas the tax might be under US$100. Some expat property owners pay as little as US$20 or $30 property tax annually.

Speculation tax: There is a 5% speculation tax on land of 300 acres or more, payable annually based on the value of the land.

Capital gains tax: There is no capital gains tax in Belize.

Registration and Title

There are three different real property title systems in Belize:

Registered Land Act system, in which application for transfer is made, and a new Land Certificate is issued to the purchaser. Belize is moving to this system throughout the country, but at present it is not yet available everywhere. However, it has now been implemented in many areas popular with foreign buyers, including on Ambergris Caye. Under this system, an application is made for title transfer and a new Certificate of Title is issued to the grantee. Any existing "charges" will be shown on the Land Register for that parcel of land. The owner holds a Certificate of Title, and this, together with the relevant Land Register entries is the proof of ownership.

Conveyance system, which involves the transfer of land by conveyance and registration. This is the system used in much of the United States. In order to assure that the seller actually owns the land, a title search must be made in the Lands Unit in Belmopan to unearth the chain of title and to un- cover any encumbrances such as uncanceled mortgages. This search usually is done by an attorney or a paralegal. Unfortunately, it is sometimes difficult or impossible to trace old conveyances with any degree of certainty of results, due to the condition of the index books.

Torrens system, which involves a First Certificate of Title followed by Transfer Certificates of Title. Unlike the Torrens system in use in parts of the U.S. and elsewhere, the Belize systems is not backed up by a fund, which guarantees title. Under this system, the uncanceled charges or encumbrances and the transfers from the title are shown on the relevant Certificate, so no further search is normally needed before the new Transfer Certificate of Title is issued, following the application for transfer.

Which system you use depends on where your property is located. You won't have a choice. If for example your property is located in an area of Belize where the Registered Land Act system is in place, such as around Belmopan, parts of Corozal, Ambergris Caye, Stann Creek District and elsewhere, or in a planned subdivision, your property will be registered under that system. Land in Belize is being put into this system area by area until eventually freehold land in the entire country will be included in it. Each year, more of Belize is converted to this system and within the next few years likely all or nearly all of Belize will be in this system.

Some property purchasers in Belize complain that it can take many months or even years for the Lands Department to provide them with their Certificate of Title.

Title insurance is available in Belize, though most buying property don't use it. RF&G Insurance and other insurance companies offer title insurance. Typically, title insurance costs 1% of the purchase price. Stewart Title, a U.S.-based title insurance firm, does not have an office in Belize but provides title insurance for some properties through Belizean firms.

Need for a Lawyer

In Belize, attorneys remain trusted advisors. They're usually well-connected and well-paid pillars of the community who wield real power. Fees are not all that different from what you would pay in a small or mid-size city in the U.S.

An attorney, or other trained person, will research the title in the Lands Registry, or in the Companies Registry if the land is held by a corporation. A title opinion for land that is not in the new Title Registration system takes longer to research as an abstract of title must first be prepared that goes back at least 30 years. (The statute of limitations on land claims in Belize generally is 30 years.) Liens, judgments and other encumbrances are valid only if properly lodged. An opinion of good and clear title will be issued once the attorney has satisfactorily examined the abstract.

A roster of attorneys in Belize *(see Appendix)* reveals the surnames of prominent families with histories in Belize going well back into colonial times along with those of today's political leaders including Barrow, Young, Shoman, Musa, Courtenay and Godfrey. In any real estate transaction, you should have your own Belize attorney.

Caution about Buying Leased Land

Many Belizeans own property under a leasehold from the government. The Belize government provides building lots and other small pieces of land to Belizean citizens on a lease basis. After the Belizean clears the property and improves it with a building or some other structure, he or she can apply for a conversion to a fee simple title. However, some Belizean owners never get around to doing this or cannot afford the cost. Be sure that you are buying a fee simple, freehold property, not a leasehold property. Again, this is an area where a Belizean attorney can help you.

Financing

It is difficult for a non-resident to get a mortgage loan from a bank in Belize for buying or building, and if you can get a loan the interest rate will be high – typically 10 to 14% -- so you should be prepared to pay cash, arrange owner financing or get financing through a loan from a non-Belize financial institution on your assets back home.

Acreage and building lots in Belize are often purchased on terms under an Agreement for Sale or Contract for Deed whereby the seller keeps title to the property until it has been paid for in full. Terms vary but can range from 10% down with 10 years to pay at 10% simple interest per annum — about the best deal you can hope for — to 50% down and three years to pay at 10 to 14%, with perhaps a balloon at the end. Residential property may also have owner financing, although commonly the lowest price will be for all-cash deals. A few owners of condos and homes in San Pedro and elsewhere offer financing, typically with around 20% down.

For citizens and official permanent residents of Belize only, the Development Finance Corporation (DFC), a financial institution owned by the government of Belize, formerly made loans of US$2,500-$50,000 or more for building or buying housing. The DFC also developed housing subdivisions near Belmopan on Ambergris Caye, on what is now the Goldson Highway in Belize District, and in Corozal Town. These subdivisions offered new homes, such as a small, three-bedroom, concrete house near Belmopan for US$35,000 and a three-bedroom, two-bath home of 925 square feet at Ladyville for about US$47,000. Financing was at 12% for up to 25 years.

Belizeans did not seem to care much for most of these subdivisions, and some homes were never sold. Reportedly, some of the houses were poorly constructed and located in undesirable areas. In 2004, the DFC ran out of financial string and temporarily ceased active operations.

However, the **DFC** (www.dfcbelize.org, 501-822-2350) has been resurrected by the Belize government. It now makes loans for home purchases, home construction, home renovation, agricultural and tourism projects and even education. To qualify, the loan applicant must be a

Belizean citizen, including citizens living abroad, or official permanent resident between 18 and 70 years of age and must meet the DFC's loan standards. Rates currently are available at interest rates beginning at 9.75% with repayment periods of up to 25 years. Loan origination fees start at 2%.

The DFC is based in Belmopan (P.O. Box 40, Bliss Parade, Belmopan City) and has offices in Belize City, San Pedro, Corozal Town, Orange Walk Town and Dangriga.

Real Estate Foreclosure Auctions

From time to time there are foreclosure auctions in Belize. They sell property put up as security for bank or other financial institution loans. Usually these are advertised in the weekly newspapers in Belize City. Some banks holding foreclosed property may put notices of property to be auctioned on their websites. Foreigners can participate in these auctions. Generally, at least 10% of the successful bid price must be tendered at the time of the auction. There may be no particular problems in buying at a foreclosure auction, other than those ordinarily associated with auctions, such as the fact that among the savvy bidders may be local people who know more than you do about the property and its value. However, in Belize sometimes the owners of the property will still be in possession at the time of the auction. If so, you may face a real problem getting the owners out. Before putting up your money, you may want to consult with an attorney conversant with real estate property law and with foreclosure auctions *(see Appendix for a list of attorneys in Belize.)*

Rentals

Rental costs in Belize also vary widely, being highest on Ambergris Caye and in Belize City. In upscale areas of Belize City, you can expect to pay around US$.80 to $2 per square foot per month, or about US$800 to $2,000 a month for a 1,000 sq. ft. two-bedroom apartment. On Ambergris Caye, a one-bedroom apartment suitable for most expats goes for US$600 to $1,000 and a two-bedroom US$900 to $2,000.

Elsewhere, rentals are much lower. In rural areas and low-cost towns such as Corozal, you can find a small house in a safe area for under US$400 a month and sometimes for as little as one-half that amount. Modern three-bedroom homes near the water go for US$500 to $1,000 a month. We know of expats in Corozal who rent for under US$300 a month, and while their homes are not fancy they are comfortable, typically of concrete block construction with a couple of small bedrooms, bath, a living room and a kitchen with stove and refrigerator. In all areas, North American-style housing with air conditioning, modern appliances, and security systems will be several times more expensive than a traditional Belize rental, simple concrete or wood house, with only basic amenities and probably no appliances except for a butane stove and a small fridge.

Short-Term Rentals

If you're coming to Belize on a scouting expedition of a few weeks to a few months, consider a short-term rental. Staying in a house or apartment rather than in a hotel can help you decide if Belize is really for you. Unfortunately, there are not a lot of short-term vacation rentals in Belize. Most of them are concentrated on Ambergris Caye, but there are a few in other areas including Placencia and Corozal. In most areas, however, you can find a hotel with housekeeping facilities.

Free Land?

You may have heard about a program of homesteading or otherwise getting free land in Belize. Yes, there is such a program in place, but there are big catches: First, you must be a Belizean citizen or have lived in the country as an official resident for at least three years. Second, land is only available in certain areas. Mainly it is small tracts or building lots. Third, you have to lease the land from the government, clear it and actually construct a home or make other improvements. At that point, for a nominal amount you can buy the property from the government, and you will get title. Given the time and red tape involved, and the low cost of land in Belize, it's may not be worth it to get a small piece of land worth a few thousand dollars. Frankly, if the only reason you moved to Belize is to take advantage of such a scheme, it's unlikely you'll have the financial resources to make it in Belize long enough to qualify for the program.

Kitchen cabinets custom-made of Belizean mahogany

BUILDING A HOME IN BELIZE

Building is usually cheaper than buying, especially if you act as your own general contractor. As a rule, you will get more for your housing dollar in Belize by building rather than buying a completed home. You'll often get a lot more home. However, you'll also get a lot more headaches. If you can put up with construction hassles – which are many — you can build a house with details such as built-in furniture, exotic tropical hardwood floors and ceilings and custom-made mahogany cabinets that in the U.S. would be found only in the most upscale homes.

What Does It Cost?

Construction costs vary depending on such factors the cost of transportation of materials to the building site, the terrain and quality of work. In Belize, construction costs are higher on the coast and cayes, because of the need to use hurricane resistant construction. In the case of the cayes, it costs extra to transport building materials out to the islands by boat. Building costs u s u a l l y also are higher in southern than in northern Belize. Inexpensive building materials are more readily available

111

in northern Belize since some can be imported from Chetumal or elsewhere in Mexico or are available at large home lumber and supply stores in Belize City such as Benny's.

Labor in Belize is much less expensive than in the U.S., with carpenters and masons typically getting around US$30 to $50 a day or less, depending on location. At times when a lot of home building is going on, especially around Placencia and on Ambergris Caye, labor costs may rise. Unskilled construction workers may only get US$15 to $20 a day.

While labor may be cheap, jobs usually take longer in Belize. Workers may be skilled at construction techniques common in Belize but may lack knowledge about building in the American style. Outside of urban areas, it is difficult to find w e l l - qualified craftspeople such as electricians and plumbers. Building materials vary but are mostly no cheaper than in the U.S., except for locally produced items such as tropical hardwoods which run about US$1,000 for 1,000 board feet. Also, locally produced plywood is roughly one-half the cost in the U.S. (though plywood prices vary over time due to fluctuating demand.) Cement is more expensive than in the U.S. — a 50 lb. bag typically costs around US$6 to $8 — as are most bathroom and kitchen fixtures that have to be imported. Flooring materials such as salt tiles from Guatemala and Mexico are moderately priced and of high quality. Overall, building costs in Belize range from around US$35 to $200 or more a square foot, not including the cost of land. At the bottom end, that would be a simple Belizean-style cinderblock house or frame construction, and at the top it would be high-quality reinforced and poured concrete construction with hardwood floors and trim and with many custom details such as hand-made doors and windows. Most commonly, you'd expect to pay about US$60 to $100 a square foot, so a 1,500 square foot home would cost US$90,000 to $150,000 to build, not including land. That's about one-third less than typical costs for construction in smaller cities and towns in the U.S.

Having said that, costs can vary tremendously from builder to builder. One resident of San Pedro said he got quotes for the construction of a five-bedroom reinforced concrete home that varied from US$90 to $250 a square foot.

Regardless of where or how you build, you need to be on-site to manage and oversee the construction, or pay someone you trust very well to do that for you. Expect that the process will take roughly twice as long as you expect – eight months to a year, or longer, to build a house is not uncommon.

Especially in rural areas or on the coast, a lot of the cost of building is underground – foundations, pilings, cisterns, septic tanks. You may need two or more septic tanks for a large house. Cisterns for your drinking water cost roughly US$50 cents to $1 a gallon to construct. Septic systems cost many thousands of dollars, depending on the site and type of system.

Of course, if you have a nose for saving money you can build for much less than that. We know one fellow who built a small house on a lagoon north of Corozal for about US$4,000. He collected building materials such as old planks and boards that were floating in the lagoon, scrounged others from old houses and did most of the actual construction work himself. The charity organization Habitat for Humanity has constructed a number of affordable homes in Belize. Habitat said that the cost around of a basic two-bedroom, one-bath 528 sq. ft. concrete block house with a septic tank was about US$11,000, and US$15,000 for a 720 sq. ft. three-bedroom house. This does not include the cost of land. That was around US$21 a square foot. (The cost has increased slightly in the last several years.)

In areas at risk of hurricanes and tropical storms, you'll have to put in deep pilings and raise the first floor above ground level to avoid water damage. Depending on the area and the depth and type of pilings, these can cost as much as US$3,000 to $5,000 each. Reinforced concrete is the preferred construction. Hurricane straps and rafter ties are inexpensive protection against having the roof blown away. Most insurance companies in Belize no longer will cover traditional thatch construction, and some also will not cover wood frame construction if the house is on the coast or cayes.

Insurance

Insurance if available at all will vary with the construction: Wood frame construction in coastal or island areas will incur annual premiums of up to 2 to 4% of value, whereas steel construction will see premiums of around 1.25-1.50% of value and reinforced concrete about 2% or less.

Building Codes and Permits

In the past, the only building codes in Belize have been those imposed by local municipalities. Many rural areas had no codes at all, and builders often ignored any existing codes. Those were, in some respects, the good old days.

Belize now has a building code calling for nation-wide standards of construction. The Central Building Authority (CBA) is taking a tougher stance to assure that builders follow the building code. Before construction for a house can be approved, at least three sets of drawings must be presented (including an electrical plan approved by the Public Utilities Commission) to the CBA, an application for construction made and the appropriate fees paid. Depending on the size of the building, the use of an architect and professional engineer may be required.

CBA application fee for homes under 1,000 square feet is US$25, and US$50 for homes over 1,000 square feet. Residential permit fees range from US5 to 7 ½ cents per square foot, and there are other rates for decks, pools, fences, piers, etc. Builders now need approvals for zoning, fire safety, environmental issues and others from up to 15 different governmental regulatory authorities, including the National Fire Service, Public Utilities Commission, Fisheries Department and Department of the Environment depending on where and what you are building. What you've read in the past about the lack of construction red tape in Belize is simply no longer true.

Check the CBA's website at www.cbabelize.org for more information.

The CBA has authority nationally, although it works with local building authorities. Varying local codes apply. For example, within Belmopan City limits only concrete new construction is permitted, not wood. More developed areas such as San Pedro and Belize City have the strictest building permit and code systems.

A licensed electrician must sign off on the electrical work before the building can be hooked up to Belize Electricity Ltd.

Trailers and Manufactured Homes in Belize

Trailer trash? Not in Belize. You won't find many mobile homes, trailers or "manufactured homes" (except from the Mennonites – see below). There are several reasons for this: For one, trailers aren't known for durability or safety in hurricanes. For another, the cost of shipping prefab units to Belize is high. Also, mobile homes and trailers don't stand up well to the hot, humid semitropical climate – rusting, abandoned RVs you see in the bush are proof of that. Perhaps most importantly, import duties make bringing in trailers an unattractive option compared with building locally. However, some expats do decide to import prefab buildings. The original owner of the Nautical Inn beach resort in Seine Bight on the Placencia peninsula brought in pre-fab hexagonal buildings from North Carolina and had them set up on the beach by local laborers.

Mennonite Prefab: Cheap Alternative

An inexpensive alternative to building from scratch in Belize is to have a prefabricated Mennonite house set up on your lot. Mennonite builders in Spanish Lookout and elsewhere build and sell small frame buildings, which they will deliver and install on pilings on your site.

This is a quick way to get a home up in Belize, and even some small resorts use these buildings. The prefab buildings typically are made of local hardwoods and come with mahogany or glass louvered windows. You can get them as unfinished shells or complete down to electrical wiring and plumbing. Usually there is a choice of roofing materials – zinc, tin (painted or unpainted) or asphalt shingles. The cabins are set up on 6"x6" posts typically 8 feet apart and about 3 feet off the ground. You may want to upgrade the specs to your own standards -- for example using 2"x4" framing rather than smaller studs. You can buy these prefab houses from standardized plans or custom order.

Prices vary, but here are typical prices, usually including transportation to your mainland lot and in some cases 12.5% GST:

20 ft. x 24 ft. (480 sq. ft.) US$14,000-$19,000

20 ft. x 36 ft. (600 sq. ft.) US$17,000-$24,000

20 ft. x 40 ft. (800 sq. ft.) with 6 ft. x 20 ft. porch US$20,000-$30,000

Delivery and set up and transportation to the cayes and to remote areas on the mainland could increase the price substantially. Also, septic systems, cistern, electrical hook-ups, kitchen appliance, permits and other charges could increase the cost considerably.

Here's a breakdown of costs in BELIZE dollars as of 2015 for a 20'x40' (800 square feet) hardwood house from Plett's Home Builders in Spanish Lookout (prices subject to change):

Basic price for 3 BR/2 BA 20x40 hardwood house	BZ$31,200
15 6"x6" hardwood posts installed to 3 ft. floor level	BZ$900
Transportation to Dangriga area	BZ$2,857
5 additional doors	BZ$1,125
Plywood interior partitioning of rooms	BZ$3,825
Ceilings	BZ$1,875
Walls cased with plywood	BZ$2,250
Electrical breaker box	BZ$200
Light switches and bulbs	BZ$500
28 electrical outlets	BZ$1,400
2 sets of 3-foot exterior stairs	BZ$300
Shower tub	BZ$1,500
1 shower stall, 2 toilets, 2 washbasins	BZ$1,760
12.5% GST	BZ$6,212
Total	BZ$55,904 (US$27,952)

Sources of prefab Mennonite houses include:

Linda Vista Lumber & Houses, Route 40, Spanish Lookout, Cayo, 501-823-0257; www.lindavistabelize.com

Midwest Lumber Mill, Spanish Lookout, Cayo, 501-823-8000

Plett's Home Builders, Spanish Lookout, Cayo, 501-823-0398; www.plettshomebuilders.com

Tobar's Home Construction, Mile ½ Iguana Bridge, Spanish Lookout, Cayo, 501-824-2660; www.tobar-construction.com

Household Expenses

You'll get some good --and some bad-- surprises when you open your household bills in Belize. On the positive side, you won't be getting a bill for fuel oil or gas to heat your home. Very few houses in Belize even have a furnace or heater, since winter temperatures rarely fall even into the 50s. If a cold front comes through, just put a blanket on the bed or pull on a cotton sweater.

However, electricity (it's often called "current" in Belize) is much pricier than in the U.S. or Canada. Figure about US24 cents per kilowatt-hour, which is a little over twice the average in the U.S. High electric rates are why most Belizeans don't have air conditioning, or if they do have A/C, it's only in the bedrooms. Belize Electricity, Ltd., is the sole provider in Belize. About 40% of the electricity used in Belize is purchased from Mexico.

The Chalillo Dam in Cayo, along with three other dams, are supposed to help Belize become energy-independent, but arguably at the cost of wildlife habitat. So far, the dams have not lowered electrical costs in Belize, nor have they made the grid significantly more reliable. Outages and surges still occur − occasionally to frequently, depending on your perspective and need for 24/7 power. If you're off the grid, as many still are in remote rural areas, either you do without power or run a diesel generator. Wind, hydro and solar energy are making some headway in Belize, although despite recent declines in the price of solar systems, initial set-up costs in Belize are high. A small community of some 20 homes on Caye Caulker, for example, generates all its power from alternate sources, mainly wind turbines. Due to the cost of batteries and other materials, they say that their long-term costs are about US$1 a kilowatt.

Water and sewerage bills vary around the country, but a typical monthly cost per household is about US$10-$20. "Pipe water," as it's known in Belize, is costlier on Ambergris Caye and Caye Caulker. If you live in a rural area, you'll probably have your own water system, either a well or a cistern to collect rainwater, and a septic tank for wastes. Thus, your only expenses will be the initial cost of the systems, plus any electricity you use.

Most households in Belize run stoves and hot water showers on butane. Butane is sold in Belize instead of propane, since there's not an issue with butane freezing. Rates vary according to energy prices, but on average, a small household may use US$30-$80 worth of butane a month. Trucks deliver butane tanks to your home, or at least to the road in front of your home.

Aside from your telephone, electric and butane bills, the only other utility expense you may face is garbage pickup. Belizeans refer to it as "dirt." Your dirt bill will probably not run more than US$10, and pickup is free in some areas. Also, cable television bills generally are in Belize than you're used to back home. Typical monthly rates are US$20-40 but are increasing in some areas.

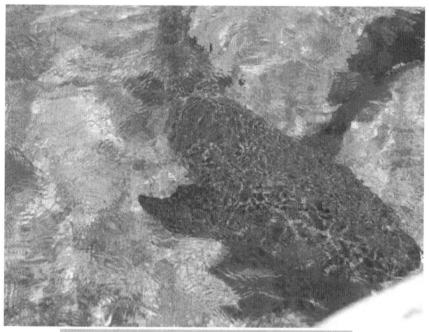

Nurse shark at Hol Chan – nicer than land sharks

BEST PLACES TO LIVE OVERVIEW

Here, in thumbnail sketches, are your main choices for living, retiring and investing in Belize. In the chapters that follow, we'll explore in more detail the options in each of these areas, including a closer look at what each area offers, the cost of living, price and availability of real estate, examples of property for sale and rent and other practical matters. We'll also provide information on transportation, hotels, restaurants and sightseeing to help you make a scouting trip to Belize.

NORTHERN CAYES

The two largest of the Northern Cayes are Ambergris (pronounced Am-BUR-griss Key) and Caye Caulker, sometimes known as Caye Corker.

Ambergris Caye

Ambergris Caye is the most popular place for retirees and other expats to live in Belize. It offers the beauty of the Caribbean in a fairly compact, accessible package. You can dive, snorkel, swim and fish to your heart's content. San Pedro, Ambergris Caye's only town, has Belize's biggest selection of restaurants and nightlife.

Island life presents its own special set of pleasures and problems. On Ambergris Caye, residents say island fever strikes from time to time. Most residents go into Belize City regularly to conduct business, shop for items not available on the island or to get dental care. Many expats take vacations in the U.S. or Mexico, or long weekends in Cayo district or elsewhere in Belize.

While beachfront house and lot prices are no longer the bargain they once were, they are not necessarily expensive by U.S. coastal standards. You can buy a buildable beach lot on North Ambergris for US$75,000 and up, or build a small but pleasant seaside home for US$200,000 to $300,000, including land. Costs on the back or lagoon side are lower.

Prices for quality beachfront land, especially near San Pedro, rose rapidly during the 1990s and early 2000s, at least until the big recession hit the U.S. in 2008-2009, and now are in the US$3,000 to $5,000 a front foot range. In and near town they are higher.

Most of the island's economy is focused on tourism. If you aren't busy selling real estate or running a hotel or restaurant, the island offers some volunteer opportunities. Some expats help out at the local library, or do church work (the island has one Catholic church and several Protestant denominations). The San Pedro chapter of the Lions Club is the island's most active civic organization. Its weekly barbecue is delicious, cheap and a fund-raiser for the group's good works.

Caye Caulker

Ambergris Caye's sister island is smaller and, if anything, even friendlier. Residents here have managed to maintain close ownership of land on the island, though some lots and houses are available on the open market. A few condos are going up. We see Caulker as a real growth area for real estate over the next few years, barring a major hurricane. A few apartments are for rent, starting at around US$400 to $600 a month.

COROZAL IN NORTHERN BELIZE

Most visitors to Belize either never get to Corozal or pass through quickly en route somewhere else. But Corozal Town and nearby Consejo village, not to mention the Cerros area and Sarteneja village, offer a lot for those staying awhile: low prices, friendly people, a generally low-crime environment, the beautiful blue water of Corozal Bay and the extra plus of having Mexico next door for shopping. There's even a new Sam's Club in Chetumal, just across the border. Corozal is one of the undiscovered jewels of Belize. There's not a lot to do, but it's a great place to do it.

The Sugar Coast – sugarcane is a main agricultural crop here as it is in the adjoining Orange Walk district – is a place to slow down, relax and enjoy life. The climate is appealing, with less rain than almost anywhere else in Belize, and fishing is excellent. The sunny disposition of residents – Mestizos, Creoles, Maya, Chinese, East Indians and even North Americans – is infectious. Real estate costs in Corozal are among the lowest in Belize. Modern North American-style homes with three or four bedrooms in Corozal Town or Consejo Shores go for US$100,000 to around US$250,000, but Belizean-style homes start at less than US$40,000. Waterfront lots are available for as little as US$75,000 to $125,000, and lots near the water are US$15,000-$30,000. Rentals are relatively inexpensive – US$200-$350 for a Belizean-style house or US$400-$1,000 for a modern American-style house.

Several sizeable real estate developments, including Orchid Bay, are building homes and condos and selling lots in areas along Chetumal Bay between Corozal Town and Sarteneja.

ORANGE WALK DISTRICT IN NORTHERN BELIZE

Orange Walk Town — the name came from the orange groves in the area — could be any number of towns in Mexico. There's a formal plaza, and the town hall is called the Palacio Municipal. The businesses and houses along the main drag, called Queen Victoria Avenue or the Belize-Corozal Road, have barred windows, and some of the hotels and bars are in fact brothels. In this setting, conservative Mennonites from Shipyard and Blue Creek who come to town to sell produce look strangely out of place. Except in Belize.

Not many would want to live in Orange Walk Town itself. However, Orange Walk Town is a gateway to a magical area of Belize — the big sky, fertile land and unpeopled forests of Belize's northwest shoulder, bush and jungle pressed against the Guatemala border.

CAYO DISTRICT IN WESTERN BELIZE

Cayo has a lot going for it: wide open spaces, cheap land, relatively few bugs and friendly people. This might be the place to buy a few acres and grow oranges. The major towns are San Ignacio/Santa Elena, with a population of around 20,000, about 10 miles from the Guatemala border, and Belmopan City, the miniature capital of Belize, with a population of approaching 20,000. Agriculture, ranching and, increasingly, tourism are the major industries here. About 30 years ago, the first small jungle lodges began operation around San Ignacio. Now there is a flourishing mix of hotels, cottages and jungle lodges near San Ignacio and in the Mountain Pine Ridge, along with a lot of natural attractions and outdoor activities – canoeing, caving, hiking, horseback riding, to name a few. The country's most accessible Maya ruins are here, as well as Caracol, in its heyday a competitor city-state to Tikal. Between Belize City and San Ignacio, Belmopan is the downsized capital of Belize, but the attractions are in the surrounding countryside. The Belize Zoo (in Belize, not Cayo, District) is nearby, as are several excellent jungle lodges. Along the scenic Hummingbird Highway are caves, wild rivers and national park areas. Small farms are available for US$25,000-$150,000.

HOPKINS ON THE SOUTHERN COAST

On the southern coast of Belize in Stann Creek District between Dangriga and Placencia, Hopkins today is what Placencia was like just a decade or so ago. Expatriates are moving to Hopkins, a friendly Garifuna village that got telephones only in the mid-1990s, and to real estate developments nearby. New small seaside resorts and luxury condo developments are going up in Hopkins and Sittee Point. Although at times the sand flies can eat you alive here, you can get in some excellent fishing and beach time, with day trips to the nearby Cockscomb Basin Wildlife Sanctuary or Mayflower/Bocawina National Park and boat trips to the reef. You'll love Hopkins if Placencia is too developed for you.

Sanctuary Belize, between Placencia and Hopkins, is one of Belize's largest developments. Though controversial in many ways, it has marketed aggressively in the U.S. and has sold many lots.

PLACENCIA ON THE SOUTHERN COAST

Placencia has the best beaches on the mainland, and it's an appealing seaside alternative to the bustle of Ambergris Caye. The paving of the Placencia Road, which was completed in 2012, has made access to the peninsula much easier.

This peninsula in southern Belize has some 16 miles of beachfront along the Caribbean, a backside lagoon where manatees are frequently seen, two small villages, a few dozen hotels and restaurants and an increasing number of expatriates and foreign-owned homes. In recent years, the Placencia peninsula has been undergoing a boom, a boom that was slowed only temporarily by Hurricane Iris in 2001. Building lots by the score have been sold to foreigners who think they'd someday like to live by the sea.

Beginning around 2004-2005, condo development on the peninsula took off, and hundreds of condo units were built in condo zones in Placencia, San Pedro and elsewhere. However, construction screeched to a halt as the housing crunch and recession seized up markets in the U.S. and elsewhere, and one large condo project on the peninsula shut down, while plans for others were shelved, at least temporarily.

Seafront real estate costs are higher in Placencia than anywhere else in Belize, except Ambergris Caye. Beachfront lots cost US$2,500 to $4,500 per front foot, making a seaside lot around US$125,000 to $225,000 or more. Lots on the lagoon or canal are less expensive. There is little North American-style housing available for sale or rent, and many expatriates are building their own homes, with building costs ranging upwards of US$100-$200 per square foot, depending on type of construction.

The Cocoplum project, spearheaded by Stewart Krohn, is a model for well-planned development in Belize. The Placencia Hotel and Residences is not.

The unknown kicker here is the opening in early 2016 of the Norwegian Cruise Lines cruise port on an island just off Placencia. Who knows what the impact will be of hundreds of thousands of cruise daytrippers waddling around Placencia and environs?

PUNTA GORDA AREA IN SOUTHERN BELIZE

Rainy, beautiful and remote, Punta Gorda in far southern Belize is the jumping-off point for unspoiled Maya villages and for onward travel to Guatemala and Honduras. The completion of the Southern Highway, now the best major road in Belize, has made access to the far south a lot easier, and work is far along on a new paved road connecting the Southern Highway to Guatemala. Improvements in transport should begin to pay off for Toledo, both in terms of tourism and as a place for expatriate living.

"PG," as it's known, is Toledo District's only population center, with about 6,000 people, mostly Garifuna, Maya and immigrants from Guatemala. Maya villages, hardly changed for centuries, are located around PG. Cayes and the south end of the barrier reef offer good snorkeling and fishing. Lumbering and fishing are about the only industries. Undeveloped land is inexpensive, with acreage beginning at a few hundred dollars an acre. Few North American-style homes are for sale. Quality rentals are fairly expensive due to demand from missionaries and lack of supply.

PRIVATE ISLANDS

The days of buying your own private island for a song are long gone, but if you have money to burn and the willingness to rebuild after the next hurricane, one of Belize's remote islands could be yours, beginning at about US$100,000 and going up to several million. In 2005, Leo DiCaprio, the star of *Titanic*, bought Blackadore Caye, a 104-acre island near San Pedro, for a reported US$2.4 million, or about US$23,000 an acre.

Developers have been selling lots on a few small cayes. Keep in mind that transporting materials to the island, building there and maintaining the property likely will be much, much higher than on the mainland.

Beachfront Land Costs in Belize

Many dream of living on a Caribbean beach. Here's the reality of what you'll pay for beachfront lots in Belize today. These are typical selling prices per front foot on the beach. If the lot has 75 feet of beach frontage, multiply that by the per-front foot cost in U.S. dollars. While the overall size and depth of the lot affects the total price, a 200-foot deep lot may be only a little more expensive than a 100- or 150-foot deep lot. It's the frontage on the water that matters most. The top end of the price range is for better-quality, buildable lots on higher ground. Large tracts with extensive beachfront typically would be less than prices shown here.

Corozal Town Area: US$1,000-$2,500
Cerros/Sarteneja Peninsula: US$900-$2,000
Ambergris Caye: US$2,500-$8,500
Placencia Peninsula: US$2,500-$4,500
Hopkins/Sittee Point Area: US$2,000-$4,500
Toledo District: US$500-$2,000

Yesterday: Old sandy street in San Pedro

NORTHERN CAYES IN DETAIL

Ambergris Caye

The two main Northern Cayes are Ambergris Caye and Caye Caulker. The first area we'll look at is the best-known destination in Belize for both visitors and prospective expats -- Ambergris Caye.

GRADING THE AREA FOR RETIREMENT, RELOCATION AND INVESTMENT

Ratings are on an A to F scale, just like your old high school report card. A is the top grade; F is failing. Grades are on a curve, relative compared to other areas in Belize.

Popularity with Expats   A
Safety   B

Overall Cost of Living	C-
Real Estate Costs	D
Investment Potential	B
Leisure Activities	B+
Restaurants	A
Cultural Activities	D+
Infrastructure	B-
Business Potential	B+
Medical Care	C+
Shopping	B-

ADVANTAGES OF AMBERGRIS CAYE: • Largest expat community in Belize • Busy resort island atmosphere with the country's best restaurants and hotels • Offers some of Belize's best beaches • Provides excellent water sports opportunities – diving, boating, fishing • No need for a car • Reasonably safe though burglaries and thefts are common

Ambergris Caye is the most popular destination in Belize, for expats and travelers. There are good reasons for that: Ambergris Caye has a pleasant, laid-back attitude. Folks are friendly. There's a wide selection of hotels and restaurants and quite a few little shops. And of course, there's the Caribbean – big and blue and beautiful, with the barrier reef only a few hundred yards off the shore. This isn't a large island, although it's by far the biggest in Belize. It's only 25 miles long and 4 miles wide at its widest point, about one-half the size of Barbados. Much of the island is low mangrove swamp, and there are a dozen lagoons.

With the paving of the former golf path on North Ambergris, now underway as of this writing, and the prospect of a possible international airport also on North Ambergris, you can expect to see continued growth of tourism and foreign investment on the island.

A Tour of the Island

The experienced Caribbean traveler may recognize San Pedro Town immediately: In some ways, it's the Caribbean of 30 years ago, before the boom in international travel, a throwback to the days before cruise ships turned too many Caribbean islands into concrete mini-malls hustling duty-free booze and discount jewelry. Wood houses

126

and shops are painted in bright tropical colors fading in the sun.

Yet, first impressions may hide the huge changes that have taken place in Ambergris Caye, especially in the past 10 or 15 years. Newer buildings are reinforced concrete, optimistically girded for the next big hurricane. Once limited to construction "no higher than a palm tree," now there are five-story buildings on the island, and large steel, concrete and glass bank and office buildings. While many people still get around by foot and bicycle, and the back streets are still sandy, there are more and more paved streets are busy with golf carts. Keep a close eye, as the electric ones sneak up behind you silently. Unfortunately, also on the island are an ever-increasing number of pickups and cars. In fact, there are so many taxis and private cars that there are occasional traffic jams downtown, and at times you take your life in your hands walking on the street. To the north of town, over the new bridge over the channel, the large expanse of North Ambergris is being opened up to additional development due to the paving of a road up through part of the north.

The name of Front Street (dozens of Caribbean islands have main streets named Front, Middle and Back) was changed years ago to the more romantic-sounding Barrier Reef Drive. It is one-way, with carts and vehicles allowed to go north only for most of its distance, to Caribeña Street. On weekends, the street is closed to all but pedestrians. Middle Street, or Pescador Drive, is one-way south from the intersection with Caribeña Street, also is paved and heavily trafficked. Many hotels, restaurants and larger businesses are on Barrier Reef Drive. Just beyond the primary school and the bite-sized San Pedro Library (here, you don't need a library card, and even visitors can check out books, free, or a buy a used paperback for a dollar or two), you'll see Ruby's and part of the old San Pedro: the San Pedro Holiday Hotel, a pioneer in the hotel industry on the island; Spindrift, home of the chicken drop; and then, near "Central Park," Big Daddy's and Jaguar's clubs are across the street from each other, and the Catholic church, cool and welcoming, stands guard. Farther up on the right there's Fido's, a popular bar and restaurant, and the Mayan Princess. On the left is the big, modern Belize Bank building. As Barrier Reef Drive peters out, dead ahead is the ultra-deluxe The Phoenix resort and Red Ginger restaurant.

To the east, beyond the line of buildings, only a few feet away, accessible through many alleys, is the Caribbean. There's a narrow strip of beach and seawall between the buildings and the sea, used as a pedestrian walkway. A number of piers or docks jut out into the sea. The patch of white you see a few hundred yards out is surf breaking over the barrier reef. Even if you're a strong swimmer, don't try swimming out to the reef from the shore, especially not in or near town. There is a lot of boat traffic inside the reef, and over the years several swimmers have been killed or injured by boats. Pescador Drive, the other main north-south venue, is also busy. It's home to several restaurants, including Elvi's Kitchen, which got its start out of the owner's window, Cocina Caramba, The Reef and others. Farther north on Middle Street, San Pedro becomes slightly more residential, and more local. You'll see the San Pedro Supermarket, Ritchie's and Island Supermarket (there's another one south), electric and telephone facilities, a small high school, a children's playground and then the Boca del Rio or "the river mouth" or "the channel."

Bridge over the "river" becomes a paved road north of the bridge

Cross the Bridge to North Ambergris

In early 2006, a new bridge opened over the river. Until then, you

128

crossed the channel on a hand-pulled ferry. The bridge originally was for golf carts, bikes and pedestrians only, but now regular taxis, trucks and other vehicles are permitted to cross. Golf carts are charged US$5 round-trip. For longer-term stays you can buy a monthly bridge pass, around US$75.

Part of the former golf cart path on North Ambergris is now a paved road. Plans are for it to be paved as far north as La Beliza, formerly Blue Reef resort, about 8 miles north. As this area is partly swampy, a lot of fill is needed.

Prime Minister Dean Barrow said in 2015 that he would like to see the former Basil Jones airstrip redeveloped as an international airport. There's long been talk of an airport on the north part of the island, and it's anyone's guess whether the Prime Minister's vision will come true.

Farther up, a golf cart and walking path wends its way north, mostly on the back side of the island, past several new or under-construction condo and residential developments, expat homes, restaurants and resorts. The cart path, the unpaved part of which can wash badly when it rains, is often bumpy and muddy.. One of the first things you see after crossing the bridge is a small movie theater and what is possibly the ugliest developments in all of Belize, Reef Village Resort and timeshare. In late 2015, it had the distinction of being the lowest rated by TripAdvisor of all 54 regular hotels on Ambergris Caye (besides the hotel category, TripAdvisor also has a B&B and Inns, Specialty Lodging and Vacation Rentals categories.)

About a mile and half above the bridge is a new outdoor food court and bar, The Truck Stop. You can drive your cart past Captain Morgan's, made briefly famous by "Temptation Island," an early reality TV show, and with its timeshares, condos and small casino, as far as Belizean Shores, Seascape, Las Terrazas, Rojo Bar and Azul Resort, Matachica and Portofino. In good weather you can go past the paved portion all the way to Robles Point beyond La Beliza. But it is a long drive, even with the newly surfaced section. Be sure to take plenty of bug spray, and wear light-colored clothes, because on North Ambergris away from the water, mosquitoes can be terrible, especially in the late summer and fall after seasonal rains.

A ferry service, Coastal Xpress (www.coastalxpress.com, 501-226-2007), has seven boats that provide water transportation up and down the island, making 10 regular stops. The boats carry pedestrians only, with regular stops from the Amigos del Mar dock in San Pedro Town as far to La Beliza, generally from around 5:30 a.m. to 10:30 p.m. At other times and to non-regular stops as far north as Tranquility Bay, Coastal Xpress operates as a private water taxi. Rates vary according to distance travelled, with regular stops from US$5 to $14 per person one-way. A one-day pass is US$25, and monthly and other passes also are offered.

Beyond most of the resorts is a large area that is developing for private homes, but some of it is still undeveloped. Over the years, many schemes have been floated for this part of the island, once part of a private holding called the Pinkerton Estate. A large chunk of this area has been saved from Cancunization thanks to establishment of the Bacalar Chico national park and marine reserve. The park, which opened in 1996, comprises 12,000 acres of land and 15,000 acres of water. At present the park is accessible by boat from San Pedro, from the Belize mainland at Sarteneja and elsewhere and also from the Mexican village of Xcalak. The park is home to a surprisingly large population of birds and wildlife, and there are a number of Maya sites. This northern tip of the island is separated from the Mexican Yucatán only by the narrow Bacalar Chico channel. Indeed, Ambergris Caye once was physically part of the Yucatán peninsula, the channel having been dug by the Maya. In recent years, several remote beachfront resorts have opened some 8 to 12 miles north of town, including La Beliza, El Secreto and Tranquility Bay. Some of these are more like being on a remote offshore island than on Ambergris Caye.

Heading South

Head south from town rather than north, and you're on Coconut Drive. A cluster of hotels and other businesses are near the airstrip, including SunBreeze, The Palms and Ramon's Village, which nearly completely burned down in August 2013 but was quickly rebuilt. Tropic Air's attractive new terminal, which opened in 2009, even has an aquarium in the waiting area. In 2008, Coconut Drive as far south as Victoria House was paved with concrete cobblestones.

You'll pass the Changes in Latitudes B&B, Exotic Caye with its thatch cabaña condos (partially destroyed in a 2015 fire), Corona Del Mar, Coconuts Hotel, Caribbean Villas, which has a good beach bar, and Xanadu. You'll also pass Island Supermarket, San Pedro's largest (and most expensive) grocery, and Bowen & Bowen's warehouse facility. At the warehouse you can buy Belikin, soft drinks and bottled water by the case for less than you'd pay in groceries. Some of the buildings, you'll note, are painted Belikin green. Nearby is a modern new service station, selling gas for all the cars owned by Sanpedranos. The road veers sharply right, then back left. The area west of the main drag here, or to your right going south, is the San Pablo residential area, and on the lagoon a cluster of cheap prefab homes put up by the government in a flood plain, after Hurricane Keith. Also to the west side is Black and White, a well-known local bar and hangout, along with Hutz (formerly the Pink Hotel), which has a bar.

Considerable development is taking place along the sea. Villas at Banyan Bay (taken over by its lender, Belize Bank, during the global recession), the Grand Colony condos, Banana Beach, Mata Rocks, Royal Palm, the beautifully upgraded Victoria House, Royal Caribbean, Caribe Island, Sunset Beach, Miramar, Athens Gate and Pelican Reef are also in this area. By this point, you're nearly 3 miles south of the center of San Pedro Town. If you continue farther south, by foot or cart, you're back in a residential area, with a number of upmarket houses including one owned by musician Jerry Jeff Walker, along with shacks, mansions and other assorted digs. A little farther on was the planned site of South Beach Belize, a controversial development by the guy who built Reef Village. It never really got off the ground, like so many big ideas in Belize.

No Longer a Fishing Village

Once a fishing village, San Pedro and the entire island are now mostly focused on tourism and real estate development. The island has more than 100 hotels, inns and guesthouses, plus dozens of restaurants. Most of the hotels are owned by Americans, Canadians and Europeans. One study showed that only about 15% are owned by Belizeans.

Expats still of working age who aren't involved in the hospitality industry often gravitate to selling real estate. For those who can't find enough to occupy themselves, substance abuse is always a risk, more so in San Pedro's freewheeling resort atmosphere than in most other areas of Belize. "Booze is ubiquitous here, and bar-hanging quite the social custom. And, in San Pedro as much as in most U.S. cities, you can now add other chemicals. If you're vulnerable, unimaginative, not a self-starter, passive-dependent, maybe Peoria would be a better bet," said a former expat who lived on the island for several years.

In the past, expats used to say that their hospitals were TACA, American and Continental airlines. For top-flight medical care, Americans on the island may still fly to Miami or Houston, or at least pop over to Belize City or to Chetumal or Mérida, but there are now a number full-time physicians on the island, along with a medical polyclinic that is not quite a full-fledged hospital.

Most residents and visitors say they feel safe on the island. Burglary and petty thefts are relatively common *(see chapter on crime)*, but violent crime isn't. Still, there are several murders a year, and residents say immigration from Belize City and elsewhere on the mainland has raised the crime rate.

Ambergris Caye Practicalities

Banks: Retail banks on the island include all four of Belize's banks: Belize Bank, Heritage Bank, Atlantic Bank and ScotiaBank. Caye Bank, on Coconut Drive south of town, is an international (offshore) bank and cannot do retail banking in Belize.

Groceries: There are a number of small groceries on the island. Among the largest are San Pedro Supermarket at the north end of town, Richie's (across the street from San Pedro Supermarket) and Island Supermarket with locations north and also south of town, at this writing for sale. Other small groceries are located around the island, including Marinas south of town. Super Buy on Back Street is where many locals shop. Another Super Buy is south near Marinas. Mata Grande, a small grocery, served North Ambergris residents for a number of years. A new grocery near Grand Caribe, Beach Basket, is another option north. Most of these and other groceries each have approximately the inventory of a large convenience store in the U.S., plus items such as frozen meats. An excellent bakery and breakfast spot or for fresh sandwiches is The Baker, south of town near Super Buy South, and a long-time local bakery is Casa Pan Dulce (formerly La Popular).

Fruits and vegetables can be purchased from street vendors or at small specialty shops in town. Costs for most food items, especially imported items, are higher than in the U.S., sometimes twice as high. Belikin beer can be ordered by the case from the Belikin distributor just south of town, near the Island Supermarket. However, even by the case beer in Belize isn't cheap – you'll pay over a U.S. dollar a bottle, including deposit, but that's still a savings over supermarket prices. At last check a case of Belikin or Lighthouse at the Bowen & Bowen distribution center (501-226-4441) south of town was around US$31 including refundable bottle deposit; stout is a little more. Bowen also delivers for an extra charge. Liquor is sold in grocery stores – imported brands cost about twice U.S. prices, but several local rums are under US$10 a fifth.

There are wine shops on the island, including Wine DeVine, on Coconut Drive near the airstrip, and Premium Wines & Spirits (a branch of a Belize City store) on Barrier Reef Drive. You'll generally pay twice U.S. prices for most wines, due to high import duties and taxes.

Other Stores: Ambergris Caye has hardware stores and other shops that provide the basics, but for some items you'll want to visit Belize City. There are gift shops galore on Front and Middle streets and also a few along Coconut Drive south of town.

Medical: There are now medical clinics on the island and several physicians, nurses and other medical professionals. However, there is still no full-fledged hospital. The San Pedro Polyclinic II (501-226-2536), which is the closest thing to a hospital, was established in great part due to the long-time efforts of the San Pedro Lions Club. In 2005, the year the new clinic opened, the San Pedro club was named the Lions Club of the Year, selected from more than 46,000 clubs in 193 countries.

Some of the other medical services on the island:

Lions Clubs Health Clinic 501-226-4052, emergencies 600-9071

Los Pinos Clinic 501-602-6383 and 226-2686

San Pedro Chiropractic Clinic 501-600-7119

Hyperbaric Chamber 501-226-2851 (or Antonia Guerrero, 600-5475 or Eleazar Portillo, 610-4560

Ambergris Hopes Clinic 226-2660, emergencies: 606-2316

Dr. Lerida Rodriguez 501-226-2197 or cell 620-1974

Dr. Teresa Damera 501-226-2686 or cell 602-6383

Dr. Giovanni Solorzano, San Carlos Medical Center, 501-226-2918 or cell 614-9251

Dr. Daniel Gonzalez 501-226-2660, cell 606-2316

Dr. Miguel Allison 501-226-4052

Wings of Hope Medical emergency air ambulance, 501-223-3292

Infrastructure: San Pedro Town has a modern water and sewerage system. The power grid now extends far up North Ambergris, but most residents there have to depend on cisterns and wells for water and on septic systems for sewerage. Cable TV and DSL and cellular internet are available on much of the island, except the far north.

Note: *For more information on what to do and see on Ambergris Caye, as well as for specific hotel, restaurant and nightlife reviews, see the Checking Out Ambergris Caye section. The same format applies to other areas of Belize.*

Real Estate on Ambergris

Property prices on Ambergris Caye are among the highest in Belize. As elsewhere, prices vary tremendously depending on location and on the specific property. Houses and lots in predominantly Belizean areas, mostly on the back or lagoon side of the island, tend to be much less expensive than seafront property preferred by foreign investors and residents. Demand in recent years generally has been strong for beachfront lots and beachfront homes. Appreciation has run 10 to 20% per year for many years, according to local real estate brokers, although this appreciation rate slowed in the 2001-2003 period, due to the high-tech bust in the United States, and stalled completely in 2008-2010, with the worldwide deep recession. Prices in Belize are to a great extent dependent on economic conditions in the United States and, to some extent, in Canada. When the U.S. sneezes, Belize catches a cold. With conditions improving in the U.S., Canada and Europe, things are again looking up in Belize.

Agents point to beachfront property on North Ambergris, which went for US$450 a front foot in the late 1980s that is offered for US$3,000 to $8,000 or more a front foot now.

Upfront taxes, especially on new condos and homes, can discourage middle-income buyers. With the 17.5% surcharge up front (5% stamp duty and 12.5% GST), buying a newly built US$300,000 condo would entail an additional US$$52,500 cash outlay upfront, not including attorney fees and other fees and charges. However, in most cases the GST and stamp duty are rolled into the offering price, so the extra costs are "hidden" from the buyer. The GST is not added to resales, unless they have been substantially renovated.

Condo development continues on the island. Some 700 new condo units were constructed in the first decade of the 21st century, most on North Ambergris Caye. A number of hotels have converted some or all of their units to "condotel" status. The idea is to sell now for immediate cash, then make 40 to 60% of revenues in management fees for running the hotel for absentee owners. Sales, however, have not always met expectations, as some investors are wary of condominium laws in Belize – condos are fairly new to Belize – and some have been burned by disputes with developers. At least one condotel project on North Ambergris shut down (it later reopened as a new resort), several stopped construction before completion of all phases and a couple were taken over by their bank lenders.

A few developers offer limited financing, typically 20% down, with the balance payable over 10 years at around 12% interest. Usually, there's a balloon payment at the end of the term.

Timeshares have not fared well on Ambergris Caye or anywhere in Belize, though a number of condo hotels offer timeshares in a low-key way. Buyers have been few, and many who did buy quickly became dissatisfied with their purchase. The town council has passed regulations restricting activities of timeshare touts.

Building lots: Caribbean seafront building lots on Ambergris Caye range from around US$3,500 to $8,000 per beachfront linear foot, and some are even higher.

Less-expensive lots generally are on upper reaches of North Ambergris, which is accessible mainly by private boat or water taxi and has no electricity or other utilities. There you can find small beachfront lots from around US$75,000 and sometimes less; lots one row back from the beach on the far north of the island are from around US$20,000 or $25,000; and back lots from around US$10,000 to $15,000. Waterfront lots on the lagoon or backside of the island start at around US$800-$2,500 per waterfront foot, with most under US$2,000 a foot. In general, lots a row back from the sea are just 30% of those directly on the water. Buyers should be aware that some beachfront lots have mangroves, not sand, on the waterside, and a permit is required to cut mangroves (though many mangroves have been illegally removed). Higher ground not subject to flooding obviously is more desirable, and more expensive, than low-lying property.

Homes: Two- or three-bedroom modern houses on the beach on North Ambergris Caye (access typically via water taxi, although the paving of the golf cart path is changing that) range from around US$200,000 (generally for a simple, wooden Belizean-style house) to well over US$1 or $2 million. A few goes for even more millions, or at least are advertised for those amounts. Those south of San Pedro Town on the sea start at around US$300,000. Small homes not on the water but with sea views are available from around US$150,000, but many run several hundred thousand dollars. At the top end, deluxe, recently built beachfront three and four bedroom homes may go for US$750,000 to $1,500,000 or more. Homes with "sunset views" – that is, on the west side or lagoon side of the island – start at around US$75,000 for a simple house but some can reach the middle six figures. Island life ain't cheap, baby.

Condos: Small one-bedroom condos without sea view start at around US$100,000, though most are US$125,000 or more. One-bedroom condos with sea views run about US$135,000 to $250,000. High-quality two- or three-bedroom condos with sea views range from around US$250,000 to $600,000 or higher. The condo market in San Pedro and elsewhere was hit hard during the depth of the real estate recession beginning in 2008-2009, but the market in San Pedro has since recovered to some extent.

Home construction: Building costs on Ambergris are relatively high, due to the need to dig deep foundations and install pilings for stability in the sandy soil, and to build with hurricane protection in mind. There's also a more strict permitting process on the island. Bringing building supplies in by barge also adds to the cost. Expect to pay US$80-$200 or more a square foot for reinforced concrete construction, less for wood (used mainly on the backside of the island). Shallow wells can be dug fairly cheaply, but the water may be brackish. As elsewhere in Belize, labor costs are lower than in the U.S., but many building materials are more expensive. An exception is native hardwood lumber, which is beautiful and relatively cheap.

Builders: Several homebuilders have become very well off building vacation and second homes for Americans and other expats. Among the builders and construction management companies on the island are the following. Caveat: Ask other owners about their experiences with these builders:

Armando Graniel, Graniel Construction, San Pedro; 501-226-

2632, e-mail sunset@btl.net. Graniel has built many of the homes and resorts on the island.

Daniel Camal, San Pedro; 501-226-2563; e-mail dcamal@btl.net.

Bob Campbell, San Pedro; 501-226-5203. Bob and Diane Campbell built El Pescador Villas, Seascape, Indigo and other upper-end projects on the island.

Mike Coleman Construction, 501-670-4538; e-mail colemanm@hughes.net.

Jim Hanna, Design/Builder, P.O. Box 128, San Pedro Town, email jm_hanna@yahoo.com, 501-226-3830.

Tom Harding, Harding General Contracting, San Pedro; 501-226-2184, harding@btl.net. Harding supervised the construction of the late Barry Bowen's Chan Chich Lodge and with his wife, Josie, ran the lodge for many years before moving to San Pedro.

Wayne Alfaro, San Pedro; 501-226-2097.

Properties for Sale

Here are some sample listings offered by individuals and real estate companies in 2015-2016. Prices shown are asking prices. Due to issues of timeliness, we have not included the offering individual or real estate agent. Consider these as representative of property on the market at this time. For similar offerings go to websites of real estate firms and other property-oriented websites listed in this book. Also, check out the Ambergris Caye MLS, a local multiple listing service at www.mlsambergriscaye.com.

• 400 feet-deep lot with 90 feet of beachfront, plus with 2nd row 90 feet x 300 feet lot behind it, combined totaling almost 1½ acres. Located in the Habaneros subdivision 9 ½ miles north of San Pedro Town.

• Lot with 100 feet of waterfront on the lagoon at Ambergris Bay, US$110,000.

• Luxury villa 5 miles north of town, four bedrooms plus fifth bedroom in apartment, 3 ½ baths, 26 ft. ceilings in living and dining areas, impressive kitchen with Subzero fridge, three sinks, Wolf stove and double oven, infinity pool with deck, great views of sea and barrier reef, US$1,995,000

• 13 acres west of San Pedro across Laguna de San Pedro, with 1,700 total feet of water frontage. No utilities. Boat access only, US$750,000 with terms possible.

• Ground-floor one-bedroom 788 sq. ft. condo at Belizean Shores, a

48-unit condotel about 3 miles north of San Pedro, property taxes US$150 a year, US$170,000

• Beachfront lot in Punta Azul area 11 miles north of San Pedro (20-25 minute boat ride), with 72 feet of beachfront and 140 feet depth, access to electricity, cell service and wireless internet, US$175,000.

• Three-acre +/- development parcel with 450 feet of beachfront ¼ mile north of bridge, with 265 feet of depth, US$3,750,000, financing available.

• Two-bedroom, two-bath house ½ mile north of bridge in Tres Cocos area, 150 feet from sea, lagoon and sea views, tiled pool, renovated kitchen, double lot, concrete construction built to Cat 4 hurricane standards, US$575,000.

• 560 sq. ft., one-bedroom, one-bath condo at Mayan Princess in heart of San Pedro, on in-town beachfront, fully furnished, currently in rental pool, US$135,000.

• Three-bedroom, two-bath wood house about 1 mile south of San Pedro, with three decks on two levels, views of lagoon, all utilities, US$135,000.

• Lagoon-front lot on back side of island, about 3 ½ miles north of San Pedro town center, 70 feet of lagoon frontage and 130 feet deep, property taxes US$90 a year, US$165,000.

• Acre lot on west side of island, with 315 feet of frontage on the lagoon, in the Tres Cocos area about ½ mile north of town, US$315,000.

• Two bedroom, two bath 1,188 sq. foot second-level condo at Villas at Banyan Bay, fully furnished, US$425,000.

San Pedro Real Estate Agents

This is not an exhaustive list of the agents on the island.

Ambergris Seaside Real Estate, Barrier Reef Dr., San Pedro, Ambergris Caye, 501-226-4545, www.ambergrisrealestate.com.

Belize Sotheby's International Realty, P.O. Box 204, Barrier Reef Dr., San Pedro, Ambergris Caye, 501-226-4309, www.belizesir.com.

Coldwell Banker Belize, 11 Coconut Dr., San Pedro, 501-226-4559, www.buyrealestatebelize.com.

Coral Beach Realty/Century 21, Barrier Reef Drive, San Pedro, 501-226-2681, www.coralbeachrealty.net.

RE/MAX Isla Bonita, 10 Coconut Drive, San Pedro Town, 501-

226-4400, www.remaxbz.com.

Sundancer Properties, Pescador Dr., San Pedro, tel. 501-226-4473, www.sundancerproperties.com.

Sunrise Realty, P.O. Box 236, #1 Barrier Reef Dr., San Pedro, 501-226-3737, www.sunriserealty.bz.

Rentals on Ambergris Caye

The best way to find a rental house or apartment on Ambergris Caye is to come to the island and look around in person. The *San Pedro Sun* newspaper, the hard copy paper edition, has a few rental classifieds, and Ambergriscaye.com (www.ambergriscaye.com) has occasional rentals posted. Here are some other sources of short-term house rentals:

Caye Management (Barrier Reef Drive, San Pedro, 501-226-3077, www.cayemanagement.com) has many rental houses and condos on the island, but these are virtually all short-term vacation rentals.

B-Lease (P.O. Box 184, San Pedro, tel. 501-610-4845, www.bleasemanagement.com) is a property management company that specializes in longer-term rentals of at least six months.

Also, look into short-term condo rentals at the resorts and condotels. One option is **Banana Beach,** which in the past has offered low-season room and one-bedroom rentals. Condotels including **Paradise Villas, SunBreeze Suites, Sunset Beach Condos, Caribe Island, Hol Chan Resort, Royal Caribbean Resort** and **Royal Palm** may offer monthly rentals, especially in the off-season between Easter and early December. Off-season, you may find one-bedroom efficiencies in the low four figures U.S., sometimes including utilities.

Airbnb (www.airbnb.com), **Vacation Rentals by Owner** (www.vrbo.com) and **HomeAway** (www.homeaway.com) are other sources of rentals. Though owners listing on these sites usually are seeking nightly or weekly rental prospects, they may also consider monthly or longer rentals.

Frenchie's Dive Shop, Caye Caulker

Caye Caulker

GRADING THE AREA FOR RETIREMENT, RELOCATION AND INVESTMENT

Ratings are on an A to F scale, just like your old high school report card. A is the top grade; F is failing. The ratings are relative to other places in Belize.

Popularity with Expats	C+
Safety	B
Overall Cost of Living	B
Real Estate Bargains	B
Investment Potential	B+
Leisure Activities	C
Restaurants	B
Cultural Activities	D
Infrastructure	C
Business Potential	C+

Medical Care   D+
Shopping   D

ADVANTAGES OF CAYE CAULKER: • Small, laid-back island atmosphere • Provides excellent opportunities for water activities – boating, fishing, diving • Less expensive than San Pedro • No need for a car

Caye Caulker is Ambergris Caye's "little sister" island – smaller, less developed and a cheaper date. Caulker, whose name derives from the Spanish word for coco plum, *hicaco*, has the kind of laidback, sandy-street, tropical-color, low-key Caribbean charm that travelers pay thousands to experience, but here they can have it for peanuts. Well, almost. Less than 10 miles and about 30 minutes by boat from San Pedro or 45 minutes from Belize City, Caye Caulker is definitely worth a visit, and perhaps you'll like it well enough to stay.

Here are some of the key comparisons between Caye Caulker and Ambergris Caye:

Caye Caulker is physically much smaller, under 5 miles long and half a mile wide at its widest point, roughly one-tenth the size of Ambergris Caye. Hurricane Hattie in 1961 divided the island in two parts. North of "the Split" it is mostly uninhabited mangrove, and much of this area is protected as a nature reserve. As on many islands, there are basically just three streets running down the island, Front, Middle and Back streets being the main ones, though there are few street signs and locals usually give directions just by saying "go down to yellow house and turn right." Most of the 300 or so listings in the Caye Caulker section of the Belize telephone directory don't even include a street name or address, just the person's name and phone number. Nearly all of 1,500 people on the island live in the village south of the Split.

Unlike Ambergris Caye, where most of the main streets are now paved, Caye Caulker has streets of hard-packed sand and far, far, far fewer cars than San Pedro. Almost everybody gets around on foot or bike.

As on Ambergris, a majority of local residents are Mestizos who originally came to the island from Mexico, and who until recently made their living by fishing, but the island also has Creoles, some of whom consider themselves Rastafarians, gringos and others.

While it is quickly going upmarket, Caye Caulker remains to some extent a budget island. In the 1960s and 1970s, the island was on the "back-packer trail," a cheap place for longhaired visitors to relax and smoke a little weed or sip a beer. Today, a very expensive hotel on Caulker goes for around US$250 a night, and most of the hotels charge under US$100 double, with some as low as US$15. Many of the older buildings on the island are wooden clapboard, often painted in tropical colors, but more recently constructed houses and hotels are of reinforced concrete. Only a few hotels on the island have swimming pools.

Caye Caulker has much the same mix of tourist-oriented businesses as San Pedro, but in most cases there are fewer of everything. The island has perhaps 25 simple restaurants, if you include those that operate out of somebody's back window or BBQ grill, a few casual bars, a handful of dive shops and tour guides, several pint-sized groceries, a few gift shops, a bank and several cybercafés.

Beaches? Caulker has much less beachfront than Ambergris Caye, and what beaches it has don't compare with the better stretches of beach on Ambergris Caye, Hopkins or Placencia. Beach reclamation projects did widen and improve the beach along the east side of the village (though storms have taken away and then given back sand). Swimming in the shallow water close to shore is mainly from piers and at "the Split," which is very popular for sunning and swimming, and there's a good bar with cold beer close by.

In the past, the pipe water on Caulker was not as good as on Ambergris Caye. On Caulker, it often had a sulfur smell and came from shallow wells, some which were close to septic systems. However, a reverse osmosis water plant is now operating on the island, but not all homes and businesses are on it.

Caye Caulker, like most other coastal areas and cayes, also has sandflies. Especially on calm days, at certain times of year, they can be a nuisance.

Ambergris Caye used to have many more restaurants than Caye Caulker, and it still does. However, in the past several years (2013-2015), a flood of new restaurants has opened on Caulker, and you now have a much broader selection of types and quality of restaurants.

Caye Caulker Practicalities

Banks: Caye Caulker has only one bank, Atlantic Bank. It has an ATM that accepts international debit cards.

Groceries: Chan's Mini-Mart on Middle Street near the Caye Caulker Plaza Hotel is the most-frequented grocery, although there are other places to buy beer, booze, snacks and other basics on Front Street and elsewhere. Near Chan's are some fruit and vegetable vendors.

Other Stores: Caye Caulker doesn't have much shopping, beyond some gift shops on Front Street, a couple of art galleries and a few other shops. Most residents go to Belize City for their big shopping trips.

Medical: Caye Caulker doesn't have a hospital, but there is a small medical clinic (Front Street at the south end, 501-226-0190), staffed as of this writing by a Belizean nurse and a Cuban doctor. It is open daily, usually until 7 p.m. and has a supply of commonly needed medications. For a real emergency, fly or take a water taxi to Belize City. Your hotel will assist in getting you to Belize City the fastest way.

Infrastructure: Caye Caulker now has a reverse osmosis municipal water system in the village. Sewerage is still an issue. DSL and cellular internet are available. North of the Split residents must rely on their own resources for power, water and sewerage.

Real Estate on Caye Caulker

Most of the development on Caulker is concentrated in the one small village, although North Caye, across the Split, is getting more development. Many families have long ties with the island and aren't interested in selling. Thus, the number of available properties is small. When properties do come on the market, the owners sometimes have an inflated idea of their value. One small budget hotel was offered for years for US$3,500,000, not much less than the total annual gross tourism revenue of the entire island!

Indeed, small is the key word to keep in mind when looking for property on Caye Caulker. Most lots are small, around 1/10th of an acre. Typical houses for sale have under 1,000 sq. ft. of indoor space, not including decks, porches or rooftop verandas.

Properties on Caye Caulker

Several real estate companies in San Pedro also have occasional listings on Caye Caulker. Here are some of the properties for sale on

Caye Caulker in 2016. Prices shown are asking prices.

• Fully furnished second floor one bedroom, one bath mini condo, 440 sq. ft., on Front Street, US165,000.

• Small two-bedroom concrete house, built in 2007, on 60 x 80 foot lot, 540 sq. ft. of interior space, plus more than 600 sq. ft. of outdoor living space including covered rooftop veranda, US$179,000.

• 60 x 90 foot lot at south end of island, second lot back from sea, US$49,000.

• Waterfront 75 x 93 foot lot in Eden Isle subdivision south near airstrip. No road or easement in front of it, US$129,000.

• Lots on North Caye (north of the Split), some with sea or lagoon frontage and some back from the water but with water views, most about 60 x 90 feet, access by boat, no utilities, US$25,000 to $220,000, owner financing available with 20% down.

Real Estate Agents on Caye Caulker

Caye Caulker Realty (Diane Auxillou), P.O. Box 63, Caye Caulker, 312-890-4006 in U.S., www.cayecaulkerrealty.bz

RE/MAX Island Real Estate (Sara Warner), Front Street, Caye Caulker, 501-226-0404, www.cayecaulkerproperties.com

Boats moored off a caye

OTHER ISLANDS IN DETAIL

GRADING THE AREA FOR RETIREMENT, RELOCATION AND INVESTMENT

Ratings are on an A to F scale, just like your old high school report card. A is the top grade; F is failing.

Popularity with Expats	B-
Safety	B-
Overall Cost of Living	D
Real Estate Bargains	D
Investment Potential	B
Leisure Activities	B-
Cultural Activities	F
Infrastructure	F
Business Potential	C-
Medical Care	F
Shopping	F

ISLAND ADVANTAGES: • Beautiful island living • Easy access to recreational activities on the water

Belize has some 400 islands in the Caribbean. The vast majority are small spits of sand and mangroves. Most are either privately owned (by old Belize families or by wealthy foreigners) or are government property.

Keep in mind that although a private island offers the ultimate in peace and quiet, you are likely to be entirely on your own. You'll need to arrange – and pay for – security and caretaking, both when you are on the island and when you are away. Building on a remote caye offers its own set of challenges, starting with getting building materials and workers to the island. Once you've built, you'll need to supply the island with food and water, along with other necessities of life. And what will you do with the garbage?

Islands Properties Offered

Islands shown below are among those on the market in Belize's Caribbean Sea in 2016. Prices listed are asking prices.

• Jewel Caye, 6½ miles off Hopkins, this 2-acre island is in the Cockney Range, US3,150,000.

• Drowned Caye in the Drowned Caye Range, 95 acres, 10 minutes by boat from Belize City, US$2,000,000.

• Lark Caye, 8 acres about 6 miles from Placencia, US$600,000.

• Manta Caye, 8-acre island with resort (now closed), US$5,500,000.

• Scipio Caye, 5 miles east of Placencia, 4 acres with 700 feet of beachfront, US$750,000.

• Turquoise Caye, a 4.75-acre island on the backside of Ambergris Caye, US$725,000.

• Placencia Island, lots for sale on subdivision of this island off the tip of Placencia peninsula, from US$167,500.

• Caribbean Caye in Blue Ground Range, about 7 miles from Hopkins, 2.4 acres, US$599,000.

• Secret Island, 2.5 acres about 7 miles off Riversdale on the Placencia peninsula, US$350,000.

• Hat Island at Lighthouse Reef Atoll, ½-acre coral island within the calmer waters of the atoll, US$680,000

Real Estate Agents

Real estate agents all over Belize occasionally offer islands for sale. In addition, several companies specializing in islands for sale also offer Belize cayes. These companies include **Private Islands Online** (www.privateislandsonline.com) and **Private Islands** (www.privateislands.bz)

Mural of Sarteneja village

COROZAL IN MORE DETAIL

GRADING THE AREA FOR RETIREMENT, RELOCATION AND INVESTMENT

Ratings are on an A to F scale, just like your old high school report card. A is the top grade; F is failing. Grades are relative compared to other areas in Belize. Note: Ratings for Corozal reflect its proximity to Chetumal, Mexico.

Popularity with Expats	B
Safety	B-
Overall Cost of Living	B+
Real Estate Bargains	A-
Investment Potential	C+
Leisure Activities	B (Chetumal)
Restaurants	C
Cultural Activities	C+
Infrastructure	B
Business Potential	C
Medical Care	B+ (Chetumal)
Shopping	B+ (Chetumal)

ADVANTAGES OF COROZAL AREA: • Low housing costs whether you're renting or buying • Proximity to Chetumal, Mexico, for medical care and shopping • Sizeable (several hundred) and growing expat community • Pleasant location on the Bay of Chetumal (sometimes called Corozal Bay) • Few sandflies in most areas and fewer noxious bugs than in some other areas of Belize • Pleasant sub-tropical climate with lower rainfall than southern Belize • Generally safe, friendly area, though property theft is an issue • Easy access by several modes of transport to Ambergris Caye and other areas of Belize and to the Yucatán

Few Belize casual visitors to Belize, except medical missionaries and tourists passing through from Mexico, pay much attention to Corozal District and its main population center, Corozal Town. Yet this part of Northern Belize is one of the friendliest, safest, least expensive and most interesting areas of the entire country.

For visitors, it's a place to slow down, relax and enjoy at least a few days of easy living by the beautiful turquoise waters of Corozal Bay and the Bay of Chetumal. True, there's not a whole lot to see here, not many tourist sites, no real beaches though nice swimming is yours in the bay and lagoons, and few memorable hotels or restaurants. But the climate is appealing, with less rain than almost anywhere else in Belize, and the sunny dispositions of residents are infectious. Corozal Town and environs is one of our top picks for expatriate living. It offers inexpensive rentals and affordable real estate. You'll want to be sure to visit here, if you are interesting in living or retiring in Belize.

Corozal District is 718 square miles in area, with a district population of 46,000, according to the Statistical Institute of Belize estimates for mid-2015. The largest town by far is Corozal, with 11,700 residents. Spanish is spoken more widely than English here, although you can get by in English at least in Corozal Town. The town is laid out on a small grid, with the most appealing part along the bayfront, with its colorful houses and parks.

Nearby on and near the Philip Goldson Highway are "suburbs" — the small villages of Ranchito, Xaibe, Calcutta, San Antonio and others. The Corozal Free Zone, just south of the Santa Elena border crossing from Mexico, is starting to make a name for itself as a place for businesses to set up free from many of the restrictions and high import duties of the rest of Belize. Mexicans come here for cheap gas. The Free Zone employs some 2,000 Belizeans. There are three casinos at the border, on the Belize side, including a branch of the Princess and a large casino, Las Vegas, which also sports a new 106-room upscale hotel. These casinos, like the Free Zone, mostly depend on business from Mexico.

The district can be divided into two main sections. The west part is still sugar cane country, once anchored by Libertad, the now-closed sugar cane processing plant and farther north by Corozal Town on Corozal Bay. The main road artery of this hemisphere is the Goldson Highway, a good two-lane paved road. From the southern edge of Corozal District near San Pablo village, it is about 28 miles to the Mexican border at Santa Elena. The border is about 9 miles from Corozal Town. The Consejo area about 7 miles north of Corozal Town on an all-weather unpaved road, on Corozal Bay, has attracted a small number of expats at Consejo Shores, Mayan Sands and other residential developments.

The eastern hemisphere consists of the Cerros/Copper Bank area and Sarteneja peninsula. This peninsula has far more trees than people. It is an area mostly of swamp and savannah, with the bulk of the peninsula's small population living in villages along the beautiful Progresso

Lagoon and Chetumal Bay. Little Belize, a Mennonite area, is the largest population center, with around 2,000 residents. For visitors, a main reason to come here is the Shipstern Nature Preserve, a 22,000-acre park originally started and funded by a Swiss organization. The fishing village of Sarteneja (pop. 1,800) is charming as well. An all-weather mostly unpaved road runs from Orange Walk Town to Sarteneja village, a distance of about 40 miles. You can also get to the peninsula from Corozal Town via a free, hand-pulled vehicular ferry across the New River and another hand-pulled ferry over the mouth of Laguna Seca. Several residential developments, including Cerros Sands and the aggressively marketed Orchid Bay, are on the bay, and Progresso Heights is on the Progresso Lagoon. While a number of lots have been sold at these developments, so far there are only a handful of homes built. Orchid Bay, despite its rather isolated location, is something of an exception, with a sizeable number of completed homes, condos and even a restaurant/bar and a bed and breakfast inn.

Corozal is one of the safer places in Belize. Even so, burglary and property theft are fairly common. One survey of expats in Corozal Town some years ago found that about 80% had been victims of theft, burglary and even home invasions over a period of four years. The town of Corozal and surrounding villages are on the power grid and generally have municipal water supplies with potable water. Sarteneja and other remote areas have less modern infrastructures.

One of Belize's two main land border crossing points is north of Corozal Town at Santa Elena (the other is at Benque Viejo del Carmen in Cayo, and a third is planned for Toledo District.) The Rio Honda marks the boundary between Belize and Mexico. Once across the border, some knowledge of Spanish is helpful. Chetumal has large supermarkets (San Francisco is one) and a modern mall with department stores, a multiplex cinema and food court. There are McDonalds and Burger King fast-food restaurants in Chetumal, along with a Sam's Club, Walmart and other big box stores.

Corozal is one of the safer places in Belize. Even so, burglary and property theft are fairly common. Follow the usual traveler's precautions.

Corozal Practicalities

Banks: Scotia Bank, Belize Bank, Heritage Bank and Atlantic Bank have branches in Corozal Town.

Groceries: Corozal Town has more than a dozen small groceries and tiendas and a market with fruits and vegetables. (No, despite the name, the author does not own Lan's grocery.) Large supermarkets are in Chetumal.

Restaurants: Among the best of the small bunch of restaurants in Corozal Town are Patty's Bistro, June's Kitchen, Corozo Blue's and the bayside restaurant at Tony's Inn.

Other Stores: Corozal has a selection of small home furnishings, construction supplies and hardware stores, many run by Chinese immigrants. Chetumal across the border has larger stores of all kinds. There also are nearly 300 stores in the Free Zone, most of them selling cheap clothing and other items from Asia.

Medical: Corozal Town has a district hospital and several doctors and clinics. Nearby Chetumal offers low-cost and often high-quality dental and medical care.

Infrastructure: Corozal Town and surrounding villages are on the power grid and generally have municipal water supplies with potable water, along with sewerage. They also have DSL and cellular internet. If in doubt, ask locally. Sarteneja and other areas have less modern infrastructures. Remote areas depend on water from cisterns or wells, power from solar or wind and sewerage from septic systems, along with satellite internet. Some developments, such as Orchid Bay, have built their own sophisticated infrastructure.

Real Estate

Corozal Town and environs has some of the belter property bargains in Belize – whether you are renting or buying.

Corozal District, like the rest of Belize, has its share of blue-sky real estate peddlers, often operating via the internet. Watch out for sellers of lots in remote areas. Some are claiming that their lots on a part of a golf or hotel development. Such developments may be years or decades in the future, if they are ever built at all.

Properties in Corozal

Here are some of the property listings offered by individuals and brokers in 2015-2016. Prices shown are asking prices.

• Seaview lot in Consejo Village, about 77 feet on road, depth of up to 97 feet, US$55,000.

• Two-bedroom, two-bath modern house with a/c in Corozal Town, cistern plus town water, US$138,000.

• 60' x 90' lot in new development on north edge of Corozal Town, US$8,000.

• Three-bedroom, two-bath concrete home in Santa Rita Heights, about 2 miles north of center of Corozal Town, fenced, municipal water, cable TV, partially furnished, US$59,975.

• Waterfront lot in Consejo Village, 100 feet on the water, 90 feet deep and 100 feet frontage on village road, US$219,000.

• 100-acre farm less than 3 miles off Philip Goldson Highway (Northern Highway), cleared and ready to farm or use as pasture, in two parcels, US$79,000.

• Fully fenced two-bedroom, one-bath concrete bungalow over more than 1,000 sq. ft., located in Finca Solana. The home on a 104' x 55' lot and was built in 2009. One block from the bay, US$109,500.

• Four bedroom, 2½ bath two-level home in Consejo Shores, with water view. About 3,200 total square footage. Swimming pool. US$260,000.

Real Estate Agents

Belize Land Consultants, P.O. Box 35, Corozal Town, 501-423-1005. Bill Wildman, a land surveyor, developed Consejo Shores, www.consejoshores.com. Members of his family are now involved in the Consejo Shores development.

Belize North Real Estate Ltd. P.O. Box 226, Corozal Town, 501-422-0284, www.belizenorthrealestate.bz.

Corozal Belize Properties, 29 Consejo Beach Trail, P.O. Box 346, Corozal Town, 501-636-8400, www.corozalbelizeproperties.com.

Orchid Bay, Orchid Bay Sales Office, 771 Santa Fe Drive, Denver, CO 80204, 470-223-5493; www.orchidbaybelize.com.

Real Estate Developments

Here are selected real estate developments in Corozal District. Most market primarily to foreign buyers. Keep in mind that Cerros Sands, Orchid Bay and Progresso Heights are all a 30 to 60-minute or more drive on unpaved roads from Corozal Town, depending on road conditions and ferry wait times. Consejo Shores, Mayan Seaside and other developments around Consejo are about a 10- to 15-minute drive on an unpaved road from Corozal Town.

Cerros Sands, near Cerros Maya, 501-402-0297; www.cerrossands.com. Cerros Sands is a 92-acre development near the Cerros ruins, across the bay from Corozal Town. Lots start at around US$18,000, with some bayfront lots starting around US$99,000. There are no public utilities at the development. While some lots have been sold, only a couple of homes have been built in the development. A beach bar/restaurant is open.

Consejo Shores, Consejo, 501-423-1005; www.consejoshores.com. Consejo Shores, with 350 acres and 7,000 ft. of bayfront, was one of the first and remains the premier residential development in Northern Belize. Around 150 homes have been built in the community. Open parkland allows access to the bay, and there is a small 9-hole golf course. Bayfront building lots with around 80 feet of waterfront have risen in price and are now selling by the developer for $165,000, though occasionally resales may be lower. Seaview lots back a row or two from the bay are US$29,000 to $39,000, while other residential lots start at around US$17,000. Modern three- and four-bedroom homes have sold for as little as US$100,000, and US$400,000 gets you close to the top end of the market.

Mayan Seaside, Consejo, www.mayanseaside.com. This development near Consejo village has about 105 lots, most of which have been sold. About 30 homes have been built or are under construction. Lot owners in the development pay a US$250 per year maintenance fee.

Orchid Bay, between Copper Bank and Sarteneja, U.S. phone 470-223-5493; www.orchidbaybelize.com. The 114-acre **Orchid Bay** on the Bay of Chetumal is being developed by Great Land Holdings, Ltd., which has some 4,000 acres in the area. Beachfront condos at Orchid Bay are now selling in the US$300,000+ range. Waterway villas, starting around US$250,000, and various casitas are also offered. Lot prices range from around well under US$100,000 to over US$200,000. There is a B&B inn on the property, Crimson Orchid Inn, and a restaurant/beach club with swimming pool. The development has an ambitious sales program and promotes popular group tours of the property from the U.S. and Canada.

Progresso Heights, on Progresso Lagoon near Progresso Village, 888-235-4934 or 561-859-1433; www.progressoheights.com. Hundreds of lots, mostly around ¼-acre in size, are included in the master plan, and more than 300 lots reportedly have been sold. Lot prices start at around US$16,000 for cash, or US$20,000 with financing (at up to 15 years at 6.99%, with 20% down). Lot owners in the development pay a US$250 per year maintenance fee. A clubhouse with swimming pool, a community pier and d i r t a n d marl roads have been constructed. About 10 homes have been built or are under construction in the development, though on a recent visit the entire development looked virtually deserted.

Rentals

Rentals in Corozal Town start at under US$300 a month, and for US$300 to $500 you can get a comfortable house in town. For rentals in the Corozal Town area, check with **Belize North Real Estate Ltd. Consejo Shores** or other real estate firms *(see above)*. In **Consejo Shores**, a nice development on the Bay of Chetumal about 7 miles from Corozal Town, U.S.-style three- and four-bedroom homes rent for US$500 to $1,000 a month. **Orchid Bay** also has some rentals, with one-bedroom casitas going on www.vrbo.com for around US$100 a night, less for weekly or monthly rentals.

Tropical bougainvillea flourishes in Belize

ORANGE WALK IN MORE DETAIL

GRADING THE AREA FOR RETIREMENT, RELOCATION AND INVESTMENT

Ratings are on an A to F scale, just like your old high school report card. A is the top grade; F is failing. Grades are relative compared to other areas in Belize.

Popularity with Expats	D
Safety	B-
Overall Cost of Living	B+
Real Estate Bargains	B+
Investment Potential	C-
Leisure Activities	C
Restaurants	C-
Cultural Activities	D
Infrastructure	C+
Business Potential	C

156

Medical Care   C+
Shopping   C

ADVANTAGES OF ORANGE WALK: • Low land prices in rural areas • Offers some of the most natural areas of Belize, with excellent birding and wildlife spotting • Proximity to Mennonite centers of Shipyard and Blue Creek • Good agricultural area

In what is now Orange Walk District, the early greatness of the Maya empire was on display at Lamanai and elsewhere. During the centuries before the time of Christ, the Maya built temples that were higher than any modern building in Belize, and one at Lamanai still stands about 100 feet above the jungle floor. Many Maya sites in Orange Walk were occupied up to colonial times. For a while the Maya were even able to resist the Spanish *conquistadores*, in the 17th century driving the Spanish out of the area around Lamanai and burning Catholic churches. Mestizos fleeing the Maya rebellions in the Yucatán settled modern Orange Walk around 1849, and Corozal about the same time.

Mahogany logging in the late 18th and early 19th centuries was the first major modern industry of the region, with some 5,000 giant mahogany trees harvested every year. A big British-based company, Belize Estate and Produce Company, once owned one-fifth of the land in Belize and was a major force in British Honduras' economy and politics until the mid-20th century. When the mahogany industry died down due to over logging, sugar cane and citrus became staple crops. But boom and bust continued, and with the global oversupply of sugar, small Orange Walk farmers turned to marijuana cultivation. The U.S. government, with its take-no-prisoners approach to drug control, forced Belizean authorities to shut down airstrips, spray chemicals on fields and destroy this cash crop. Today, subsistence agriculture and the remnants of sugar cane and citrus farming occupy the time of rural residents. Rum is distilled near Orange Walk Town, logging still is going on and Mennonites farm productively in the Shipyard (home to conservative Mennonites), Little Belize and Blue Creek (progressive) areas.

The road west from Orange Walk Town, past Cuello distillery, Yo Creek, and then back south to August Pine Ridge village and San Felipe village leads through agricultural areas to the 240,000-acre Programme for

Belize Rio Bravo Conservation area and the 250,000-acre private estate of the late Sir Barry Bowen. Or, if you go southeast from San Felipe, you end up at Lamanai near Indian Church village. Two world-class jungle lodges, Chan Chich at Gallon Jug, and Lamanai Outpost Lodge on the New River Lagoon, await you in this part of Orange Walk District. Another route is via Shipyard, on an unpaved road just south of Orange Walk Town.

Orange Walk Practicalities

Banks: ScotiaBank, Heritage Bank, Atlantic Bank and Belize Bank all have branches in Orange Walk Town.

Groceries and Other Stores: M & A Supermarket and P & P Supermarket, both fairly small, are among your choices. The main drag, Queen Victoria aka Belize-Corozal Road, has a large variety of shops and stores. There's a public market in the middle of town.

Medical: Orange Walk Town has the Northern Regional hospital, though it is not one of the more modern hospitals in Belize. Chetumal, Mexico, about an hour away, offers low-cost and often high-quality dental and medical care. About the same distance to the south is Belize City, with its private and public hospitals and many physician and dental offices. Mérida, Mexico, also is a popular place for Belizeans and expats to get expert medical care at modest costs. In fact, the ADO Express bus from Belize City to Mérida is often called the "hospital run."

Restaurants and Hotels: Among the good restaurants in Orange Walk Town are Nahil Mayab, El Establo and Maracas Bar & Grill. Among the good lodging in and near town are Hotel de la Fuente, St. Christopher's and the new El Gran Mestizo Riverside Cabins. In remote areas are two outstanding lodges, Chan Chich Lodge and Lamanai Outpost Lodge, plus La Milpa Field Station.

Infrastructure: Orange Walk Town and some larger villages have municipal water and sewerage systems. More remote areas have to rely on wells and cisterns for water, septic systems for sewerage and satellite for internet.

Real Estate

The real estate market in Orange Walk District is not very active. Undeveloped land in large tracts starts at under US$200 an acre and goes up to around US$2,500 an acre for well-sited medium-sized tracts with good road and utility access.

Property Listings

Here are properties available in 2016 in Orange Walk District. Prices shown are asking prices.

• 1.16 acres with 140 feet of frontage on Philip Goldson Highway (formerly Northern Highway) in Carmelita village, US$13,000.

• 130 acres in three tracts near Guinea Grass village about 4 miles from Shipyard, with frontage on New River and power on road passing the properties, US$169,000.

• Lot in Pasadita area of Orange Walk Town, 75 x 75 feet, filled and ready to build on, US$7,500 – up to five other adjoining lots available, with totaling about ½ acre, US$45,000.

• 147-acre fenced cattle ranch near Yo Creek, less than 8 miles from Orange Walk Town, over 1,400 feet frontage on secondary road, US$150,000.

• Starter home on ¼-acre lot in Carmelita village about 8 miles from Orange Walk Town, concrete construction, US$29,500 with some owner financing.

• 15,000 acres near Blue Creek Mennonite community – about two-thirds of acreage is in timber, US$1,000 an acre.

Real Estate Agents

Real estate companies in Belize City and elsewhere in Belize handle property in Orange Walk.

Sign at Belize Zoo on way to Cayo

WESTERN BELIZE IN MORE DETAIL

GRADING THE AREA FOR RETIREMENT, RELOCATION AND INVESTMENT

Ratings are on an A to F scale, just like your old high school report card. A is the top grade; F is failing. Grades are relative compared to other areas in Belize.

Popularity with Expats	B
Safety	B-
Overall Cost of Living	B
Real Estate Bargains	B+
Investment Potential	C+
Leisure Activities	B+
Restaurants	B
Cultural Activities	C

Infrastructure	B
Business Potential	B
Medical Care	C+
Shopping	C+

ADVANTAGES OF CAYO: • Relatively low cost for rural land and for houses in San Ignacio and Belmopan • Offers some of Belize's most beautiful inland scenery • Access to outdoor activities on beautiful rivers and mountains • Friendly mix of Mestizo and Maya residents • Agricultural area for citrus, cattle ranching and other • Good place to escape from hurricanes

To exaggerate just a bit, Cayo is the "Wild West" of Belize. For would-be expats, it's an area where you can buy a small spread (or a large one) to raise citrus or Brahma cattle. For tourists, it is the turf in the traditional "surf 'n turf" visit to Belize — a few days on the cayes, typically Ambergris Caye or Caye Caulker, combined with some time on the mainland exploring ruins, rivers and rainforests.'

Cayo District has an area of more than 2,000 square miles, beginning near Belmopan and extending west and southwest to the Pine Ridge and into the Chiquibul wilderness and Maya Mountains. Belmopan City, Belize's capital, about 48 miles west of Belize City, has a reputation as a Nowheresville. Truth to say, the capital is not exactly a jumping place, but nearby is the Hummingbird Highway, the most scenic road in Belize. Also in the area are several top-notch jungle lodges. Belmopan is also in a growth spurt, with the population reaching around 18,300 in mid-2015 and a lot of new development going on. San Ignacio, with its sister town Santa Elena, total population around 20,000 in 2015, have an unassuming small town atmosphere.

Nothing in the twin towns of San Ignacio and Santa Elena will knock your boots off. There are few big cultural sights or museums, though there is an attractive new Welcome Center with historical artifacts in downtown San Ignacio. The shopping and other urban activities are somewhat limited. But San Ignacio, often just called Cayo or El Cayo, is a pleasant little burg. Locals are friendly, easy-going folk, mostly Mestizos with the usual Belizean mix of other, from Maya to Creoles to Chinese and Americans. Here you can buy groceries, check your email, do your banking and get a good cheap meal.

Progressive Mennonites have a large farming and commercial presence in the Spanish Lookout area northeast of San Ignacio. Some of the largest stores in Belize are in Spanish Lookout, with some of the lowest prices. Around San Ignacio, mostly to the southwest, are the green rolling hills of cottage country. Some of Belize's best lodges are here. With a few exceptions, to call them jungle lodges is a bit of a misnomer. Most are set in partially cleared pastures or fields.

Much of the land here is in cattle farms and citrus orchards. As you go west, you begin to see the influences of Guatemala. Maya women wash clothes in the river, and Benque Viejo del Carmen (population 6,500) strikes many as more Latin American and less Caribbean than most Belizean towns. But cross the border to Melchor de Mencos, Guatemala, and you're really in another world, one of more poverty, crime and where English is rarely spoken.

International Living in 2016 named Cayo as one of the top places in the world to retire.

In mid-2005, an oil drilling company, Belize Natural Energy, then run by two Irishwomen and three geologists, found oil near Spanish Lookout. The wells there currently are pumping light sweet crude at the rate of several thousand barrels a day.

Cayo District Practicalities

Welcome Center: A new Cayo Welcome Center is in downtown San Ignacio, near Burns Avenue. In addition to tourism information and some interesting historical and cultural displays, the complex has dining, shopping and a pay parking lot.

Banks: All four Belize banks -- Heritage Bank, ScotiaBank, Belize Bank and Atlantic Bank -- have branches in San Ignacio. ScotiaBank also has an office in Spanish Lookout near San Ignacio. Heritage Bank, Atlantic Bank and Belize Bank also have offices in Belmopan. Currently, only Heritage Bank has an office in Benque Viejo del Carmen.

Groceries: The two largest and generally cheapest grocery stores in the San Ignacio area are Mega Food in Santa Elena and Costless, near Cahal Pech at 7 Benque Viejo Road. Both are owned by the same people. Currently they are both open daily, until 9 p.m. Monday through Saturday but only until 1 p.m. on Sunday. Celina's Superstore on Burns Avenue is a friendly place to shop for groceries and other items. The San Ignacio market near downtown across from the football field has fruit, vegetables and some clothes and household items. Saturday morning is the best time to visit, but some stands are open daily. There also are fruit and vegetable stands downtown near the Welcome Center.

Restaurants: San Ignacio has many good small dining spots, including Ko-Ox Han-Nah (formerly Hannah's), Fuego Bar and Grill, Sanny's, Erva's, Mr. Greedy's Pizzeria, Hode's, Serendib and others. Benny's Kitchen in San José Succotz is a local favorite. Belmopan has several good places to eat, including Corkers, which is the best of the bunch, Bull Frog Inn and Caladium. There's also a good Indian food shack.

Medical: A private hospital, La Loma Luz, is in Santa Elena. Among public facilities, there is a district hospital in San Ignacio in a newish facility off the road to Bullet Tree and a regional hospital in Belmopan. Mopan Clinic is in Benque Viejo.

Infrastructure: Belmopan, San Ignacio/Santa Elena and Benque Viejo have municipal water and sewerage systems. More remote areas of Cayo are off the electrical grid and have to depend on cisterns and wells for water and on satellite internet.

Note: As with all other areas of Belize, see the Checking Out Cayo District chapter for more information on what to see and do in the area as well as in-depth reviews of hotels, restaurants and nightlife.

Real Estate

Cayo covers a fairly large area, with a lot of agricultural land along with wild bush. It includes the capital, Belmopan, and the largish town of San Ignacio/Santa Elena, plus Spanish Lookout and Benque Viejo. Thus property values vary widely. Land in tracts of under 50 to 100 acres along the beautiful Hummingbird Highway is selling in the range of US$1,000 to $4,000 an acre. These tracts usually have some road frontage and electricity. Larger accessible tracts in Cayo are going for US$500 to $1,000 an acre, but some opportunistic owners are asking blue sky numbers such as US$10,000 an acre or more. The same blue sky prices are being asked for some homes, especially those offered by real estate agents. Belizean-style homes start at around US$30,000, but you can pay up to half a million or more for a large U.S.-style home on an estate tract.

Property Listings

Here are a few of the properties available in 2015-2016, offered by individuals and real estate firms. Prices shown are asking prices.

• Small Belizean-style wood house in Kontiki neighborhood of San Ignacio, US$30,000.

• 5+ acres in Mountain Pine Ridge, with clear stream through property, US$45,000.

• Modern concrete three-bedroom home on 2 acres, fully fenced, about midway between Belmopan and San Ignacio, with caretaker's house included, US$189,000.

• 50 acres on Privassion Creek in Mountain Pine Ridge, across creek in Don Elijo National Park, US$150,000.

• 200+ acres near Blackman Eddy, about 2½ miles off George Price Highway, accessible via year-round dirt road, mostly jungle and bush, could be cleared for farming and ranching, US$289,000.

• 150 acres in Barton Creek area, with long creek frontage, US250,000.

• Small house with additional caretaker's house and a cabin on 10 acres of landscaped property, with frontage on the Macal River, near Mile 62 of the George Price Highway, US$600,000.

• One-quarter acre building lots in Cristo Rey village, all utilities, US$12,000.

• 25 acres with 1,000 feet of frontage on the Mopan River, US$169,000.

• Small two-bedroom concrete house on Banana Bank Road near Belmopan, all utilities, US$39,000.

• 1-acre building lot in Belmopan, US$35,000.

• 50 x 100 feet building lot overlooking San Ignacio, US$6,000.

• 1,420 acres in Yalbac Hills near Valley of Peace village, with 500 acres of cleared pasture for cattle, remainder high bush with timber, US$1,136,000.

Real Estate Agents

Ceiba Realty (Jonathan Lohr), 76 George Price Highway (Western Highway), Santa Elena, 501-824-4050; www.ceibarealestatebelize.com

Diamond Real Estate, Market Square, San Ignacio, 501-824-4450, www.diamondrealestatebelize.com

Rainforest Realty, 22 Benque Viejo Road, San Ignacio, 501-804-0195, www.rainforestrealty.com

Tropic Real Estate, Mile 60, George Price Highway (Western Highway), Unitedville, 501-824-3675; www.realestatebelize.com

Sign for Chef Rob's restaurant in Hopkins

DANGRIGA/HOPKINS IN DETAIL

GRADING THE AREA FOR RETIREMENT, RELOCATION AND INVESTMENT

Ratings are on an A to F scale, just like your old high school report card. A is the top grade; F is failing. Grades are relative compared to other areas in Belize.

Popularity with Expats	B-
Safety	B-
Overall Cost of Living	B
Real Estate Bargains	C+
Investment Potential	B-
Leisure Activities	B
Restaurants	C+

Cultural Activities	C
Infrastructure	B
Business Potential	B
Medical Care	C+
Shopping	C+

ADVANTAGES OF HOPKINS/DANGRIGA AREA: • Lower prices for beachfront property than on Ambergris Caye or Placencia • Friendly, interesting Garifuna culture • Provides excellent opportunities for water sports – boating, fishing, diving • Proximity to Cockscomb Basin Wildlife Sanctuary and other natural areas

This part of Stann Creek District is Belize at its most exotic, with Garifuna settlements that may remind you more of a coastal village in Senegal than Central America. Rural Maya villages that look much as they did hundreds of years ago. A few miles inland are a wild jaguar preserve and the highest mountains in Belize. The Cockscomb Basin Preserve west of Hopkins is real rainforest jungle, and the tallest peaks in Belize, Doyle's Delight at 3,688 feet and Victoria Peak at 3,675 feet, are in the Maya Mountains.

Unlike most of the rest of Belize's mainland coast, the Hopkins area has real beaches. The beaches here are similar to those in Placencia *(see below)* —ribbons of khaki-colored sand, with a good deal of seagrass in the water off the beach. Swimming is possible, especially in areas where the seagrass has been removed, as at the end of a dock. The snorkeling off the shore usually is not very good, although you can see some fish and possibly even a manatee.

The barrier reef is about 12 to 15 miles offshore from Hopkins and Dangriga, so it takes a while to get out to the reef for diving.

The Garifuna (usually pronounced Gah-RIF-u-nah) people who settled in this area have a fascinating history. Before the time of Columbus, Indians from the South American mainland came by boat to the island of St. Vincent in the southeast Caribbean. They conquered, and then intermarried with, Arawak Indians, adopting much of the Indian language. They went by the name Kwaib, from which the names Carib and Garifuna, meaning cassava-eaters, probably evolved.

Then, in the 17th century, slaves from Nigeria were ship-wrecked off St. Vincent. They too mixed with the Caribs or Garifuna. For years, Britain tried to subdue these free people of color, but the Garifuna, with the support of the French, fought back until the late 1700s, when the French and Garifuna finally surrendered to the British. In 1797, several thousand surviving Garifuna were taken by ship to Roatán in Honduras. Over the 150 years or so, many Garifuna moved from Roatán up the coast of Central America to Belize, where they worked in logging. The largest migration to Belize took place in 1823, and today that is commemorated nationally on November 19 as Garifuna Settlement Day.

Many settled in Stann Creek Town, what is now Dangriga. Hopkins, Seine Bight and, in Toledo, Punta Gorda Town and Barranco village also have sizable Garifuna populations. Initially, Dangriga was called Black Carib Town and then Stann Creek. The Garifuna in Belize are working hard to continue their language and culture. They have a complex system of religious beliefs, combining African and South American elements as well as Catholicism. Dugu or "Feasting of the Dead" is one of the ancestral rites practiced by Garifuna. There is a good small museum near Dangriga, Gulisi Garifuna Museum, with displays on the Garifuna people, their culture and their art.

Dangriga itself is not a very popular area for expats, but the Hopkins/Sittee Point area south of Dangriga is attracting a lot of attention, especially among those wanting a home on or near the beach or river. An American developer based in Texas, British-American Cattle Company, subdivided a large tract near Hopkins and before retiring sold a sizeable number of lots. Not too many homes have yet been built in this area, but more building is likely to take place over the next few years. Several upscale seafront condo developments, including Belizean Dreams and Hopkins Bay, have opened, with units sold to investors who let a management company rent out the units on a nightly or weekly basis.

Hopkins is a delightfully friendly and still mostly unspoiled village, though it is changing fast. In Hopkins and nearby are several excellent beach resorts, notably Hamanasi, along with many smaller, less expensive lodging options. You'll find some good spots for dining as well. The Sittee River and the Caribbean waters offer some of Belize's best fishing. The barrier reef isn't close to shore here, but once you get to the reef there's good diving. There's also good diving in the Southwater Marine

Reserve. Inland you're only a few miles from the world's first jaguar preserve, Cockscomb. Also within a short drive are Maya ruins and waterfalls at Mayflower, along with a revitalized jungle lodge, Mama Noots, with the country's longest zipline.

In Dangriga you'll find some shopping and a regional hospital for medical care. The access roads from the Southern Highway to Sittee village and the coast are mostly paved, and the road to Hopkins village from the Southern Highway has been rebuilt and surfaced. If there's a rub to this paradise, it's the sand fleas, which can be fierce in this area.

Dangriga/Hopkins Practicalities

Dangriga is the hub of this area, and for medical care, shopping and other services this is where you will need to go. Hopkins has only a few small shops.

Banks: Belize Bank, Heritage Bank and ScotiaBank have branches in or near Dangriga. There are no banks in Hopkins, although there is a Belize Bank ATM.

Groceries: There are several sizeable groceries in Dangriga. Try the one near Pen Cayetano's home and studio.

Restaurants: The restaurant at Pelican Beach Resort is the best Dangriga has to offer. Hopkins has several small restaurants owned and operated by local ladies, including Innie's that serve good local food and low prices. Chef Rob's, now at Parrot Cove Resort, is one of the top restaurants in the south. The restaurant at Beaches and Dreams is very good.

Medical: The Southern Regional Hospital (501-522-2078) at Mile 1.5 of the Stann Creek Valley Road opened in 1999. Dangriga is a regional medical center for southern Belize, including Placencia.

Infrastructure: Dangriga and Hopkins have municipal water and in most areas sewerage systems. These areas as well as most villages are on the electrical grid. Cable TV, DSL and cellular internet are available. More remote areas are not on the grid and must depend on their own resources for water, sewerage and satellite internet. Some Maya villages have homes with no running water.

Real Estate

Prices have gone up considerably in recent years in the Hopkins/Sittee

169

area, due to resort development in and around Hopkins. Beachfront lots generally go for US$150,000+ though occasionally one is available for less. Larger lots of more than half an acre with both Caribbean and canal or lagoon access are around US$150,000-$250,000. Seaview lots are much less, starting around US$35,000, and lots on the Sittee River can be had for US$40,000. These lots have utilities (electricity, telephones, public water and cable TV) and road access. Small recently built homes in this area, near but not on the water, are going for US$125,000 to $400,000+, occasionally with some owner financing available. New or resale beachside luxury condos are US$300,000 to $600,000.

Properties in Dangriga/Hopkins

These are offerings by individuals and real estate agencies in 2015-2016. Prices shown are asking prices.

• Seafront lot with 75 feet frontage on the Caribbean in False Sittee Point subdivision, with bonus 75 x 75 feet canal frontage lot, US$250,000.

• Double building lot on Hopkins Road about 3½ miles from Hopkins village, US$40,000.

• Seaview residential corner lot in False Sittee Point subdivision, 80' x 150', all utilities, property taxes US$18 a year, US$45,000.

• Three-bedroom, three-bath 2,500 sq. ft. condo villa in Hopkins Bay North development, fully furnished, views of Caribbean, US$589,000.

• About 81 acres on Coastal Road, with creek frontage, about 10 miles from Dangriga, US$99,000.

• Newly built two-bedroom, one-bath concrete home, with one-bedroom, one-bath apartment on ground level, on three-fourths of an acre on Sittee River, US$234,000.

• Two-story concrete house in Dangriga Town, with sea views, total of seven bedrooms and three baths, now rented as two separate units, US$139,000.

Real Estate Developments

Here are selected real estate developments in the Dangriga-Hopkins area. Most market primarily to foreign buyers. As always in Belize, it's buyer beware. For example, a large "development" was divided on paper into more than 1,000 lots. Located near Mullins River and called "Dreamscapes," (several different versions of the name were used) the "developer," allegedly a disbarred Florida attorney who had served time in prison on a federal felony racketeering charge, reportedly sold lots to buyers, some of whom had never seen the property, for some US$20,000 to $30,000 each. In 2015, a group of investors, who sued in a Florida court, claimed that some 300 lots had been sold, but that none of the money had been escrowed, and that besides the grading of a few roads nothing had been done to the property to prepare it for home building. Stay tuned.

Hopkins Bay, 412-860-1418; www.hopkinsbayrealestate.com Developers of the successful Belizean Dreams condos near Jaguar Reef Resort originally put together the Hopkins Bay project at the north end of Hopkins village. Now, a "Canadian-American-South African consortium" is offering lots and villas on a 48-acre tract. A number of condo units, which range in price up to around US$750,000, are offered for sale. A master plan calls for a casino, marina, hotels and golf course, but those are years in the future if they materialize at all.

Sanctuary Belize, Dangriga, 1401 Dove St. #610, Newport Beach, CA 92660, 949-757-0949 or 830-443-4595; www.sanctuarybelize.com. Sanctuary Belize, a large and at times controversial development formerly called Sanctuary Bay, on a 14,000-acre tract of land, of which about 9,000 to 11,000 acres (various numbers have been put forth over the years) is a protected reserve. The property is located between the Placencia peninsula and Hopkins, bordering the Sapodilla Lagoon and the Sittee River.

Sanctuary Belize has something of a checkered history. Two Americans initially involved in Sanctuary served prison terms in the U.S. Andris Pukke, founder of a U.S. credit counseling company accused of cheating 300,000 debtors out of millions of dollars and reportedly the original owner/developer of Sanctuary Bay, and Peter Baker, a long-time Pukke friend and associate who was also a principal in Sanctuary Bay, were jailed by a U.S. District Court judge in Maryland. Pukke was held in contempt of court for failing to turn over assets to a fund set up, in a U.S. Federal Trade Commission agreement, to repay the debtors. Peter Baker, the son of Joan Medhurst, whose firm in the 1990s had the international public relations contract for the Belize Tourism Board, was jailed because the judge concluded Baker and Pukke colluded to shield assets both in Belize and in California.

For a while after the U.S. legal actions, sales and development at Sanctuary Bay essentially were on hold. Since then, with new management, headed by John Usher, a Belizean, in place and with a slick new website, Sanctuary has regained traction. It has been promoting aggressively in the U.S. and Canada. Ads invite prospects to come to Belize on five-day property visits for an attractive price. Andris Pukke is now a consultant to Sanctuary and reportedly visits the development frequently. Sanctuary has approximately several hundred building lots of ½-acre to 10 acres in its initial phases, surrounded by a 11,000-acre wildlife sanctuary. A large number of lots have been sold, according to the current management. Some of the development infrastructure, such as graded roads, a beachfront clubhouse and a marina, is in place. Originally offered for under US$80,000 to US$229,000, some resale lots are on the market. Newly released lots at Sanctuary start in the "low 100s," according to management but most are priced much higher. A number of homes have been built, and in 2013 Sanctuary took over operation of a nearby beach resort, Kanantik, to house visitors to the property, who come to Sanctuary on sales junkets. However, Kanantik now also advertises itself as a regular beach resort. Sanctuary also built a small "tent resort" near its beach club and swimming pool for potential buyers coming to look over the property.

Real Estate Agents

Belize Property Agents, Mile 6, Hummingbird Hwy., Dangriga, 501-522-0511; www.belizepropertyagent.com

Caribbean Property Consultants, P.O. Box 149, Dangriga, 501-523-7299; www.belizeproperty.com

The Shak restaurant in Placencia

PLACENCIA IN MORE DETAIL

GRADING THE AREA FOR RETIREMENT, RELOCATION AND INVESTMENT

Ratings are on an A to F scale, just like your old high school report card. A is the top grade; F is failing. Grades are relative compared to other areas in Belize.

Popularity with Expats	B
Safety	B
Overall Cost of Living	C+
Real Estate Bargains	C-
Investment Potential	B
Leisure Activities	B
Restaurants	B+
Cultural Activities	D
Infrastructure	B-
Business Potential	B-

Medical Care	C
Shopping	D+

ADVANTAGES OF PLACENCIA: • 16 miles of beaches on the peninsula • Growing number of expats buying property and building here • Excellent fishing and water sports • Popular resort area • New cruise port on island off the peninsula

Placencia's boosters boast that it has the best beaches on mainland Belize. The 16 miles or so of beaches on the peninsula indeed are a beautiful resource, a narrow, long loaf of toast-colored sand. Like most beaches in Belize, these are only fair for swimming, as there's a good deal of seagrass, except where hotels have removed it around piers. You can snorkel here and there, but for world-class snorkeling you'll have to take a boat out to the reef or to one of the small offshore cayes with patch reefs, a 10- to 20-mile boat trip. There is closer snorkeling at False Caye off Maya Beach and in a couple of other areas.

Several marine national parks and reserves are within an hour or two by boat, including Laughing Bird Caye, Southwater and Port Honduras. The Caribbean is incredibly beautiful, above and below the surface. Above, the crystal clear water sparkles in the sun. Poke your head below, and you find a whole new universe of color and activity, from tiny tropical fish to dolphins, manatees and whale sharks.

The peninsula is beginning to take off in development, but contradictions abound. Unpainted wood shacks stand next door to luxury resorts, where a week's stay costs more than a local worker might earn in a year. Local families who a few years ago fished for a living have opened restaurants, bars and hotels, and they don't always have all the management skills down pat. There's a modern water system, and most of the peninsula is on the power grid, yet local schools barely have any books and, until a Cuban volunteer medical team came to the peninsula, locals had to go to Independence or Dangriga to see a doctor.

The biggest change is that after years of promises the road from the Southern Highway to Riversdale and then down the peninsula was finally paved. What formerly was a series of mud holes is now one of the best roads in Belize, with its main disadvantage being the annoying speed bumps. Another development: a new international airport, funded by private interests on the peninsula and elsewhere in Belize, was partially built in the area just northwest of Riversdale. It remains incomplete and unopen. Whether this airport actually will open and handle international flights is still, well, up in the air.

Another BIG change is the Norwegian Cruise Lines cruise port at Harvest Caye off Placencia. *See Checking Out Placencia for more information.*

In October 2001, Hurricane Iris did extensive damage to the southern part of the peninsula. Except for a few open spaces where trees have not been replanted or houses rebuilt, the peninsula is back to normal now. The area is attracting a mix of expats: A few with cash and a dream have opened resorts. Some are middle-class baby boomers that are buying lots and hope to build a vacation or retirement home. A few are marginalized escapees from the North American rat race, who live hand-to-mouth and seem to spend most of their time boozing.

Hundreds of condo units were under construction or planned, and then the Great Recession hit. Several major projects were cancelled or postponed. At least one large project, Bella Maya, closed.

Tourism is still a hit-and-miss seasonal thing on the Placencia peninsula. Except for a few well-marketed properties, annual occupancy at peninsula hotels is well averages under 35%. During the winter, especially around holidays, and around Easter, hotels fill up and it can be tough to find a decent room. But, off-season, the peninsula slows down, some hotels and restaurants close and most of the peninsula reverts to its sleepy self. Quite a few peninsula resorts are, actively or passively, up for sale. Many have been on the market for years; nearly all continue with business-as-usual, regardless of sale status.

Land on the peninsula is low-lying and flat. The Maya Mountains are visible to the west. Placencia, a Creole village, with a population of about 800, is at the southern tip of the peninsula. A long concrete sidewalk runs up the center of the village. A stroll up and down the sidewalk will give you a good introduction to life in the village. A Garifuna village, Seine Bight (population over 1,000), is a little farther north. Maya Beach, not a village but a collection of houses and small resorts, is known for its good beaches.

Placencia Practicalities

Shops and services, such as they are, mostly are clustered in Placencia village, though a few are located in Seine Bight and in Maya Beach.

Banks: Atlantic Bank, Belize Bank and ScotiaBank have branches and ATMs in Placencia. Heritage Bank has a branch across the lagoon in Independence.

Groceries: There are several small groceries on the peninsula. Wallen's Market (on the main road in Placencia village, across from the soccer field), is one of the oldest, but there are other choices in the village, including Ming's and Everyday. A newish, modern grocery, Top Value, opened farther up the peninsula, on the east side of the main road just north of Placencia village, and there are small groceries in Seine Bight and Maya Beach. Placencia village also has several small bakeries. John the Baker Man has long been making pastries and breads in his home in the village. For a bigger selection of groceries and better prices, you may want to go to Dangriga, Belmopan or Belize City. A truck from Dangriga makes weekly deliveries selling fresh fruit and vegetables, but there are small fruit and vegetables stands in Placencia.

Restaurants: The dining scene on the peninsula has greatly improved in recent years. The Bistro at Maya Beach Hotel is one of the best restaurants in Belize. Rumfish y Vino in Placencia village is a nice spot for drinks and little plates, as there are other good choices including La Dolce Vita and The Secret Garden. Several of the hotels, including Turtle Inn, Singing Sands and Laru Beya, do a good job with food and beverage. Among the more modest spots, Dawn's Grill 'n Go, De Tatch, Yoli's, The Shak and Omar's offer good local food and reasonable value. The highly notable Tutti Frutti has authentic Italian gelati, by far the best we've tasted anywhere in Central America. Heck, maybe anywhere outside Italy.

Other Services: There is a gas station in Placencia village, another a little north of the village, fairly well equipped building supplies stores and a number of gift shops.

Medical: A small medical clinic is located near the school in Placencia village, and another clinic is in Seine Bight. Cuban doctors, on loan from Fidel and Raul, may still be in residence when you are there. Otherwise, for medical attention you may need to go to Dangriga or across the lagoon to Independence.

Infrastructure: The Placencia peninsula is now on the power grid, has good water straight from the Maya Mountains and in most areas a sewerage system. The peninsula has cable TV and DSL and cellular internet.

Note: For more information on what to see and do in Placencia and for detailed reviews of hotels, restaurants and nightlife, see the Checking Out Placencia chapter.

Real Estate: Real estate has been booming on the Placencia peninsula, though with the 2009-2012 global recession the boom diminished to a whimper. Since then, however, sales are clawing back. With limited land on the narrow peninsula, and considerable demand from Americans seeking a place on the Caribbean, prices zoomed upward in recent years. Desirable beachfront lots are now going for US$3,000 to $4,500 a front foot, or around US$185,000 to $260,000+ for a deep lot with 75 ft. of beachfront, while lots a row or two back are US$50,000 to $100,000. Lagoon and canal lots are US$35,000 to $75,000, and some more. Most condos are also expensive – US$150,000 to $225,000 for a one-bedroom and US$200,000 to $400,000+ for a two-bedroom. Small wood homes in Placencia or Seine Bight villages might be had under US$100,000, but modern reinforced concrete homes farther north on or near the beach are US$200,000 to $400,000 and up, often way up. Rentals are few and far between on the peninsula. You may be able to find a rental in Placencia village for around US$300 to $500 a month. A nicer home north of village may go for US$700 and up.

Real Estate Developments

Among the real estate developments on the peninsula are these:

Coco Plum (www.cocoplumbelize.net): This is *the* quality residential development on the peninsula. Established by Stewart Krohn, who for years operated Channel 5 TV and Great Belize Productions, and his partners, the 224-acre master-planned gated community is a low-density development with most lots over one-half acre. All roads are paved, and utilities are underground. Eventually it is expected to have a resort hotel and other amenities. Lots range from around US$130,000 to over $500,000. Several homes already have been built. HOA fees are US$450 annually, plus, after building, an additional fee of US$225 per bedroom annually. Villas at Coco Plum, a condo development, was carved out of Coco Plum land but is separate from the Coco Plum residential development.

The Placencia, The Placencia Residences and Copal Beach

(www.theplacencia.com, www.theplacenciaresidences.com and www.copalbeach.com). The Placencia is an ambitious hotel, condominium and residential development north on the peninsula. Condos on the seaside are offered from US$350,000 to around $1 million. Some of the these condos are part of The Placencia hotel, which must have one of the lowest occupancy rates on the peninsula; we've never seen more than a handful of guests here. Residential lots on the filled lagoon side are priced at up to around $800,000. Homes are mostly US$1 million and up. The status of a long-planned international airport northwest of the peninsula is unclear. Earlier, plans for a casino and golf course were announced, but their future also is unclear. The high-rise Copal Beach luxury complex, just north of The Placencia, has condo units ranging in price from around US$1 million up. Who buys these things, anyway?

Villas Los Porticos (www.losporticosvifllas.com), two-bedroom, two-bath condos in Phase 3, from US$270,000 to US$375,000.

Properties on the Placencia Peninsula

Here is a selection of properties offered by individuals and real estate companies in 2015-2016:

• Lagoon-front lots at Crimson Park, with water frontage from 70 to 135 feet, US$85,000 to $165,000.

• Beach lots with 85 feet frontage on the sea in the Plantation II area, about 15 miles north of Placencia, lots with 170 feet depth, US$249,000.

• Three-bedroom, four-bath concrete luxury home on lagoon side, completed in 2009, in gated Placencia Residences subdivision, 3,300 sq. ft. of living space, approx. 7,500 sq. ft. lot, lagoon views, fully air-conditioned, some marble floors, owners' dues of US$1 per sq. ft. per year includes yard maintenance and access to Placencia Hotel facilities, US$1,750,000.

• Residential lot near Wendy's restaurant, on lagoon side of Placencia village, 64 x 104 feet, all utilities, US$130,000.

• Interior building lot in 224-acre Coco Plum development, electric and water underground utilities in place, paved roads, gated, security, access to beach, from US$129,000.

• Two-bedroom, two-bath 1,100 sq. ft. condo at Belize Ocean Club, fully furnished, US$325,000.

• One-bedroom, one-bath 750 sq. ft. concrete home on 100 x 150 feet lot in Buccaneer Subdivision just north of Placencia Airport, sea and lagoon views, US$199,000 with some owner financing.

• Two-bedroom condo at Villas at Coco Plum, 1,392 sq. ft., one of 12 finished units out of planned 35 on the beach. US$315,000.

Short-Term Rentals

Besides the properties listed below other condos and resorts may have furnished units for rent on a weekly, monthly or seasonal basis, especially during the off-season.

Barnacle Bill's, Maya Beach (tel. 501-523-8010, www.barnaclebills-belize.com) has two nice one-bedroom cottages on the beach at Maya Beach, for around US$665 a week May to November and around US$770 the rest of the year. These rates include utilities but not 9% tax.

Placencia Beach Club, 22 Harbor Place, Placencia, 501-665-2675, (www.placenciabeachclub.com) is a cabaña resort with furnished, utilities and taxes included, monthly rentals for one-bedroom units from US$1,600 off-season to US$2,000 in-season.

Real Estate Agents

CPC Real Estate Solutions Ltd., 1 Placencia Village Square, Placencia Village, 501-672-9000 or 501-669-9000, www.belizeproperty.com

Yearwood Properties, Placencia Road, Placencia; tel. 501-523-3462; www.placenciabelizerealestate.net

Fruit and vegetable sellers in PG

TOLEDO IN MORE DETAIL

GRADING THE AREA FOR RETIREMENT, RELOCATION
AND INVESTMENT

Ratings are on an A to F scale, just like your old high school report
card. A is the top grade; F is failing. Grades are relative compared to other
areas in Belize.

Popularity with Expats	D+
Safety	B+
Overall Cost of Living	B
Real Estate Values	B
Investment Potential	C
Leisure Activities	C
Restaurants	D+
Cultural Activities	C-
Infrastructure	C+

Business Potential   C

Medical Care   C

Shopping   C-

ADVANTAGES TO PUNTA GORDA AREA: • Lush, beautiful tropical scenery • Excellent fishing • Diverse mix of Maya, Garifuna and other cultures • Moderate land prices • Proximity to Rio Dulce area of Guatemala • Increasing interest in area for tourism due to completion of Southern Highway and construction of new road to Guatemala with border crossing

You've probably heard stories about Punta Gorda being the end of the earth and all that. You may be surprised, then, at how inviting a town it is. With about 5,500 people, it has a mix of Mopan and Kekchi Maya, Garifuna and a dollop of Creoles, Lebanese and Chinese, plus a few American expats, missionaries and dreamers.

PG, as it's known in Belize, is colorful and friendly. There's usually a breeze blowing from the Bay of Honduras. On Wednesdays and Saturdays, the downtown market draws Maya from surrounding villages. PG's waterside setting is, like that of Corozal Town, truly pleasant, even beautiful.

Business activity in the town is not exactly hot and hopping. Hotels in and around PG stay empty most of the year, though several new ones have opened -- hope springs eternal. The hotel occupancy rate is under 30%. As yet, only a few tourists make it all the way down the Southern Highway from Belize City or Placencia. Some backpackers do pass through on their way to cheaper towns in Guatemala and Honduras. With the completion of the paving of the Southern Highway, and the planned opening of a new paved road to Guatemala's Pan-American Highway, conventional wisdom is that PG will soon explode with new hotels, real estate developments and other businesses. We're not so sure that will happen to any great extent, but certainly things are getting a bit busier.

Outside of PG, the land in Toledo District is lush, wild and wet, fed by 160 inches or more of rain each year — the only "dry" months are February through May. Emerald green valleys lay between low peaks of the Maya Mountains. Rice grows in flooded fields, and giant bromeliads line the roads. There are no beaches to speak of around PG, but the rocky shorelines are cooled by near constant breezes from the Bay of Honduras. Offshore are isolated cayes and the straggling end of the barrier reef.

The Maya have lived in this part of Belize for millennia. Among the Maya ruins here are Lubaantun ("Place of the Fallen Stones") Lubaantun was occupied only from around 700 to 900 CE. The famous, or infamous, "crystal skull" was supposedly discovered here in 1926 by F.A. Mitchell-Hedges, on assignment from the British Museum, though most experts believe the skull is a hoax. Nim Li Punit ("Big Hat") was occupied about the same time as Lubaantun, in the Late Classic period. At its height, several thousand people may have lived there. Among other notable Maya sites in the area is Uxbenka (pronounced Ush-ben-ka and meaning "Ancient Place").

The Maya were joined in the early 19th century by Garifuna from the Bay Islands of Honduras and, after the American Civil War, by a group of former Confederate soldiers and their families who attempted to settle here, with relatively little success. In modern times, Punta Gorda has held an attraction for missionary groups, mostly fundamentalists from the U.S. Who knows? You may find PG is precisely your kind of place, too.

Punta Gorda Practicalities

Banks: Belize Bank and ScotiaBank have branches and ATMs in PG.

Groceries: All of the groceries in Punta Gorda are small. Try Mel's Mart or one of the several Supaul Stores (usually referred to by color, "green Supaul's," "white Supaul's," etc. The old PG market, where vendors sell fruit, vegetables and other items, has been renovated.

Restaurants: Asha's Culture Kitchen, Mangrove Inn, Marian's Bayview, The Snack Shack, Gomier's and Grace's. At the lodges, the restaurant at the luxurious Belcampo Lodge is charming but expensive.

Medical: Punta Gorda Hospital (south end of Main Street) can provide basic emergency care; you may want to upgrade to the Southern Regional Hospital in Dangriga or to hospitals in Belize City.

Infrastructure: Punta Gorda has power, municipal water and sewerage system. Cable TV, DSL and cellular internet are available in PG. Many remote areas of Toledo District are not on the grid, and residents must depend on their own resources for water, sewerage and satellite internet. Some Maya villages have homes with no running water and no power.

Real Estate

Toledo does not have a very active real estate market, and it is difficult to establish market value. Accessible land in smaller tracts (under 50 acres) often goes for US$1,000 to $2,000 an acre. Larger parcels with access and river frontage are usually US$500 to $1,000 an acre. Building lots in or near Punta Gorda not on the bay are inexpensive – usually no more than a few thousand dollars, but waterfront lots are more expensive. Smaller concrete houses on the bay in PG have sold for under US$75,000.

Properties Offered in Toledo

Here are a few properties offered by individuals and real estate companies in 2016. Prices shown are asking prices.

• 55x110 foot waterfront commercial lot in renovated market in PG, US$125,000

• 200 acres near Mafredi village off Blue Creek Road, in Toledo, about half in high ground, most of remainder low-lying land formerly used for rice farming, price reduced to US$149,000.

• 50 acres with frontage on Moho River, about 10 miles from PG, currently accessible by sea or river, US$50,000.

• Four-bedroom, two-bath 1,200 sq. ft. concrete home on 29 acres near Barranco village, including pickup truck and motorcycle, US$124,500.

• Teak, mahogany and cacao plantation near Machaca, Toledo, with 80 acres planted in teak, 40 in cacao, 30+ in mahogany, 150 in rainforest, total 300 acres, plentiful water from creek, US$1,050,000.

Real Estate Agents

Real estate companies in Belize City and elsewhere also have some listings for Toledo. PG tourism operators and entrepreneurs sometimes hustle real estate on the side.

CPC Real Estate Solutions Ltd., #168 Beach Front,Hopeville,Punta Gorda, Toledo, 501- 667-3254. www.belizeproperty.com

Traffic in Belize City

BELIZE CITY IN MORE DETAIL

GRADING THE AREA FOR RETIREMENT, RELOCATION
AND INVESTMENT Ratings are on an A to F scale, just like your old
high school report card. A is the top grade; F is failing. Grades are relative
compared to other areas in Belize.

Popularity with Expats	D
Safety	D
Overall Cost of Living	C-
Real Estate Bargains	C-
Investment Potential	B-
Leisure Activities	C+
Restaurants	B+
Cultural Activities	A-
Infrastructure	B+
Business Potential	B
Medical Care	A-
Shopping	A-

ADVANTAGES TO BELIZE CITY: • Access to good restaurants and social and cultural activities • Business and transportation hub of the country • Availability of stores and shopping, some with lower prices • Good medical care

Belize City has a bad rep among visitors and even among Belizeans from other areas, who sometimes dread visiting the "big city" with its rude layabouts and drug touts. In truth, the city is hardly more than an oversized town, with ramshackle buildings set close to the street in the central areas but also with its share of stately old colonial houses in the Fort George section and early 19th century landmarks such as St. John's Anglican Cathedral and the House of Culture, formerly Government House. And while crime is a considerable problem – hardly a weekend goes by without a murder or three – crime in Belize City is nothing like that you'd experience in the much bigger and meaner cities of the region such as Guatemala City and Tegucigalpa.

The city has an energy of its own. By day, Front, Queen and Albert streets swarm with shop clerks and shoppers. Restaurants are packed at lunchtime. On Regent Street you'll find lawyers and judges dressed in British-style robes. Day trippers from the cruise ships that now call on Belize City – nearly a million passengers make port here annually, much to the dismay of many resort and ecolodge owners who fear the impact of hordes of cruise tourists on environmentally sensitive ruins, caves and cayes – get on vans and boats for their shore excursions. (Some of the cruise tourists are being siphoned off to southern Belize, with the debut of the Norwegian Cruise Lines cruise port on a caye off Placencia village.)

Everywhere you'll hear the sound of Creole being spoken, as local residents greet friends and lovers amid a happy Caribbean-style gumbo of sounds and smells. At night, despite the street crime, Belize City lights up with parties, gallery openings and political and professional meetings, as Belize City remains in all but name the true political, as well as cultural and social, capital of the country.

Belize City Practicalities

As the largest urban area and commercial hub of the country, Belize City offers most of the amenities of a town of similar size in the U.S. or

Canada, although don't expect to find international big box stores like Home Depot or Best Buy.

Airlines: Belize City is the transportation hub of the country and offers more than 50 domestic flights a day by Maya Island Air (www.mayaislandair.com) and Tropic Air (www.tropicair.com) from two Belize City area airports to major destinations in Belize and to Guatemala, Honduras and Mexico. The international airport is served by major airlines including American, Avianca (formerly TACA), United, Delta, Copa and Southwest.

Goldson International Airport at Ladyville near Belize City

Buses: More than a dozen bus companies leave from the terminal in the Collet Canal area west of the city center. This terminal is still called Novelo's, though the original Novelo's bus line, for which it was named, no longer operates.

Taxis: Most taxi trips within the city cost US$5 or less. The rate to and from the city and the international airport is fixed at US$25 (for the cab, not per person).

Banks: All of Belize's domestic banks -- Atlantic Bank, Belize Bank,

Heritage Bank and ScotiaBank -- have offices and ATMs in Belize City. The larger banks have multiple offices, in several cases along with their international banking (offshore) subsidiaries. Branches in the "suburbs" have drive-up windows.

Embassies: Some diplomatic missions to Belize maintain their offices in Belize City rather than Belmopan. However, the U.S. Embassy moved to a new US$50 million compound in Belmopan in 2006.

Groceries: The two largest supermarkets in the Belize City area — indeed in all of Belize — are Save-U (San Cas Plaza by Belcan Bridge, 501-223-1291) and Brodies (Mile 2½ Philip Goldson Highway, 501-223-5587, www.brodiesbelize.com). Both are modern supermarkets with air-conditioning and free parking. Brodies was greatly expanded and redone in 2006-2007. They both have pharmacies and sell liquor, beer and wine. Brodies also has a fairly extensive dry goods section. There is another, older Brodies downtown. Premium Wine & Spirits (166 Newtown Barracks, 501-223-4984) has a good selection of imported wines.

Restaurants: Belize City has many good restaurants in all price ranges. Among the favorites are the Tender Bar & Grill, Riverside Tavern, Sahara Grill and Chon Saan Palace.

Other Stores: While there at present is no Walmart or Costco, Belize City does have a number of larger stores where you can buy appliances, hardware, home furnishings and construction supplies. Among them: Mirab Department Store (501-223-2933, www.mirabsbelize.com, for appliances, home furnishings and other items); Courts (501-223-0775, www.shopcourts.com/belize, for electronics and other goods); Benny's Home Center (501-227-3347, www.bennys.bz, for construction supplies); and Hofius (501-227-7231, www.hofiusbelize.com), a hardware store with a good reputation for appliances and kitchen equipment.

Car Dealers: Among the new car dealers in Belize City are those selling Ford, Toyota, Mitsubishi, Land Rover, Suzuki, Hyundai, Kia, Isuzu, Nissan, Dodge and Jeep.

Medical: Belize City is the medical center of Belize, with the largest hospital (Karl Heusner Memorial Hospital, Princess Margaret Dr., 501-223-1548, www.khmh.bz) and by far the largest number of physicians, dentists and other healthcare professionals. Belize Medical Associates (5791 St. Thomas St., Kings Park, tel. 501- 223-0302) is a 25-bed private hospital. *(See the Health chapter for other listings.)*

Among the several dozen physician practices in the city are Family Medical Center (3 Newtown Barracks, 501-223-2647, email b.e.bulwer@btl.net) and Caribbean Shores Medical Center (5756 Princess Margaret Dr., 501-224-4821, email fdsmith@btl.net). Among recommended dentists are Dr. Osbert O. Usher Dental Clinic (16 Magazine Road, 501-227-3415) and Heusner's Professional Dentistry (42 Albert Street, 501-272-2583).

Infrastructure: Belize City has the most advanced electrical, water, sewerage and internet/telecommunications systems in the country. Larger villages in rural Belize District also are generally well served, but more remote areas are exceptions.

Real Estate

Few expats will choose Belize City as a place to live, unless they need to be there for business reasons. Those that do likely will live in the suburbs north and west of the city, such as Bella Vista and Belama, or in the more upscale areas of town along Princess Margaret Street, King's Park and West Landivar. Homes in these areas are priced similarly to homes in nice areas of mid-sized U.S. cities, with prices of several hundred U.S. dollars for homes not being unusual.

Secure apartment rentals also are not cheap: You can expect to pay around US$.90 to $2 per square foot per month, or about US$900 to $2,000+ a month for a 1,000 sq. ft. two-bedroom apartment, and more for luxury condos such as those in Renaissance Towers and Marina Towers.

Residential areas around Belize City range from upscale suburbs to poor villages. Ladyville near the international airport has subdivisions and a variety of businesses. Farther north in Belize District, Crooked Tree is a pleasant Creole village with a lagoon setting. To the west, Hattieville is a sprawling residential area that sprang up after Hurricane Hattie in 1961. To the south off the Coastal Highway, Gales Point, another Creole village, enjoys a beautiful setting between the sea and lagoons.

Properties Offered in and around Belize City

Here are some offerings, from individuals and real estate firms in 2016:
• Residential building lot in Buttonwood Bay area, US$67,500.
• Two-story building suitable for offices, 2,400 sq. ft. on Regent Street in downtown Belize City, about 50 years old, renovated in 2009, onsite

parking, US$600,000.

• Modern concrete two-story home in on seafront in Ladyville, three bedrooms, four baths in 3,300 sq. ft., on 2/3-acre lot, US$800,000.

•10 acres in Ladyville area, all utilities, US$175,000.

• Small three-bedroom, two-bath concrete cottage off Central American Boulevard, reduced to US$75,000.

• Two-story building at Mile 2½ Philip Goldson Highway, currently used as apartments, US$237,500, with discount for cash offer.

• 19 acres in rural Belize District near Altun Ha Maya site, US$35,000.

Real Estate Agents

4 Realty (Carlos Habet), 115 Barrack Road, Belize City, 501-223-5588, http://carlohabet.point2agent.com

Belize Land Properties Ltd., 9 Third Street, King's Park, Belize City, 501-621-4754, www.belizelandproperties.com

Buy-Belize Real Estate, 101B Freetown Rd., Belize City, 501-223-2121, Belize City, www.buy-belize.com

Century 21 BTAL, 1 Mapp St., Belize City, 501-224-5420, www.century21belize.com

Emerald Futures Real Estate, Mile 3 ½, Northern Hwy., Belize City, tel. 501-670-6818, www.emeraldfutures.com

Vista Real Estate, 13 Cork St., Belize City, tel. 501-223-2427, www.belizerealestate.bz

Textures of Belize

HOTELS AND RESORTS FOR SALE

Many people have a dream of owning and operating a small beach hotel or jungle lodge.

By our count, more than 50 hotels, lodges, inns and B&Bs are currently for sale in Belize. Aside from these properties that are actively on the market via media advertising or listings with real estate companies in 2015-2016, there are a number of other hotels for sale but currently are not being promoted. Not all of the properties shown below are currently operating. All prices shown are asking prices in U.S. dollars.

We attempt to provide current and accurate information, but such information is subject to change, and owners *do* change their minds. These listings should be used for informational purposes, to provide you with an idea of what resort properties are asking for in the current market.

CAYO DISTRICT
Belize Jungle Dome, Belmopan, 5-room lodge plus 3-bedroom

house, swimming pool, on 2½ acres with Belize River frontage, US$1,0595,000.

Pook's Hill Lodge, Belmopan, 11 cabañas on 100 acres, asking US$2,300,000.

Roaring River Golf Course, 9-hole golf course on 20 acres with restaurant and five tourist rental cottages, US$1,650,000.

Mopan River Resort, Benque Viejo, former leading all-inclusive now in receivership, on 83 acres with large owners' home, 9 cabañas plus 3 suites, pool, lodge and restaurant, about 1,500 feet frontage on Mopan River, US$1,500,000.

Maya Mountain Lodge with 8 cabañas plus 7 rooms in large building 1 mile off George Price Highway on Christo Rey Road, swimming pool, on 10+ acres, US$985,000.

CAYE CAULKER

Seaside Cabanas, 17 air-conditioned rooms on seafront in main part of village, pool, bar, US$2,999,999.

AMBERGRIS CAYE

Villa Casa Buena Vista, 1 acre on 300 feet of seafront, 10 rental units, a little over 2 miles south of San Pedro, US$2,200,000.

Tranquility Bay Resort, 11 cabañas, restaurant, dive shop, 3 boats, North Ambergris Caye, US$3,300,000.

REMOTE CAYES & ATOLLS

Eco resort on Long Caye, Lighthouse Reef Atoll, about 1½ hours by boat from Belize City, 24 rooms, about 2/3 acre, with solar electric system and back-up diesel generator, 15,000-gallon water storage, reverse osmosis water systems, not operating, priced reduced to US$2,499,000.

Manta Reef Resort, Glovers Reef Atoll, 15 cabañas plus house and restaurant on 12 acres, seafront, not operating, US$5,500,000.

Resort on Long Caye, Glovers Reef Atoll, US$3,200,000.

HOPKINS AREA

All Seasons Guesthouse, 3 room, 3 separate cabins and owners' suite, on market due to death of longtime owner, US$389,000.

Beach and Dreams, 11-unit beachfront resort with restaurant, owners' quarters, new pool, van, trucks, boats and equipment included, US$2,500,000 with terms.

Unfinished Resort, currently with 2 cabañas, on almost 9 acres with Mullins River frontage, US$475,000.

Villa Verano, 10-room hotel, pool, 100 feet frontage on sea, US$3,350,000.

PLACENCIA

South Waters Resort, Point Placencia, Placencia, 4 waterfront cabañas, 3 units plus office in main building, cafe and bar, on 2 2/3 acres, US$2,500,000.

COROZAL TOWN

Copa Banana, 2 houses divided into guest rooms and an apartment, US$350,000.

Las Palmas, 23 air-conditioned rooms, space for restaurant, reduced to US$1,700,000.

PUNTA GORDA

Hickatee Cottage, near Punta Gorda, six cottage units on about 20 acres, owners' quarters, lodge building with bar and dining area, includes furniture and fixtures, US$355,000.

BELIZE CITY AND BELIZE DISTRICT

Bamboleo Inn, 7-room nearly new guesthouse in Ladyville area, 3-room owners' suite, US$429,900.

Crooked Tree Lodge, 6 cabañas on 11 acres, with about 1,000 feet of riverfront, US$1,200,000.

Watch out for the snakes in Belize, including the two-legged kind

MONEY AND HOW TO KEEP IT IN BELIZE

Belize's official currency is the Belize dollar, which for many years has been pegged to the U.S. dollar at a rate of 2 Belize dollars to 1 U.S. dollar. However, moneychangers often give a slightly higher rate than 2 Belize for 1 U.S. dollar, sometimes as much as 2.1 or 2.2 to 1, or even higher, depending on the local demand for American greenbacks. Generally, though, the premium is only 2% to 3%.

That brings us to a key fact about Belize and your money: Hard currencies, like the U.S. dollar, euro and yen, are good. Soft currencies, and the Belize dollar is one of them, are not so good. The Belize dollar is difficult to exchange anywhere outside of Belize (except at border areas of Guatemala and Mexico).

For years there has been talk of dollarizing the Belize economy, making the U.S. dollar the official currency of Belize, similar to what El Salvador and Ecuador and, to a degree, Guatemala have done, but so far that talk hasn't translated into action. There are several possible reasons.

193

For one, the Belize government is reluctant to do away with its Central Bank and surrender so much of its financial control to Uncle Sam. That's understandable. For another, Belize politicians may think that in a tough economic pinch it's a lot easier to just print money than to actually earn it. That's also understandable.

Technically, according to Belize law, only the Central Bank of Belize is permitted to deal in foreign currencies including the U.S. dollar. But this rule is widely, almost universally, flaunted in Belize, and businesses routinely take U.S. dollars in payment for goods and services and have been doing so for decades. In any event, U.S. dollars (bills, not coins) are accepted everywhere in Belize, although you often will receive change in Belizean money, or in a mix of Belizean and U.S. money.

Paper-money Belize denominations are the 100-, 50-, 20-, 10-, 5- and 2-dollar bills. Belize coins come in 1-dollar, 50, 25, 10, 5 and 1 Belizean cent units. The 25-cent piece is called a shilling.

Currency Exchange Regulations

The U.S. Embassy in Belize provided this summary of currency regulations in Belize:

Under the Exchange Control Regulations (Chapter 43 of the Laws of Belize - 1980), only the Central Bank of Belize and authorized dealers/depositories (i.e., commercial banks and Casas de Cambio, if permitted) may deal in foreign currencies. In order to pay for goods and services procured outside of Belize in a foreign currency, a foreign exchange permit must be obtained from an authorized dealer or directly from the Central Bank of Belize. The permission of the Central Bank of Belize is also required to secure a loan from outside Belize that involves a foreign currency, and also to service repayment of foreign debt. According to the Belize Investment Guide, "the necessary approvals can be easily secured in the case of genuine, approved enterprises." Foreign investors are required to register any investments made in Belize with the Central Bank in order to facilitate the repatriation of profits, dividends, etc. Officially, no person, other than authorized dealers and authorized depositories, may retain any foreign currency in their possession without the consent of the Central Bank of Belize. In practice, however, many local businesses accept payment in U.S. currency.

Foreign exchange controls can be summarized by the following rules and guidelines: Residents and non-residents need permission to buy foreign currency for whatever purpose; Authorized dealers (i.e., commercial banks) are allowed to sell foreign currency up to US$2,500 for private travel and up to US$10,000 for business travel per calendar year; requests in excess of these amounts must be approved by the Central Bank of Belize; Exporters are required to register their exports with the Central Bank, guaranteeing delivery of their foreign exchange earnings; Authorized dealers may authorize payments for imports, where goods are paid for through letters of credit or bank collection. They may also authorize payments for imports against copies of invoices and customs entries, where the documents show that the goods were obtained on credit; Belizean residents, who wish to borrow abroad and where debt service will be in hard currencies, must apply to the Central Bank of Belize for permission to do so.

Banks and Banking in Belize

Until 2015, Belize had five commercial banks, not including offshore banks. Three were based in Belize, although with outside ownership — Heritage Bank, Belize Bank and Atlantic Bank — and two, First Caribbean Bank (formerly Barclays) and ScotiaBank, were multinational banks with branches in Belize. However, in mid-2015, Heritage Bank bought First Caribbean Bank and all its Belize branches, subject to final regulatory approval.

All the banks based in Belize are fairly small, about the size of a small-city bank or savings bank in the U.S. The largest in terms of assets is Belize Bank. Belize also has several credit unions and small mortgage lending institutions.

Here are the basic facts, including contact information for the main offices, about each bank in Belize:

Atlantic Bank was founded in 1971. It is 55% owned by Sociedad Nacional de Inversiones, S.A., a Honduran company, along with individual stockholders in Belize and Honduras. Atlantic Bank has 15 offices in Belize — in Corozal, the Corozal Free Zone, Belize City (three offices), International Airport, Belmopan, Ladyville, Caye Caulker, Orange Walk (two offices), San Pedro (two offices), Placencia and San Ignacio. Atlantic Bank also has a subsidiary insurance company that offers life, property and auto insurance. According to financial statements, Atlantic Bank had assets of more than US$355 million in 2014. Main office: Atlantic Building, Freetown Road at Cleghorn Street, Belize City, 501-223-4123, www.atlabank.com.

Belize Bank traces its history back to 1902 when it was founded as the Bank of British Honduras. It is owned by BCB Holdings, shares of which trade on the Alternative Investment Market of the London Stock Exchange in the United Kingdom under the symbol BCB and also on the Bermuda Stock Exchange under the ticker symbol BBHL BH. Lord Michael Ashcroft, a British billionaire and Conservative party honcho who holds dual citizenship in the UK and Belize, is a large stockholder in BCB Holdings and formerly was chairman. Belize Bank bills itself as the largest commercial bank in Belize, with almost 50% share of loans and deposits in Belize. BCB Holdings has assets of US$655 million, and a net (comprehensive loss) of US$16.6 million, according to its most recent financial report. It has 12 offices around the country— in Corozal Town, the Corozal Free Zone, Orange Walk Town, Philip Goldson International Airport, Belize City (two offices), Belmopan, San Ignacio, San Pedro, Dangriga, Placencia and Punta Gorda. Main office: 60 Market Square, Belize City; tel. 501-227-7132, www.belizebank.com. Belize Bank also has an international banking division, Belize Bank International Limited.

Heritage Bank (formerly Alliance Bank) is the newest of the commercial banks in Belize. It has 10 offices -- in Belize City (two offices), Belmopan, Benque Viejo, Caye Caulker, San Pedro, Orange Walk, San Ignacio, Independence (near Placencia) and Pomona (near Dangriga). In mid-2015, Heritage Bank bought First Caribbean International Bank with its five offices in Belize, two in Belize City and one each in Belmopan, Orange Walk Town and Dangriga. As of this writing it's unclear as to how the banks will be integrated and which if any branches will close. Alliance Bank formerly was associated with Glenn D. Godfrey, a well-connected Belizean businessman and attorney. In 2009, Alliance reportedly was sold to a group of mostly foreign investors from Mexico and the Caribbean. The bank then ran a contest to rename the bank, and Heritage Bank was chosen as the new name. Main Office: 106 Princess Margaret Drive, Belize City, 501-223-6783, www.heritageeibt.com.

ScotiaBank, formerly Bank of Nova Scotia, is a large Canadian bank with operations in 50 countries and with worldwide assets of nearly US$800 billion. It has been operating in Belize since 1968. In Belize, it has 11 offices

-- in Corozal Town, San Pedro, Orange Walk Town, Belize City (two offices), Belmopan, Spanish Lookout, San Ignacio, Placencia, Punta Gorda and Dangriga. Main Belize office: 4A Albert Street, Belize City, 501-227-7027, www.scotiabank.com/bz.

Offshore Banks

In addition to commercial banks in Belize serving local customers, Belize has developed a small community of offshore banks, or international banks as they like to be called. These offshore banks were authorized by the Banks and Financial Institutions Act, 1995, and the introduction of the Offshore Banking Act, 1996, and the Money Laundering (Prevention) Act, 1996.

These banks are regulated by the Belize Central Bank, have physical offices in Belize and offer various services including international bankcards and demand, savings and time deposit accounts. Accounts maintained with these banks are not subject to local taxes or exchange control restrictions and may be denominated in one of several major currencies, including U.S. dollars, euros, U.K. pounds, Swiss francs and others. International banks tout their privacy for their customers, although if the Belize courts find that funds in the banks are proceeds of crime the banks are required to release the identity of the account owner. Funds are transferred into and out of Belize in foreign currencies with no conversion to Belize dollars taking place.

These banks are prohibited from doing business with Belize citizens or legal residents. The offshore banks also comply with United Nations sanctions and don't accept deposits from citizens of Iran, North Korea, Somalia, Sudan and several other countries. Most customers of international banks first establish an International Business Company (IBC). Here's information on some of the offshore banks in Belize.

Atlantic International Bank: This bank, which is now separated from Atlantic Bank, offers demand deposit accounts, savings accounts, corporate accounts, credit cards and investment/brokerage accounts to non-Belize residents. Other services include offshore trust services and establishing International Business Companies (IBCs). Main office: 4792 Cloney Drive, Belize City, 501 223-3152, www.atlanticibl.com.

Belize Bank International Limited: A division of BCB Holdings, Belize Bank International Ltd. was licensed in 2006. The offshore bank offers personal demand deposit accounts. It also offers credit cards, corporate accounts and loans and other services. Main office: 60 Market Square, Belize City, 501-227-0673, www.belizebankinternational.com.

Caye International Bank: Opened in 2003, Caye Bank is located in San Pedro. Currently, the bank offers a mix of deposit and loan services to non-residents of Belize, including demand (checking) deposits, savings deposits and CDs. Main office: Coconut Drive (P. O. Box 105), San Pedro, Ambergris Caye, 501-226-2388, www.cayebank.bz.

Heritage International Bank & Trust Limited: Formerly called Provident Bank & Trust of Belize Ltd., this international bank adopted its present name in 2010. Demand deposits, savings accounts and time deposits are offered. The bank also offers on-line banking, credit cards and other services. Main office: 35 Barrack Road, Belize City, 501-223-56783, www.heritageibt.com.

FACTA and FBAR

For a long time, wealthy U.S. taxpayers were able to hide foreign assets in countries, such as Switzerland, where bank-secrecy laws fostered tax havens. But in 2009 and 2010, after U.S. authorities obtained information about the identities of clients of Swiss banks, they began a sweeping crackdown on hidden offshore accounts. This has impacted Belize and its international banks.

The spillover also has impacted ordinary not-so-wealthy people, especially U.S. citizens or official residents, and also banks, both domestic and offshore, in Belize.

A primary reason is the Foreign Account Tax Compliance Act, called FATCA (www.irs.gov). The U.S. Congress enacted it in 2010. Foreign financial firms, including those in Belize, now must report to the U.S. Internal Revenue Service investment income and balances above certain thresholds (typically US$50,000 for individuals, but the rules vary depending on circumstances) for accounts held by U.S. customers. Nearly 100,000 banks and other companies around the world have registered with the IRS. If they hadn't, all their customers would have 30% withheld from income received from U.S. sources, such as interest and dividends. Individual U.S. taxpayers must also file on FATCA, using Form 8938, when filing their 1040 tax return.

Another big factor is FBAR, Report of Foreign Bank and Financial Accounts, another U.S. reporting requirement. FBAR applies to any U.S.

citizen or official resident who has signature authority over one or more financial accounts – bank account, brokerage account, mutual fund account, etc. -- outside the U.S. and if the aggregate value of such account or accounts totaled US$10,000 or more during any calendar year. U.S. persons falling under FBAR must report holdings to the U.S. Treasury Department (separately from any IRS filing) on Form 114 by April 15 of the year following the calendar year being reported. Penalties for willfully not reporting the foreign holdings are high – US$100,000 or 50% of the amount not reported, whichever is higher.

U.S. citizens and official U.S. resident aliens, including those with dual citizenship, who have lived or worked abroad during all or part of a calendar year, may have a U.S. tax liability and a filing requirement for both FBAR and FACTA.

Frankly, this is a pain in the butt for both U.S. taxpayers and for financial institutions inside and outside the U.S., including in Belize.

So far, more than 43,000 U.S. taxpayers have entered amnesty programs to avoid fines or prison sentences under these financial reporting laws. More than 100 people have been indicted by the U.S. One consequence is that the number of Americans renouncing their citizenship has hit records.

Registered banks in Belize and elsewhere are closing accounts for Americans, or declining to open new ones, in order to avoid increased compliance costs and the consequences for potential errors. In Belize, as in other countries popular with expats, banks have become more reluctant to open accounts for U.S. citizens, and even U.S.-based banks and brokerage firms also have restricted expats from using their services.

In 2014, the *Wall Street Journal* reported: "The reality on the ground is that overseas Americans are facing restrictions and lockouts from both U.S. and foreign financial firms," quoting Marylouise Serrato, the director of American Citizens Abroad, a leading group representing U.S. expatriates.

In 2015, several Belize international banks, including Atlantic International Bank, Heritage International Bank and Belize International Bank, lost their correspondent banking relationships with Bank of America, due to Bank of America's "de-risking" process, a consequence of increased pressure on financial institutions in the U.S. and Europe to make sure that proceeds from money laundering does not make its way into legitimate accounts and also to avoid tax evasion. One practical result of this loss of correspondent banking relationships is that bank customers would not be able to wire money to their accounts in the U.S. However, the Belize Central Bank jumped in and, as of this writing, has acted in effect as a correspondent bank for purposes of wiring money.

Belize Banking Differences

Most expats find that banking is a little different in Belize. In most cases, you can't just sashay in to your local bank office and open an account. You usually will be asked for references, including a letter from your former bank. There is no standard format for this reference letter, but it should state something along these lines: "Mr. Jones is currently a customer of our bank and has maintained a satisfactory banking relationship here since 1985. His savings, time and demand deposit accounts with us current total about US$xxx,xxx." The letter should be on the institution's letterhead and signed by an officer.

Commercial banks in some cases may also require that you have some reason before you can open a banking account in Belize, such as owning property, building a house, living in Belize part- or full-time, etc. The offshore banks in Belize are just the opposite – you can't be a citizen or official resident and bank of Belize.

All of which brings us to another key fact about your money and Belize: The accepted wisdom is to keep the bulk of your liquid assets out of Belize. You may want to open a checking account in Belize to have easy access to spending money and for handling routine local transactions, such as paying your Belize telephone or electric bill. And if you are in Belize under the Qualified Retired Persons Incentive Program, you are required to deposit US$24,000 a year in a Belize bank. But the savvy expat will maintain a banking relationship in the U.S. or similar country, with the bulk of your demand and deposit cash accounts there. You can then transfer funds by wire or other means to your account in Belize, as needed.

CAUTION: Deposits in Belize banks are not protected by deposit insurance, as they are in the U.S. under the FDIC, and in many other countries. All of your deposits are at risk should the bank fail.

Belize Bank has 26 ATMs on its countrywide network around Belize. These ATMs accept foreign-issued ATM cards on the Visa, MasterCard, Plus and Cirrus systems. Atlantic Bank has 16 ATMs that accept foreign-issued ATM cards on the Visa, MasterCard, Plus and Cirrus systems.

ScotiaBank has 14 ATMs around the country accepting foreign-issued ATM Cards. Heritage Bank has more than 20 ATMs at its branch locations, plus ATMs at seven credit unions and at the remaining First Caribbean International Bank offices absorbed by Heritage in 2015. Most ATMs have a limit of BZ$500 per day (US$250 a day).

You can use these ATMs to tap your bank accounts back home, although you will get cash in Belize in Belize dollars.

Banking hours are shorter in Belize, typically only until 3 p.m. most days, slightly later on Fridays. Most bank offices have modern conveniences such as ATM machines. While bank personnel in Belize are usually very friendly – this is Belize, after all – you can't always say the same about bank policies, especially for loans. Loan interest rates are high. Even as the U.S. prime rate was down to 3.25% in 2014 and 2015, Belize's commercial bank prime lending rate was 10.8%. Belize banks were getting 8% (a special promotional rate by Atlantic Bank) to 16% or more on business and personal loans. Fees and charges can add several percentage points to the loan interest. Visa and MasterCard credit cards issued by banks in Belize carried interest rates of 16 to 22% in late 2015. Modern consumer protection laws haven't all made it to Belize yet.

Although rates have fallen in recent years, savings still earn higher interest in Belize than in the U.S. or Canada. In late 2015, for example, money in regular savings accounts at several banks in Belize earned 2.5%. CD rates were higher but well down from the attractive rates of recent years.

On the road in Belize

MOVING TO BELIZE

If you decide to move to Belize, you have several options, including driving down with your household goods and other possessions or shipping them by sea or land. This chapter covers the mechanics of moving, including bringing pets.

Driving to Belize

Caution: Due to the drug cartel violence in Mexico, especially in border areas, many people who in previous years would have considered driving to Belize now are reluctant to do so. Those who do drive usually try to convoy with other drivers or hire a Belizean who has made the trip frequently and knows the safest and best routes.

The drive from Brownsville, Texas, the nearest entry point in the U.S. to Belize, is about 1,250 to 1,500 miles, depending on the route you take. It usually takes three to four days to drive, although it can be done faster. Total non-stop driving time is around 28 to 35 hours, depending on conditions, your driving speed and other factors.

The fastest route from Brownsville/Matamoros is via Tampico, Tuxpan, Veracruz, Villahermosa and Chetumal. From the border, take Mexico national route 101 to highway 180. Just north of Veracruz, take 150D (a toll road) to Villahermosa. (Alternatively you can stay on highway 180). At Villahermosa, take route 186 for 360 miles to the Belize border (the last 5 miles may be signed as route 307). The toll roads are expensive, around US$10 for each 100 miles, but you can make 70 mph on them, much faster than on the regular roads.

Driving in Mexico can be confusing, as road through towns and elsewhere are often poorly signed. In general, avoid going through the town centers *(Centro)*, as you can easily get lost and the hotels are more expensive. To enter Mexico (and later, Belize) by car, you need the original plus two copies of your passport, valid driver's license, vehicle registration card, original vehicle title, or if your vehicle is not paid for, a notarized letter of permission from the lien holder. Besides paying the Mexico tourist entry fee of about US$20, which allows entry for up to six months, you have to provide a credit card in lieu of posting a cash bond to guarantee that you will bring the car back out of Mexico. Your credit card (Master Card, Visa, American Express, Diners, which must be in the name of the driver) will be charged US$22.

Upon arrival at the Belize-Mexico border, if you are not returning to the U.S., you must have the Mexican temporary entry permit canceled at Mexican customs. If entering Mexico by car as a tourist, as a resident of the U.S. or Canada you can bring in such personal items as luggage, binoculars, laptop computer, TV, camping equipment, up to three liters of alcohol and fishing equipment. Do NOT even think about bringing in a gun, as you will find yourself in serious trouble. If you are transporting goods of a value of US$1,000 or more and/or are going through Mexico to Belize to stay permanently, you are supposed to use the services of a customs broker at the U.S.-Mexico border and get trans-migratory status, which costs money in fees and, some say, in bribes to Mexican federal officers along the way. A broker at the U.S.-Mexico border will cost you about US$150 to $200. Unless you plan to stay in Belize, it is best just to enter Mexico as a tourist and not go the trans-mig route.

Except on toll roads, driving after dark in Mexico is not advised. You may be stopped frequently for inspections. You should exchange enough

U.S. dollars to get you through Mexico, as U.S. dollars are not widely accepted, or are accepted at a low rate of exchange. The exchange rate for U.S. dollars in late 2015 was around 16.5 pesos to the dollar. Gasoline stations in Mexico sometimes do not accept credit cards.

Mexican auto insurance is required; liability costs from around US$75 for five days. It is now recommended that you get at least US$300,000 in third-party liability coverage. Collision insurance coverage can add to the cost, depending on the value of your vehicle. Insurance for a month or two, or even six months, is not much more than for a few days.

Here are typical quotes for 7 days and six months:

Extended coverage including US$300,000 third-party liability for nearly new vehicle valued at US$20,000: US$120 to $135

Six months: US$400 to $415

You MUST have Mexican auto insurance. Your U.S. or Canadian insurance is NOT valid in Mexico (or Belize.)

Sanborn's (tel. 800-222-0158; www.sanbornsinsurance.com) is a well-known source of information on travel in Mexico and for Mexican auto insurance, although their insurance tends to be more expensive than insurance from most other companies. Other companies include International Insurance Group (www.sb.iigins.com), which offers insurance through Grupo Nacional and ACE Seguros.

Do a Google search for other companies selling Mexican auto insurance, some of which can be purchased on-line in advance. One such is Mexican Auto Insurance (www.mexicanautoinsurance.com). Some U.S.-based insurance companies including GEICO and Progressive offer links to a Mexican insurance provider, with small discounts available for their U.S. or Canadian policyholders.

Sanborn maps, and in fact most maps to Mexico, may not be completely accurate. The Guia Roji (Red Guide) maps to Mexico are probably the best available, although ITMB maps also are good. A website with all types of helpful information on Mexico is www.mexconnect.com.

On arrival at the Mexico-Belize border, you again need your original title (no photocopies) for your vehicle, or, if you do not own it free and clear, a notarized statement from the lien holder that you have permission to take the car out of the U.S. You also have to buy Belize auto insurance, which is required by law in Belize. There are brokers at the border. Three months of insurance should cost about US$60 to $100, or one month or less about

US$35. The cost may be higher depending on the coverage you get. Crossing the border you probably will have to have your car sprayed to kill hitchhiking bugs — the fee is around US$5.

Assuming that you are entering as a tourist, you should get free entry of your vehicles for 90 days, with no duty required. (However, we have heard of a number of exceptions to this statement.) Your car information is entered on your passport so you cannot sell it in Belize. You must leave the country with the vehicle.

If you plan to stay in Belize and keep your vehicle there, you have to pay import duty and tax. The rate varies by number of cylinders and type of vehicle, but it runs about 20% to nearly 80% of book value. *(For more information, see below.)* Some say that if you want a lower appraisal of value of the vehicle, have it appraised in Belize City. You can have a customs officer drive with you to Belize City for around US$20. However, others claim that appraisals are lower at the border.

If you bring your vehicle in as a tourist and do not pay import duty, and then later decide you want to keep the vehicle in Belize, you may be hit with a fine of US$250 or more in addition to import duty. So, if you are pretty sure you want to keep the vehicle in Belize, it's usually best to go ahead and pay the import duty when you first enter Belize.

For another perspective, to give you an idea of what you may face, here's a detailed post in 2014 on driving from Mission, Tex. (near McAllen) to Belize from the Expat Exchange forum (www.expatexchange.com). The spelling and punctuation mostly have been left as is:

Here's the route: Driving Direction from Mission, Texas, to the Belize border.

Now for those of you who have new done this, it is not that bad!! I have done this trip six times down and back. I have never paid or been asked to pay a police officer. There are Federal Police checkpoints and there are military checkpoints. Both are polite and most of the time no one speaks English. Use that to your advantage. Even if you do [speak Spanish] don't act like you do. If they can't talk to you they just look at your paperwork and send you on your way. This year I drove down and back and was never searched in Mexico or for that matter even at the US border station.

Now what I have done here is detailed the route to the mile. We zeroed the trip odometer at the Mexico border station. My passenger wrote down details at every turn. Now that won't mean our reading will be exact but they should be close. Oh do yourself a favor and cash at least US$1500 into pesos!!!!!!

Exit the Mexico border station. Zero your odometer and relax. You have 1519 miles and two nights in Mexico. I will give you two options to make this trip. One puts you south of Mexico City in Puebla the first night, and 80 miles from Belize the second night. This is the way I run the route. I will drive both nights one hour in the dark. I will give you options for the first night in Querétaro, and the second night in Villahermosa. This route brings you to the Belize border around 2 pm and you spend the night in Corozal.

Exit the border merge to the left, 90 Reynosa Drive 3.9 miles turn right on Hwy 40 to Monterey.

18.8 miles to a checkpoint you must go thru it.

27.2 miles merge right onto the Hwy 40 cuota (toll road) to Monterey.

56.4 miles enter a tollbooth (210 pesos).

108 miles come to a small town, pay attention to where you are going. Mostly stay straight and on the main drag. Follow sign to Monterey.

114 miles enter another toll. (44pesos)

116.2 merge right to Saltillo still Hwy 40

127.8 miles another toll both

134.8 stay straight towards Saltillo Cuota

148.7 Another toll for the by pass around Monterey.

158.2 miles Merge right onto cuota again?? Pay another toll (66 pesos)

181.1 yes another toll BUT you don't go thru this one. Exit to Saltillo just before it. When in doubt follow signs to Saltillo (Cuota).

Just before you get over by Saltillo we screwed up and missed a turn. Day dreaming this area was mountains and very pretty. If you see a huge orange building you missed it also. Look for the signs 57 south to San Luis Potosi and Matehuala. Hope I spell these correct.

We needed gas and there was a nice spot at mile 207.

226 toll booth (50 pesos) Plenty of gas stations after this one.

346 exit left on the San Luis Potosi cuota. This is the bypass around Matehuala. There is plenty of gas station along this area.

350 miles tollbooth for the by pass cuota around Matehuala

452 miles merge left towards Mexico City, Querétaro.

466 miles a tollbooth.

473 The cuota splits stay left towards Querétaro. Now here is where you must decide! Do I push thru to Puebla or stay in Querétaro. There is n where that I have found to stay in between. And you will not get to Puebla until 8:30 pm It should be around 5:00 pm now. Your choice!! If you choose to go on to Puebla follow these. If you stay in Querétaro follow 57 thru town it is not bad. You will find a Best Western on your right just south of town

568 miles exit right real quickly it splits go right. Splits again go left. This is tricky and it happens fast but there are signs. Follow sign for the cuota to San Juan Del Rio, and Mexico City. This is the bypass around Querétaro. If you miss this don't worry I went thru last year it was easy. In fact that is how I found the Best Western you can stay at.

580 miles is another tollbooth (40 pesos)

592 miles stay left the bypass reconnects to Hwy 57 south to San Juan Del Rio and Mexico City.

620 miles another toll (70 pesos)

656 miles - you are south of San Juan Del Rio, This gets a little confusing and happens fast. Look for signs, Pachuca and Puebla. This is a bypass around Mexico City. DO NOT MISS THIS!!! Split to the right! Take the

second split to the right. It is label 75D Pachuca, Puebla. You then pull up to a tollbooth but at this one you just take a ticket, and pay at the other end.

Also you have now fuel here until mile 740. If you need fuel do it before this exit.

760 miles you come to the tollbooth it will be dark now. Give them your ticket it was 565 pesos for us. But we were towing a trailer. We can only guess the toll for you would be half that. Now they are working on the road for the next few miles until you tie back into the main road from Mexico City to Puebla.

763 mile the road splits stay left and this road is bumpy slow down.

766 miles toll booth for a crappy road. 777 miles you will see a McDonald's.

778 miles you will see a "one" Hotel a big tower on your left.

780 miles you will see the Fiesta Inn and a Holiday in right next to each other. Stay at one of these.

Next morning get up early leave at six if you can. You have a mountainous decent this morning. And then some bumpy roads.

794 miles tollbooth (55 pesos)

840 miles tollbooth and there is a volcano on your left. It had snow on the peak in January, early Feb. Hang on and take your time for awhile. You will be going down hill for the next few hours. It is steep and you go thru tunnels. Don't ride your brakes!!!

877 miles another toll (24 pesos) 895 toll booth (85 pesos) 966 toll booth (177 pesos)

1031 toll booth (155 pesos) 1069 tollbooth (17 pesos)

1076 exit right to Villahermosa Stop at the stop sign. Turn right?

1081 miles the road splits stay left to Villahermosa

1095 Inspection station, we got waved thru.

1111 miles another toll, wow imagine that.

1166 miles you have now been in some traffic for a little while. You passed the Walmart distribution center. You cross this bridge with a sign that says welcome to Villahermosa!!! Pay attention the road splits just over this bridge. Take the left split!

The best direction thru Villahermosa is to follow the main flow of traffic. Towards the airport. I always make it.

1168 under a bridge

1170 Lake on the right

1171 over a cool bridge

I think this is where it turns into Hwy 186 to Escarsega

Sign that says 11 Km to the Airport just over the bridge

Now we left Puebla at 7:00am and we are passing the Hilton south of the Villahermosa Airport at 2:30pm. We're 1177 miles into Mexico.

If you stayed in Querétaro you will be later and should stay here for you second night. Go past the Hilton, it is on your left. Two miles in front of you is a RETURNO! Circle back and spend the night.

1181 miles another tollbooth (20 pesos)

1200 miles switches from divided highway to two-lane road for the rest of your trip. The road in actually real good except for a small area here and there. But they are working on them.

1260 miles tollbooth (20 pesos)

1354 miles you are entering Escarsega take the split to the left. Burger King will be on your right. Just after that a couple hundred yards turn right towards Chetumal. You go right thru the middle of town. Looks rough but it is not. Nice Mayan statue in town.

Now somewhere after this is will get dark and sometimes there is a checkpoint at the far edge of Escarsega. The next part is very easy just follow the road to mile 1448. You have past the Becon Mayan ruins by a couple miles. You will have past the ECO Village on your left. You can stay there also. You will come to a Hotel just before the town of Xjupil. Can't miss it. DEBLIZ HOTEL on your right. Nice little place and they are always there.

Spend the night. You might even want to check Becon out. They are cool ruins. You are about 80 miles from Belize. Sleep in if you want.

Next morning head to Chetumal and at mile 1511 exit right to Chetumal

1515 miles is the last Mexico gas station. Fill up if you have not.

1518 miles exit right up and over a bridge. Once you reach the border pull over to the right you will see a small both for immigration. They will take your tourist card. Then if you have a vehicle permit listen carefully. If you are not driving that vehicle back look to the left find the Banjercio and cancel your vehicle permit.

If you are returning with the same vehicle you can wait until you get back to the US/MX boarder to cancel it. Once you have done that travel over the bridge into Belize.

Your Vehicle in Belize

Because Belize is lightly populated and fairly spread out, it's very useful to have a car or truck in Belize. A four-wheel drive is ideal, due to the many unpaved secondary and tertiary roads, which can get very bad during the rainy season. Many people consider a small four-wheel drive truck, such as Toyota Hi-Lux, as the perfect vehicle for Belize. Import duties are 10% on trucks or vans (not SUVs, which are taxed at the higher auto rates), plus GST of 12.5%. It is relatively inexpensive to buy new -- US$24,000 to $30,000+ including duty. It gets good mileage, which is important when fuel is around US$5 a gallon. The Toyota is a rugged vehicle that holds up well to tough conditions in Belize. Even better is to get a diesel-engine version, as diesel fuel costs about one-third less in Belize than gasoline, and diesel engines usually last almost forever. Other small cars and trucks are popular in Belize, including Suzuki, Mitsubishi and the smaller American models such as Ford Ranger and the Jeep Cherokee. With Belize's British heritage, the Land Rover also is popular, especially older models. However, many Belizeans drive old, large U.S. cars that were brought into Belize before the price of gas went up to its present high levels.

Most of the new car dealers in Belize are located in Belize City, with a couple in Belmopan and Spanish Lookout. Among the brands available new are Ford, Toyota, Suzuki, Kia, Land Rover, Jeep, Hyundai, Dodge, Nissan and Mitsubishi. Some Chinese brands are available in Belmopan or Spanish Lookout. Other car brands are in Chetumal, Mexico.

If you live on an island, you probably will not need a car. Smaller islands do not have any roads or vehicles. Caye Caulker has only a few emergency vehicles. Ambergris Caye has too many vehicles for its small size and limited road system and is currently limiting the import of more vehicles to the island. On Ambergris, Caulker and other islands a golf cart is a useful way to get around. You can expect to pay around US$2,000-$4,000 for a used golf cart in Belize. Maintenance tends to be costly due to the salt air. Replacing the six batteries alone costs US$300 or more. A gas cart, rather than an electric cart, is the way to go.

Liability insurance is mandatory in Belize. If you don't have it and are stopped at a road check, common in Belize, you are likely going to be arrested and will spend at least a little time in jail. Happily, auto insurance in Belize is fairly inexpensive. You likely won't pay more than US$200 to $400 a year. Your U.S. or other driver's license is good for up to three months in Belize. After that, you are supposed to get a Belize license. You must be 18 to get a driver's license in Belize. You can obtain a driver's license in Belize City or in larger towns for a fee of US$10. You will have to provide a doctor's statement that you are in good health.

Getting Your Household Goods to Belize

What to Bring: Foreign residents in Belize are split on how much to bring to Belize. Some see a savings in bringing everything you may need to Belize, especially if you have a duty exemption on household goods as an approved permanent resident or as a participant in the Qualified Retired Persons program. On the other hand, many who have moved to Belize say it's best to bring as little as possible with you. After all, you won't need a lot of clothes. You can buy furniture cheaply in Belize, and you can find appliances and other household goods either in Belize City or in Chetumal, Mexico. Amazon.com and other companies will ship books, CDs, and other items to Belize, though international shipping charges may be high. You may want to store most of your household goods in a storage facility back home. Then, after you've been in Belize for a while, on a trip back home you can get items you decide you really need.

Items you probably will want to bring to Belize if you are setting up housekeeping, as these are hard to find or expensive in Belize, or will be expensive to ship later:

- good-quality sheets and towels
- high-quality mattresses
- good dishes
- high-quality pots and pans, silverware and other kitchenware
- hobby equipment
- specialized hand and power tools
- fishing and diving gear
- top-end electronics
- computers, laptops, tablets
- smartphones
- books

Shipping Options

You can ship bulky items by sea or overland. Small items can be shipped via the postal system or an airfreight service. You can drive your vehicle down through Mexico or ship it by sea.

Ocean Freight

Sending goods such as furniture, household supplies and personal possessions in a 20-foot container from Miami is likely to cost you about US$2,400-$3,000, not including import duties, insurance, customs broker fees or storage fees. A 40-foot container may cost you US$4,000-$5,500, or more, by the time you get it to your home in Belize, again not including extra fees and duties.

Cars and trucks can also be shipped via ocean freight. Companies like Transporter Auto Services (800-799-3329, www.moveglobalnow.com) specialize in shipping vehicles, either in high cube containers or Roll-On/Roll-Off, but other companies also will accept vehicles. Normally you can pack your vehicle with personal goods.

Hyde Shipping is the most used and recommended shipping company serving Belize. It offers freight sailings from Port Everglades near Ft. Lauderdale and Miami to Belize City, at least once a week and sometimes twice a week. Hyde also provides service to Roatán, Honduras, Puerto Morelos, Mexico, and Grand Cayman. Both 20-ft. and 40-ft. containers are available, either dry or climate controlled. Contact Hyde in Florida at 10025 NW 116th Way, Suite 2, Medley, FL 33178, 305-913-4933; www.hydeshipping.com. Hyde's agency in Belize is **Caribbean Shipping Agency** (501-227-7396).

Other Options for Smaller Shipments

A few companies offer door-to-door shipment of LCL (Less Than Container Load) items between the U.S. and Belize. One is **Belize Freight** (832-764-7239 in the U.S., 501-223-2746 in Belize, www.belizefreight.com). Belize Freight ships monthly by sea from its warehouse in Houston (until late 2015 its warehouse was in Miami). It picks up by truck from about a dozen different cities in the U.S., from the New York/New Jersey area to Texas, on a rotating pick-up schedule, and delivers to most cities, towns and villages in Belize. The company provides an "all-inclusive" quote based on the size and weight of the item or items shipped, including pick-up and delivery door-to-door, custom brokerage fees, customs duty and taxes and other charges. It's not cheap, but it's convenient. If you don't need door-to-door service, you can ship your items to Belize Freight's Houston warehouse (3340B Greens Rd., Suite #450, Houston, TX 77032) and pick up the item in Belize City. Storage also is available.

Mail and Express Freight

Small items can be shipped to Belize by air or surface postal mail, which is fairly dependable and not too expensive, or by a fast but expensive airfreight service such as **FedEx, UPS** or **DHL Express**. A 10-pound package might cost from around US$100 to $300, depending on the airfreight company and the type of service.

Companies such as **MyUS** (www.myus.com) provide a turnkey purchasing, package consolidation and shipping service. You pay a membership fee, get a U.S. address and then do your shopping at Amazon.com or other U.S. companies. You have the store send your items to your MyUS mailing address. Then MyUS consolidates your packages into one shipment. MyUS then ships to Belize via FedEx, DHL Express or UPS. Shipping from the U.S. to Belize for a consolidated package weighing

20 pounds ranges from about US$160 to more than US$500, with delivery in from one to 10 days.

Preparing Items for Shipment

When shipping individual packages to Belize, new items require an invoice and used items require a packing list. A packing list is simply a list of the items enclosed in the package with their reasonable resale values. You need to insert one copy of the invoice or packing list into an envelope and tape it to the outside of the package, and mail or fax one copy of it to the freight company in advance of your shipment.

For shipping vehicles, you'll need the original title (or if there is a lien on the vehicle a notarized letter from the lienholder authorizing shipment), the VIN, license plate number, notarized power of attorney to ship the vehicle, addresses and phone numbers in the U.S. and Belize and full payment of all fees in advance.

Customs Brokers

Customs brokers in Belize can be very helpful in smoothing the way and in getting materials quickly released from customs. They will meet your goods when they arrive in Belize, fill out the paper work and have the goods forwarded to their final destination in Belize. In most cases, to ship to Belize it is now required that you work with a licensed customs broker in Belize. Plus, it will make your life a lot easier if you have a local customs broker working for you.

There are about 65 members of the **Customs Brokers Association of Belize** (www.customsbrokers.bz). Be sure to check references. Here are some brokers who have received recommendations from folks shipping to Belize:

Billy Valdes, Valdez Global, 160 N. Front St. (P.O. Box 4), Belize City, 501-227-7436 or 501-610-1180, email lizzvaldes@yahoo.com

Joseph Hamilton, Belize City, 501-227-1453

Milin Gomez, Belize City, 501-610-4569, email mily@btl.net

Calbert Reynolds, Belize City, 501-227-0381

Storage in Belize

What do you do with your goods after you get them to Belize, if your home isn't ready for occupancy? Freight companies usually will store your shipped items in their warehouse, for a fee of around US$12.5 cents per cubic foot per week. This can add up; storage of a half-container would cost nearly US$700 a month

Storage facilities in Belize, other than those owned by the government or freight companies, are few and far between. **Edgar's Mini Storage** (894 Vista Del Mar, Ladyville, 501-602-4513, www.edgarsministorage.com), in the international airport area near Belize City, was the first mini-storage facility in the country. Dave Edgar established it in 2002. The steel storage building has 32 10 x 20 ft. spaces, each with around 1,800 cubic ft. of space. Current rates for a space are US$100 a month on a 12-month lease, US$125 a month on a six-month lease and US$150 a month on a three-month lease. Rates are plus 12.5% tax. Edgar's also offers long-term off-airport parking with transportation to and from the international airport in Ladyville or the water taxis in Belize City.

Another storage facility is on Ambergris Caye. **Grumpy & Happy Storage** offers an 8-feet wide, 12-feet deep, and 10-feet high container for US$150 a month, plus 12.5% tax. Larger spaces, up to 20 feet deep, are also available. The facility is at 19 Fire Coral Street, south of San Pedro Town. Contact Grumpy & Happy Self/Mini Storage at 501-226-3420, www.belizestorage.com.

Moving with Pets

In most cases, dogs and cats can be brought into Belize without quarantine.

Bringing a pet into the country falls under live animal importation and is regulated by the **Belize Agricultural Health Authority (BAHA).** Dogs and cats are allowed to enter the country provided that owners have a valid import permit, international veterinary certificate, valid rabies vaccination certificate and inspection by quarantine officer at the port of entry. Owners must get a certificate from a veterinarian at the owner's home country. The vet examination must take place within 14 days before arrival in Belize, and the certificate must state that the animal is in good health, is free from infectious diseases and has been vaccinated for rabies not less than one month and no more than one year prior to departure for Belize.

Kittens and puppies under three months of age that can't be vaccinated for rabies can be brought in but must be confined at the owner's home in Belize until they are three months old, at which time they must be vaccinated and then confined at home an additional 30 days.

The dog or cat must be inspected at the port of entry. Those coming from countries considered of risk (for example, pets from South American where there is the risk of screwworm) need to undergo veterinary inspection. There is an additional fee for veterinary inspection.

You should apply for an import permit for your cat or dog from BAHA. Permit application forms are available for download at the BAHA website. Send the permit application by email to bahasps@btl.net or fax 501-824-3773 or 501-824-4889.

Return the completed form to Permit Unit of BAHA. The date of arrival must be specified. There is a US$25 entry and inspection fee, payable in U.S. or Belize dollars at the port of entry. Approved permits are faxed to applicant at a cost of US$12.50 to be paid at the point of entry. If you don't follow this application process, you could be subject to a violation fine on top of the regular admission and inspection fees. In addition, any pet arriving without a valid permit or without a valid rabies vaccination may be confined at the owner's expense until the vaccination is valid.

For other pets or farm animals, such as ferrets or birds, check with BAHA for the current regulations. An import permit likely will be required. You can download the permit application from the BAHA website at www.baha.org.bz.

For more information, contact BAHA:
Belize Agricultural Health Authority (BAHA)
Corner Forest Drive and Hummingbird Highway (P.O. Box 169)
Belmopan City, Belize
Tel. 501-822-1378
www.baha.org.bz

Vets in Belize

More information about pets in Belize may be available from vets in Belize, including the following:

Animal Medical Centre, 1 Dr. Michael DeShield Lane, Belama Phase II, Belize City, 501-223-3781, www.animalmedicalcentre.net

Paws Veterinary Clinic, 1 Joseph Andrews Dr., San Ignacio, Cayo, 501-621-5377, www.pawsveterinaryclinicbze.com.

Note that while there are more than 20 practicing vets in Belize, most focus on large farm animals and do not care for dogs, cats and other small pets. A list of registered veterinary surgeons, as veterinarians are called in Belize, is available at the Veterinary Surgeons Board of Belize at www.veterinarysurgeonbelize.org.

Transporting Pets to and in Belize

Small dogs and cats can usually be carried in the cabin of scheduled commercial airlines. The kennel must fit under the seat. Reservations in advance are required, to assure that no more than a certain number, typically five to seven, animals are on a flight. A vet's certificate that the animal is in good health usually must be provided, with the certificate done typically within 10 days prior to the date of travel.

American, Delta and United are some of the airlines flying into Belize that ship pets and allow them as checked luggage, with some restrictions. Pets are transported in the pressurized cargo hold. The kennel must be large enough for the animal to turn around in. Pets may not be accepted by the airline as checked luggage if the forecast temperature is too hot or too cold – typically above 85 or 90 degrees F. or below 45 degrees F. -- at any point on the air itinerary; in some cases, the airline may accept a letter from a vet stating that the animal can stand temperatures above or below these points.

Some airlines have restrictions on which breeds can be checked as luggage. American and Delta, for example, do not permit "pug nosed" dogs such as Boston Terriers, Bulldogs or Boxers. These airlines also prohibit Burmese, Persian, Himalayan and Exotic Shorthair cats in the cargo hold.

Charges vary. American, for example, charges US$200 for a checked pet, and US$125 for a pet accompanying the passenger in the cabin. United charges $125 for an accompanying dog, cat, rabbit or bird and US$239 to US$709, depending on weight, for checked pets.

Contact the airline in advance to be sure you are following all its rules for pet travel; otherwise, you may be denied boarding.

Service animals generally are exempt from these rules and charges.

Yes, There Can Be Import Duty on Pets!

You will not be charged Belize import duty on pets that accompany you on your flight. However, if you ship your pets separately, you will be charged an import duty based on a combination of the freight charges and the value of the animal, plus sales tax. The duty plus sales tax rate is about 50%. Check with Belize Customs to determine the amount of duty.

In-Country Transport of Pets

In Belize, both Maya Island and Tropic Air will carry your pet in its kennel. Tropic Air currently charges you for three seats for the pet, plus your own ticket. Maya Island Air currently charges you only for one seat for your pet, plus your town ticket. You must notify the airlines in advance that you are transporting a pet. To San Pedro and Caye Caulker, the Caye Caulker Water Taxi Association boats allow pets to be carried like luggage, at no charge. The San Pedro-Belize Express boats charge US$10. Note that these charges are subject to change.

You can drive through Mexico with your pets. Some cargo services also transport animals.

Will Your Pet Adapt to Belize?

Not all pets adapt well to Belize's subtropical climate. Mange and venereal disease are endemic. Snakebites and scorpion or bee stings can be dangerous or fatal to your pet. Rabies occasionally shows up in rural areas, vectored by vampire bats and other wild things. However, most dogs and cats seem to adapt satisfactorily to the climate and conditions in Belize.

Belizean Attitudes Toward Pets

Belizeans generally do not have the same view of pets as do Americans. They rarely allow dogs in the house, for example. Dogs are used more as watchdogs than as companions. You don't see that many cats kept as pets in Belize, except by expats. In some areas, feral cats are a problem, hunting birds and other wildlife. In rural areas, often you will see a number of wild animals including howler and spider monkeys and the smaller wild cats kept as pets (even though generally this is prohibited by law).

Shops on Front Street on Caye Caulker

WORKING OR RUNNING A BUSINESS

Imagine you're living beside the blue Caribbean Sea. You spend your days snorkeling, diving and fishing. Now imagine you get paid to do this. You pay your way through paradise by working as a dive master, or guiding tourists, or tending bar in a little thatch hut. Or you run a little hotel by the sea, welcoming guests and raking in the dough.

Sorry, but a reality check is required. About one in ten Belizeans is out of work, and those with jobs often don't make enough to live above the poverty level. The few good jobs that are available in Belize are mostly reserved for Belizeans. Many occupations, including tour guiding and waiting tables and bartending, are reserved for Belize citizens only. Residents under the Qualified Retired Persons Incentive Act can't work for pay at all. Even if you were able to legally get a job, salaries in Belize are far below those in the U.S., Canada or Western Europe, and even physicians, college teachers and other professionals may earn under US$15,000 or $20,000 a year. While some hotel and resort owners and other expat business owners in Belize do pretty well, others barely eek out a living. Costs

219

are higher than they planned for, and the frustrations of doing business in Belize are far more numerous than they expected.

We know expatriates who have carved out a comfortable niche for themselves in Belize, either working for an established Belizean company or running their own business. It is possible to do so, but it's not easy. After all, it's the United States that is a land of opportunity for job seekers and entrepreneurs. Millions of people around the world vie to get a green card to let them live and work in the States. More than 100,000 Belizeans have left Belize to work and find their fortunes, legally or illegally, in the U.S. You're going to leave the U.S. with all its opportunity, resources and huge base of consumers and set up shop or find a job in poor little Belize, with its tiny population and economic resources of a small American town? If you can't make it in the U.S., how do you expect to make it in Belize?

There are good reasons why someone might decide to move to Belize and work or invest there, mostly having to do with quality of life, but economic rewards and an easy road to fortune are not among them.

The Reality of Investing in Belize

The late John Lankford, a New Orleans lawyer who lived for several years in San Pedro before selling his property and moving back to the U.S., put the situation bluntly: "As to investing, first realize that when Belize's government or general population speaks or thinks of foreigners 'investing in Belize' they mean bringing money and handing it over. They also contemplate a long-term, possibly permanent, commitment. They are not so solicitous of your expectations to realize a RETURN on your investment, and in some cases tend to think it craven of a 'rich' first-world person to try to make money off poor Belize. The approved motivation for investing in Belize is for the benefit of Belize. The investor's benefit is gratification at helping Belize advance, and any other motivation may be seen as exploiting rather than investing. As a general rule, don't even dream of investing in Belize unless you plan to be present with your eyes on your investment every day."

Starting and Running Your Own Business

With good-paying jobs few and far between, most foreigners who want to generate an income in Belize will be looking at operating a business. The Belize government says it welcomes investors who can contribute to the Belize economy and provide work for Belizeans, particularly in tourism, agriculture and manufacturing. But it's rarely simple or easy to do business in Belize. A timeworn saying in Belize, worth repeating again, is that if you want to make a small fortune in the country, better start with a big one. Belize's small domestic market, inefficient distribution and marketing systems, heavy-handed government red tape and other factors make it difficult for entrepreneurs to achieve great success in Belize.

What Type of Business?

Several types of businesses require special permits or licenses, and these may not be granted to non-Belizeans. The idea is to avoid permitting non-Belizeans to take jobs from Belizeans. The following businesses, in varying degrees, are not usually open to foreigners: commercial fishing, sugar cane cultivation, restaurants and bars (not associated with a resort), legal and accounting services, small retail shops, beekeeping, beauty shops, sightseeing tours and operation of bus, water taxi or domestic airlines.

Businesses that are most likely to succeed in Belize include export-oriented operations whose main markets are outside Belize. The Belize market itself is small and spread out, and average Belizeans don't have the income to buy much beyond the basic necessities of life. Niche export products such as specialty or organic agricultural products may have a future. Also workable are well-marketed resorts or lodges that target international visitors and, in addition, the companies that cater to them — for example, companies that provide specialty herbs, fruits and gourmet vegetables to larger resorts.

However, the difficulty of making a go in tourism in Belize is shown by the number of hotels that are actively on the market at any one time. In the San Ignacio area, for example, at any one time about one-fourth of the hotel properties are actively for sale, and other owners likely would quickly sell for the right offer. With hotel occupancies in Belize averaging only about 40% nationally, it is difficult to earn an adequate return. Only in San Pedro, which gets a regular flow of tourists year-round, do many hotels appear to be more consistently profitable. The typical small hotel in Belize can't afford to do the international advertising and marketing necessary to compete with larger, better-capitalized resorts in other parts of the Caribbean.

Quite a few expats gravitate to selling or developing real estate. Some have been successful; many have not.

Unemployment in Belize is stubbornly high, yet many of the best-

221

trained and ambitious Belizean workers have moved to the U.S. This brain drain means that it's difficult to find skilled, motivated employees. In rural areas, many Belizeans have never held a regular job. Training must start with the basics like showing up on time and coming to work every day. Another problem is that the cost of labor in Belize, while low compared with the U.S., is relatively high compared with some other developing countries. The minimum wage in Belize is BZ$3.30 (US$1.65) an hour for manual workers, but that's several times the minimum wage of workers in Honduras or Nicaragua. The minimum wage in Mexico is around US$5 a day, less than one-half that of Belize. Most workers in Belize do earn more than the minimum wage.

Belizean workers also have comparatively strong workplace protections, including mandatory two weeks' paid vacation and participation in Belize's Social Security system, mostly funded by employer contributions of about 5% to 6.5% of wages (the percentage varies depending on the wage of the worker, and workers also contribute from 1.5% to about 3% of earnings), 13 paid holidays, 16 days of sick leave annually and a required two weeks' notice or pay in lieu of that notice should the employee be terminated after having been on the job at least a year. The workweek cannot exceed six days or 45 hours. Businesses in highly competitive export industries may be at a disadvantage if they are located in Belize.

Capital for Business

In Belize as in most countries it is difficult to borrow money to start a business. For successful, on-going businesses loans from Belize banks may be available but typically at higher interest rates than prevailing in the U.S. In recent years, 10 to 16% has been the usual rate for business loans. Business people in Belize complain that in some cases hidden fees and charges for business loans add to the overall cost. The Belize Development Finance Corporation, a government-owned entity whose mission is to help develop the Belize economy, did make loans for developing new tourism and agricultural projects, but the DFC, after reorganization, makes loans only to Belizean citizens or official permanent residents.

Steps Involved in Starting a Business in Belize

The following information is derived from Beltraide materials.

Business Name Registration

Complete an application form and submits the application to the Belize Companies Registry in Belmopan City. The applicant may also request a name search by telephone or fax for a fee.

A name search is conducted to check whether the name is unique or it is not similar to any existing business, and to ensure compliance with the rules set out in the legislation.

If business name is available, a Certificate of Business Name Registration will be issued.

Note: Foreigners will need to apply with a Belizean partner or someone with a Permanent Residency to be able to register a business name.

Incorporation

Incorporation is usually done through an attorney, and requires the submission of the company's Memorandum of Association and Articles of Association in order to be issued a Certificate of Incorporation. Attorney fees range from US$1,000 to US$2,00).

If the Share Capital is less than 10,000, the processing fee is US$292; if it is more than 10,000, the processing fee is calculated in accordance to the Companies Act, Chap. 250, Section 222, as amended.

Trade License

A business must obtain a trade license before the commencement of any type of operations in Belize. A trade license is required for each location that the trade will be carried on regardless as to whether it is the same business. The trade license must be renewed annually. This applies to companies, partnerships and sole traders including professionals.

Applications are submitted to the local city or town council and approved by the Trade Licensing Board of the municipality. The Licensing Board consists of the Mayor of the local authority, who is the chairman of the board, and four other members.

Annual license fees are calculated based on the annual rental value of the property and penalties are imposed for non-payment of fees. The police and Council Field Officers often go out to investigate whether there are businesses operating without a trade license. If the business does not have a trade license, it may be closed down. The Trade License must be displayed on the premises for the public viewing.

Business Tax Registration

All businesses must register at Income Tax Department to obtain a

Taxpayer Identification to pay tax. These businesses include sole proprietorship, companies and partnerships.

The following persons/entities are subject to payment of Business Tax:

Persons carrying on a trade or business who earn BZ$75,000 or more per annum where such receipts are the only source of livelihood of the person;

Persons practicing a self-employed profession or vocation, earning BZ$20,000 or more per annum where such receipts are the only source of livelihood of the person;

Persons engaged in the business of investment or earnings from real or personal property;

Persons engaged in the provision of personal services.

Business Tax Rates

Note: The percentage of business tax paid is based on the gross receipts of the business before any deductions for expenses, losses or other costs.

Receipts from radio, television or newspaper business	0.75%
Receipts from domestic airline business	1.75%
Receipts from service stations (fuels and lubricants)	0.75%
Receipts from other trade or business	1.75%
Receipts from rents, royalties and other sources from real estate (except a real estate agency or business)	3%
Receipts from a profession, vocation or occupations	6%
Receipts from licensed insurance company	1.75%
Commissions and winnings from gaming	5 to 15%
Receipts of a bank/financial institution	8 to 15%
Management fees, rent of plant and equipment, technical services, paid to non-resident	25%
Receipts of telecommunications companies	19%
Gross earnings of casinos	15%
Gross earnings of real estate business/agency	15%

General Sales Tax Registration

General Sales Tax (GST) is a tax on consumer spending collected in stages on business transactions and imports when goods change hands or services are performed.

All persons engaged in a taxable activity with an annual turnover exceeding BZ$75,000 must register with the Department of General Sales

Tax in accordance with the Sales Tax Act No. 49 of 2005. Note that it is not the business activity that is registered but the person conducting those activities. This person can be a company, partnership, sole proprietor, trustee or estate. Persons must register within one month of the day on which the person first becomes eligible.

Social Security Registration

All persons or entities employing one or more persons must register for Social Security with the Belize Social Security Board. The application must be made within seven days of employing an employee.

Employers pay 5.02% to 6.5% of the employee wages into the Belize Social Security system, based on the wages of the employee (the percentage is highest for employees with the lowest wages). Employees contribute from 1.5% to 2.98% (the percentage is lowest for employees earning the lowest wages.)

Opening a Local Bank Account

Belizeans and Permanent Residents

Customer must bring a valid identification (Social Security card and/or passport), along with a recent utility bill (not older than three months) to confirm place of residence. A minimum deposit will be required to open the account, and this may vary among banking institutions.

To open a checking account, the bank would require a Bankers' Reference from an established banking institution, or that the customer maintains a savings account prior to opening a checking account.

Non-Belizeans

Customer must bring in two Bankers' References from established institutions, along with his/her passport or a notarized copy, and one other form of identification. The customer also must bring in a recent utility bill (not older than three months).

Companies

For a company to open an account, identification is required for each beneficial owner and authorized signatory. Authorized signatories must each submit two Bankers' References from established institutions. Certified copies of the company's Certificate of Incorporation and Memorandum and Articles of Association also are required.

Incentive Programs

Belize has several incentive schemes designed to encourage investment in the country, including the Fiscal Incentives Act, the International Business and Public Companies Act, Export Processing Zone Act and Commercial Free Zone Act. However, a U.S. Commerce Department advisory notes, "many foreign investors have complained that these investment promotion tools are rarely as open and effective as they are portrayed." The programs of most interest to those thinking of starting a business in Belize are the Export Processing Zone Act, the Commercial Free Zone Act and the Fiscal Incentives Act. For more information on these programs, contact **Belize Trade & Development Service (BELTRAIDE),** 14 Orchid Garden Street, Belmopan, 501-822-3737, www.belizeinvest.org.bz.

The International Business Companies Act (IBC) makes it possible for foreign companies to get tax exemptions on all income of the IBC, all dividends paid by an IBC, all interest rents, royalties to non-Belizean residents and capital gains realized. There are several thousand companies registered as IBC's in Belize. However, IBCs are not available to citizens or official residents of Belize.

Working in Belize

In theory, unless you are a Belize citizen or a permanent resident under the regular permanent residency program (as a resident under the Qualified Retired Persons Incentive Act program you can't work for pay, though you can own a business or rental property in Belize) you cannot work in Belize without a work permit from the government. You also need a Belize Social Security card. In practice, we have heard about a few foreigners without work permits who have part-time jobs and take in-kind or cash payments. If you're caught working without a permit, however, both you and your employer could be in trouble. You could be deported, or even jailed, and fines are imposed on employers found with illegal workers. The government has cracked down on foreigners working in Belize, and on at least a couple of occasions senior management at resorts alleged to be working without a work permit were arrested and jailed.

There are two basic types of work permits. One is a work permit that is obtained by an employer in Belize for an employee. The employer has to prove that the company can't fill the job with a Belizean and has exhausted all avenues for finding a qualified Belizean applicant, including advertising the position for at least three weeks. Examples of jobs that may require a foreign applicant are hotel restaurant chef or a specialized computer software engineer. Application must be made by the employer to the Immigration Department with proof that the foreign employee is qualified, three passport photos, a valid passport and a small application fee.

Another type of work permit is the temporary self-employment certificate. This category applies to foreign investors and others seeking self-employment or who are starting a business in Belize, where it is assumed that the venture will lead to the creation of jobs for Belizeans. The applicant has to show proof of adequate funds for the proposed venture — for example, a bank statement. Also, the applicant has to have a reference from the relevant government Ministry or other organization showing that the venture is reasonable. If opening a tourist operation a reference from the Ministry of Tourism or the local village or town council where the operation is to be located may be required. For the temporary self-employment certificate the residency period is waived.

Work permit fees (subject to change):

Professional workers	US$1,500
Technical workers	US$1,000
Self-employed workers	US$1,000
Religious/voluntary workers	US$100
Entertainers, in groups	US$500 to $750
General workers in banana, citrus and sugar industries	US$100

Permits must be renewed annually and the above fees paid each year. With rare exceptions, work permits are not granted for waiters, domestic workers, farm hands and anyone involved in retail or other types of sales. For information and application forms, contact the Immigration and Nationality Department in Belmopan. If that sounds like a lot of red tape, it is. The Belize government is trying to discourage foreigners from working in jobs in Belize that Belizeans can perform. Belize is also trying to discourage illegal immigration from Guatemala and other Central American countries.

One American who moved to Ambergris Caye from Florida, said, "It was very hard for me to find work. My husband found work as a bartender the first week we were here, but he is Belizean, so he didn't have the problem of a work permit to deal with. I found that businesses are reluctant to hire you if you don't already have a permit in hand. The problem is, the price of work permits has gone up for professionals. None of the employers want to spend that amount of money when they don't know if you will stay or go."

Another American, Katie Valk, who was an executive in the music business in New York City before moving to Belize about 30 years ago, recalls the frustrations of trying to get a work permit: "It was not at all difficult adjusting. Belize was a perfect fit for me. Finding work wasn't a problem for me, either. Getting a work permit was, however, and it took a tremendous amount of stick-to-it-ness, patience and energy."

Typical Salaries in Belize

Salaries and wages in Belize vary widely, even for the same position, just as they do in the U.S. or Canada. Overall, wage levels in Belize are about one-fourth of those in the U.S., or lower, although a few business people and entrepreneurs in Belize make as much or more than their American counterparts. In general, wages are highest in Belize City and San Pedro and lowest in remote rural areas. All figures are in U.S. dollars:

Maid/Domestic Worker	$10-$20 per day
Day Laborer	$15-$30 per day
Skilled Carpenter or Mason	$25-$50 per day
Nurse	$8,000 per year
Doctor in Public Health Care	$15,000-$20,000 per year
Primary School Teacher	$8,000 a year
High School Teacher	$10,000 a year
College Professor	$12,000-$20,000 a year
Shop Clerk	$90-$150 a week
Office/Clerical Worker	$100-$150 a week
Secretary	$125-$150 a week
Lodge/Resort Workers	$15-$25 a day
Minimum Hourly Wage	$1.65 a hour

Eating a fresh papaya on the beach

DAILY LIFE IN BELIZE

What's daily life like in Belize? Of course, it varies from person to person in Belize as it does anywhere in the world. But here's a composite picture of a typical week in the life of an expat living in the Corozal area.

Monday You get up around 6 a.m. and watch the sun rise over Corozal Bay, while enjoying your regular breakfast of fresh fruit. This morning it's bananas and watermelon. The bananas cost about 5 U.S. cents each at the market, and the watermelon was about US$3. Here, only about 17 degrees north of the equator, the sun rises about this time every day and goes down again about 12 hours later. There's only a limited variation in the length of the day. You sit on your screened porch with a view of the bay. The weather is warm, as usual in the high 60s or low 70s F. this time of day. A refreshing breeze from the water eliminates the need for air-conditioning. The only time you turn on your small unit in your bedroom is in the summer, when there are still periods when the prevailing offshore breezes die down, sometimes for a couple of weeks at a time. After breakfast, you putter around in your yard, tending the fruit trees. You have lime, mango,

229

star fruit and banana. Then you decide to go into town to buy some groceries and do your banking. You stop and get some gas at the Shell station. It costs nearly US$60, for a around 12 gallons to fill up your Jeep. Then you go to the grocery. It's about the size of a large convenience store in the U.S. You buy two pounds of red beans (US$1.60) and a fifth of One Barrel rum (US$9). Before the ScotiaBank office closes, you stop in and cash a check on your local account. You decide to have lunch at Miss June's. Stew chicken with beans and rice and a Belikin come to US$6. After lunch, you come home and take a siesta. You watch a little cable TV, and then you and your partner decide to go out to dinner. For a splurge, you decide to go to Tony's. You sit in the seaside palapa, with a breeze off the bay, and enjoy chicken fajitas and rum and tonics for under US$30 for two.

Tuesday After breakfast, you get ready to drive down to Belize City to take care of some business with your attorney. It's the maid's day to come in. You pay her US$20 a day. It's about a two-hour drive to Belize City. Traffic is light all the way on the paved two-lane road. The only town of any size between Corozal and Belize City is Orange Walk Town, which looks much like a small town in Mexico. Just south of Orange Walk at the New River is Belize's only road toll -- BZ75 cents. As you approach the outskirts of Belize City, traffic tightens up. Cars pass right and left, apparently heedless of pedestrians along the road or any speed limit signs. At one of the new roundabouts coming into Belize City, traffic is backed up. Until the last few years, the entire country of Belize only had a couple of red lights. Now there are quite a few in Belize City and a handful elsewhere. As usual, you get turned around in Belize City. It's not a big city, hardly more than an overgrown town, but the narrow streets lined with ramshackle buildings confusingly end up at canals and suddenly turn one-way. The city has a colorful street life, with people of all races and backgrounds jostling for space and sharing a word. Finally you get to Albert Street, where your attorney has her office. Luckily you find a parking place on a side street, though you worry that leaving your vehicle parked here is asking for trouble. As you walk to the office, you're approached by a thin Creole who tries to sell you weed. You tell him you don't need any today, and he goes on his way. Since moving to Belize, you've picked up a little Creole -- most everybody in Belize knows how to *wap wa li Kriol,* or speak some Creole. You've also learned some Spanish, helpful in Corozal. After you finish your legal business, you return to your car and find it undisturbed. Nearby you see a tour bus full of pale-skinned, plump Americans, gawking at the street life of the city. A cruise ship must be in town. On some days, there are three or four ships in port at once, with thousands of day trippers tendered into the Tourist Village, built expressly for cruise industry. The harbor is too shallow to allow the big ships to dock. On your way back to Corozal, you stop for a late lunch at Victor's restaurant, at Petville near Orange Walk Town. It's a little joint serving Creole and Maya dishes. You decide just to have the roast pork with rice and beans. It's hot, close to 90 degrees, and a cold Belikin tastes good. Lunch comes to a little over US$8. After you get back home, you do some research on the internet. With your new satellite dish, you get fast access, especially for downloads, though you notice the latency problem sometimes. You pay around US$60 a month, plus installation was about a grand. Technically, your satellite service isn't sold in Belize, but since you have a U.S. address for billing and a U.S. credit card, you had no problem getting it set up. A lot of businesses and hotels, along with some individuals, use satellite for internet access, although DSL and cellular internet is available in most places, and access via digital cable is offered in Belize City and a couple of other areas. Unfortunately, the power goes out. Power in Northern Belize comes from Mexico, and occasionally -- sometimes more than occasionally -- there are blackouts. This time, the power is off for about three hours. There's no explanation of why it went out.

Wednesday You decide to get in a little fishing today. So, early in the morning, you head out with a friend who has a small powerboat. After about an hour on the bay, you make a stop in the fishing village of Sarteneja to check out a skiff a fellow there has for sale. Sarteneja boat builders are known all over Belize. Then you grab a cold Fanta and some tacos at Liz's Fast Food, for around US$3. You spend a few hours trolling for snapper, and you also catch and release a couple of tarpon. Your friend free dives and eventually comes up with three conchs. Heading home, you make plans next week to go diving on the reef north of San Pedro, as there's no good diving or snorkeling in the bay. After a home-cooked dinner of conch ceviche and grilled snapper, you watch TV and retire early.

Thursday Today, you decide to poke around the house, doing some repairs and piddling in your garden. Not everything grows well in the thin limestone-rich soils of Northern Belize, but you've had good luck with tomatoes, peppers, several kinds of squash including cho-cho, which your neighbors say looks like the face of an old granny without teeth, and all kinds of herbs including lemongrass and basil.

Friday A lower molar is giving you a little problem, so you call a dentist you know in Chetumal, and his office says you can come in at 11 this morning. You drive to the border and then to your dentist's office in Chetumal. The office is modern and clean and seems to have all the latest equipment. Your dentist says a filling has come out, and he replaces it. The cost? US$50. It might have cost you US$250 in the States. Then you visit San Francisco, a large supermarket in Chetumal, where you pick up some antibiotics and other medicines for your partner. You don't need a prescription, and the total cost is less than one-half what you'd pay in the U.S. You have lunch at Los Cocos, where an expansive meal with good Mexican beers came to less than US$9. You take in a first-run movie (in English with Spanish subtitles) at the multiplex at the mall. At Sam's Club you buy a new blender for your kitchen. Since you're a permanent resident, the US$18.75 exit fee from Belize to cross the land border into Mexico or Guatemala doesn't apply, though coming back you pay US$5 in duty and GST on the blender.

Saturday After running errands, you stop by Xaibe village to pick up some hand-pressed coconut oil. Some locals claim the amber-colored liquid is a super food and good for all kinds of medical ailments. In the afternoon, you invite friends over for a cookout. The grind meat (Belizean for ground beef) for hamburgers isn't as good as you'd like, but it's a successful party nonetheless. After the meal, you sit out on the deck and look at the lights from Chetumal across the bay.

Sunday You go to church in Corozal Town, and then after a light lunch at home, you drive a few miles up to the Four-Mile Lagoon for a dip in the lagoon and a cold drink at a Cool Spot. After reading for a while, you snack on fresh fruit for Sunday supper, then go to bed early. You have to be rested and ready for another hard week in paradise.

Belize visitor enjoys a cold Belikin and coconut shrimp at Blue Water Grill in San Pedro

CHECK-IT-OUT TRIP TO BELIZE

Before you get very far along in thinking about Belize as a place to live or retire or for a vacation home, you MUST visit Belize and see it for yourself. Don't sit at your computer dreaming about this little English-speaking paradise – come see for yourself if it's for you.

Entry and Exit Requirements: You must have a valid passport to enter Belize, with at least six months before expiration, but visas are not required for citizens of the U.S., Canada, the U.K. and most Caribbean and European Union countries. You should also have an onward or return ticket. Immigration in Belize won't ask for it, but the airline you fly in on most likely will. Entry is granted for up to 30 days, with renewals of up to a total of six months permitted (renewals cost US$25 per month for the first six months, then US$50 a month.) When leaving Belize by air, there is a US$39.25 exit fee for those who are not citizens or official residents of

233

Belize, who pay a lower rate. Many airlines include the fee in the ticket price. When leaving by land, at either the Benque Viejo border with Guatemala or Corozal border with Mexico, or by sea, there is a US$15 border fee, plus a $3.75 conservation fee, for a total of US$18.75. Students with valid student ID pay US$7.50. Children under 12 accompanied by parents are exempt.

What to Pack and Bring: Belize is a very casual country. You don't need evening clothes or even a coat and tie or other U.S.-style business dress. You'll live in tee shirts, shorts, loose-fitting slacks and casual shirts. A really dressy occasion for men might require a guayaberra or collared shirt and long pants; for women a simple skirt or dress. Leave all your fancy jewelry and Rolex watches at home. They will impress only thieves. Also leave your rain gear at home. It probably will rain, but most raincoats just make you sweat. At most, you could bring a light weight plastic poncho that folds up into a small package.

Here are ideas for your packing list:

Lightweight cotton clothes or quick-drying cotton/synthetic blends.

Comfortable walking shoes. Consider light boots or walking shoes for hiking and sandals for the beach.

Extra swimsuits.

Unlocked cell phone.

Maps, guidebooks and paperback books (if you prefer paper to digital versions). If available at all in Belize, books and maps will cost more than back home and may be out of date.

Cap or hat — be sure it's one that won't blow off in windy conditions on the water.

Sunglasses — the darker the better.

Small flashlight with extra batteries, baggies in various sizes, a roll of duct tape, a large garbage bag, pen and writing pad, and Swiss Army-style knife — with these you can go anywhere and do almost anything.

Replacement battery and memory stick (if needed) for your digital camera — you'll shoot many more photos in Belize than you think you will. Film is readily available in Belize, but it's expensive.

Health kit consisting of your prescription medicines and a copy of your eyeglass prescription, plus aspirin, insect spray with 30% DEET, sunscreen (more than you think you'll need), baby oil or Avon Skin-So-Soft for sandflies, Pepto-Bismol or other tummy medicine, antibiotic lotion, bandages, sun-burn lotion, toilet tissue, moist wipes, seasick pills and other over-the-counter medicines.

Optional:

Lightweight laptop or iPad or other tablet device, useful for getting on the internet at hotels and for storing books and other reading material. Some may prefer to substitute a smartphone.

Battery-operated radio if coming during peak tropical storm and hurricane season (July-November).

Snorkel mask — you can rent snorkel and dive gear in Belize, but rental masks often don't fit well.

Fishing gear.

Cotton sweater or light jacket may be needed in the winter, especially on the water or in the higher elevations of the Mountain Pine Ridge.

Frisbees, baseball-style caps with U.S. sports logos, tee shirts and boxes of crayons make good small gifts for kids. School supplies also make good gifts for children.

Money and Credit Cards: U.S. dollars (bills, not coins) are accepted everywhere in Belize, at a fixed rate of 2 Belize dollars to 1 U.S. dollar, although you often will receive change in Belizean money, or in a mix of Belizean and U.S. money. While there's no need to exchange U.S. dollars, sometimes you will get a better rate than 2 to 1 by exchanging at the border with moneychangers. At times when there's a shortage of U.S. dollars in Belize, you may be able to get up to 2.10 to 2.15 Belize for each U.S. dollar.

Canadian dollars, Euros and other currencies are not widely accepted. These should be exchanged at banks or moneychangers. The Belize Bank branch at Goldson International Airport offers currency exchange seven days a week. Traveler's checks in U.S. dollars are still accepted by most hotels and at some stores, restaurants and other businesses, but the use of traveler's checks is becoming less common due to the prevalence of ATM machines. You usually need to show your passport when paying with a traveler's check. Banks and some businesses only give about 1.96 Belize to 1 U.S. for traveler's checks.

Visa and MasterCard are widely accepted, except at small shops. American Express is accepted by some hotels and larger businesses. Discover, Diners and other cards are rarely accepted. Sometimes there is a surcharge for credit card use, usually 3 to 5% but occasionally more.

Surcharges are becoming less common, due to complaints by consumers and moves by credit card issuers. Ask about surcharges before using your card.

In addition to a possible local surcharge, increasingly credit card companies are levying international currency conversion and foreign usage fees, from 1 to 3% or even higher. Most products and services in Belize will be charged in Belize dollars, so the currency conversion charges apply. Even if the charges are listed in U.S. dollars, some credit card companies charge an international exchange fee anytime a charge is made outside your home country. Some American Express, Capital One Visa/MC, Bank of America and other cards have no foreign transaction fees.

As explained elsewhere, most bank offices in Belize have modern ATM machines, and now most accept ATM cards issued outside Belize. If you can't tap your funds with your ATM card, most banks in Belize will issue an advance on your Visa or MasterCard. The fee for this is usually less than US$10, depending on the bank, plus whatever fees and interest your bankcard charges. Getting a cash advance may take a little time and paperwork.

Your bank back home may levy a foreign ATM fee of up to US$5 per ATM use, plus a foreign transaction fee of 1 to 3% of the money withdrawn, and the local bank in Belize may also hit you with a fee, so try to minimize the number of ATM withdrawals you make.

Savvy travelers bring a combination of cash in small U.S. currency denominations, an ATM card and credit cards, and perhaps a few traveler's checks, just in case your cards and cash are stolen or lost.

Dress: Belize is a casual place. You don't need evening clothes or a coat and tie or other U.S.-style business dress. Heavy winter clothes are unneeded, though a light cotton sweater will come in handy at times. Most of the year, you'll live in tee shirts and shorts or other casual clothes.

Best Times to Visit Belize: Anytime is a good time to visit, but here are the "best times" for different activities and budgets:

Best time to avoid tourists: September-October
Best time to avoid rain: February through April
Best time for underwater visibility: March-June
Best time for lowest hotel prices: After Easter to U.S. Thanksgiving
Best time to visit Toledo District and the far south: February-May
Best time to visit Cayo: October-February (when it's not so hot)

Best time to visit Placencia: January-May

Best time to visit cayes: December-July

Best time to avoid hurricanes and tropical storms: December-June

Air Travel to Belize: At present, six major airlines fly to Belize: **American** (which recently merged with US Air), **Avianca** (formerly TACA), **Copa** (which in late 2015 began offering two weekly flights between Panama City, Panama, and Belize City) **Delta, United** (which merged with Continental) and **Southwest** (which began service to Belize in late 2015). The gateways for nonstop flights from the U.S. include Atlanta, Charlotte, Dallas, Houston, Los Angeles, Miami and Newark. Avianca has service from San Salvador, and Copa has service from Panama City. In addition, Belize-based **Tropic Air** has service between Belize City and Cancún, Mérida, Flores, Guatemala City, Roatán, San Pedro Sula and Tegucigalpa.

The international airlines use mostly Boeing 737, Airbus A320 or other smaller equipment to Belize, with the usual tight seating in coach and grossly overpriced seating in first or business class, if there is any seating at all beyond coach.

Flights from Atlanta, Miami, Dallas, Charlotte and Houston take only two to three hours of airtime.

At present there is no scheduled non-stop or direct service from Canada or Europe. In-season, usually there are a few charter flights, in winter only, from Toronto.

One of the chief complaints from Belize travelers is the high cost of airfare. Tickets from the U.S. to Cancun or Cozumel often are one-half the cost of tickets to Belize City. From the chief gateways you can expect to pay US$500 to $900 round-trip. Airlines flying to Belize occasionally have internet specials with prices as low as US$300, but you have to act fast as the windows for purchase and travel are narrow.

Our advice: Sign up for internet fare notices on the airlines that fly to Belize. Keep checking the on-line reservation sites such as Expedia.com or Travelocity.com. Also check meta-reservation sites – they compare fares from a variety of other sites – such as Kayak.com. A travel agent specializing in Belize, such as **Barb's Belize** in Stuarts Draft, Va. (540-337-1103 or toll-free 888-321-2272, www.barbsbelize.com) may be able to find lower fares for you. The owner, **Barbara Kasak,** is very knowledgeable about Belize.

Another source of airfare deals and hotel and tour bookings in Belize is **Katie Valk,** an American who has lived in Belize for many years. Email her at **Belize Trips** in Belize at info@belize-trips.com or visit www.belize-trips.com. Her U.S. telephone number is 561-210-7015.

Another idea is to fly into Cancún or Cozumel on a cheap scheduled or charter flight and bus it from there. There is now a first-class ADO bus service daily between Cancún and Belize City. Also, there is a water taxi from Chetumal, Mexico, to San Pedro and Caye Caulker. *See below for more information and travel tips.*

Arriving by Air -- What to Expect: The Belize International Airport (also known as the Philip S. W. Goldson International Airport, named after a long-time People's United Party politician) is about 9 miles north of the center of Belize City, off the Philip Goldson Highway (formerly Northern Highway) at Ladyville. The airport is small but fairly modern, having opened in 1990. It is believed to be the only "major" airport in the world with a mahogany ceiling in the original building. A new domestic terminal area opened in late 1998 and since then the runway has been extended. After your airplane taxis to the terminal building, you disembark the old-fashioned way, down a set of moveable stairs. You cross the tarmac and enter the immigration and customs area. Most days, you feel the humidity right away. The immigration officer will look at your passport and usually ask the purpose of your visit and how long you are staying. You can be granted a visitor's entry permit of up to 30 days, but that's not automatic. If you say you are staying 10 days, the officer may grant only that period or two weeks at most. If you think there's any chance you may want to stay a little longer than your current reservations, be generous about estimating the time you'll stay. The officer will then stamp your passport and enter the arrival and departure date.

From here, you move to a small baggage claim area, where there is a small duty-free shop selling duty-free liquor and a few other items. (When entering Belize, you are permitted to bring in only one liter of alcohol, but you can buy an additional four liters of booze at the airport arrival duty-free shop, where you need to pay in U.S. dollars.) You then go through customs. Belize now has a Green/Red customs system. If you have nothing to declare, you can go through the Green line, though an officer may still ask to see inside your bags. On a typical flight, probably one-third of passengers have at least one bag inspected. Customs and immigrations officers generally are courteous and efficient, though like government officials in most countries they are not known for being overly friendly. Treat them with respect, and you'll be treated similarly. Do not even think of offering a bribe. That is not how things work in Belize, at least not at this level. The entire immigration and customs process usually takes from 15 minutes to half an hour.

After your bags pass customs, you can go into the main airport lobby or out to the taxi or rental car area. Porters are available to assist with bags, if necessary. A tip of US$1 per bag is standard, more if special services are provided. If you are continuing on a domestic flight, move quickly to the Maya Island Air or Tropic check-in area, as the domestic carriers use small airplanes, and they fill up quickly. The rectangular passenger lobby, which is usually bustling with people, has a Belize Bank office (you do NOT need to change U.S. dollars to Belize dollars —see above), a few tourist shops and airline ticket counters. Upstairs to your left are bathrooms (clean) and a restaurant adjoining the "waving area" with views of the airstrip. There is another restaurant in the newer terminal section, and a small bar in the international and domestic departure area.

Taxis are available right outside the passenger lobby door. The cabs at the airport – they have green license plates – are regulated and you shouldn't be ripped off. The fare is fixed at US$25 (BZ$50) to anywhere in Belize City — that's for the cab, not per person, although a small additional amount may be charged for extra luggage. In Belize, you do not need to tip taxi drivers unless they perform extra service such as carrying luggage. There are no buses directly into Belize City from the airport. You can walk 2 miles to the Goldson Highway, or pay a taxi around US$6 to take you there, and flag down a bus into Belize City (about US$1).

Rental car kiosks, including local offices of international franchised auto rental companies such as **Avis, Budget** (www.budget-belize.com), **Hertz** (www.carsbelize.com) and **Thrifty**, along with locals **Crystal** (www.crystal-belize.com), the largest rental firm in Belize, **Jabiru, AQ, Pancho's** and others, are across the street on the other side of the airport parking area, a short distance. There is a small motel, Global Village Hotel, on the Philip Goldson Highway just south of the airport entrance road, and this hotel usually will provide a free shuttle from and to the airport.

Air: Belize has two domestic carriers, **Tropic Air** (800-442-3435 from

the U.S. and Canada, or 501-226-2012 in Belize, www.tropicair.com),
which has service to 11 airports in Belize, plus seven destinations in Mexico,
Guatemala and Honduras; and **Maya Island Air** (501-223-1140,
www.mayaislandair.com), which serves nine airports only in Belize.

Tropic Air operates 11 Cessna Grand Caravans (208B), two Gippsland
Airvans and one Cessna 172. These aircraft are configured for from three to
14 passengers. Maya Island operates eight Cessna Caravans, three Britten
Norman Islanders, one Gippsland Airvan and one Cessna 182.

As of late 2015, Tropic has scheduled service at Belize City (both
international and municipal airports), Belmopan City, Caye Caulker,
Corozal Town, Dangriga, Orange Walk Town, Placencia, Punta Gorda,
San Ignacio/Benque Viejo and San Pedro. Internationally, it services
Cancún and Mérida in Mexico, Flores and Guatemala City in Guatemala
and Roatán, San Pedro Sula and Tegucigalpa in Honduras. Maya Island
Air has scheduled service at Belize City (both international and municipal
airports), Caye Caulker, Corozal Town, Dangriga, Placencia, Punta Gorda,
San Pedro and Savannah. Both airlines also offer charter flights and may
offer non-scheduled stops at other airstrips in Belize such as Kanatik in
Stann Creek or Caye Chapel near Caye Caulker.

Currently, Maya Island Air permits passengers to have one checked
bag of up to 50 pounds, one carry-on and on small personal item (such as a
computer or purse) as a carry-on, all at no charge. Additional checked items
are charged excess baggage fees ranging from BZ 41 cents to BZ$1.13 per
pound. Tropic Air allows one small carry-on (such as a purse or computer
bag) and two free checked bags on domestic flights. On Tropic's
international flights, the first checked bag is free, and additional bags are
US$35 each.

Domestic flights from the municipal airport, about a mile from the
center of Belize City, are cheaper than from the international airport in
Ladyville. For example, a flight to San Pedro on Ambergris Caye costs
approximately US$90 one-way from international, and US$55 one-way
from municipal. Savings to most other destinations are less significant. Of
course, you have to pay a cab to transfer from one airport to the other –
US$25 for up to four persons.

Usually there is little or no savings on roundtrip fares over two one-
way fares, but there are exceptions so it's worth checking the airlines'
websites. Except for occasional off-season specials, fares are about the same

year-round, with no advance-purchase or other discounts. Sometimes you can get a 10% or larger discount by paying cash rather than paying by credit card. It pays to ask.

The airlines fly only during daylight hours, except at peak tourism periods when they have permission to continue flying into San Pedro until all waiting passengers are taken care of.

Which airline is better? In some ways, it's a toss-up. Tropic is larger, with 250 flights daily to 17 destinations in Belize and surrounding countries, but Maya Island has added new aircraft and several new terminals (at Belize municipal, Placencia and elsewhere). For most people, the decision comes down to which airline has the more convenient flight on a specific day and time. Fares are similar, although there are some small differences to specific locations.

Are advance air reservations necessary? Except at peak high-season travel periods, you can probably get on a convenient flight without advance reservations. Still, having a reservation gives you a little extra edge, and we recommend you book ahead if possible. It's essential you do so at holiday periods such as Easter and Christmas.

Buses: Travel by bus in Belize is inexpensive. You can travel the whole length of the country from the Mexican border in the north to Punta Gorda in the far south for about US$25 or go from Belize City to Cayo in the west for US$4 to $5. It's also a good way to meet local people and to get a real feel for the country.

In Belize City, local and the Mexican-based ADO buses use the main bus terminal on West Collet Canal. It is still known as Novelo's, the name of a former bus company. Buses to Guatemala stop at the Marine Terminal near the Swing Bridge in Belize City. Other places have a bus terminal or a central point where buses stop.

There now is limited bus service within Belize City. Around half a dozen lines offer service in the downtown area and in the north and west parts of the city. Fares are around BZ$1 to $2.

Bus travel in Belize falls somewhere between the chicken bus experience in rural Guatemala and the deluxe coaches with comfortable reserved seats and videos in Mexico. Belize buses are usually recycled American school buses or old Greyhound diesel pushers. There are two types of buses in Belize – regular buses that pick up and let off passengers on demand, and express buses that are faster because they make stops only at a few places.

The country has a franchised bus system, with the government granting rights for certain companies to operate on specific routes. Belize City is the hub for bus service throughout Belize. Bus companies licensed to operate on the Philip Goldson Highway in the Northern Zone include BBOC, Cabrera's, Chell's, Morales, Tillett's, T-Line and Valencia. (Bus lines subject to change.) Northbound buses depart from Belize City about every half hour from around 5:30 a.m. to 7:30 p.m. Some of the northbound buses continue to Chetumal. Bus companies authorized to operate on the George Price Highway in the Western Zone include BBOC, D&E, Guerra's, Shaw and Westline. Westbound buses depart Novelo's bus station roughly every half hour beginning at 5 a.m., with the last departure around 9:30 p.m. Bus companies operating in the Southern Zone – most running between Belize City and Punta Gorda via Belmopan and Dangriga -- include James Bus Line (the best bus company in the south), Cho, G-Line, Ritchie's and Usher. In addition, several lines are licensed to operate mainly in rural areas of the Southern Zone. These include A-Jay's, Chen, Martinez, Radiance Ritchie and Polanco. Keep in mind that many of these "bus lines" have just one or two buses. The small lines tend to come and go.

In some cases you can make advance reservations with the larger bus operations by calling the bus companies, although most people don't make reservations. If boarding at a terminal, you pay for your ticket at the window and get a reserved seat. If boarding elsewhere, you pay the driver's assistant.

Fuente del Norte (www.grupofuentedelnorte,com) and **Linea Dorado** (www.lineadorada.info) provide bus service between Flores, Guatemala, and Belize City. The fares are around US$25 one-way. In Belize, the buses pick up and drop off at the Marine Terminal near the Swing Bridge in Belize City. The Guatemalan buses are not supposed to pick up or drop off passengers anywhere else in Belize, but drivers sometimes will do so. Fuente del Norte buses also run daily between Flores and San Pedro Sula, Honduras, and San Salvador, El Salvador.

Mexican bus line **ADO** has two express services to Belize City – a daily one from Cancún and one from Mérida (where Belizeans often go for medical care) that runs three or four days a week. The ADO buses are much nicer than Belize buses, with 44 reserved reclining seats, videos, bathroom and air conditioning. From Cancún, the ADO bus leaves from the Cancún bus station in downtown Cancún City. In Belize City, ADO uses the main Belize City bus terminal (still known as Novelo's) located on West Collet Canal.

From Cancún to Belize City, the ADO bus departs from Cancún terminal daily at 10:15 p.m., with stops at Playa del Carmen, Tulum, Corozal Town and Orange Walk Town. It arrives in Belize City about 6 or 6:30 a.m. The current fare (subject to increase) is 576 Mexican pesos one-way or about US$35 at current exchange rates. Trip time is about 8 hours.

Shuttles: Another option for traveling around Belize is to use a private shuttle service. There are around a dozen of these shuttle services, some based in Belize City and others in Corozal, San Ignacio and elsewhere. While the shuttles cost more than buses, because they use small vans they are more comfortable and less crowded than buses. In some cases, shuttles will make stops on demand, and some drop and pick up as far away as Cancún. Among the shuttle services in Belize are **Belize VIP Transfer Service** (www.belizetransfers.com) and **Moralez Travel Service** (www.gettransfers.com), both based in Corozal Town; **William's Belize Shuttle** (www.williamshuttlebelize.com) in Cayo; and **Discounted Belize Shuttles and Tours** (www.discountedbelizeshuttlesandtours.com) and **Belize Shuttles and Transfers** (www.belizeshuttlesandtransfers.com), in Belize City.

Water Taxis: If you are going to San Pedro or Caye Caulker, you have the option of taking a water taxi. There are now two main water taxi companies, with boats that hold up to 50 to 100 passengers, connecting Belize City with San Pedro and Caye Caulker. From Belize City it's a 45-minute ride to Caulker and 75 minutes to San Pedro. Going between Caulker and San Pedro takes about 30 minutes. The water taxi business in Belize is in flux; schedules and rates are subject to change. **Ocean Ferry** (501-223-0033, www.oceanferrybelize.com) boats leave from the Marine Terminal in Belize City at 10 North Front Street near the Swing Bridge. **San Pedro Belize Express** (501-223-2225, www.belizewatertaxi.com) boats leave from the Brown Sugar dock at 111 North Front Street near the Tourism Village.

Ocean Ferry, which currently has five departures daily from each location, charges US$24.50 round-trip between Belize City and San Pedro and US$14.50 between Belize City and Caye Caulker or between San Pedro and Caye Caulker. San Pedro Belize Express, which has around eight or nine departures from each location, charges US$35 round-trip between Belize City and San Pedro, and US$25 between Belize City and Caye Caulker or between San Pedro and Caye Caulker.

San Pedro Belize Express also has service every other day between the municipal pier in Chetumal, Mexico, and San Pedro and Caye Caulker, a trip of about 90 minutes to San Pedro, for US$50 one-way Chetumal-San Pedro and US$100 round-trip. To and from Caye Caulker the trip is nearer two hours and is US$55 one-way or US$110 round-trip. Another water taxi company, **San Pedro Water Taxi,** (501-226-2194, www.sanpedrowatertaxi.com) also has service, sometimes daily, sometimes not, between Chetumal and San Pedro and Caye Caulker. One-way fares are US$60 between San Pedro and Chetumal and US$65 between Caye Caulker and Chetumal. Round-trip fares are US$130 and US$120 respectively. The fares usually do not includes US$5 port fees in Mexico or exit fee of US$18.75 leaving Belize. You may also have to pay a 295 Mexican peso fee leaving Mexico, if you have not already paid it, and 295 pesos when you enter Mexico for the first time.

Another company, **Thunderbolt,** has daily service between Corozal Town and San Pedro for US$25 one-way. The trip takes 90 minutes to two hours, and the boat will stop in Sarteneja on demand. In Corozal, the Thunderbolt leaves from the Reunion Pier in the center of town.

A local ferry company, **Coastal Xpress** (www.coastalxpress.com), provides scheduled boat transportation up and down Ambergris Caye, with rates from around US$5 to US$14 one-way.

There are several water taxis daily between Punta Gorda and Puerto Barrios, Guatemala (US$25 one-way). **Requeña** (www.belizenet.com/requena) is probably the best operator. A weekly boat, **D-Express,** operates between Placencia and Puerto Cortes, Honduras for US$60 one-way. Also, the **Starla** boat (504-9545-9322 in Honduras) runs weekly between Belize City and Puerto Cortes for US$75, with a stop at Dangriga. Belize City to Dangriga costs US$50.

From Dangriga to Tobacco Caye, you can arrange a boat (around US$20 one-way) but service is not scheduled. Ask at the Riverside Café in Dangriga.

The **Hokey Pokey** operates about eight round-trips a day between Independence (Mango Creek) across the Placencia Lagoon, and Placencia (MnM Hardware). Cost is US$5.

Belize Bus and Travel Guide (www.belizebus.wordpress.com) is an excellent source of information on bus and other travel options in Belize.

Health: The standards of health and hygiene in Belize are fairly high, similar to that in Costa Rica. Not many visitors become ill from traveler's diseases or from drinking the water. While malaria, dengue fever and other tropical diseases are present in Belize, they do rarely affect visitors in the more popular destinations of Belize. Most travelers to Ambergris Caye or Placencia and other popular areas don't get any special shots or take other precautions before they come. No shots are required for entry into Belize, except for yellow fever if you are coming from an infected area such as parts of Africa. However, it's always a good idea to keep tetanus-diphtheria, Hep A and B and other vaccinations up to date.

Malaria prophylaxis may be advised for mainland travel, especially to remote areas in southern Belize or in Guatemala. Chloroquine, taken once a week, starting two weeks before arrival, is usually all you need in most of the region. Better be safe than sorry. Check with your doctor or the U.S. Centers for Disease Control, tel. 404-332-4559 or visit www.cdc.gov for the latest information.

The biggest trip-spoiler in Belize is probably sunburn. You're only 18 degrees of latitude north of the Equator, and the sub-tropical sun is much stronger than back home.

Accommodations -- What to Expect: Belize has some 600 hotels, with about 5,000 total rooms. Most of these hotels are small, owner-operated places; about 70% have 10 or fewer rooms. Only two hotels have more than 100 rooms: the 180-room Ramada Princess Hotel & Casino and the 102-room Radisson Fort George. Both are in Belize City.

Travelers to Belize today can expect to find a variety of accommodations to fit almost any budget or preference. Among the uniquely Belizean accommodations are the so-called jungle lodges. These are mostly in remote areas, but despite the remote locations you don't have to forego life's little luxuries, such as cold beer, hot showers and comfortable mattresses. The best of these places, including Chaa Creek in Cayo, Hidden Valley Inn and Blancaneaux in the Mountain Pine Ridge and Chan Chich in rural Orange Walk, are as good as any jungle lodge in the world.

Usually, the birding and wildlife spotting around the lodges are excellent, and they offer all the amenities you enjoy after the day's adventures are done. Most, though not all, have bay thatch cabañas built with a nod to Maya-style construction, but done up in much more luxury and style than traditional Maya cottages. While the top places are first-class in every way, with rates to match — often US$200 to $400 or more a night in season — you don't have to pay much to get an authentic jungle lodge experience. Places like Clarissa Falls, Crystal Paradise and Parrot's Nest, all in Cayo, are bargains.

Another delightful type of lodging in Belize is the casual and small seaside resort. The best of these are sandy barefoot spots, with a friendly Belizean feel you won't find in other parts of the Caribbean. A couple can spend a night at the beach for US$50 to US$150.

All around Belize you can find small places with clean, safe rooms at budget prices. The Trek Stop, Aguada and Casa Blanca in Cayo, Sea Breeze in Corozal Town or Tipple Tree Beya Inn in Hopkins are examples. At these places you can get a nice little room for around US$50 or less.

At the other end of the scale, for those who demand luxury, a whole wave of upmarket hotels hit Belize starting in the 1990s. No longer is it necessary to stay in a hotel with linoleum floors and mismatched furniture. On Ambergris Caye and other cayes, places like Victoria House and The Phoenix have rooms that could earn a spot in *Architectural Digest*, with rates from US$200 to $500+ a night. On the mainland, Chaa Creek's newer digs are gorgeous. Blancaneaux's villas are luxurious, as are the seafront villas (with furnishings imported from Bali) of its sister resort, Turtle Inn in Placencia. In a few areas, mainly San Pedro, you can enjoy the extra space of a condo-style unit at a regular hotel-style price. Grand Caribe, Villas at Banyan Bay, Grand Colony, The Palms, Coco Beach and Pelican Reef are great examples of condotels. In between are all shapes and sizes of personality inns, mostly run by their owners.

Many owners are struggling to earn a decent income, and they can't always afford to have the softest sheets or newest TVs in the rooms. But, whether the owners are Belizean, American, Canadian, British or from a galaxy far, far away, they're almost always friendly and helpful, willing to sit down with you and help you plan your day.

Do You Need to Book Ahead?

Can you wing it in Belize? Or do you need to book hotels in advance? The answer, except around busy holidays such as Christmas and Easter, used to be that you could just wing it. Average annual occupancy at Belize hotels was under 40%, and rooms in all price levels were plentiful most of the time. However, beginning in the late 1990s, tourism grew to record levels. Quite a few hotels, especially those offering the best value or top service and location, are heavily booked in-season. when visiting Belize in-season, roughly Christmas and March through Easter, it's a good idea to book ahead for at least the first night or two. This doesn't mean that if you arrive without reservations you'll have to sleep on the beach with the sand flies — you'll be able to find a room somewhere — but your first choices may well be booked and you may have to spend valuable vacation time hunting for a room. Tours and dive trips can easily be booked after you arrive.

Using the Internet to Find and Book Rooms: Belize is wired. Most hotels in Belize have websites and email. You can use their web sites (listings in this book include internet addresses) to help you choose your accommodations, but remember that these sites are advertising and naturally put the best face on things. Nearly all hotels in Belize are small, and though many won't admit it for fear of alienating travel agents and travel wholesalers, they would prefer you book direct, preferably via the internet. That saves them 10 to 25% in agent commissions, plus the cost and trouble of faxing, mailing brochures and telephoning back and forth. In many cases, booking direct also will save you money. Some, but not all, hotels offer discounts for direct bookings via the internet. Many don't advertise this, but it won't hurt to ask.

The cheapest way to communicate with hotels in Belize is via email. Unfortunately, not all hotels in Belize check their email regularly and respond to messages in a timely way. In addition, many hotels have to deal with spam email seeking bookings, with the scam coming in after the booker sends a credit card number. Also, email in Belize may be down, sometimes for several days at a time. You may have to follow up with a telephone call or fax.

Eating Well in Belize: We don't know who started the rumor that you can't get a good meal in Belize. The fact is, you can eat gloriously well, at modest prices. Rice and beans is the quintessential Belizean dish, but this is not the rice and beans your momma used to fix — unless she's from Belize or perhaps New Orleans. Rice and beans (or beans and rice, which is slightly different) in Belize means spicy and smoky, with plenty of recado (also known as achiote) and other seasonings, perhaps flavored with salt pork and some onions and peppers and cooked in coconut milk. Usually these are served with a chunk of stew chicken, fish or pork. The whole thing might cost just US$5 or $6 in a pleasant restaurant. If you're not happy in Belize, you're probably not getting enough rice and beans.

Along the coast and on the cayes, seafood is as fresh as the salt air. In-season (mid-June to mid-February) spiny lobster — grilled, broiled, steamed, even fried — is fairly inexpensive and good. But a big filet of snapper or grouper, prepared over a grill with lime juice, is just as tasty and even cheaper. Conch, in season October to June, is delicious grilled or stewed in lime juice as ceviche, but we like it best in fritters, chopped and fried in a light batter.

Every ethnic group in multicultural Belize has its own taste treats. Among them: Sere and hoodut, the best-known Garifuna dishes, fish cooked in coconut milk with plantains. Boil-up is a Creole favorite, fish boiled with plantains, yams and potatoes, and served with a tomato sauce and boiled bread. The Maya dish most popular with tourists is pibil, pork and other meats seasoned, wrapped in banana leaf and cooked slowly in an underground oven. Of course, with Mexico next door, Belize has a wide variety of Mexican dishes, including tamales, burritos, garnaches (corn tortillas fried and topped with beans, salsa and cheese) and panades (deep-fried tortillas filled with fish). A few restaurants serve local game, including iguana, venison and gibnut, a rabbit-like rodent dubbed "the Royal Rat" because it was once served to Queen Elizabeth II.

We find most of the beef in Belize to be poor, although you can get an tasty steak in Belize if you look hard enough. But the pork — it's heavenly. The pork chops are tender and flavorful, the bacon a little different from most we've had, but delicious with fresh farm eggs. Only brown eggs are legal in Belize, by the way, to protect Belize's chicken farmers — if you see a white egg it's an illegal alien. For breakfast, fruit is the thing — fresh pineapple, mango, papaya, watermelon, orange. With fry jacks (a sort of fried biscuit, the Belizean version of beignets) and a cup of rich Guatemalan or Gallon Jug Estates Belizean coffee, we're set for the day.

For the most part, Belize dining isn't fancy, but even Belize is branching out in some of the newer worlds of cuisine – French, Thai, Vietnamese, Japanese, Chinese, Italian and more. Extraordinary Italian gelato is delicious at Tutti-Frutti in Placencia.

To drink, there's nothing more refreshing than a fresh lime juice or watermelon juice. Belikin beer may not be up to the high standards of some of the beers of Mexico and Costa Rica, but it's good enough for us, and the Belikin stout will make you strong as an ox. Local rums such as One Barrel are cheap and flavorful.

Nightlife: Many visitors to Belize, after full days of hiking, caving, diving or snorkeling, are just too pooped to stay up late and party. At remote jungle lodges and dive resorts, often the lights go out by 10 p.m. Belize City and Ambergris Caye have the most clubs and bars. Visitors thinking about a tropical romance or a visit to one of the several brothels in Belize City, Orange Walk Town, Cayo or elsewhere should be aware that AIDS is a serious and growing problem in Belize. There are an estimated 8,000 people in Belize with HIV, a large number considering the country's small population of over 360,000.

Gambling: A law passed in 1999 permitted gambling, and several casinos have opened in Belize; others are planned. Belize City has the Ramada Princess Hotel and Casino, with about 500 electronic machines plus live tables for poker, blackjack and other games. The Princess also has a branch in San Ignacio and in the Free Zone in Corozal. Two other casinos are in the Free Zone in northern Belize, including the large Las Vegas Casino, where a nice, new, 100+ room hotel associated with the casino opened in late 2015. San Pedro has a gaming spots at Captain Morgan's. Casinos have been proposed for Placencia in southern Belize, but when and whether they will open is anyone's guess.

Personal Knowledge: For each area of Belize, we've sketched out the options for getting there, outlined what to see and do and selected our favorite hotels, restaurants and bars in all price ranges. In almost every case, the author has stayed at or eaten at these places (in a few cases we've relied on reports from trusted associates), so you're getting first-hand recommendations.

Of course, you can also use TripAdvisor (www.tripadvisor.com), Yelp (www.yelp.com) and other social media sites to get further opinions.

Fried chicken is a Belize staple

CHECKING OUT BELIZE CITY

Note: *The order of the "Checking Out" chapters differ somewhat from the "In More Detail" chapters above. This is because that when coming to be on a Check-It-Out scouting trip, you most likely will arrive in Belize City. Many people also check out the various locations of interest in the order they are presented here, although of course that depends on your preferences and interests.*

Coming into Belize you most likely will land in Belize City. Many Belize travelers will tell you the best way to see Belize City is through your rear view window. However, with an open mind to its peculiarities, and with a little caution (the city has drug, gang and crime problems, though this rarely affects visitors, and the areas usually frequented by visitors are watched by tourist police), you may decide Belize City has a raffish, atmospheric charm. You might even see the ghost of Aldous Huxley or Graham Greene at a hotel bar.

Getting to Belize City

Belize City is the hub of transportation in Belize. *For information on how*

*to get to Belize City, see the preceding chapter on Visiting Belize on a Check-It-Out
Scouting Trip.*

What to See and Do in Belize City

Belize City, if nothing else, has character. It's full of interesting faces,
streets full of color and charming old colonial houses. The city rewards the
travelers with a surprising number of interesting sights and memorable
places, among them the colonial-era buildings in the **Fort George** and
Southern Foreshore sections. For the most part, the colonial buildings
are wood with zinc roofs.

Belize is divided into the North Side and South Side, with the Swing
Bridge effectively diving the two sides. The Fort George section on the
North Side is bordering the Belize City Harbour, is Belize City's most
photogenic area.

There are at least a half dozen buildings and sights especially worth
seeing, including the Fort George Lighthouse, the Museum of Belize and
the Swing Bridge, the Supreme Court Building and St. John's Anglican
Cathedral House of Culture. These are described briefly below, roughly
from north to south. The Fort George Lighthouse and Bliss Memorial and
the Museum of Belize are on the North Side of the city. As noted, the Swing
Bridge divides the North and South Sides. The Supreme Court, House of
Culture and St. John's Cathedral are on the South Side.

All of these places are safe enough to visit during the day, but should
be avoided after dark unless you are with people who know the area. At the
very least, take a taxi to them.

Fort George Lighthouse and Bliss Memorial. Fort George
Point, For George area, North Side. Admission free. The Fort George
Lighthouse, on the tip of Fort George Point near the Radisson Fort George
Hotel, was designed and funded by Belize's great benefactor, Baron Henry
Edward Ernest Victor Bliss. The Edwardian nobleman never actually set
foot on the Belizean mainland, but he sailed his yacht in the 1920s to the
coast of British Honduras. For unknown reasons, in his will he bequeathed
most of his fortune to the people of Belize. The date of his death in 1926,
March 9, or on a weekend date close to it, is celebrated as a national
holiday. Bliss is buried here, in a small mausoleum perched on the seawall.

Museum of Belize. 8 Gabourel Lane, North Side, 501-223-4524,
www.museumofbelize.org, open Tuesday-Friday 9-4:30, Saturday, 9-4,

251

admission US$5. This fascinating museum was the main Belize City jail from the 1850s to 1993. Displays on Belize history and culture include ancient Mayan artifacts, colorful Belize postage stamps, colonial-era bottles and an actual jail cell. Exhibitions change regularly.

Swing Bridge. The bridge spanning Haulover Creek actually swings, when needed to allow a boat through or by special request of visiting dignitaries. Four men hand-winch the bridge a quarter-revolution so waiting boats can continue upstream. The large creek over which it swings was so named because before the bridge lifestock were "hauled over" the stream, an inlet of the Belize River. The bridge, made in Liverpool, England, opened in 1923. It was upgraded in 1999. It's the only one of its kind left in Central America and one of the few in the world.

Near the Swing Bridge at 91 Front Street is the **Image Factory** (501-223-4093, www.imagefactorybelize.com, open 9-5 Monday-Friday, 9-noon Saturday), an art gallery and foundation that is the focus of Belize's contemporary art and cultural scene. The Image Factory also has a nice selection of books on Belize for sale.

Belize Supreme Court. Regent Street, South Side. The 1926 Belize Supreme Court building was modeled after its wooden predecessor, which burned in 1918. The current building, of reinforced concrete painted white, has filigreed iron stair and balcony rails, similar to what you might see in New Orleans (the construction company was from Louisiana) and above the balcony a four-sided clock. Belize's Supreme Court for Belize and Cayo districts meets here four times a year (there are two other Supreme Court buildings, one in Corozal Town and one in Dangriga.) You can't enter the building, but you can admire it from the outside.

House of Culture. Regent Street, South Side, 501-227-3050, www.nichbelize.org, open Monday-Friday 8:30-5 (until 4:30 p.m. Friday), admission US$5. Formerly Government House, the city's finest example of colonial architecture is said to have a design inspired by the Sir Christopher Wren. Built in 1814, it was once the residence of the governor-general, the queen's representative in British Honduras. After Hurricane Hattie in 1961 the house became a place for tony social functions and a guesthouse for visiting VIPs. Queen Elizabeth stayed here. Now it's open to the public. View art, silver, glassware, and furniture collections.

St. John's Cathedral. 8 Albert Street at Regent Street, South Side, daily 8-7, admission free. This cathedral, built staring in 1812, is the oldest

Anglican church in Central America and the only one outside England where kings were crowned. Four kings of the Mosquito Coast (a British protectorate in Honduras and Nicaragua) were crowned here. The cathedral, built of brick brought to British Honduras as ballast on English ships, is thought to be the oldest building in Belize, other than Mayan structures. Its foundation stone was laid in 1812. The roof is constructed of local sapodilla wood, with mahogany beams.

Suburbs

Outside the downtown area to the west of the city, **Old Belize** (Mile 5, George Price Highway, 501-222-4129, www.oldbelize.com) has a cultural and historical museum (open daily 10-8:30, admission US$2.50, a beach area, a zip line, waterslide and a marina.

To the north of the city centre, **Travellers Liquors Heritage Center** (Mile 2½, Philip Goldson Highway, open Monday-Friday 8-5, 501-233-2855, www.onebarrelrum.com) is a small museum dedicated to the history of Traveller's brand rum, and rum in general, in Belize. You can enjoy free samples and watch rum being made in the back.

Belize City Lodging

Rates shown are plus 9% hotel tax and in some cases a service charge, usually 10%. Hotels are listed alphabetically.

City Centre Area

Best Caribbean Pickwick Hotel. 160 Newtown Barracks, 501-223-2950; www.bestcaribbean.bz. Opened in 2014, this hotel is on the fourth floor of a commercial building (you take an elevator up to the hotel). It is named after a famous private club, the Pickwick Club, in this area. The small hotel has 24 air-conditioned rooms. The 13 deluxe rooms have 45-inch flat screen TVs, king beds and sea views. The hotel is across from the Ramada Belize City Princess Hotel and Casino (we don't recommend you stay there) and the locally popular BTL Park, where you can sometimes rent paddle boats or jet skis. Guests have free use of a swimming pool and can play tennis on two courts, for a fee. Rates are US$128 to US$138 double, plus tax.

The Great House, 13 Cork Street, 501-223-3400; www.greathousebelize.com. The Great House offers spacious air-conditioned rooms with polished pine floors in a modernized and expanded colonial house, originally built in 1927. It is in the historic Fort George area, located a short stroll from the harbour and directly across the street from the Radisson Fort George. All 12 rooms, half on the second and half on the third floor (there's no elevator), have a balcony, private bath, mini-fridge, safe, TV and phone. There is also a pretty good, if somewhat pricey, restaurant in the courtyard, the Smoky Mermaid. Doubles are US$173 double May-October and US$183 double November-April, plus tax.

Radisson Fort George Hotel and Marina. 2 Marine Parade, 501-223-3333 or toll-free from U.S./Canada, 800-333-3333; www.radisson.com/belize-city-hotel-bz/belize. This is the flagship of the city's international-style hotels, and the most expensive, though you may be able to get reductions from the rack rates. As the Fort George Hotel, it was the first major hotel built in the country, opened in 1953 with 36 rooms. Today, all rooms have cable TV, fridge and minibar, and those in the Club Wing, reached by the only glass elevator in Belize, have sea views. Most of the rooms, including those in the Villa Wing (once a Holiday Inn) across the street, have been remodeled. There are good restaurants, a bar, and the grounds are an oasis of calm on the edge of the sea. The hotel has two pools and a private dock. The marina can take large boats of up to 250 feet in length with a 10-foot draft. Management is solid, and the staff is friendly and helpful. In-season rates start at around US$250 double, a little less the rest of year.

Near International Airport and Between Airport and City Centre:

Best Western Biltmore Plaza. Mile 3½ Philip Goldson Highway, 501-223-2302, toll-free U.S./Canada 800-528-1234; www.belizebiltmore.com. If you must have a U.S.-style motel, this is an adequate choice between the international airport and downtown. It does have a pool and an okay bar, but the restaurant isn't much. (Go to the Sahara Grill across the highway instead). Rates in-season start around US$140 double, plus tax, but it pays to get a "premier" room at around US$160 and up. Parking, while limited, is in a guarded and fenced lot.

Black Orchid Resort. 2 Dawson Lane, Burrell Boom Village, 501-225-9158 or 866-437-1301 in U.S./Canada; www.blackorchidresort.com. This is a relaxing, if somewhat pricey, alternative to the crime and bustle of Belize City, and it's about the same distance from the international airport as the city centre. The Belizean-owned resort is on the Belize River, and you can launch a canoe, kayak or powerboat from the hotel's dock, or just laze about the riverside swimming pool and thatch palapa. The air-conditioned gardenview rooms start at US$150 double in-season, US$125 off-season, plus 9% tax and 10% service) are large, with custom-made mahogany furnishings. Riverview rooms are more expensive, US$225 in-season and US$195 off, plus tax and service. New luxury suites top out over US$300 with tax and service. The on-site restaurant serves good Belizean food and gets quite a few locals. Tours are available.

D'Nest Inn. 475 Cedar Street, 501-223-5416; www.dnestinn.com. D'Nest Inn is a B&B run by Gaby and Oty Ake. Gaby is a retired Belize banker, and Oty is originally from Chetumal. The Caribbean-style house is on a canal 50 feet from the Belize River. It's in an area called Belama Phase 2, a generally safe, middle-class section between the international airport and downtown. Oty's gardens around the house are filled with hibiscus, roses and other blossoming plants. The four guest rooms – all on the second floor up a flight of stairs -- are comfortable rather than deluxe, furnished with antiques such as a hand-carved, four-poster bed, but they also have modcons like free wi-fi, air-conditioning, and cable TV. Some could use a little sprucing up. With a private entrance and your own key, you come and go as you like. Rates are US$82-92 double and include a delicious breakfast. Recommended, mainly due to the gracious hospitality by the owners.

Global Village Hotel. Mile 8½, Philip Goldson Highway, 501-225-2555; www.globalvillagehotel.com. If you have an early morning flight out or you're overnighting en route somewhere else, the Global Village Hotel (actually it's more of a motel than a hotel) is a decent choice near the international airport. The 40 rooms are clean and modern, at around US$55 double, including a basic continental breakfast and airport shuttle. This Chinese-owned place is located just south of the turnoff to the international airport.

Villa Boscardi. 6043 Manatee Drive, Buttonwood Bay, 501-223-1691; www.villaboscardi.com. This quiet and tasteful bed and breakfast is in an upscale part of Belize City north of the city centre, It's usually rated the best B&B in the city. In fact, it's near the current prime minister's home. European-owned, Villa Boscardi has eight clean, attractive rooms, all with air conditioning, private bath, fan, desk, hair-drier, cable TV, wi-fi and phone. Rates are around US$100-$115 double, plus tax.

Dining in Belize City

In addition to the better choices listed below, greasy fried chicken is available as takeaway from small restaurants all over the city — a Belizean favorite known as "dollah chicken" whatever the price. The big hotels have their own restaurants, quite expensive but with varied menus and good service.

If you're shopping for groceries while in the city centre, **Brodies** is worth a look. It's on Albert Street, just past the park, and their selection of food is good if expensive, reflecting the fact that much is imported. Milk and dairy products, produced locally by Mennonite farmers, are delicious and good quality. Naturally enough, local fruit is cheap and plentiful, though highly seasonal — Belizean citrus fruits are among the best in the world. Fruits and vegetables are available at the Queen Square market near the Novelo's bus station. It has been renovated. Two modern supermarkets, a branch of **Brodies** and **Save-U**, are on the Goldson Highway on the way to the international airport. This Brodies outpost has been remodeled and expanded, with dry goods as well as groceries, and is the largest and most modem supermarket in the country.

Most restaurants in Belize City are closed for lunch on Sunday, and many are closed all day. Some are also closed for lunch on Saturday.

The pricing system for restaurants in all areas is as follow:

Inexpensive: Under US$7

Moderate: US$8-$19

Expensive: US$20-$39

Very Expensive: Over US$40

Prices don't include tips or alcoholic drinks. If not otherwise stated, the price range is for one person for dinner.

Chon Saan Palace. 1 Kelly Street, tel. 501-223-3008. This has been considered the best Chinese restaurant in Belize City for 30+ years, although the Friendship restaurant on the Goldson Highway now is preferred by some. Chon Saan serves fresh seafood and is Hong Kong style. Good fried chicken, too. Moderate.

Neries and Neries II. Corner of Queen and Daly Streets., 501-223-4028, with another location at Douglas Jones St., 501-224-5199. Popular local joints, serving Creole favorites including cow foot soup, barracuda, stew chicken and gibnut. Inexpensive to Moderate. Open for breakfast, lunch and dinner. Take a taxi after dark.

Riverside Tavern. 2 Mapp Street at North Front Street, 501-223-5640. Opened in 2006, this Bowen family-owned restaurant has become very popular. It's still our favorite spot to eat in the city. Riverside Tavern has the biggest and best burgers in Belize City and arguably in all of Belize, with a variety of other well-prepared dishes, including steaks. You can dine outside overlooking Haulover Creek or inside in cold air-conditioning, with views of the large bar and its TV sets. Parking is safe, in a fenced, guarded lot right in front of the restaurant. Recommended. Moderate to Expensive.

Sahara Grill. Vista Plaza, Mile 3½, Philip Goldson Highway, 501-203-3031. Reasonably priced Lebanese/Middle Eastern food. Try the chicken kabobs, falafel or hummus. Popular lunch spot, but also open for dinner. Closed Sunday. Inexpensive to Moderate.

Tender Bar & Grill. 8 Fort Street, Pier 1, 501-605-1620. Focuses on the cruise ship crowd – it's located where the cruise ship tenders drop off passengers, hence the name -- but other visitors and some locals praise it for its breezy waterside location, cheap drinks (the "soup of the day" sometimes is a two-buck daiquiri), good seafood and Belizean dishes such as stew chicken. Music is loud. Moderate.

Bird's Isle (90 Albert Street, South Side, 501-207-2179) is an institution in Belize City. Its location on the water is still nice, but the food of late is only so-so. If going after dark by all means take a taxi.

Where to Party in Belize City

Unless you know the city well, and go out with friends, it's best to do your drinking and partying at the bars of the city's main hotels, such as the Radisson Fort George and Ramada Princess Hotel & Casino, or in the more upscale restaurants, such as the Riverside Tavern. Don't venture out alone after dark in Belize City. If you need to go somewhere, take a taxi.

Rural Belize District
BABOON SANCTUARY

The **Community Baboon Sanctuary** (Burrell Boom village, 501-245-2009, open 8-5 daily, admission US$7) is a community organization of around 200 members in seven villages who banded together in 1985 to protect black howler monkeys, called baboons by local people. The effort was successful, and there are now about 3,000 monkeys in the sanctuary.

Spend a few minutes in the small visitor center and then take a guided tour to see monkeys. **Black Orchid Resort** *(see above)* is nearby, as is **Belize River Lodge** (501-225-20002, www.belizeriverlodge.com), the oldest fishing lodge in Belize.

CROOKED TREE

Crooked Tree, a reference to the crooked cashew tree, is famous for the number and variety of birds that flock here, especially in the dry season (February to early June). The sanctuary and village are a little over 30 miles north of Belize City. You may see the jabiru stork, the largest bird in the Americas. It stands nearly as tall as a human, with a wingspan of up to 12 feet. Even if you're not a birder, you'll appreciate the beauty of the Crooked Tree lagoon. Coming from the Philip Goldson Highway across the causeway toward Crooked Tree village, an old and predominantly Creole settlement, you'll see cattle cooling themselves in the lagoon, with their egret pals. Check in at the visitor center at the end of the causeway. You'll get a map and can walk or drive around the village, nearby bush trails and the lagoon front. Or ask about a local guide. Canoes are available for rent, too. Admission: US$4.

Crooked Tree Lodge. Crooked Tree Wildlife Sanctuary, 501-626-3820; www.crookedtreelodgebelize.com. Formerly Paradise Lodge, this lodge on more than 11 acres was rebuilt and redone by a Belizean-English couple. It's now the best place to stay in Crooked Tree. There are six nice cabañas (starting at around US$60-$75 plus tax) on the shores of Crooked Tree Lagoon. A main lodge building houses a restaurant and bar. Camping (US$10) also available. As of this writing, the lodge is for sale.

Birds Eye View Lodge. Crooked Tree Wildlife Sanctuary, 501-203-2040, fax 222-4869; www.birdseyeviewlodge.com. Birds Eye View Lodge is a modern two-story concrete hotel, just a few steps from the lagoon, covered with climbing vines and flowers. The hotel's 20 renovated rooms are modest but clean – rooms on the second floor generally are larger and you have access to the patio with great views of the lagoon. The Belizean management and staff are friendly. The hotel's dining room serves tasty Creole fare. Doubles are around US$80 to $120 in high season, plus hotel tax and 10% service. Continental breakfast is US$6, lunch is US$12, dinner US$15. The hotel can arrange birding, local tours, canoe rentals and such.

ALTUN HA

Altun Ha (off Old Northern Highway about 35 miles north of Belize City via the Philip Goldson Highway, Old Northern Highway and Altun Ha access road, daily 9-5, admission US$5) is currently the most-visited Maya site in Belize, mainly because of day trippers from cruise ships and from Ambergris Caye who go on day tours that include a quick visit to this Pre-Classic site settled some 2,000 years ago. There's a visitor center, gift shop and craft sales area. If you decide you want to stay overnight near Altun Ha, or just have a nice lunch, the main choice is **Maruba Resort Jungle Spa** (Mile 40.5, Old Northern Highway, Maskall village, 501-713-799-2031 or 800-617-8227, www.maruba-spa.com). Overnight rates start at around US$200 and go up to several times that amount. We don't recommend that you buy the viper rum, in a bottle with a snake in it.

GALES POINT AREA

The Northern and Southern lagoons near Gales Point, about 55 miles south of Belize City by road, are excellent places to spot West Indian manatees. There is a "manatee hole" fed by warm under-water springs, about 200 yards off the peninsula point northeast, where manatees are commonly seen. Some of the manatees have been tagged with radio transmitters, which permit researchers to track their movements. Tours from Gales Point will take you on manatee watching trips, or you can arrange with someone in the Creole village of Gales Point to take you out. The village has a manatee guides association. When out manatee spotting, please be respectful of your fellow mammals. Responsible guides (and visitors) don't get too close to these huge, gentle creatures, nor do they try to swim with them or touch them. Gales Point is off the regular tourist track in Belize. There is no longer bus service to Gales Point from Dangriga or elsewhere, so you'll need a car or take a taxi from Dangriga. Very basic accommodations are available in local homes in Gales Point village. Near Gales Point are several miles of beach — not so good for swimming, but hawksbill turtles nest here.

Manatee Lodge. Gales Point (P.O. Box 1242, Belize City), 501-532-2400; www.manateelodge.com. If you like the British Honduras colonial atmosphere, with a truly lovely setting on a lagoon, this might be your cup of tea. There are eight rooms with polished hardwood floors, private baths, 24-hour electricity and jalousie windows in an old white frame building beside the Southern Lagoon. Doubles start at about US$90 plus 9% tax and 10% service. Package plans including transportation from Belize City, meals and tours are available, starting at around US$600 per person for three nights. Canoes are complimentary. Among other tours, the hotel offers a half-day boat tour, which includes manatee watching and a visit to Ben Loman cave.

Part of now paved Barrier Reef Drive in San Pedro

CHECKING OUT AMBERGRIS CAYE

Getting to San Pedro

Getting to San Pedro is easy as caye lime pie, but it does require at least one stop along the way. There is no international air service direct to San Pedro's little airstrip, although the current Belize government supports building a new international airport on North Ambergris.

From Belize City: You can either fly or take a water taxi to San Pedro (or to Caye Caulker). It's a 20-minute flight to San Pedro; the boat trip takes about 75 minutes. The two Belize airlines, Maya Island Air and Tropic Air, each have about one flight per hour every day to San Pedro, starting at around 7:30 a.m. and ending around 5:30 p.m. In peak visitor season, additional flights may be added to accommodate demand.

Flights originate from both the International Airport in Ladyville about 9 miles north of Belize City, where your international flight arrives, and Municipal Airport, a small airstrip in Belize City. In some cases the same Maya Island and Tropic flight picks up passengers at both airports, making the short hop between the two in a few minutes.

Should you fly to San Pedro from International or Municipal? The answer depends on whether you'd rather save time or money. It's easier just to fly into international and walk over to the domestic terminal and catch your connecting puddle jumper.

But you'll save a little money, especially if traveling in a party of several people, by flying from Municipal. Adult and child one-way fares on both Maya Island and Tropic are approximately US$95 from international, including security charges; from municipal, adult one-way is around US$55. So you're saving roughly US$40 per person. Round-trip fares are just slightly less than twice one way. Only rarely are there bargain fares or discounts for advance booking. Sometimes, mainly in the summer, the Belize airlines will offer discounts if you pay cash, rather than use a credit card.

Transferring between the airports requires a 20-minute taxi ride. A taxi from international to municipal is US$25 for up to four passengers. A tip isn't necessary unless the driver carries a lot of your luggage, in which case add a couple of bucks. Taxis – they have green license tags – are plentiful and await passengers just outside the main lobby on the international airport. You can do the math.

Do you need to make reservations for Maya Island or Tropic flights in advance? Off-season, it's not really necessary, though having a reservation won't hurt. In-season, a reservation might save a wait. Most hotels on Ambergris Caye will arrange for your air travel to the island at the time you make your hotel reservations, and there's usually no extra cost to you (the hotel gets a small commission). You also can book direct with the airlines by telephone or over the internet. Here's contact information:

Maya Island Air: 501-226-3838; schedules, fares and reservations at www.mayaislandair.com.

Tropic Air: 800-422-3435 or 501-226-2012; schedules, fares and reservations at www.tropicair.com.

Astrum Helicopters (George Price Highway, near Belize City, 501-222-5100, www.astrumhelicopters.com) offers VIP transfers of guests to selected hotels on Ambergris Caye and elsewhere. Astrum also offers helicopter charters, tours, and aerial photography trips, plus medevac service.

If you are going to San Pedro or Caye Caulker, you also have the option of taking a **water taxi.** There are now two main water taxi companies connecting Belize City with San Pedro and also Caye Caulker. From Belize City it's 75 minutes to San Pedro.

Ocean Ferry (501-223-0033, www.oceanferrybelize.com) boats leave from the Marine Terminal in Belize City at 10 North Front Street near the Swing Bridge. **San Pedro Belize Express** (501-223-2225, www.belizewatertaxi.com) boats leave from the Brown Sugar dock at 111 North Front Street near the Tourism Village.

Ocean Ferry, which currently has five departures daily from Belize City to San Pedro, charges US$24.50 round-trip between Belize City and San Pedro. San Pedro Belize Express, which has around eight or nine departures to San Pedro from Belize City, charges US$35 round-trip between Belize City and San Pedro.

Coming from Mexico or Northern Belize:

An option that became available recently is to fly from Cancún to Belize City (the international airport) on **Tropic Air.** From there you can fly or water taxi to San Pedro. Currently there are two flights daily from Cancún International Airport, one in the early afternoon and one in the late afternoon. The regular one-way fare is a rather pricey US$292. Tropic also flies from Mérida to Belize City.

A cheaper option from Cancún to Belize City is to take the ADO *bus (see below).*

Another option from Chetumal is ferries. **San Pedro Belize Express** (501-223-2225, www.belizewatertaxi.com) has service every other day between the municipal pier in Chetumal and San Pedro a trip of about 90 minutes to San Pedro, for US$50 one-way Chetumal-San Pedro and US$100 round-trip.

Another water taxi company, **San Pedro Water Taxi,** (501-226-2194, www.sanpedrowatertaxi.com) also has service between Chetumal and San Pedro. One-way fares are US$60 between San Pedro and Chetumal and US$120 round-trip.

Water taxi fares usually do not include US$5 port fees in Mexico or the exit fee of US$18.75 when leaving Belize. You may also have to pay a 295 Mexican peso fee leaving Mexico, if you have not already paid it on arrival (if you flew into Cancún, it probably was included in your air ticket.)

Note that the water taxi business in Belize is changing. Check locally on providers, schedules and prices.

Many travelers, however, will come from Mexico or from northern Belize. To get to San Pedro, you have several options:

1) Take the **ADO Express** overnight bus from Cancún to Belize City, then fly or water taxi to the island. In late 2011, ADO began two express services to Belize City – a daily one from Cancún and one from Mérida (where Belizeans often go for medical care) that now runs three or four days a week. The ADO buses are much nicer than Belize buses, with 44 reserved reclining seats, videos, bathroom and air conditioning. From Cancún, the ADO bus leaves from the Cancún bus station in downtown Cancún City. In Belize City, ADO uses the main Belize City bus terminal (still known as Novelo's) located on West Collet Canal.

From Cancún to Belize City, the ADO bus departs from Cancún terminal daily at 10:15 p.m., with stops at Playa del Carmen, Tulum, Corozal Town and Orange Walk Town. It arrives in Belize City about 6 or 6:30 a.m. The current fare (subject to increase) is 576 Mexican pesos one-way or about US$35 at current exchange rates. Trip time is about 8 hours.

2) Transfer services in Corozal and elsewhere in Belize will also pick you up in Cancún or elsewhere in Mexico and bring you to Corozal or to Belize City. Belize **VIP Transfer Service** (www.belizetransfers.com) is one of several. You'll pay US400 for up to four persons from Cancún to Corozal, US$350 from Playa del Carmen, US$300 from Tulum, US$45 from Bacalar and around US$30 from Chetumal.

3) There is a water taxi from Corozal directly to San Pedro. There's one boat a day, operated by **Thunderbolt.** It departs Corozal from the pier near Reunion Park at 7 a.m. and returns from San Pedro at 3 p.m., stopping at Sarteneja on demand. Fare is US$25 one-way. Check departure times locally, as they may change, and service may be reduced at times in the off-season.

4) If you are coming from Corozal you can fly nonstop to San Pedro, a trip that takes about 25 minutes. **Tropic Air** has five flights a day from Corozal to San Pedro, for around US$72 one-way. **Maya Island Air** has several flights a day, for about the same price.

WHERE TO STAY: TOWN? NORTH? SOUTH?

Probably the biggest decision you'll make about Ambergris Caye is where to stay. We're not talking about a specific hotel but about the general area. The area you choose will determine to a great degree the experience you have on the island. You have four basic options:

1) in the town of San Pedro

2) just to the south of San Pedro near the airstrip, within walking distance of town

3) on the south end, beyond easy walking distance to town

4) on the north end of the island above the channel.

There is no one "best" place to stay. Each of these four areas has advantages and disadvantages. Which area you choose depends on what you want from your vacation. If you're looking for privacy and the feeling of being away from it all, consider the south end or the north end of the island. If you prefer easy access to restaurants, nightlife, shops and other activities, you'll likely be happier in San Pedro town or just to the south. There's little advantage to any one area in terms of beaches, although the beaches in town tend to be more crowded with boats than those outside of town and in general are less desirable for swimming.

HEART OF TOWN: Hotels in the town of San Pedro, with a few notable exceptions, are older spots, among them the original tourist hotels on the island. They are, again with a few exceptions, less expensive digs. If you're looking to save a buck or two, this may be the place for you. You also will be right in the heart of things, no more than a few sandy blocks from some of the best restaurants, bars, shops and dive operations on the island. Party animals will want to stay here or just the south of town. Accommodations here include Ruby's, Holiday Hotel, Spindrift, Lily's, Martha's, Sanpedrano, Mayan Princess, Hotel del Rio and Ocean Tides. More expensive options in town include The Phoenix, SeaBreeze Suites and Paradise Villas.

AIRSTRIP SOUTH: If you want a larger variety of moderate and upscale lodging but still want to be within walking distance of the attractions of San Pedro Town, think about staying at the south edge of town and the area just to the south of town. The San Pedro airstrip is here, but you should have few or no problems with airport noise, since the planes are small one- and two-engine prop jobs. This is a good compromise between the activity of town and the remoteness of the north end and far south end. Among the hotels here are SunBreeze, The Palms, Belizean Reef Suites, Ramon's Village, Exotic Caye, Coconuts, Coral Bay Villas, Caribbean Villas, Belize Yacht Club and Changes in Latitudes.

SOUTH END: Although most of this area is beyond a quick walk to town, this is a major growth area for tourism on the island. Some of the nicer upmarket hotels are located here, and more are on the way. An increasing number of restaurants and amenities also are located here. At the far end, you're two to three miles from San Pedro, so for visits to town you'll need to rent a golf cart (US$60 to $75 for 24 hours), ride a bike (some hotels offer them free to guests), take a taxi (about US$5 to town) or take a hotel shuttle, if available. Among the choices here are Villas at Banyan Bay, Grand Colony, Banana Beach, Mata Rocks, Royal Palm, Victoria House, Caribe Island Resort, Royal Caribbean, Sunset Beach and Pelican Reef Villas.

NORTH AMBERGRIS: By all accounts, the area north of "the River" or "the Cut" – a narrow channel of water separating the south and north ends of the island – is where much of Ambergris Caye's growth will occur over the next decade or two. Houses, hotels and restaurants have been going up here at an increasing pace.

At present, though, access is limited by the fact that there are only two ways to get to the north end: One is by boat, usually a water taxi, either scheduled or on-demand. The other is via a bridge, which opened in 2006. In 2014-2015, part of the former golf cart path up North Ambergris was paved. Currently paving is under way to the Portofino area and eventually will go about 8 miles north of the bridge to around La Beliza Resort (formerly Blue Reef). Crossing the bridge costs US$2.50 each way for a golf cart or other vehicle, US$1 for a pedestrian. Work trucks pay much more. Weekly and longer passes are available. A monthly pass is US$75. The Coastal Xpress water taxi is US$5 to $14 per person one-way, more to resorts farther north. When going north, bring plenty of bug spray for use when you're away from the water.

You also may want to stock up on snacks, groceries (if you're doing a lot of cooking in your condo) and some rum. Isolated resorts on North Ambergris may have set, and limited, restaurant and bar hours. You never know when the munchies will strike!

Accommodations on the north end include Cocotel Inn, White Cove Resort, Ak'Bol Yoga Retreat & Eco Resort, Grand Caribe, El Pescador, Capricorn, Captain Morgan's, Coco Beach, Belizean Shores, Seascape Villas, Las Terrazas, Azul, Matachica, Portofino, Tan Ha, La Beliza and Tranquility Bay.

Not on Ambergris but close by, off the backside of the island, is the ultra-expensive all-inclusive, Cayo Espanto.

Here are approximate distances, in driving miles, of hotels and resorts from Central Park, more or less in the center of San Pedro Town. Your mileage may vary.

SOUTH END

Pelican Reef	2.8 miles south
Athens Gate	2.6 miles south
Miramar Villas	2.5 miles south
Sunset Beach Resort	2.5 miles south
Royal Caribbean Resort	1.9 miles south
Victoria House	1.8 miles south
Mata Rocks	1.4 miles south
Banana Beach Resort	1.4 miles south
Grand Colony	1.3 miles south
The Villas at Banyan Bay	1.2 miles south

AIRSTRIP AREA AND SOUTH

Xanadu	1 mile south
Caribbean Villas	1 mile south
Coral Bay Villas	1 mile south
Coconuts Caribbean	.9 miles south
Corona del Mar	.9 miles south
Exotic Caye Beach Resort	.8 miles south
Changes in Latitudes	.6 miles south
Pedro's Hotel	.6 miles south
Ramon's Village	.4 miles south
The Palms	.4 miles south
Belizean Reef Suites	.3 miles south
Sunbreeze Hotel	.3 miles south

IN TOWN

Ruby's	.2 miles south
Holiday Hotel	.2 miles south
Coral Beach Hotel	.2 miles south
Spendrift Hotel	.1 miles south
Martha's Hotel	.1 miles south

Hostel La Vista	.0 miles
Mayan Princess	.0 miles
Hotel Sanpedrano	.0 miles
Conch Shell	.1 miles north
SeaBreeze Suites	.1 miles north
The Phoenix	.3 miles north
Paradise Villas	.3 miles north
Blue Tang Inn	.4 miles north
Caye Casa	.5 miles north
Ocean Tides	.5 miles north
Hotel del Rio	.7 miles north

NORTH AMBERGRIS

Ak'Bol	2.0 miles north
Grand Caribe	2.5 miles north
Cocotal Inn	2.5 miles north
El Pescador	2.9 miles north
Capricorn	3.0 miles north
Capt. Morgan's Retreat	3.1 miles north
Coco Beach	3.1 miles north
Seascape Villas	3.2 miles north
Belizean Shores	3.3 miles north
Las Terrazas	3.8 miles north
Azul Resort/Rojo Bar	5.1 miles north
Matachica	5.2 miles north
Portofino Resort	6.0 miles north
Xtan Ha	7.1 miles north
La Beliza	8.1 miles north
Sueño del Mar	11.5 miles north
Tranquility Bay	12.0 miles north

How to Get the Best Hotel Rates

Ambergris Caye hotel rates are not cheap, running US$150-$400+ double in high season, although rooms are available for under US$25, and you can pay US$600 or more a night. Rates in San Pedro, however, are about the same as in resort areas of Mexico and Costa Rica and generally are far less than on Caribbean islands such as St. Maarten/St. Martin, Anguilla or St. Thomas.

There are several things you can do to enjoy lower prices. The most obvious is simply to go off-season, when most hotels drop rates 20 to 40%. Exact dates vary from hotel to hotel, but the low season generally starts just after Easter and runs until about mid-November. The island has more than 60 hotels and condotels. Annual occupancy rates on the island average in the 50% range, and there are normally rooms available even in high season, although some popular spots may be full in-season. Easter and Christmas/New Years periods are usually almost fully booked.

With most hotels having excess capacity, particularly in September and October and to a lesser degree also in the other off-season months, discounts of several types are available. In the off-season, many hotels have "walk-in" rates. These rates, typically 15 to 20% off the already discounted summer rates, can be real values.

Some hotels on Ambergris Caye also post special discounted rates for September to mid-November period, the slowest time of the year for tourism. Often you can get an extra day or two free – for example, stay four nights and get the fifth free.

Some hotels also offer sizable discounts for stays of a week or longer, or have a value package such as "stay seven nights/pay for five." Frequently, hotels offer discounts for internet or other direct bookings, saving them travel agent or wholesaler commissions. These direct booking discounts usually range from 10 to 20%, and occasionally are as much as 40%.

We've noted recently that more and more properties are posting rack rates on their websites and then showing "Special" or "X% Off" rates. These may or may not be true discounts.

When booking, always ask, "Is that your best rate?" or "Do you have a lower rate?" or "That's a little more than I was hoping to pay – is there a way I can get a better rate?" Keep probing to find out if you're getting the best price. Most hotels require a deposit to hold reservations, usually nonrefundable or only partially refundable.

Nearly all hotels on the island accept Visa and MasterCard. Some accept American Express. Only a few accept Discover. If credit cards are not accepted, this is noted in the hotel reviews. A few hotels still surcharge credit cards by 5% or so, but this practice happily is rare now.

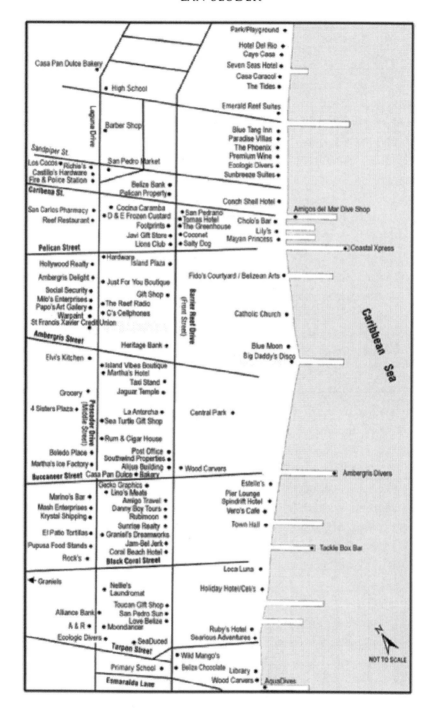

A further note about seagrass and seaweed: In the last year or two (2015 and 2016), there has been an unusually abundant crop of seagrass or Sargasso seaweed on beaches in Belize, especially on Ambergris Caye. The hotels do what they can to keep their beaches cleared, but often it gets ahead of them, piles up and raises an unpleasant odor. Keep telling yourself that this is part of the natural ecosystem of the sea and the barrier reef.

Types of Lodging

You have several different types of lodging from which to choose on Ambergris Caye:

Condotels: These are condominiums run like a hotel. Units are individually owned and rented to visitors by on-site management that typical takes 40 to 60% of the gross. They have most of the same amenities as a regular hotel, except usually not a restaurant. Most condotels on Ambergris Caye are not the large sprawling condo complexes found in Florida or Hawaii. They are small, only two or three stories high, with from one to three dozen units. Typically they have a mix of one- and two-bedroom units; some have three-bedroom suites. The advantage of a condotel is that you get a lot more space, including a kitchen, for a price not much more than for a regular hotel. The drawback is that most condotels do not offer the range of services of a hotel, such as room service. Condotels range in price from under US$100 to over US$600 a night. Among the condotels on Ambergris Caye are Villas at Banyan Bay, Belizean Shores, Coral Bay Villas, Mayan Princess, Grand Colony, Grand Caribe, Pelican Reef Villas, Athens Gate and Xanadu.

Beachside cabañas and cottages: These come in two flavors – thatch and not. Thatch cabañas have thatch roofs and palapa-style walls, usually over concrete block or wood frames. Among resorts with thatch cabañas (in some cases, only some units are thatch) includes Portofino, Captain Morgan's, Ramon's Village, Exotic Caye, Xanadu and Victoria House. Note that a fire destroyed much of Ramon's Village in 2013, but it was quickly rebuilt. Another fire destroyed three buildings at Exotic Caye in 2015. As of this writing the structures have not been rebuilt; it is likely the entire complex eventually will be replaced with a more upscale resort. Other properties have more traditional wood-frame or concrete cottages or cabins. Beachside cabañas are available from around US$75 to more than US$600 a night.

Hotels: Many of the hotels, even larger ones, on the island are personality inns. Most are small, with fewer than 40 rooms, and all are low rise. Hotels come in all price ranges, from US$15 to over US$400 a night. Nearly all the hotels, except for a few budget places, are on the water.

Privately owned houses for vacation rental: Scores of private homes and villas are available on Ambergris Caye for weekly rental. Rates start at around US$1,500 a week and go up to US$8,000 or more. Check Air BnB (www.airbnb.com), Vacation Rentals by Owner (www.vrbo.com) and TripAdvisor (www.tripadvisor.com) for listings and availabilities. Also, a local company, Caye Management (www.cayemanagement.com) has some listings.

Longer-term rentals: Monthly rentals of houses and apartments are available, starting at around US$400 for a small apartment, though most rentals are US$500 to $2,000 and up. The best way to find a rental is to ask around in person.

Camping: There are currently no campgrounds on Ambergris Caye, and camping, unless on your own land or on other private land with permission, is prohibited. Caye Caulker has a small private campground, and primitive camping is available on some outlying cayes, including Half Moon Caye.

What to See and Do on the Ambergris Caye
You come to Ambergris Caye to relax, enjoy good food and drink and take part in beach and water activities, especially snorkeling and diving.

Snorkeling and Diving
Hol Chan Marine Reserve (www.holchanbelize.org), which includes Shark Ray Alley, is the most popular snorkeling site in Belize. On nice days, especially when cruise ships are in port in Belize City, small dive and snorkel boats are lined up at Hol Chan and especially at Shark Ray Alley, where you can swim with nurse sharks and sting rays. The reserve, which covers about 3 square miles, is located 4 miles off the southern tip of the island, accessible only by boat. Hol Chan, Maya for "Little Channel," is on the west side of a narrow cut or channel, only about 80 feet wide, in the barrier reef. Note that due to the wave and tidal activity through the narrow channel, snorkelers and divers must be cautious. Several snorkelers have died in accidents here. Weak swimmers and small children probably should not get in the water here, especially on windy days with rough seas and heavy currents. In San Pedro Town is the Hol Chan visitor and information

center on Caribeña Street, open daily 9 to 5. The marine reserve fee is
US$12.50 per person, usually collected by the dive and snorkel tour
operators that take visitors out to the reserve. Fishing is not permitted within
the reserve. It is also illegal to touch or hold sharks, rays or other sea life
here, although guides routinely do it. Snorkel trips to Hol Chan typically
cost around US$45 to $65, depending on the operator and whether or not
marine reserve fees and snorkel gear are included. Two-tank local dives to
Hol Chan and elsewhere on the reef near San Pedro generally are US$75-
$85 plus any rental fees. When booking dive or snorkel trip, ask if the
reserve fee and equipment rental are included. See below for some of the
many dive and snorkel operators on the island.

Bacalar Chico Marine Reserve (501-226-2833) is at the opposite
end of Ambergris Caye from Hol Chan. Mexico Rocks. It comprises about
23 square miles of sea and land area, from the Mexican border at the north
tip of Ambergris Caye, where Maya traders cut a narrow channel between
what is now Belize and Mexico, to the Robles Point area of the island. It
includes areas of both the Caribbean Sea and Corozal Bay. At Rocky Point
in the reserve the reef comes close to the shore, the only point on the island
where it does. There is a loggerhead and green sea turtle nesting site
between Robles and Rocky Point. Offshore is a seasonal spawning area for
Nassau and yellowfin groupers and is breeding area for the endangered
queen conch. Manatee and bottle-nose dolphins visit Bacalar. On land are
a surprisingly large number of animals, including on occasion all five of
Belize's five wild cats, plus crocodiles and hundreds of species of birds. On
the small cayes on the back side of Ambergris are the "bird isles" where you
can see breeding colonies of roseate spoonbills, white ibises, tricolor heron,
egrets, cormorants, frigatebirds and others. There at least nine known Maya
sites in the reserve. **Bacalar Chico Expeditions** (www.bacalarchico.org)
is an organization established by Green Reef Environmental Institute of
Ambergris Caye. Bacalar Chico Expeditions trains guides to operate tours
of the reserve, runs diving, fly fishing, kayaking and canoeing and other trips
to Bacalar Chico. It also operates education programs and stays at cabins
near the reserve.

Belize Barrier Reef runs all along the east side of Ambergris Caye.
It comes almost to the shore at Robles Point but is about a half mile from
the beaches along most of the island. You can watch the waves break on the
reef. The reef, part of the Meso-American Barrier Reef, is a UNESCO

World Heritage Site.

Mexico Rocks is a popular snorkeling site off North Ambergris, a little over 4 miles north of San Pedro. Water depth is only about 10 to 12 feet. A patch reef system known for its live formations of staghorn, elk horn, brain and other coral, along with tropical fish, it is now a Marine Protected Area.

Dive and Snorkel Shops

Nearly every hotel on Ambergris Caye has a dive shop or a relationship with one. Most are pretty good, although your experience may vary depending on the particular dive master and crew you happen to draw. Prices are higher than you'd probably like, especially compared with Honduras and Mexico.

Here are a few of the well-thought-of shops (not a complete list):

Ambergris Divers Belize (www.ambergrisdivers.com)
Amigos del Mar (www.amigosdivebelize.com)
Belize Pro Dive Center (www.belizeprodivecenter.com)
Ecologic Divers (www.ecologicdivers.com)
Hugh Parkey's Dive Connection (www.hpbelizeadventures.com)
Island Divers Belize (www.islanddiversbelize.com)
Ramon's Village (www.ramons.com)
White Sands Dive Shop (www.whitesandsdiveshop.com)

Other Attractions

There are not many cultural or historical attractions on the island, but there are a few:

San Pedro House of Culture (Angel Coral Street, 501-226-4531, 8-5 daily, free admission) is the newest National Institute of Culture (NICH) House of Culture in Belize. It's small, but it's a start. There are a few artifacts from Marco Gonzalez Maya site (see below) along with some exhibits relating to life in San Pedro.

Marco Gonzalez (501-662-2725, www.marcogonzalezmayasite.com) is the most significant of about 19 known Maya sites on Ambergris Caye. At the height of the Maya settlement of Ambergris Caye, an estimated 20,000 Maya lived on the island (about the present-day population of the island). There's evidence that during the Maya period the island was larger than it is now, since the sea level here has risen as much as 2 feet over the past two millennia, capturing much of the land area. Many Maya were engaged in trading with other Maya cities to the north and south. Marco Gonzalez dates back to around 100 BC with occupation until at least 1500 CE. The site is located at the far south end of the island, about a half-hour golf cart ride from San Pedro Town. Marco Gonzalez has been partially excavated, but much of it was looted. Since 2011, the site has been under the supervision of the National Institute of Culture. There's a visitor center, and tours are available for US$10, not including transportation to the site, which costs around US$8 if you don't provide your own transportation.

If you're staying on Ambergris Caye, do try to see the "other side" of Belize, notably the mainland. Even Caye Caulker will give you a different perspective. It's easy to get to either by water taxi or air.

Ambergris Caye Lodging

These hotel reviews are candid and are not influenced by advertising (we accept none) or by comps. Keep in mind that hotel reviews, like movie reviews, are matters of opinion. Your mileage may vary.

Also, keep in mind that things change – rates, amenities, management. We routinely check with properties for current and projected rates. Note that rates for the Christmas, New Year's and Easter holidays may be higher than those shown here, and minimum stays may be required for those prime holiday periods.

SAN PEDRO TOWN

(Listed from the north to south. From Hotel Del Rio, Ocean Tides and Caye Casa, it is about a 10-minute walk along the beach to the main part of town.)

Hotel Del Rio. Boca Del Rio Drive, 501-226-2286; www.hoteldelriobelize.com. At this small seafront operation, you have the choice of several types of rooms and cabañas, some with thatched roofs. This is not a fancy resort, but it has personality some other places lack. In-season doubles are US$60 to $150, off-season US$50 to $130, plus 9% tax. Weekly rates are US$600 except at Christmas. Worth considering if you're watching your pennies and want a bit of thatch ambiance.

Ocean Tides Beach Resort. 57 Boca Del Rio Drive, 501-631-6863; www.tidesbeachresort.com. Formerly The Tides and started by well-known Sanpedrano divemaster Patojo Paz, under new ownership this little resort has been upscaled and slightly expanded. It still focuses somewhat on divers, and you'll often see wet suits and dive gear hanging over the balcony. The three-story hotel has rooms and suites with pleasant furnishings. No restaurant, but several good ones are nearby, and there's a small beach bar and a pool. Rates range from around US$100 to US$275, plus tax, depending on the time of year and unit. Dive packages also available.

Caye Casa. Beachfront, San Pedro, 501-226-2880 or 888-480-4535 in U.S./Canada; www.cayecasa.com. Caye Casa, developed by the multi-talented Julie Babcock, is on the beachfront at the north end of town. Although there's some seagrass off the beach, swimming is good from the pier. The resort has three types of accommodations – rooms, casitas and deluxe one- and two-bedroom villas. Though modern, it has tropical colonial touches, such as thatch-roof porches. Rates in-season range from US$125 for a room to US$410 for a two-bedroom villa, off-season from US$110 to $350. Rates are plus a total of 15% tax and service charge. The hotel will pick you up from the airstrip or water taxi at no charge.

Paradise Villas. Pescador Drive, San Pedro. Paradise Villas is an older but still attractive low-rise condo colony at the north end of town. The units, individually owned, are managed and rented by several different companies, plus several owners of one or two units. This can make it difficult to compare rates and accommodations. Choose from one-, two- and three-bedroom condos. Though units vary in furnishings and amenities, they are basically similar. There's an attractive seaside pool area, and a small artificial reef at the end of the pier (built by the condo owners) to attract fish for snorkeling. Rates vary slightly among the different agents, but most are in the range of US$125 to $275 in-season and US$100 to $235 off-season, plus tax. Rates are higher at Christmas. Among the companies offering rentals here are Paradise Villas in Belize (www.paradisevillasinbelize.com), Nellie Gomez (www.nelliesproperty.com) and Tradewinds Paradise Villas (www.tradewindsparadisevillas.com), which manages eight Paradise Villas units. You may also find units offered through Vacation Rentals By Owner (www.vrbo.com).

Blue Tang Inn. Sand Piper Street, 866-881-1020 in the U.S./Canada, 501-226-2326; www.bluetanginn.com. Blue Tang Inn, at the north end of town, is sometimes billed as a B&B, although we think inn describes it better. The 14 studio-type suites with kitchenettes in this three-story beachfront building are in good conditions, and there's a "cozy" swimming pool. There's also one small apartment. Rates US$129 to $229 off-season, US$155 to $255 in-season, plus 9% hotel tax. (For those who aren't divers, a Blue Tang is a colorful tropical fish seen around the barrier reef.)

The Phoenix. Barrier Reef Drive, San Pedro; 501-226-2083; www.thephoenixbelize.com. This beachfront condo resort is one of the best and most luxurious lodging spots on the island, if not in all of Belize. The winner of several "Best of" awards, The Phoenix is on the site of what used to be a retreat for Catholic nuns and later the location of the Paradise Hotel, one of classic old resorts on the island. The 30 condo units are absolutely gorgeous. The two-bedroom, two-bath units are around 1600 sq. ft., with deluxe kitchens, custom Belizean hardwood cabinets and trim, broadband internet and all the upscale amenities. There also are one-bedroom and three-bedroom units. If you can, get a ground floor unit right on the beach. There are two swimming pools, and an upscale restaurant, Red Ginger. Rates are US$425 to US$675 in-season and US$350 to US$575 in low season, plus tax. No service charge is added. Highly recommended.

Conch Shell Inn. 11 Foreshore Street, San Pedro; 501-226-2062; www.ambergriscaye.com/conchshell/. This heart-of-town, beachfront two-story hotel, is an option for money-conscious travelers who just want a clean, simple place to stay. There are fans but no air-conditioning in the 10 rooms. Second-floor rooms are probably a little cooler, as they catch the breeze off the sea, and quieter, too. Recently renovated. Rates US$74 to $94 double mid-November to mid-April, US$64 to $84 off-season, plus tax. Free wi-fi and mini-fridges.

Sanpedrano. Barrier Reef Drive, San Pedro; tel. 501-226-2054. Budget, six-room spot near but not on the water, located over a convenience store. Clean rooms starting at around US$35 with fan, US$45 with air-con, plus tax. Free wi-fi.

Mayan Princess. Barrier Reef Drive, (P.O. Box 79), San Pedro; 501-226-2778 or 800-250-6972 in U.S./Canada; www.mayanprincesshotel.com. This three-story, seafront condotel, painted a distinctive coral pink, has 23 large one-bedroom suites (king or queen beds) with air conditioning, kitchenettes, phones and cable TV. Rates are a good value at US$120 double off-season, US$155 in-season, plus 9% hotel tax and 10% service. Get 10% off if you book at least 90 days in advance. Dive packages available. Amigos del Mar dive shop is nearby. No pool, but each suite has a balcony with wonderful views of the sea, although swimming here in the middle of town isn't the best on the island. However, the whole atmosphere is comfortable and homey.

Hostel La Vista. Barrier Reef Drive, San Pedro, 501-627-0831; www.hostellavista.com. Right in the middle of things, across from Central Park and the sea, and next door to Jaguar nightclub, this purple hostel with green trim has space from around US$20 per person, plus tax. There's an eight-bed dorm, a six-bed dorm, some private rooms and a kitchen, plus space outside to lounge in a hammock. Free wi-fi and air conditioning. Before it opened as a hostel in late 2014, it was the old Sands Hotel, which was one of the early hotels on the island, dating from the 1970s. Because it's prime real estate, it probably won't last forever as cheap lodging.

Spindrift. Barrier Reef Drive, San Pedro, 501-226-2174; www.AmbergrisCaye.com/spindrift/. This three-story concrete hotel won't win any awards for design, but it is on the water in the center of town, with 20 rooms with A/C, four with fans and three one-bedroom apartments with kitchenettes. The lounge on the first floor hosts the "famous chicken drop" at which drinkers bet on where a chicken will poop. Rates year-round around US$53 to $150 including tax and service.

Holiday Hotel. Barrier Reef Drive, San Pedro, 713-893-3825 in the U.S./Canada; www.sanpedroholiday.com. This was one of the first hotels on the island, opening with five rooms June 15, 1965. Built by Celi McCorkle, an island native and near-legend in the hospitality industry, the three-story Holiday Hotel has been well maintained and remains a pleasant spot convenient to most everything in town. All rooms have A/C and some have refrigerators. Island Divers Belize dive shop is located on the hotel's pier. Celi's Deli across the street and the Caprice Bar are handy. Room rates are perhaps a bit higher than you'd expect: Off-season doubles are US$97 to $135, US$134-$212 in-season. Rates plus 9% tax and 6% service charge.

Ruby's. Barrier Reef Drive, San Pedro; 501-226-2063; www.rubyshotelbelize.com. This 23-room hotel at the south end of town is the favorite of many budget-oriented visitors. Rooms in the old wooden building section of the hotel, which opened in 1987, are basic but clean, some with shared baths; those on the street side can be a little noisy. Newer rooms, also basic, have private baths and some have air-conditioning. Some have sea views. Rates off-season range from around US$20 to $38 with fans,

US$50 with air-conditioning; in-season, rates are US$22 to $42 for rooms with fans, US$65 with air. Get inexpensive breakfasts and light meals in the first-floor restaurant, Ruby's Deli, which opens early to catch the fishing crowd. The hotel is often full. Free wi-fi.

SOUTH EDGE OF TOWN/AIRSTRIP SOUTH:
(Listed from north to south, with those nearest town listed first.)
SunBreeze Beach Hotel. Coconut Drive (P.O. Box 14) San Pedro, 800-688-0191 or 501-226-2191; www.sunbreeze.net. The SunBreeze has a good location, just steps from the San Pedro airstrip (but you won't be bothered by airport noise) and within walking distance of most of what there is to do in town. SunBreeze has been upgraded and considerably improved. A number of the rooms have been refurbished. There's a freshwater pool, above ground but nice. The pool is just steps from the Blue Water Grill restaurant. Many other restaurants are within a few blocks. SunBreeze has 43 large rooms, configured in a two-story motel-style U-shape. Five of them are billed as "premier" with amenities such as Jacuzzi tubs. All have strong air conditioners, telephones, color cable TV and tile floors. SunBreeze is directly on the water, with a dock and an independent dive shop, but there's a seawall and no real swimming beach. A good beach is at Ramon's nearby. The SunBreeze has handicap-accessible rooms, somewhat uncommon in Belize. Rates for doubles, in-season, US$188 to $248; off-season, US$156-$215, plus 9% tax and 6% service. Discounts may occasionally be offered. The same Belize City-based company, Roe Group, also operates San Pedro's **SunBreeze Suites** (www.sunbreezesuites.com) north in town, with small suites from US$173 off-season and US$199 in-season, plus tax and 6% service, along with the Belize Biltmore Plaza in Belize City and Hidden Valley Inn in the Mountain Pine Ridge. Roe Group has many other business interests in Belize.

The Palms. Coconut Drive (P.O. Box 88), San Pedro, 501-226-3322; www.belizepalms.com. This three-story condotel on the water has a lot going for it: attractive and well-decorated condominium apartments plus a small casita near the pool, which is small and on the back side but surrounded by tropical greenery, a sandy beach and a convenient location at the south edge of town. Rates off-season: casita, US$170; one-bedroom condo, US$219; two-bedroom US$244 to $271; three-bedroom, US$349; in-season: casita, US$204; one-bedroom, US$259, two-bedroom, US$289 to $319; three-bedroom, $399. Rates are for up to four persons, except in the casita, which is for double occupancy, but do not include plus 9% hotel tax and 10% service charge. Three-night minimum stay required.

Ramon's Village. Coconut Drive, San Pedro, 800-624-4215 in the U.S./Canada or 501-226-2071; www.ramons.com. Anyone who has heard of San Pedro has probably heard of Ramon's Village, the creation of Ambergris native and pioneering hotel operator Ramon Nuñez. Now American-owned, over the years it grew from a small, moderately priced collection of thatched cabañas on the beach into a much larger group of multiunit buildings and individual cabañas, with more than 70 rooms, suites and cottages. In August 2013, much of Ramon's was destroyed in a fire, but it was rebuilt and quickly reopened for the Christmas 2013 season. Ramon's retains its sand-and-thatch ambiance, and the resort has one of the better beaches on the island. Certainly, the beach is the best in or near town, part of the hotel's 500-foot water frontage. A small artificial reef near the 420-foot pier brings fish to snorkelers. The pool is gorgeous. Ramon's has a room service, free wi-fi, a popular bar and a restaurant called Pineapple. It has a big dive operation, which it says is the oldest in Belize, with two big dive boats and four skiffs. Lodging is divided into several categories, depending on location and size. All are air-conditioned and have free wi-fi. Across the street, not on the water, is a sister property, the Belizean Princess, with small cottages at lower rates. Ramon's location, just south of the airport, and a five-minute stroll from town appealing, although street traffic in this area is active, to say the least. Ramon's does a first-rate job of marketing, especially to travel agents, and it enjoys one of the highest occupancy rates on the island. Rates vary depending on location and date. In-season, cabañas are US$180 to $295 double, and suites are US$345 to $510. Off-season rates are a few dollars less. Rates at the cottage colony annex across the street are US$155 double in-season, US$150 off. All rates are plus 9% tax and 10% service.

Corona Del Mar. Coconut Drive, San Pedro; 501-226-2055, www.coronadelmarhotel.com. This is a low-profile lodging spot, but regulars know it offers pleasant rooms, recently renovated apartments on the water, a penthouse suite and a cottage, at fairly moderate rates (although they have increased some with the renovations and additions). It now has a pool. Point of history: Corona del Mar was the first hotel on the island with an elevator. Off-season rates US$90 to $180 (US$250 for the

LAN SLUDER

penthouse, cottage US$180); in-season US$130 to $250 (penthouse US$350, cottage US$225), all plus tax and 6% service. As elsewhere on the island, rates are higher during the peak Christmas season. Friendly, homey place and one of the better values on the island.

Pedro's Hotel. Seagrape Drive, San Pedro, 501-226-3825 or 800-213-8347 from U.S./Canada; www.pedroshotel.com. This budget hotel south of town isn't on the beach, but it does offer affordable, even cheap (for San Pedro), accommodations. The 32 standard rooms start at US$50 off-season, and the 12 "deluxe" rooms start at US$70. Rates plus 9% hotel tax. All hotel rooms have A/C, free wi-fi and cable TV, and you have a choice of one king or two twin beds. On the grounds is a sports bar with pool table and projection TV. If you're looking for something cheaper, check out **Pedro's Inn Backpackers Hostel** (www.backpackersbelize.com) with 14 hostel-style rooms, each with two beds. Rates are around US$12.50 per person, plus tax. The hotel has two small swimming pools, and guests have access to the nice beach at **Caribbean Villas,** a short hike away. The owner of Pedro's Hotel, the hostel and also Caribbean Villas, garrulous Englishman Peter Lawrence, claims Pedro's has the best pizza in Belize.

Changes in Latitudes B&B. 36 Coconut Drive, San Pedro, 501-226-2986; www.changesinlatitudesbelize.com. This small gay-owned inn has six small but pleasant and very clean rooms on the first level, plus a suite upstairs sleeping up to six. The included breakfast is served from 7 to 11 a.m. Changes in Latitudes isn't directly on the water, but it's close, perhaps 150 feet. The owners have redecorated all the rooms (all have private bath, A/C and fan.) Rates start at US$85 double off-season, US$125 in-season, plus hotel tax (no service charge). There's a minimum stay of three nights at most times, and five nights during peak holiday period from mid-December to mid-January.

Coral Bay Villas. Coconut Drive (P.O. Box 1), San Pedro, 501-226-3003 or 214-396-3218 in U.S.; www.coralbaybelize.com. This small condo resort has six one-bedroom beachfront suites in a white two-story concrete building with red tile roof. There's a new pool. Rare US$135 double, off-season, US$175 in-season, plus tax. No service charge. Complimentary bikes and kayak.

Xanadu Island Resort. Coconut Drive, San Pedro, 501-226-2814 or 866-351-4752 in U.S./Canada; www.xanaduislandresort.com. Xanadu, located about 1 mile south of San Pedro, bills itself as the "world's first monolithic dome resort," a description that might sound good to an engineer but doesn't exactly get our poetic juices flowing. Happily, the resort's five monolithic domes look much nicer than they sound. The building process is costly, but the result is a masonry dome with foam insulation that, according to the resort, can withstand winds of up to 300 mph. The domes are covered with thatch palapa roofs, giving them a tropical look. Inside, the 20 condo suites (studio lofts, one-, two-, and three-bedroom) are attractively furnished in earth tone colors, with central air-conditioning, fans, phones, free wi-fi and cable TV. You get the use of bikes and kayaks gratis. Jet skis, small sailboats, windsurfers and kite boards, plus golf carts, can be rented on-site. There's a nice stretch of seaside sand, though with a seawall, a 350-foot pier and a lovely freshwater swimming pool, with lush landscaping. The resort has no restaurant, but there's a snack bar, and for self-catering a small grocery is just outside the resort. Several restaurants also are nearby. Xanadu consistently is rated on TripAdvisor and other social media sites as one of the top resorts on Ambergris Caye. Rates range from US$220 (studio) to $650 (three-bedroom beachfront) in-season and US$180 to $545 May to mid-December, plus hotel tax and service. Rates higher at Christmas and Easter periods.

Caribbean Villas. Coconut Drive, San Pedro, 501-226-2715 or 800-213-8347 in U.S.; www.caribbeanvillashotel.com. The folks who originally built and ran this place for many years, Wil and Susan Lala, sold out in 2004, and new management added a beach bar and swimming pool. Later, the owner of Pedro's Hotel, Peter Lawrence, took over Caribbean Villas. The resort has a variety of accommodations, pleasant but not deluxe, in the two-level whitewashed buildings with tile roofs, from small studios to two-bedroom suites. You'll enjoy the nice beach area and pier, with a little artificial reef for snorkeling. The open-air bar near the water serves booze and pretty good food. Rooms are air-conditioned, with phones and TVs. There's free wi-fi, but it may not reach inside all rooms. Rates are a good value, considering San Pedro prices, at US$135 to $245 year-round, higher at holidays. Three-night minimum, with seven-night minimum at holiday periods. All rates plus tax (no service charge). There's also an all-inclusive option, with all meals, local beers, rum and other drinks, for US$99 per person per day. In 2015, Caribbean Villas hosted the first gay pride week on Ambergris Caye.

SOUTH END:

(This area begins about a mile south of town. Properties are listed from north to south, with those nearest town listed first.)

Villas at Banyan Bay. Sea Grape Drive (P.O. Box 266), San Pedro, 866-352-1163 or 501-226-3739; www.banyanbay.com. At this 42-unit condotel, you have all the pleasures of home ... if your home happens to be just steps from the Caribbean. Many of the guests here appear to be families, taking advantage of the big two- and three-bedroom units. The kids love the big, three-tiered pool, and dad and mom go for the fully equipped kitchen and the whirlpool off the master bedroom. The beach here, Mar de Tumbo, less than a mile and a half south of town, is one of the best on the island, although as most beaches in Belize, it does have some seagrass. There's a dive shop, Belize Pro Dive, on the pier. The food at Rico's Restaurant on-site doesn't always knock us out, but service is good, and it has a beautiful setting on the water for drinks or dinner; breakfast is handy and well done. Overall, we're impressed by the high degree of maintenance. The apartments look almost as good now as when they were built. The woodwork and cabinets are mahogany. The cathedral ceilings in the main living area sport a stunning array of tropical hardwoods. Some units here were sold as timeshares, before the resort was taken over by its lender during the Great Recession. Rack rates: US$275-$475 for a two-bedroom condo in-season, depending on location and number of people, and US$250 to $350 in the summer. For a three-bedroom beachfront unit, for up to six people, you'll pay US$675 in-season, US$550 off. Discounts may be available.

Grand Colony Villas. Sea Grape Drive, San Pedro, 501-226-4270 or 866-620-9521 from U.S./Canada; www.grandcolonyvillas.com. Built in 2005, the Grand Colony Villas are among the most upscale – and expensive – condotels on the island. The 15 large two- and three-bedroom villas have 10-foot ceilings, marble and hardwood floors, mahogany doors and cabinets and deluxe furnishings. There is also a three-bedroom presidential suite. Rates: US$599 to $899 in-season and US$499 to $799 off-season, higher during holidays, plus 9% tax, for up to four persons in the two-bedroom units and up to six in the three-bedrooms. The rates include transfers from the San Pedro airport, wi-fi, use of bikes, paddle boards and kayaks. The beach here is one of the best on the island.

Banana Beach. Coconut Drive, San Pedro; 501-226-3890, 877-288-

1011 in U.S. and Canada; www.bananabeach.com. This older South End resort has affordable rooms and one- to four-bedroom suites with kitchens, two swimming pools and a setting just steps from the sea and Mar de Tumbo beach (however, there's a low seawall directly in front of the hotel, and the usual seagrass). The 35 original one-bedroom units are in a single three-story building, designed in a style similar to Mexican hotels, around a courtyard with swimming pool. These units and indeed most of the resort are overdue for a facelift. A three-story addition, which went up in 2002, has a variety of "expandable" suites, regular rooms and also some one-bedroom efficiencies. There is an air-conditioned restaurant, El Divino, featuring steaks and martinis, but prices are on the high side. The hotel's tour office, Monkey Business, can set you up with tours, cart rentals and diving. Off-season, they start at US$95 double for a room or US$120 for a courtyard suite, US$145 for a seafront one-bedroom suite and top out at US$430 for a four-bedroom seafront suite. In high season, rates range for US$110 to $495. All rates are plus 9% tax and 6% service and include continental breakfast.

Mata Rocks. 45 Coconut Drive, San Pedro; 888-628-2757 or 501-226-2336; www.matarocks.com. Mata Rocks is a small, long-established beachfront hotel with 17 rooms and junior suites, comfortable rather than deluxe, just south of Banana Beach hotel. With its white stucco and wood exterior, Mata Rocks has a relaxed, laid-back atmosphere. The little thatch Squirrel's Nest beach bar often hops, however, and if you want to pop into town, about 1½ miles away, bikes are complimentary. All units have A/C and little fridges, and the junior suites have kitchenettes. There's a small pool. In-season, doubles are US$155 to $180 for rooms and US$205 to $220 for junior suites. Summer rates range from US$120 to $180, with some discounts offered. Rates are plus tax and include continental breakfast.

Royal Caribbean Resort. Coconut Drive, San Pedro, 501-226-4220; www.royalcaribbeanbelize.com. The little yellow cabins lined up in rows at Royal Caribbean, which opened in 2005, remind some people of army barracks. However, inside the cabins are fairly spacious, with tile floors, wicker furniture, and kitchenettes, and all have cable TV and air conditioning. There's a pool, beach bar that serves some food and 300 feet of beach. Prices are US$140 to $175 double off-season and US$150 to $185 in-season. All rates plus tax.

Victoria House. Coconut Drive (P.O. Box 22), San Pedro, 800-247-

5159 or 713-344-2340; www.victoria-house.com. If what you want is an upscale but casual resort vacation, Victoria House is just about perfect. About 2 miles south of town, Victoria House is a quiet hideaway on 19 acres, with a variety of accommodations ranging from comfy motel-like rooms in two buildings at the back of the resort to rooms and suites in the main lodge to thatch casitas to deluxe villas and gorgeous condos. There has been lots of remodeling and upgrading in recent years, including adding a second fabulous main pool, along with a group of condo villas at the south edge of the resort. These condo villas are our pick for some of the most beautiful beach accommodations in Belize. The hotel's restaurant, Palmilla, remains an asset. A full meal plan is US$75 per person per day, but many guests prefer not to be locked into a meal plan and dine around the island. Admiral Nelson's, the freestanding bar cabaña on the beach, is ideal for sipping rum drinks or Belikins. Head to the lovely sandy beach area for relaxing, or swim off the pier. The hotel also has a gift shop and a dive operation. A spa is opening in 2016. With its long-time management team, service is top-notch everywhere at this resort. Victoria House is a popular place to get married, and the hotel has honeymoon packages. Rack rates for rooms in-season, December-May, US$199 to $335, suites US$375 to $545; villas, condos and houses, US$650 to $1975, all plus 9% tax and 10% service. Prices are a little lower off-season and higher during holiday periods. Highly recommended.

Athen's Gate. Coconut Drive, San Pedro, 501-226-4151, 713-609-9457 in U.S.; www.athensgatebelize.com. Athens Gate, which features some Greek design flourishes, has 12 two- and three-bedroom luxury condo units in four-story buildings (and there is no elevator!) There's an infinity swimming pool with waterfall, and the condo has 100 feet of beachfront. Rates for two bedroom units are US$375 to $450, and for three-bedroom US$500 to $575, but currently in-season rates are discounted 30% and off-season 40% off. Rates are plus tax, but service charge is not added. "Tipping is up to you." Neither Athens Gate nor Pelican Reef Villas nearby has anon-site restaurant, but there are several places to eat nearby.

Pelican Reef Villas Resort. Coconut Drive, San Pedro, 501-226-4352, 281-394-3739 in U.S.; www.pelicanreefvillas.com. While listening to the pool's tinkling waterfall, it is easy to believe you've stumbled upon a hidden tropical treasure, when really the faux cave is a swim-up bar and Pelican Reef is only 2 miles south of San Pedro's bustle. This condotel is one of the most popular on the island, despite relative spendy rates. Service here is top-notch, and the resort has won a number of "best of" awards. Large alabaster buildings with butter-yellow trim house the 24 two-bedroom (US$289 to $549 in-season, plus 9% tax and 6% service) and three-bedroom (US$449 to $699 in-season for up to six people, plus 15% tax and service) suites. Rates are lower off-season (May-mid-December). The resort sometimes offers discounts, with rates for two-bedroom units as low as US$175 plus tax and service, off-season. Tastefully decorated, with fully equipped kitchens, mahogany cabinets, granite countertops and plush sleigh-beds, the villa suites are gorgeous, and the oceanfront views are stunning. The same owners developed Athens Gate nearby. Highly recommended.

NORTH AMBERGRIS ABOVE BRIDGE

These hotels are all north of the river channel and the bridge. With the paving of much of the former cart path to the north, it's much easier to go by golf cart or by taxi to resorts and on North Ambergris. Within the immediate future, the golf cart is supposed to be paved to about 7 miles north of the bridge. Many people, however, still take a boat or the scheduled water taxi Coastal Xpress. Hotels are listed south to north, with those nearest town listed first.

New paved road on North Ambergris Photo by Greg Riggs

Grand Caribe Suites and Residences. Tres Cocos, North Ambergris, 501-226-4726 or 800-488-5903; www.grandcaribebelize.com. Tim Jeffers' latest project on the island is a winner! Set in an arc on a 5-acre beachfront site about 2 miles north of town, Grand Caribe's 72 luxury condos, in eight four-story, red-tiled-roof clusters, plus a large villa, all face the sea and a fine stretch of sandy beach. Grand Caribe debuted in 2008, with additional units finished over the next several years. It has since won several awards as one of the top resorts in Belize. The one, two-, three- and four-bedroom suites, for two to eight people (US$449 to $1,049 in-season, US$379-$1,049 off-season, plus 9% hotel tax and 10% service/resort fee). If you stay at least four days, or a week or longer, there are significant rate drops. The suites have Brazilian floor tiles, kitchens with granite countertops and mahogany countertops, and high-quality furnishings. Rare in Belize, some units have elevator access. There's also a five-bedroom beachfront villa, for up to 10 people. The regular rate is US$20,000 a week plus 19% fees and taxes. Resort amenities include a restaurant, Rain, with indoor and rooftop dining, room service, concierge service, a new grocery store, Beach Basket, free wi-fi, five swimming pools, pool bar and a fitness room. The resort's windsports shop rents aquatic sports equipment to guests and the public. An unusual feature of Grande Caribe is the long, curving pier with berths for a number of boats. Highly recommended.

White Sands Cove Resort. North Ambergris (P.O. Box 192, San Pedro), 602-733-1322 or 501-226-3528; www.whitesandscove.com. This little colony, about 2 miles from town, was closed to visitors for a time but has reopened. Those who want to be within a short bike or taxi ride to town, but a bit away from the hustle and bustle, seem to like it. The 14 units go for from US$116 to $395 a night, depending on time of year and size and location of unit. There's a pool.

Ak'bol Yoga Retreat & Eco-Resort. North Ambergris, 501-226-2073; www.akbol.com. This hip little resort has seven simple thatch cabañas (US$145-$165 in-season, US$10-$120, plus 9% tax and 6% service), some with sea views, around a natural stone swimming pool. You'll love the outdoor showers in the cabañas. On the lagoon side is a three-story building with 30 single rooms with shared baths for those attending yoga retreats. Rates for these rooms start at US$50 double, year-round, plus 15% tax and service. Daily group yoga lessons, open to the public, are US$15 per session. Private lessons are US$75. Ak'bol regularly holds yoga retreats with visiting masters. Soul Kitchen, the restaurant, serves local foods such as salbutes, panades, and pupusas at modest prices, and it also offers pizzas and vegetarian dishes.

Cocotal Inn & Cabanas. North Ambergris, about 2½ miles north of the center of town, 501-226-2097; www.cocotalbelize.com. Looking for small, comfy, affordable spot on the beach? Cocotal could be it. There are only six units - four cottages and two suites in the main house. Our favorite is the casita, with vaulted hardwood ceiling and a four-poster queen bed. It's closest to the beach and also overlooks the pool. All have fully equipped kitchens, so you can cook your own meals, or hop on one of the complimentary bikes and ride to a nearby restaurant. If you're thirsty, there's a beer and soft drink honor bar. Kayaks also available at no charge. The helpful owners are on-site. Rates are US$150 to $260 in-season, US$115 to $200 off. All rates plus 9% tax.

El Pescador. North Ambergris (P.O. Box 17, San Pedro), 501-226-2398 or 804-661-2259; www.elpescador.com. Since 1974, El Pescador has been the island's leading fishing lodge. Today, it's bigger and more upmarket than it used to be, with three pools, upscale villas and other resort amenities, but it's still devoted to anglers and angling. After fishing for tarpon, bonefish, permit and jacks, but you can enjoy a fine meal, served family style in the dining room, or enjoy a drink and a cigar on the verandah. The lodge has 14 comfortable units, recently redone, in a rambling two-story colonial-style building with lots of mahogany. Adjoining the lodge are newer three-bedroom villas, and these are deluxe, with prices to match. Most can be divided and reserved as either one- or two-bedroom units. Nightly rates for rooms are US$275 in-season and US$185 off-season; villas are US$400 to $850 per night depending on the number of bedrooms in-season, US$280 to $595 off. Rates plus 9%, with a three-night minimum, and meals are extra. El Pescador offers all-inclusive fishing packages, which include guide, boat, transfer from Belize City, local drinks, all meals and taxes, but there also are dive and resort packages. Fishing packages start at US$1,895 per person for three nights with two days of fishing (two persons per room and two per boat) and range up to over US$5,915 per person for a week (one person in a room and one per boat.)

Seascape Villas. North Ambergris, 501-226-2119 or 888-753-5164; www.seascapebelize.com. This collection of villas on four beachfront acres 3½ miles north of town, built by noted island developers Bob and Diane

Campbell, opened in 2006. Villas have sunken living rooms, slate floors, outdoor garden with hot tub and unobstructed views of the sea. Four rental villas are privately owned but available for rent when the owners aren't in residence. In-season, expect to pay around US$550 to $975 per day for up to six people, and US$459 to $559 off-season, plus tax.

Coco Beach Resort. North Ambergris (P.O. Box 1, San Pedro), 844-360-1553 or 501-226-4297; www.cocobeachresort.com. This is the newer, more upscale sister resort to Belizean Shores. It's about 3½ miles north of town. Coco Beach has deluxe one- and two-bedroom suites, plus penthouse suites and casitas. On-site is the Cocoblanca Restaurant. In-season rates are around US$280 to $850, plus tax, off-season rates lower. Discounts from rack rates frequently offered.

Belizean Shores. North Ambergris (P.O. Box 1, San Pedro), 844-360-1553 or 501-226-2355; www.belizeanshores.com. Belizean Shores is an older but still popular condotel, developed by the same company that did the newer Coco Beach Resort, on North Ambergris with good rates and a lot of space in the units. The pool is a beaut, with a swim-up bar, and huge. The beach is small but fairly nice. There's a 350-foot pier, a tennis court, basketball court and a dive shop. The resort has a restaurant, lower off-season, plus tax. Discounts frequently offered.

Las Terrazas Resort & Residences. North Ambergris, 4 miles north of town; 800-447-1553 in U.S./Canada, 713-780-1233 or 501-226-4249; www.lasterrazasbelize.com. Las Terrazas, which opened in late 2007, is a luxury 37-unit, three-level condominium resort with one-, two- and three-bedroom suites. Rates are US$300 to $600+ in-season, plus tax and service, depending on the unit and number of people; lower rates off-season. The condos have 9-foot ceilings, travertine tile floors, fully equipped kitchens with Brazilian granite countertops, and all the amenities including cable TV and wi-fi. A two-level pier sweeps out into the sea. O Restaurant is at the resort, but other restaurants are not far away. White Sands Dive Shop in on-site.

Azul Resort. North Ambergris, 501-226-4012; www.azulbelize.com. Azul has only two beach villas, but, man, they are nice. The two-level villas have 20-foot ceilings with beams of mylady wood. Custom kitchens feature Viking appliances, and the cabinets and most of the furniture are made of zericote wood. Each villa has a 50-inch plasma flat-screen TV and Bose theater system. On the rooftop, you can relax in your own hot tub. The two beach houses share a beautiful pool, 400 feet of beach, and about 11 acres of prime property. Rates start at US$550 a day double, plus tax. Rojo Beach Bar is next door for drinks in a romantic beachside setting and some of the best food on the island, but it's not guaranteed to be open when you're there, and other changes may be coming. Matachica and its bar and restaurant, however, are literally steps away.

Matachica Resort & Spa. North Ambergris, 501-220-5010; www.matachica.com. When it opened in late 1997, Matachica raised the bar on what constitutes deluxe lodging on Ambergris Caye. Matachica's original owners designed this resort, located about 5 miles north of San Pedro, to the hilt. Each of the cabañas had a fruit theme -- mango, watermelon, banana and so on -- a theme that began with the exterior color and was carried through down to the tiles in the baths. It all might have been a little much for some, but others said the colors reminded them of Gauguin. New owners (who also bought the former Five Sisters lodge in the Mountain Pine Ridge) made some much-needed renovations, added a pool and new cabañas. The resort now has 30 one-bedroom and one two-bedroom cabañas. The beach here is postcard lovely, though swimming isn't that great. We recommend the beach-front units, if available. They get a breeze and sometimes the A/C in the back units can't keep up due to the high thatch roofs. If a spa is your thing, Matachica has the Jade Spa & Gym. Mambo, the hotel's expensive restaurant, offers an eclectic menu, albeit emphasizing seafood. It's definitely a romantic spot for dinner. Doubles US$275 to US$625 in-season and US$225 to $495 off-season, plus tax and service. Package rates also available. No children under 14.

Portofino. North Ambergris (P.O. Box 36, San Pedro), 501-220-5096 or 800-813-7880; www.portofinobelize.com. One of Portofino's drawing cards is that it has thatch cabañas, fairly rare on the island. The resort, which opened in 2001 on the site of an old resort, the Green Parrot, has lushly landscaped grounds, a restaurant, dive shop, thatch units including beach cabañas, tree house suites, beachfront suites, honeymoon suite with whirlpool and a four-bedroom villa. Rooms have A/C, wi-fi, mini-fridge and cable TV. There's a circular swimming pool. Complimentary kayaks and free boat transfers to town, about 6 miles away. Rates: US$310 to $450 double in high season, US$280 to $380 in low, plus taxes and 10% service charge.

X'Tan Ha. North Ambergris, 844-360-1553 or 501-226-2846;

www.xtanha.com. Formerly the Belize Legacy condotel, which closed during the Great Recession, X'Tan Ha (pronounced ISH-tan-HA) has been reborn as a small resort a little over 7 miles north of town. Just offshore is Mexico Rocks, one of the most popular snorkeling spots around Ambergris. It has one-bedroom units with kitchens. Kayaks, paddleboards and a water trampoline are complimentary. There's a restaurant, Temple Run Tavern. A burger and fries is around US$15 while fish dishes are US$25 at dinner. A beach bar is on the water. Two pools. Rack rates start at around US$275 in-season plus tax but are often discounted.

La Beliza Resort. North Ambergris, 786-472-9664; www.vivabelize.com/la-beliza/. About 8 miles north of San Pedro Town, this was originally called Blue Reef, which opened in 2005 with construction continuing in 2006-2007. La Beliza is now part of a group of about a half dozen properties under one management in Belize, including Jaguar Reef and Almond Beach in Hopkins and Sleeping Giant Rainforest Lodge and part of Ian Anderson's Caves Branch on the Hummingbird Highway, among others. It has 18 one- and two-bedroom condo units. The apartments are attractive, with granite tile floors and 10-ft. ceilings, and all have sea views. The swimming pool also overlooks the water. La Beliza has no restaurant, but staff will cook meals for you and deliver to your condo. There's little within easy walking distance, so for company you'll have to try biking or carting south or depend on the hotel's boat (US$35 transfer one-way from the San Pedro airport) or the Coastal Xpress water taxi, a 20-minute ride each way. This is the last stop north for the water taxi, and it does make stops at resorts on the way to town. (Coastal Xpress has weekly passes for US$75 per person.) "Soon come" the golf cart path up North Ambergris will be paved all the way to this resort. Year-round rack rates at La Belize are US$340 to $499, plus 9% hotel tax and service, but significant discounts are frequently offered, often bringing the real rate down by US$100 to $200 or more per night.

Tranquility Bay. North Ambergris, in Bacalar Chico Marine Reserve, 501-236-5880; www.tranquilitybayresort.com. You're really, really away from things at Tranquility Bay, about 10 miles and a 35-minute boat ride from San Pedro Town. It's too far to go to town by the cart path, and the Coastal Xpress water taxi doesn't schedule stops this far north, so you have to depend on the resort's little boats. The good news is a new management team is making some improvements and upgrades, the restaurant is pretty good and that this far north you are closer to the barrier reef than at other resorts on the island. The reef is about 250 yards offshore, within swimming or kayaking distance if you're comfortable in the sea. You're also close to nature, as Tranquility is the only resort in the Bacalar Chico reserve. The one-bedroom cabañas are US$290 double in-season, $210 off,. Also available are two-bedroom units (US$340 to $370 in-season, $268 to $307 off.) A budget room is US$170 in winter, US$135 May to mid-December. Rates are plus 9% tax and 10% service and include breakfast. All lodging is air-conditioned and has kitchenettes, but there are no TVs. As of this writing, the resort was for sale.

PRIVATE ISLANDS NEARBY

Cayo Espanto. 888-666-4282 in U.S./Canada or 910-323-8355; www.aprivateisland.com. Ready, willing and able to pay nearly US$20,000 a couple for a week's pampering, not including airfare to Belize? Then Cayo Espanto, a tiny private island on the backside of Ambergris, about 3 miles west of San Pedro, may be for you. At Cayo Espanto, the resort staff lines up, as on the old TV show "Fantasy Island" to greet you on arrival. Cayo Espanto's American owners quickly figured out that, in Belize's economy, it's not that expensive to hire a bunch of workers to keep the staff-to-guest ratio at two to one. So if you like attentive service, you definitely will get it at Cayo Espanto, including your own "houseman" who cares for your every need day or night. Start with breakfast in bed and end the evening with pisco sours (all meals and most drinks are included in the price) on your private dock, before bundling off to your king-size bed with its luxurious Yves de Lorme sheets. Currently there are seven villas, four one-bedroom, two two-bedroom and one over-the-water bungalow. The villas are quite large, and all but one have small private "plunge" pools. We especially like the units with open-air design, with walls that fold out let the Caribbean in, such as Casa Estrella. Meals are created by Cayo Espanto's crew of award-winning chefs and brought to your villa. You can dine at your own table by the sea. The resort offers a full range of tours, dive and snorkel trips, fishing and all the rest, but most guests seem to spend most of their time at their villas (and for the US$75 more per hour they're paying to stay here, who wouldn't?) You can also get spa services in your villa. The rates are like the money-is-no-object rates on villa rentals on St. Barths: US$1,595 to $2,295 double in winter, and US$1,495 to $2,195 off-season — that's per night, not

293

per week -- including meals and most drinks. However, 9% tax and 15% service/resort fee are additional. There's a minimum stay of five nights (some exceptions to this may be made). Rates are higher during the Christmas season. Occasional promotional rates may be offered. Is it worth it? Cayo Espanto stays pretty busy, so obviously there are people who figure it is.

Dinner seaside at your villa at Cayo Espanto

Dining on Ambergris Caye

Ambergris Caye has Belize's widest selection of restaurants, ranging from inexpensive local spots and pizza joints to a couple that will have you reaching for your Platinum Amex. The emphasis is on seafood, of course, but many restaurants also serve chicken and pork, and even steak. Lobster is usually the most-expensive item on the menu (in-season mid-June to mid-February), at around US$20 to $35. Pasta and Mexican-style dishes also are popular. After all that pricey seafood, an honest plate of Belizean beans and rice will taste real good. Vegetarians can get by okay in San Pedro, even if you don't eat seafood. Rice and beans are ubiquitous (but often these are seasoned with lard or meat). Many Mexican places do up vegetarian burritos, and of course pizza is available at many spots. Fruit plates, with mangos, pineapple, watermelon and other local fruits, are a part of breakfast at a lot of places. Many restaurants will do vegetarian versions of their specialties – just ask.

Dress on the island is very casual. Even at the spiffiest places, tee-shirt and shorts are okay, although some guests at the top restaurants will wear casual resort clothes – a light summer dress or a golf shirt with khakis. Socks optional.

Reservations are usually not necessary, except where noted. During the season, at popular dining spots, you may have to wait a few minutes, or longer. Grab a Belikin and relax while you wait.

Keep in mind that small restaurants on a resort island can change overnight, with the loss of a cook or a setback in the personal life of the owner. Always ask locally if the restaurant you're thinking about is still good.

Price ranges shown are for typical meals for one (usually dinner), not including tip, tax or alcoholic drinks. Price ranges:

Inexpensive: Under US$7
Moderate: US$8-$19
Expensive: US$20-$39
Very Expensive: Over US$40

IN TOWN OR NEARBY
Listed alphabetically.

Blue Water Grill. At SunBreeze Hotel, Coconut Drive, 501-226-3347. Blue Water Grill aims high, and usually hits the spot. Try the mixed seafood grill or the local snapper dusted in cumin. The crispy Coconut Shrimp is a winner. Many dishes are Asian-influenced. Tuesdays and Thursdays sushi is offered. Blue Water is often jammed. Open for lunch and dinner daily. Expensive/Very Expensive.

Cocina Caramba. Pescador Drive, 501-603-1652. Owner Rene Reyes made a big success out of Caramba by simply serving good food in large portions at moderate prices. This spot is usually packed. Just about any of the seafood and Mexican dishes are tasty and well-prepared. Open for lunch and dinner. Closed Wednesday. Moderate.

Caliente. Spindrift Hotel, Barrier Reef Drive. This restaurant gets attention for its spicy versions of traditional favorites such as conch ceviche, its big variety of seafood and Mexican dishes and for its delicious soups. Locally popular for lunch, and open for dinner, too. Moderate/Expensive.

Caroline's Cookin'. Coconut Drive, beside airport, 501-226-3188. Great spot for breakfast, but jerk dishes, conch fritters, burritos and pork chops are good for lunch or dinner. Open for breakfast, lunch and dinner. Moderate.

Coconut Café, Coconut Drive, 501-226-4311. Casual spot on the beach at Exotic Caye with breakfast menu of pancakes, burritos, banana bread and eggs served all day. Also pizza and wraps. Open for breakfast and lunch. Most items under US$12. Closed Wednesday. Moderate.

DandE's Frozen Custard. Pescador Drive next to Cocina Caramba, 501-608-9100. Dan and Eileen (DandE, get it?) Jamison, who used to run the local weekly paper, the *San Pedro Sun*, now operate this custard and sorbet shop. For something with an island flavor, try the mango sorbet or the soursop frozen custard. Inexpensive.

El Fogón. Trigger Fish Street, 501-206-2121. A fogón is an open-hearth grill that harkens back to the old Belize. El Fogón cooks Creole and Mestizo favorites that Belizeans love, and you will, too. It's family-run and a good value, especially at lunch. Dinner, focusing on seafood, is more expensive. Open for lunch and dinner. Closed Sunday. Moderate.

Elvi's Kitchen. Pescador Drive, 501-226-2404. Yes, it's a little touristy, and, yes, it's a little more expensive than some, but Elvi's still does a fine job with fish and just about everything. Doña Elvia Staines began her restaurant as a take-out burger stand in 1974. It has grown in fame and fortune year after year, until today it is one of the best-known restaurants in Belize. There are still burgers on the lunch menu along with shrimp and fish burger versions. At dinner, you choose from large selection of seafood, chicken and other dishes, and almost all of it is good, with prices mostly under US$20 for entrees. The sand floor and the frangipani tree around which the main dining room is built add atmosphere. Open for lunch and dinner. Closed Sunday. Moderate/Expensive.

Estel's-by-the-Sea. Barrier Reef Drive, 501-226- 2019. Charlie and Estella Worthington run this little seaside restaurant near Central Park. With its sand floor this place can boast of real island atmosphere. It's a favorite spot for breakfast, with all the usual egg-and-bacon basics including fried potatoes, but you'll also enjoy the burritos and *huevos rancheros*. Estel's may have the best Bloody Marys on the island. Opens early, closed

Tuesday. Moderate.

Fido's. Barrier Reef Drive, 501-226-3714. (Pronounced FEE-doh's.) Extremely popular, centrally located spot for a beer and a bite. Sit under the big palapa by the sea and enjoy burgers, fish and chips or lobster burrito. Live music many nights. Moderate.

Neri's Taco Place. Chicken Street. New to San Pedro, Neri's is hugely popular for its cheap and delicious local food. You order at a window and if there's space eat at a picnic table outside. A little hard to find, it's one street back of El Fogón just north of the airport. Open for breakfast and dinner (breakfast only on Sundays.) Inexpensive.

Red Ginger. Barrier Reef Drive, at The Phoenix, 501-226-4623. With its stylishly minimalist décor, this restaurant could be in L.A., but it's actually at The Phoenix condos at the north end of San Pedro. No sea views here - you gaze at deep red and rich cream walls, with brown earth-toned accents, and tropical wild ginger plants in glass vases. The specialty is seafood. The service is a notch above most other places in San Pedro. Expensive/Very Expensive.

The Reef. Pescador Drive, 501-226-3212. This old local favorite serves tasty Belizean fare such as stew chicken with rice and beans in large portions at small prices. Open for lunch and dinner. At lunch, there's a daily special for a few dollahs. Inexpensive to Moderate.

Ruby's. Barrier Reef Drive, 501-226-2063. If you can't sleep or are heading out for a day of fishing, get up early and grab a casual breakfast at Ruby's. For a few dollars, you can enjoy coffee, burritos and the best coconut tarts on the island. Later in the day, there are sandwiches and daily specials. It starts serving before 5 a.m., and usually stays open until late afternoon. Closed Sunday. Inexpensive.

Wild Mango's. Barrier Reef Drive, 501-226-2859. Award-winning chef Amy Knox brought her "New Wave Latin" cooking to this little spot at the south edge of town, on the water. She quickly made Wild Mango's one of the top restaurants on the island. One of the specialties is ceviche, a variety of different ceviches. You can try a sampler. Knox also delivers some great Mexican dishes and, of course, seafood. The snapper is particularly good. Open for lunch and dinner. Closed Sunday. Moderate/ Expensive.

Street vendors offer food that is cheap, good and safe to eat. Most are in stalls at Central Park. You can get a whole plate full of delicious food for a few bucks. Don't worry – it won't upset your tummy. Also don't miss the Lions Club barbecue on Friday night. The barbecue is great and the flan is out of this world. The money also goes to a good cause – improved health care on the island. Inexpensive/Moderate.

SOUTH OF TOWN

Antojitos San Telmo. Coconut Drive, 501-226-4575. It's just a joint, but a good joint, with snacks like tacos and burritos for almost nothing. Good service, too. Open for breakfast and lunch (close at 3 p.m.) Inexpensive.

The Baker. Sea Grape Drive, 501-629-8030. Now located near Xanadu Resort and next door to Marina's grocery, across from Antojitos San Telmo, The Baker is the island's best spot for delicious baked bread, croissants, pastries and sandwiches. Open from 7:30 a.m. to 5:30 p.m. Monday-Friday and 7:30 to 2 pm on Saturday. Inexpensive to Moderate.

Black Orchid Restaurant. Coconut Drive, 501-206-2441. Located about 2½ miles south of town, beyond the croc pond and just before Athens Gate condotel, Black Orchid gets five stars for hard work and trying to please guests. Relaxed atmosphere, open to the fresh air, with good fish, lobster and other dishes. Open for lunch and dinner. Expensive/Very Expensive.

Casa Picasso. Sting Ray Street, 501-226-4443. Closed for several years, Casa Picasso reopened under new ownership and almost instantly became a big new hit. Many consider it the best restaurant on the island. Billed as tapas dining with global flavors, besides tapas it features wonderful local seafood, pork and other entrees, with paired wines. There are interesting takes on most everything. Expensive/Very Expensive. Closed Sunday and Monday. Reservations suggested.

Hidden Treasure. Escalante area, 501-226-4111. Hidden away indeed on a back street in a residential neighborhood south of town, at dinner you dine by candlelight, in the sultry tropical air under a pitched roof set off by bamboo, mahogany and cabbage bark wood. Although under new management, one of the longtime signature dishes, Mojarra a la Lamanai, remains on the menu – it's a snapper fillet topped with bell peppers, onions, tomatoes and capers in a coconut sauce and cooked in a banana leaf. In season, the local lobster, butterflied and topped with lemon butter sauce, is around US$30. Open for dinner only. Closed Tuesday. Expensive/Very Expensive.

Palmilla at Victoria House. Coconut Drive at Victoria House, 501-226-2067. The main restaurant at Victoria House, Palmilla, once dependent on unexciting buffets, has had a marked change for the better under its current chef. For dinner, dine by romantic candlelight. Breakfast by the pool with views of the sea isn't to be missed. Expensive to Very Expensive.

Palapa Bar on North Ambergris   Photo by Greg Riggs

NORTH AMBERGRIS

Aji Tapa Bar and Restaurant. Beachfront, Buena Vista area, North Ambergris (about 2½ miles north of town), 501-226-4047. Relax in a shady, romantic seaside patio, with views of the beach and barrier reef in the distance, and snack on shrimp in garlic and other small plates. For a special treat, try the seafood paella. Aji is under new management, so things may change. Closed Tuesday. Expensive.

Mambo. North Ambergris at Matachica Resort & Spa, 501-220-5010. If you'd visited the island a few years ago, you'd never have thought Ambergris Caye would get this kind of place. The restaurant space is open, appealing and upscale. Everything is designed to the hilt – even the menus show hours of design time. On those menus is a selection of sophisticated Italian dishes and seafood, along with daily specials. But you need to bring plenty of money or plastic. Prices are high, at least by Belizean standards. Open for breakfast, lunch and dinner. Reached by water taxi. Very

Expensive.

Palapa Bar & Grill. Beachfront, North Ambergris, 501-226-2528. If you were going to invent the platonic Caribbean bar on the beach, this might be it. Actually, the thatch-roof, two-level Palapa Bar & Grill is not on the sandy beach but at the end of a pier jutting out into the sea. It's about half a mile north of the bridge. The food is mostly just bar stuff, burgers and BBQ wings and fish platters. The beer is cold and the drinks are not very expensive. It's the setting that makes it all work. Sometimes it gets a little too gregarious, like when the bartender takes out the "shot stick," but, heck, have another shot and a Belikin, and before long you may jump in the water and float on an inner tube with other gassed up patrons. At night, it's an adult wonderland of lights and booze. Sometimes, the wind really kicks up. No wonder it's been going strong for more than 20 years. Moderate to Very Expensive (depending on how much you drink.)

Rendezvous. Next door to the former Journey's End hotel, 501-226-3426. This probably was the first Thai-French fusion restaurant in Central America, and surely it's the best. Started nearly two decades ago by an expat couple that formerly lived in Southeast Asia (sadly, the wife, Colleen, passed away recently), Rendezvous has an intimate setting, on the second floor of a colonial-style house by the water. The menu changes from time to time, but you can expect dishes such as Pad Thai or chicken in a red curry coconut sauce. Due to the death of the co-owner, the restaurant is for sale, and its future is unclear. Expensive to Very Expensive.

Rojo Beach Bar. North Ambergris, 501-266-4012. About 5 miles north of the bridge, Rojo was once known as among the island's top places to eat, in a romantic beachside setting next to Azul's two beachhouses. It's still romantic, and there's still a pool to splash in, but now it's mostly a bar, and the dining has been scaled back, with lobster, king crab and such by Chef Danny Choc. Co-owner and chef Jeff Spiegel isn't so much hands on anymore. Closed Monday and Tuesday. Expensive to Very Expensive.

Where to Party on Ambergris Caye

For visitors, San Pedro is the nightlife capital of Belize. Still, it's not exactly a world-class party town. Nightlife usually consists of drinks and dinner at a local restaurant, with perhaps a later visit to one of the "clubs" or hotel beach bars, a few of which rev up late and don't stop until the wee hours. Quite a few expats on the island have made a second career out of drinking.

Big Daddy's near Central Park is probably the hottest spot on the island, and things sometimes go late and loud here. Across the street, **Jaguar** hops, too, especially toward the weekend. The real action at these spots often doesn't get started until midnight. **Fido's** is always busy, with lots of people dropping in for a drink or to hear some music. **Palapa Bar, Wahoo Lounge, Sandy Toes, Rehab Bar, Lola's Pub** and **Hurricane's** are popular bars where you can get a cold beer or something stronger. **Pedro's** is a local expat hangout, with hot pizza and disgusting shots of Jaegermeister; some days there's a poker game going in the back room. **Cholo's Sports Bars** and a couple of other small local bars have pool tables. **Kama Bar** (currently for sale) has a nice North Ambergris setting for drinks and snacks. **Wine de Vine** has wine by the glass in the afternoon as well as selling wine (at prices about twice what you'd pay in the U.S., due to import duties and taxes.)

Several hotels have popular beach bars, including the **Pier Lounge** at the Spindrift Hotel, (home of the chicken drop), **Caprice** at the Holiday Hotel, Ramon's **Purple Parrot,** Exotic Caye's **Crazy Canucks** (the hotel was seriously damaged in a 2015 fire) and Mata Rocks' **Squirrel's Nest** beach bar. You can stroll along the beach south of town and slake your thirst at a half dozen beach bars.

If, after a long day in the sun you're too pooped to pop a Belikin, you'll be glad that many of the island's hotels have cable TV, with about the same channels as you'd get in the U.S.

A long-time small casino on the island, the Palace Casino – where the slogan was "It Ain't Vegas" – has closed. A casino now is open at **Captain Morgan's.** Again, it ain't Vegas. For more action, you can try the **Ramada Princess Hotel & Casino** in Belize City. There also are three casinos in the Commercial Free Zone near Corozal Town (a 25-minute flight away and a taxi ride away), of which Las Vegas Casino is the largest and newest.

Coffee and art on Front Street, Caye Caulker

CHECKING OUT CAYE CAULKER

Getting to Caulker

You can fly to Caulker's little airstrip on **Tropic Air** (www.tropicair.com) or **Maya Island Air** (www.mayaregional.com) from Belize City. Flights from either International or Municipal to San Pedro will stop, on demand, at Caye Caulker. Fares are the same as to San Pedro – US$95 one-way from the international airport and from municipal US$65. Flights from San Pedro to Belize City also drop passengers at Caulker's airstrip, again for the same fare as to Belize City itself.

Most visitors to Caulker, however, come by boat. Two water taxi companies, with fast boats that hold up to 100 passengers, connect Belize City with Caye Caulker.

From Belize City it's a 45-minute ride to Caulker. **Ocean Ferry** (501-223-0033, www.oceanferrybelize.com) boats leave from the Marine Terminal in Belize City at 10 North Front Street near the Swing Bridge. **San Pedro Belize Express** (501-223-2225, www.belizewatertaxi.com) boats leave from the Brown Sugar dock at 111 North Front Street near the

302

Tourism Village. Ocean Ferry, has five departures daily from to Caulker. It charges US$14.50 between Belize City and Caye Caulker. San Pedro Belize Express, which has around eight or nine departures to Caulker, charges US$25 between Belize City and Caye Caulker.

The water taxi business in Belize is in flux; schedules, rates and companies are subject to change.

GETTING ORIENTED

The water taxis boats mostly come in at two piers on the front side of the island. If you come ashore at the main public pier, the pink and green Trends Beachfront hotel is on your right, and the mustard-colored Seaside Cabañas is on your left.

Walk a few sandy feet and you'll come to Front Street. Go right, or north, and in 15 minutes or so you'll pass several good hotels, some restaurants, shops and tour operators, plus a few touts, and end up at "the Split," the main place to swim on the island. Go left or south and you'll find some of the island's better beachfront properties. Many of the island's restaurants, shops and hotels are on Front Street or on the beachfront. Go straight west, and you're in the heart of the village.

In general, hotels to the south are quieter than those north toward the Split. However, if you're staying south, it's a bit more of a walk to restaurants and most bars. For those who really want to get away from things, try the North Island, the area north of the Split. However, this part of the island is accessible by boat, and except for some off-the-grid homes, there's little development.

If you come by air, the little airstrip is at the south end of the island. You can walk the 20 minutes or so back to the heart of the village, or you can get a golf cart taxi.

What to Do and See on Caye Caulker

Caye Caulker isn't so much about seeing and doing as being. This is a little island to kick back, relax and just enjoy life.

From Caulker, you can do visit most of the same attractions as from Ambergris Caye. See the Ambergris Caye section above for information on **Hol Chan Marine Reserve** and other dive and snorkel sites. The **Caye Caulker Marine Reserve** is Caulker's own mini-Hol Chan snorkeling area, just 10 minutes from Caulker.

In addition, you may also want to visit **Swallow Caye Wildlife Sanctuary** (www.swallowcayemanatees.org), 9,000 acres of protected sea and mangrove habitat for manatees and other wildlife. Swallow Caye trips are around US$85.

There is no shortage of tour operators and snorkel and dive shops to take you out. There are at least three dive shops on the island and perhaps a dozen snorkel and tour operators, most of which have locations on the beachfront along Front Street.

Frenchie's Diving Services (beachfront pier, toward the Split, 501-226-0234, www.frenchiesdivingbelize.com) is the island's oldest dive shop under continuous ownership. It has four dive boats, the largest of which is a 38-footer.

Belize Diving Services (Chapoose Street, near soccer field, 501-226-0143, www.belizedivingservices.com) is a well-respected dive operation, founded in 1978, and owned since 2009 by Chip and Dani Petersen. It has a 46-foot dive boat.

You'll pay US$100 to $145 including marine reserve fee for a two-tank dive trip to the Caye Caulker Marine Reserve or to Hol Chan, and up to about US$265 for three-tank dive trips to Lighthouse Reef Atoll and the Blue Hole, including US$40 reserve fee. Day trips to Turneffe Atoll are less than to Lighthouse Reef.

Among the well-established snorkel and land tour operators are the following:

Anwar Tours (501-226-0327, www.anwartours.com)

Carlos Tours (501-600-1654)

Tsunami Adventures (501-226-0462, www.tsunamiadventures.com)

Local snorkeling trips around Caye Caulker are about US$35 per person, while snorkel trips to Hol Chan are around US$65 to $75. Land tours for cave tubing or to visit Altun Ha Maya site are around US$85 per person.

Caye Caulker also is home to a growing scene of other water and windsports, including paddleboarding and windsurfing and of course fishing. Check out:

Raggamuffin Tours (501-226-0348, www.raffamuffintours.com) has overnight sailing trips a 56-foot ketch, plus a three-day sailing trip to Placencia, with a stop-over for camping on Tobacco Caye. The Placencia trip goes for US$350 per person including meals. It also does day sails and snorkel trips.

KiteExplorer offers (501-635-4967, www.kitexplorer.com) offers beginner to advanced kiteboarding, windsurfing and paddle surfing.

Anglers Abroad (Sea Dreams Hotel, 501-226-0602, www.anglersabroad.com) does half-day fishing trips for around US$220 and full-day for around US$350, including guide, boat and lunch.

Caye Caulker Lodging

This is not a complete list of island hotels, but these are among our favorites in all price ranges. They are arranged by location, either north or south of Main Street and the main "front pier" where some water taxi boats arrive, and then (roughly) by price range, from most to least expensive.

North of the Main Front Pier:

CayeReef Condos. Front Street, Caye Caulker, 501-226-0381; www.cayereef.com. CayeReef Condos are relatively new upscale accommodations. The six condo apartments are on Front Street not far from the Split, with a small swimming pool at the front, hidden behind a wall. You can book either a two-bedroom entire unit or just one of the bedrooms. All units are fully air-conditioned, with tile floors, custom kitchens, private verandas with sea views (second and third floors), free wi-fi and cable TV. The units have Belizean art on the walls and flat-screen TVs. There are great views of the reef from the fourth floor roof top patio, where there is a rooftop whirlpool. Rates vary by the floor level – the higher the floor the higher the rate. In-season two bedroom units are US$210 to $247, and one-bedroom units are US$173 to $210. Off-season, the two-bedrooms are US$159 to $206, and the one-bedrooms are US$124 to $165. All rates plus tax and are higher at Christmas-New Years.

Iguana Reef Inn. Middle Street next to soccer field (P.O. Box 31, Caye Caulker), 501-226-0213; www.iguanareefinn.com. This is the Ritz-Carlton of Caye Caulker. Sort of. The suites have air-conditioning, Belizean furniture, queen beds and local artwork. A swimming pool was added in 2006, and there's a nice bar with some 20 brands of rum. Considering the size and amenities of the 11 suites, the rates, US$159 to $259 in-season, and US$139 to $189 off-season, plus tax, are reasonable, and they include continental breakfast and complimentary kayaks and bikes. A penthouse suite on the third level with two bedrooms and two baths is pricey in-season at US$469, and a cabaña is US$289 (US$389 and $209 off-season, respectively). If there's a downside, it is that the hotel is on the backside of the island and not on the Caribbean, though the plus of that is from some suites you have a view of sunsets over the lagoon. The hotel's website is a good source of information about the island.

Sea Dreams Hotel. Front Street near the Split, Caye Caulker, 501-226-0602; www.seadreamsbelize.com. This is a great spot for anglers or just those who want to enjoy a relaxing stay at a well-run place. The "lobby" is sand with a large tree in the middle of it. Sea Dreams, located off Front Street on the west side, near the Split, has a variety of accommodations, including five courtyard rooms, three two-bedroom apartments, a penthouse and a cabaña, a bungalow and a house. All have A/C, cable TV and wi-fi; larger units have full kitchens. Sea Dreams has a roof-top terrace with panoramic views, plus a pier/dock on the lagoon side. Rates from around US$115 to $225, plus tax, including full breakfast. Owner Haywood Curry is known as an excellent fly fisherman. Co-owner Heidi Curry helped found Caulker's first high school.

Caye Caulker Condos. Front Street (P.O. Box 52, Caye Caulker), 501-226-0072; www.cayecaulkercondos.com. Want a suite with a full kitchen to prepare some of your own meals? Try these condo apartments not far from the Split. Each of the eight cozy units, on the west side of Front Street, has a private verandah facing the water, less than 100 feet away; those on the second floor have the better views. There's now a small pool, too. All the units have A/C, tile floors, satellite TV and wi-fi. Bikes are free. There's now a swimming pool, too. Rates US$99 to $139 double in-season, US$79-$99 off-season, plus 9% hotel tax.

Caye Caulker Plaza Hotel. Avenida Langosta and Calle del Sol (P.O. Box 3, Caye Caulker), 501-226-0780; www.cayecaulkerplazahotel.com. This modern 30-room, concrete hotel has a central location in the middle of the village. It's about a 5-minute walk to either the sea or the lagoon. While not on the water, you do have sea and lagoon views from the fourth-level roof-top deck. Rooms are clean, with mini-fridge, cable TV and really cold air-conditioning! In-season, rates are US$90 to $110, off-season US$75 to $95, plus tax.

De Real Macaw. Front Street, Caye Caulker, 501-226-0459; www.derealmacaw.biz. This friendly American-owned lodging, on the west side of Front Street but still close enough to catch the breezes, has a variety of accommodations -- rooms, a beach house, cabañas and a two-bedroom condo. More-expensive units have A/C. There's a porch with hammocks. Rates are US$25 to $130 for most of the year and US$20 to $110 September to mid-November, plus tax. Some units have minimum stay requirements.

Yuma's House. Beachfront just north of public pier, Caye Caulker, 501-206-0019; www.yumashousebelize.com. For US$17.50 per person, you can grab a bunk bed at this hostel on the beach. Formerly it was the very laidback Tina's; now it is less laidback, with no children under 15, a zero drugs policy, no guests that aren't registered can enter the property, quiet time after 11 p.m. and other rules that are strictly enforced. A few private rooms with shared baths are about US$42.50, plus tax. Rates a little lower mid-May to mid-December. Though the hostel dorms are basic, you're right on the water, and the price and location mean this place is usually packed with young people. Reservations are a good idea – see the Yuma's website for a schedule for when reservations are accepted.

Sandy Lane Guesthouse and Cabañas. Corner Chapoose and Langosta Streets, Caye Caulker, 501-226-0117. This longtime budget favorite has nine rooms, some with private baths and some with shared baths, and four basic cabañas. Rates are a bargain at around US$13 to $17 for rooms and US$30 for the cabañas. There is a common kitchen outdoors.

South of the Main Front Pier:

Seaside Cabanas. Main Street, beachfront (P.O. Box 39, Caye Caulker), 501-226-0498; www.seasidecabanas.com. Rebuilt after a 2003 fire, this seafront hotel, with 17 rooms plus a seafront suite, is a high-profile spot near the village's main front pier. You're just a short walk from many of the island's restaurants, bars and shops. Painted a mustard color, with a combination of tropical thatch and concrete constructions, the Seaside buildings are in a U-shape around a pool. Una Mas is the bar. Several of the rooms have private rooftop terraces for sunning or watching the sea in privacy. The hotel has in-room phones and free wi-fi. Rates around USS129 to $199 in-season and US$115 to $189 off-season, plus 9% tax. The hotel is for sale but is operating normally.

Colinda Cabañas. Beachfront, Caye Caulker, 501-226-0383; www.colindacabanas.com. Colinda Cabañas (the owners are named Colin and Linda) enjoys a great reputation and many repeat guests. Located away from the main part of the village toward the south end of the island, it has three beachfront suites, two second-row suites, five cabañas and a two-bedroom house on the breezy sea side of the island with a fine view of the reef. You can lounge on hammocks or possibly swim from the 175-foot private pier with thatch palapa. Year-round rates range from US$69 to $159, plus tax. Weekly or longer bookings and returning guests enjoy a US$10-a-night discount. Complimentary bikes, kayaks and snorkeling gear. Wi-fi is free but the signal isn't strong in some rooms.

Barefoot Beach Belize. Beachfront, south of the public pier, Caye Caulker, 501-226-0205; www.barefootbeachbelize.com. Formerly the Seaview Guest House, the current owners have turned this little seafront place into one of the more popular spots on Caulker. There are a total of 17 rooms, including seven budget rooms in "The Huts." Rates in-season range from US$55 to $129, and US$40 to $99 off-season, plus tax. Don't confuse this place with the similarly named Barefoot Caribe.

OASI. Front Street, Caye Caulker, 501-226-0384; www.oasi-holidaysbelize.com. Located about 5 minutes south of the main public pier, in a quieter area, OASI has four lovely rental apartments with air conditioning, wi-fi, cable TV, fully furnished kitchens and verandahs with hammocks. It is set in tropical grounds, with a fountain, barbecue grill and small bar for guests, Il Baretta, which serves real Italian espresso, wine and drinks. Complimentary bikes. Rates are a good value at US$95 to $105 double in-season, US$85 to $95 in low season. All rates plus 9% tax. Get the top floor apartment if you can. Recommended.

Tree Tops. Beachfront, (P.O. Box 29, Caye Caulker), 501-226-0240; www.treetopsbelize.com. Set back a little from the water, Tree Tops is run by Austrian-born Doris Creasy. All rooms have air-conditioning available, cable TV and a fridge. The four regular rooms are US$70 to $90 double year-round. Two third-floor suites (US$120 year-round), Sunset and Sunrise, have king-size beds and private balconies with views of the sea. Rates plus 9% tax. A small courtyard is a great place to read or just lounge in a hammock. Belize needs more places like this one – the guest rooms are clean as a pin, the entire place is meticulously maintained, and the owner is helpful. Highly recommended.

Pancho's Villas. Pasero Street (P.O. Box 80, Caye Caulker), 501-226-0304; www.panchosvillasbelize.com. Owned by the same people who run Pancho's Auto Rentals in Belize City, Pancho's Villas has six rooms and three one-bedroom suites in a yellow three-story concrete building. All units have air-conditioning and ceiling fans, cable TV, wi-fi, fridge and microwave. The seafront is a short walk away. Rates US$70 to $95 in-season, US$60 to $85 off-season, plus tax. Weekly and monthly rates available.

Maxhapan Cabañas. 55 Avenue Pueblo Nuevo, Caye Caulker, 501-226-0118. This little spot is in the center of the village and not on the water, but it's very popular because it's neat and clean and a good value. Set in a small, sandy and shady garden, there are only three rooms in a two-story cabaña and in a one-level building. They have tile floors and a veranda with hammocks. Complimentary bikes and snorkel gear. Rates start around US$65 plus tax.

Caye Caulker Vacation Rentals

For small vacation rental house on Caulker, expect to pay around US$350 to $1,000 a week, or US$75 to $200 a night. Rentals incur the 9% hotel tax.

Caye Caulker Accommodations. (P.O. Box 88, Caye Caulker), 501-226-0382; www.cayecaulkeraccommodations.com. This company manages more than two dozen houses and other rental units (some listings shared with other firms) on the island. Several have pools.

Caye Caulker Rentals. Front Street, Caye Caulker, 501-226-0029; www.cayecaulkerrentals.com. This rental agency has some two dozen houses for rent, some from as low as US$50 a night, and others, including beachfront houses, from under US$500 a week.

Casitas Carinosa. (P.O. Box 48, Caye Caulker), 501-226-0547; www.cayecaulkercasita.com. Amanda Badger offers three nice rental options, all with pools – Amanda's Place, with two studio apartments, the three-bedroom Casita Carinosa and the one-bedroom Casa Amancer. Weekly rates range from US$575 to $1,295, plus 9% tax.

Dining on Caye Caulker

Caye Caulker has more than 30 restaurants, mostly small spots with a few tables and sand or wood floors, where you can get a tasty meal for a few dollars. A few are more upmarket. Some don't accept credit cards.

With the increasing popularity of Caye Caulker, there has been a boom in the restaurant business on the island over the past two or three years. More than a dozen new eateries have opened. Locals also operate "pop up" restaurants – just a grill where they prepare fresh fish or chicken for you at modest prices.

Note that some restaurants close during the slow September-October period or at the whim of the owner. Opening times and days may vary seasonally

Price ranges shown are for typical meals for one (usually dinner), not including tip, tax or alcoholic drinks. Price ranges:

Inexpensive: Under US$7

Moderate: US$8-$19

Expensive: US$20-$39

Very Expensive: Over US$40

Restaurants here are listed alphabetically.

Alladins. Beachfront, near the Split, Caye Caulker, 501-660-1550. Alladins serves tasty, authentic Middle Eastern dishes such as kebabs, falafel, hummus and baba ghanoush at modest prices. Inexpensive to Moderate.

Amor y Café. Front Street, Caye Caulker. Formerly Cyndi's, Amor y Café is another good place for breakfast, along with love and coffee. Open for breakfast daily. Inexpensive to Moderate.

Au French Corner. Front Street at Avenida Hicaco, Caye Caulker, 501-624-7374. Who would have thought you could get authentic French savory and sweet crepes on Caye Caulker? The new Au French Corner, with a chef from Paris – really – pulls it off. There are banana crepes, curry crepes, spinach crepes, strawberry nutella crepes, breakfast crepes, dessert crepes and others. Open for breakfast Wednesday to Saturday and dinner Tuesday to Saturday. Moderate.

Caribbean Colors Art Café. Front Street, Caye Caulker, 501-668-7205; www.caribbean-colors.com. Come for the art by Lee Vanderwalker. Stay for the coffee, omelets, salads and sushi. Open for breakfast, lunch and dinner. Closed Tuesday. Moderate.

Glenda's. Back Street, Caye Caulker, 501-226-0148. Come to Glenda's for a cinnamon roll, johnnycake and fresh-squeezed orange juice for breakfast, and come back at lunch for rice and beans. Open for breakfast and lunch Monday to Saturday. No credit cards. Inexpensive.

Habaneros Restaurant. Middle Street, Caye Caulker, 501-626-4911. Caye Caulker's most upscale dining and some think the best. Try the Lobster Newburgh (in lobster season) or voodoo cakes. Everything tastes better with frozen mojitos. Dinner daily. Live music many evenings. Expensive. Reservations suggested in-season.

Il Pellicano Cucina Italian Restaurant. 49 Pasero Street, Caye Caulker, 501-226-0660. Authentic Italian food prepared by Italians. Open for dinner. Closed Tuesday. Expensive.

Pasta Per Caso. Avenida Hicaco, Caye Caulker, 501-634-5641. It's always seemed odd to us that visitors to a tropical island would choose Italian food for dinner, but in the case of Pasta Per Caso, we can understand it. The chef, from Milan, here does fresh pasta with light and tasty sauces, usually just two dishes each evening for you to choose between. Desserts are good, and try the Compari orange and rum punch. Open for dinner. Closed Tuesday and Wednesday. Expensive.

Roses Grill & Bar. Calle del Sol, Caye Caulker, 501-206-0407. This "open door" restaurant under a large thatch palapa is one of the best-known spots on the island, and the tables are often packed. However, some think Roses is a victim of its own popularity and that it's not as good as it once was. The specialty is seafood, and it's all fresh. Dinner daily, open for breakfast and lunch during high season. Moderate to Expensive.

Syd's. Middle Street, Caye Caulker, south of public pier, 501-600-9481. Locals often recommend Syd's, one of the old-time places on the island. It serves Belizean and Mexican faves like beans and rice, stew chicken, garnaches, tostadas along with lobster and conch, when in season, at prices lower than you'll pay at many other eateries. Breakfast, lunch and dinner daily. Moderate.

Wish Willy Bar & Grill. Located on a side street off Front Street near the Split, across from Frenchie's. At Wish Willy you eat in the back yard of the owner, Maurice. He tells you what's on the menu today. It may be fresh fish, lamb or chicken. In most cases, the prices are low, and the rum drinks cost less here than almost anywhere else on the island. You may have to share a table with other guests, and the service is sometimes slow, but keep in mind the money you're saving. Moderate.

Sign on Caye Caulker

WHERE TO PARTY

For Belikin and booze, the **Lazy Lizard** at the Split is probably the most popular bar on the island. Its slogan is "A sunny place for shady people." Closed Monday.

For live music, on Fridays check out the guitar jam at the **Barrier Reef Sports Bar & Grill**, beachfront near the water taxi piers. **Habaneros** has live music with its dinner most evenings. **I&I,** on Traveler's Palm Street near Tropical Paradise, a funky joint with rope swings and hammocks instead of chairs, blows reggae and other music nightly. In the back is a tree house.

Cabaña on Thatch Caye, off Dangriga

CHECKING OUT OTHER CAYES

Belize's two main northern cayes, Ambergris and Caulker, are the largest and by far the most popular of Belize's islands, both by expats and visitors. However, Belize has more than 400 other islands in the Caribbean. Most are small, remote and unpopulated. They are wonderful if typically somewhat expensive to visit, and building and living on the islands also is expensive. Here, briefly, are some of the options for lodging.

Note on fishing licenses: If you plan to fish in Belize, whether around the cayes or even from a pier on the mainland, in most cases you now need a saltwater fishing license. Costs are US$10 per day, US$25 per week or US$50 per year. Your fishing guide or hotel can assist in getting you a license, or, failing that, contact Belize Coastal Zone Management (www.coastalzonebelize.org, 501-223-0719).

NEAR BELIZE CITY

Historical St. George's Caye is only about 8 miles or 20 minutes by boat from Belize City. It was the site of perhaps the most famous event in Belize history, when, as the story goes, in September 1798 a ragtag group of

Baymen defeated a larger Spanish fleet from Mexico. St. George's Caye Day on September 10 celebrates the culminating Belizean victory. Today, St. George's Caye is home to one dive resort and to a number of weekend and holiday homes of Belize City's economic and social elite. Ask about the small aquarium on the island.

St. George's Caye Resort. St. George's Caye, 800-813-8498; www.belizeislandparadise.com. This long-established resort, now under new management, has 12 cabañas, including some that are set over the water, and a main lodge building with seven rooms. It's the exact opposite of a large resort. You get personal attention here, and sometimes you may be the only guests at the hotel. Cabaña rates are US$119 to $159 per person. Simple rooms are US$99 per person. All units have air-conditioning. Full meal plans are an additional US$60 per person per day. There are also dive and other packages, starting at US$826 to $1,066 per person for four nights. Rates are plus 9% tax. Rates include transfers from the international airport (minimum four-night stay), unlimited use of kayaks, Hobie Cats, windsurfers and snorkeling equipment and wireless internet in the main lodge. There is a salt-water pool. A bar serves beer and drinks.

Royal Palm Island Resort. Little Frenchman Caye, 501-223-4999 or 888-969-7829; www.royalpalmisland.com. This resort on 7-acre Little Frenchman Caye is about 9 miles off Belize City and within about a mile of the barrier reef. Accommodations are in air-conditioned two-bedroom beachfront cottages. All-inclusive rates include full breakfast, lunch with beverage of choice, three-course dinner with beverage of choice, mini-bar in room and return transfers from the international airport. Day trips to the island from Belize City are around US$100 including lunch. All-inclusive rates are from US$342 to $430 per person per day, depending on the time of year. Rates include taxes and service.

Hugh Parkey's Belize Adventure Lodge. Spanish Lookout Caye, 501-223-4526; www.belizeadventurelodge.com. Named after a well-known dive and hotel operator who with his wife Therese for many years ran the famous Fort Street Guesthouse in Belize City. He died of a heart attack in 2002, while diving in Mexico. This lodge formerly featured a swim-with-dolphins program, which happily was discontinued. Now it has 12 cabañas on 186-acre Spanish Caye about 25 minutes from Belize City. The cabañas are built over water. Five day/four-night dive packages, including transfers, lodging in an over-the-water cabaña, meals and four dives are around US$950 per person, based on double occupancy. Prices include taxes but not rental dive equipment or entries to some marine parks.

Islands Off Dangriga
RAGGED CAYE RANGE

Royal Belize. Ragged Caye Range, 800-348-0546; www.royalbelize.com. Want to rent a private island for yourself and your closest friends? There are four deluxe, air-conditioned cottages on the island 25 minutes by boat from Dangriga. For around US$5,600 a night (US$4,400 September to mid-November) on an all-inclusive basis, including transfers from Belize City, meals, drinks and many water activities, you can enjoy the entire island for your party of up to 10 people. For weddings and other groups, the island comes with manager, concierge and cook. Off-island tours are not included in the all-inclusive rates. Minimum four-day stay, and taxes are additional. All on-island activities are included in the rates, including use of a Hobie Wave Catamaran, paddleboards, kiteboards, kayaks and snorkeling equipment. Rates for couples may also be available at times.

SOUTHWATER CAYE MARINE RESERVE

About 10 miles off Dangriga, **Tobacco Caye** is a tiny 5-acre coral island. It is getting more attention these days because it offers snorkeling off the shore. Some people think Tobacco Caye is a funky island paradise; others think it's a bit junky. The accommodations on Tobacco Caye are all quite basic, essentially simple wood cabins without air-conditioning.

There's no scheduled water taxi service, but you can hook a boat at Dangriga to take you out – around US$17.50 one-way. **Captain Buck** (501-669-0869) is reliable, as are **Campa** (501-666-8699) and **Captain Doggie** (501-627-7443). Check at the **Riverside Café,** where the boat captains hang out. Campa has the largest and newest boats.

Paradise Caye Cabins. 501-532-2101 or 800-667-1630 in U.S./Canada; www.tobaccocaye.com. Paradise has six simple but clean over-the-water cabins at the north end of the island. Rates around US$25 per person for room-only, US$50 per person including meals. All plus 9% tax. If you're buying meals separately, they're US$7.50 for breakfast or lunch, US$10 for dinner. Paradise Cabins is part of the Belize Adventure Group, which also runs Island Expeditions, Island Adventures and

Bocawina Rainforest Resort.

Tobacco Caye Lodge. 501-532-2 033; www.tclodgebelize.com.
Rooms in six duplex wood cabañas, with all meals, are around US$55 per
person in-season and US$48 per person off-season, plus 9% tax.

Other choices on the island include **Reef's End Lodge**
(www.reefendslodge.com, which has the island's only dive shop, and **Jo-Jo's
by the Reef** (www.jojosbythereef.com.)

Southwater Caye, about 15 acres in size, is one of the most beautiful
small islands off Belize. The south end of the caye, where Pelican Beach's
cottages are located, has a nice little beach and snorkeling right off the
shore.

Pelican Beach Resort, Southwater Caye. (P.O. Box 2,
Dangriga), 501-522-2044; www.pelicanbeachbelize.com. This is a
wonderful place, but it's not cheap. The resort has three charming but not
deluxe duplex cottages, two stand-alone casitas plus five rooms in the main
building on 3½ acres at the south end, the best end of this beautiful island.
In-season, nightly rates are US$350 double in a Pelican Pouch room to
US$475 double in a freestanding casita, including three meals. Off-season,
rates are only slightly less -- US$315 to $430. Rates do include taxes and
service. Boat transfers from Dangriga are around US$70 person extra.
Packages are also available, which include lodging, meals and transfers. A
three-night package is US$850 to $885 per person, including taxes and
service, a few dollars less off-season.

Other choices on the island is the expensive **Blue Marlin Lodge**
(501-520-2243, www.bluemarlinlodge.com), with good dive and fishing
options, and the less expensive **International Zoological Expeditions
Cottages** (501-520-5030, www.ize2belize.com), which caters to
educational groups in a dorm, but which also has private cabins and a dive
shop.

Note: Visitors to Southwater Caye Marine Reserve (including those
staying on Tobacco Caye and Southwater Caye) pay US$5 a day per
person marine reserve fee, or US$15 for up to a week's stay.

COCOPLUM RANGE

These islands are about 9 miles off Dangriga. Unlike Southwater Caye
and Tobacco Caye, they are not directly on the reef, so the shore snorkeling

316

is fair at best.

Thatch Caye. (P.O. Box 133, Dangriga), 501-532-2414 or 800-435-3145 in U.S./Canada; www.thatchcayebelize.com. There are five overwater bungalows, one three-bedroom over-the-water villa and four seaside cottages on this "hand built" island. (The developers spent years putting up bamboo sea walls and raised boardwalks.) You can head out for a day of fishing, diving, sea kayaking, or snorkeling, then enjoy a delicious meal in the thatched-roof dining room, sip an ice-cold drink and surf the web on the free wi-fi in the bar before heading to your seaside or over-the-water cabaña where you'll be lulled asleep by the trade winds. Nightly all-inclusive rates, including lodging, all meals, drinks, marine reserve fees and use of non-motorized water sports equipment and round-trip transportation from Dangriga, are US$595 double per night for both island cabañas or over-the-water bungalows. Taxes aren't included, and rates are higher during holidays. Diving, fishing and wedding packages are also available. Thatch Caye strives for sustainability, with solar and wind power, and discourages the use of air-conditioning.

Coco Plum Island Resort. Cocoplum Caye, 800-763-7360 in U.S./Canada; www.cocoplumcay.com. Coco Plum Island Resort is an adults-only all-inclusive on a 16-acre island, a short distance from Thatch Caye. It has 14 cottages, all air-conditioned and painted in bright tropical colors. The larger cottages have kitchenettes. A four-night package with all meals, drinks, boat transfers from Dangriga, two snorkeling tours and use of snorkeling equipment and kayak is US$2,720 in-season, US$2,440 off-season. Taxes but not gratuities are not included in packages. Some more-expensive packages include flights from Belize City and a number of mainland and other tours. The snorkeling off the shore is only so-so, but most packages include snorkel trips to the reef a few miles farther out. Diving, fishing and romance packages also available.

Islands Off Placencia

Whipray Caye, about 11 miles off Placencia, is a spot for anglers, as you can wade out about 50 yards in the flats and fish for tarpon, permit and other game fish. Julian Cabral, a well known Placencia fishing guide, owns the island and with American wife Beverly Montgomery-Cabral operates **Whipray Lodge** and the **Sea Urchin** bar and restaurant (501-610-1068, www.whipraycayelodge.com.) The three basic cabins can accommodate up to eight people. There's also good snorkeling here.

The Atolls

Atolls are characterized by a large lagoon surrounded by coral reefs. While atolls are common in the South Pacific, they are rare in the Western Hemisphere. Of the four known atolls in the Western Hemisphere, three are in Belize – Glovers, Turneffe and Lighthouse. (The fourth, Chinchorra, is in southern Mexico.)

GLOVERS ATOLL

Glovers Atoll (also spelled Glover's Atoll) is the smallest of the three atolls in Belize, with an area of about 140 square miles. Some 45 miles from the mainland, Glovers offers some of the best diving and snorkeling in the Caribbean. The atoll, named after a pirate, John Glover, has some 800 coral patches in the lagoon. It, like the Belize Barrier Reef, is a UNESCO World Heritage Site. Around the atoll are 50 miles of walls dropping from 40 to 2,500 feet or more. There's a US$30 marine reserve fee. Fishing is restricted in this reserve – if you are fishing, reserve rangers will collect a weekly fee of US$25 per person.

Isla Marisol. (P.O. Box 10, Dangriga), 501-610-4204 or 855-350-1569; www.islamarisol.com. Southwest Caye, where Isla Marisol is located, is owned by a Belizean family, which obtained the island in the 1940s. Lodging at this resort is in 12 wood cabins with air-conditioning and zinc roofs and two suites in a house. There's a restaurant and bar. Four-night packages, including lodging, meals and transport from Dangriga, start at about US$2,150 per couple. Fishing and dive charges are extra (for example, one-tank dives are US$56 plus 12.5% tax per person). Isla Marisol's sister resort on the mainland is Fantasy Island Eco-Resort.

Off the Wall Dive Center and Resort. Long Caye, 501-532-2929; www.offthewallbelize.com. Off the Wall, run by Jim and Kendra Schofield, focuses on diving, but there's excellent snorkeling and fishing as well. Facilities are rustic — five small wood cabins, composting toilets and outdoor rainwater showers. Meals are served in a beachfront thatch palapa with sand floor. There is no a/c, no room phones, no room TVs, with solar-powered lights and candles, which many find just about perfect. Great snorkeling is available from shore, and you can also fish for bonefish, permit, grouper and jack right from the lodge's pier. Rates US$1,495 plus tax per person weekly for lodging and meals; gratuities and rum and beer are additional. Boat transfers from Dangriga, leaving on Saturday, are included. Dives are extra −a 12-dive package is US$450 plus 12.5% GST. Any needed dive and fishing equipment rental also is extra.

Glovers Atoll Resort. Northeast Caye (P.O. Box 563, Belize City), 501-520-5016; www.glovers.com.bz. Don't let the name mislead you − this isn't your typical resort. The Lamont family, who came to Belize in the 1960s, offer very basic accommodations on Northeast Caye, about 45 miles out in the Caribbean at a reasonable price in a beautiful setting. You won't get running water or electricity here, but you can enjoy one of the most stunning parts of the Caribbean Sea. Around the 9-acre island you can dive or snorkel right from the shore. Weekly per-person rates year-round: Simple palmetto thatch cabañas are US$249 and those built over the water are US$299; thatch cabañas on beach, US$249; dorm room is US$149, camping, US$99. Children under 12 are half price. Rates include transportation by boat to and from Sittee River near Hopkins but not 9% hotel tax. The weekly boat from Sittee River leaves Sundays. If you can't make the Sunday boat, charters are expensive: One-way US$350 for up to six passengers from Sittee River Village or Dangriga, and it takes 1½ to 2 hours to island. From Placencia the charter is US$400, and from Belize City, US$800. You'll need to bring most everything you need, including toilet paper, food, beer, cooler with ice and other supplies. Bottled water (US$1.50 a gallon) and kerosene (US$1 a pint) and a few grocery items are usually available on the island. Simple meals are offered, but they're fairly expensive. You can rent kayaks, canoes, and dive and snorkel gear. Glovers Atoll Resort is quite a remarkable place, but not for everyone.

Also check out the **Slickrock Adventures** lodge on Long Caye (800-390-5715 from U.S./Canada, www.slickrock.com), with rates around US$1,500 per person for a five-night trip. Another good option is **Island Expeditions** (800-667-1630 from U.S./Canada, www.islandexpeditions.com), which has a tent camp on Southwest Caye. Three-day packages cost from around US$640 per person.

LIGHTHOUSE REEF ATOLL

Lighthouse Atoll is about 45 miles off the mainland coast, east of Belize City. The atoll is famous (thanks to Jacques Cousteau) for the Blue Hole inside the lagoon. The Blue Hole, an underwater sinkhole or cenote, is about one-quarter mile across and about 500 feet deep. Divers usually find the Blue Hole less interesting than they expected it would be, with very little sea life other than some sharks, but it's worth doing once. Several divers have died here, and it is not for novice divers. Half Moon Caye, a 45-acre coral island, is one of the most beautiful of all the Belize cayes, and it was part of Belize's first marine reserve. There's a daily fee of US$40 per person to visit the reserve. Currently, an eco lodge at the atoll is not operating and is for sale.

TURNEFFE ATOLL

Turneffe Atoll is about 25 miles from the mainland, to the east of Belize City. The central lagoon, which has some 200 small mangrove islands, is about 240 square miles in area. There is also a smaller northern lagoon. Like Belize's other atolls, Turneffe offers magnificent diving and great fishing. The eastern and southern side of the atoll offers the best diving. Probably the most famous site is The Elbow, on the southern tip. Spur and groove diving is here only for experienced divers.

Turneffe Flats. U.S. office: P.O. Box 10670, Bozeman, MT 59719, 501-232-9032 or 888-512-8812 in U.S./Canada; www.tflats.com. It's remote, it's beautiful and it's air-conditioned. The lodge, on the northeast side of the atoll, provides boat transport from Belize City to Turneffe on Saturdays. The trip takes about 90 minutes. Dive packages are around US$2,750 in-season and US$2,550 per person for a week, depending on the time of year inclusive of lodging, meals, three dives a day and transport to the island but not booze, tips, park fees or taxes. Weekly fishing packages are more, around US$3,780 to $4,280 per person. Three- and four-night packages also are available, as are many other packages.

Blackbird Caye Resort. 866-909-7333; www.blackbirdresort.com. Now under new management, Blackbird Caye Resort is about 25 miles from Belize City, with about 4,000 acres and some two miles of beachfront on Blackbird Caye at Turneffe Atoll. Accommodations are in duplex and triplex cabañas, a beach house, a beachfront suite and in three levels of rooms. Dinner is served in a large thatch palapa, and there's a pool with bar. All-inclusive packages that include transfers by air to the caye (Blackbird has an airstrip), lodging in an oceanfront suite, meals, diving and more, for US$4,000 per person for a week and US$3,200 for four nights. Rates do not include a resort fee, tips or drinks. There are myriad other packages and rates.

Turneffe Island Resort. 501-532-2990 or 800-760-0241 in U.S./Canada; www.turnefferesort.com. Accommodations are in eight private cabañas or in 12 superior-level or deluxe-level rooms on Big Caye Bokel at the southern end of the central lagoon. Weekly packages range from US$2,090 to $4,590 per person, depending on type of activities, the time of year and other factors. Three- and four-night packages also available, starting at US$1,340 per person. Rates include boat transport to the island but not taxes, tips or alcohol.

CHECKING OUT COROZAL

How to Get There
From Mexico: ADO (in Mexico 525-133-2424, www.ado.com.mx)
and other Mexican bus lines serve Chetumal, capital of the Mexican state of
Quintana Roo and, with a population of more than 300,000, far larger than
any city in Belize. Buses run frequently from various towns and cities in the

Yucatán, including Playa del Carmen and Mérida. Fares for first class buses — with reserved seats, videos, and bathrooms — are around 312 pesos or US$20 at current exchange rates from Playa del Carmen to Chetumal. It's a little over four hours from Playa del Carmen and six from Mérida. At the Chetumal bus station, you change to a Belize bus to Corozal Town (fare US$1.50), or take a taxi to the border or use a transfer service. Buses leave Chetumal for Corozal Town and points south beginning well before daybreak. At the border, which sports a new Belize customs and immigration office, marked by a bridge over the Rio Hondo, you get off the bus to go through customs and immigration and then reboard for the 15-minute ride into Corozal Town. A taxi into Corozal Town from the border is around US$10.

Another option for some is the **ADO Express** between Cancún and Belize City and also between Mérida and Belize City. The daily Belize-City-Cancún bus is a comfortable, air-conditioned bus with reserved seats and videos. It costs 576 pesos one-way (about US$35 at current exchange rates.) Schedules change, but as of this writing the ADO Express departs from the Cancún bus terminal at 10:15 p.m. with stops at Playa del Carmen, Corozal Town and Orange Walk Town. It arrives in Belize City about 6:30 a.m. From Belize City, the current schedule is departure from the Belize City Novelo's station at 7:30 p.m., with stops at Orange Walk (9 p.m.), Corozal (10 p.m.), Tulum (4 a.m.), Playa del Carmen (5 a.m.) and Cancún International Airport (6:30 a.m.). The ADO Express Mérida, also known as the hospital run, due to the number of Belizeans who get medical care in Mérida, currently isn't daily but three or four days a week.

Transfer services in Corozal and elsewhere in Belize will also pick you up in Cancun or elsewhere in Mexico and bring you to Corozal. One of the good transfer services is **Belize VIP Transfer Service,** formerly Menzies Tours (www.belizetransfers.com, 501-422-2725). You'll pay around US400 for up to four persons from Cancun to Corozal, US$350 from Playa del Carmen, US$300 from Tulum, and US$45 from Bacalar or US$30 from Chetumal. Other shuttle services also operate.

It's also possible to **rent a car** in Cancún, Playa del Carmen, Chetumal or elsewhere and drive it into Belize (only a few Mexican agencies permit this). You will have to stop at the Belize border and purchase Belize auto insurance.

From points south in Belize: Corozal Town is about 83 miles by road from the international airport in Ladyville and 9 miles from the Mexican border. Figure about two hours by car on the Philip Goldson Highway (formerly Northern Highway) from Belize City. Belize Bus Owners Cooperative (BBOC), Cabrera's, Chell's, Joshua's, Morales, Tillett's, T-Line and Valencia are among bus lines on this route, with frequent service in both directions, starting early in the morning and continuing to the early evening. Fares are about US$6 between Belize City and Corozal Town. Buses on this route use the main bus terminal in Belize City, Novelo's on West Collet Canal; in Corozal Town the bus station is on the main road toward the north end and just a few minutes walk to the main part of town. By regular (local) bus the trip takes about three to four hours. Most buses on this route are retired school buses or other older equipment, and currently there are no express buses.

From San Pedro, Ambergris Caye:

Maya Island Air (www.mayaislandair.com) and **Tropic Air** (www.tropicair.com) each fly four or five times daily between Corozal's tiny airstrip and San Pedro, Ambergris Caye (around 25 minutes and roughly US$72 one-way). The airstrip is about 2 miles south of Corozal Town, a US$5 cab ride.

A **water taxi** with enclosed seating area, **Thunderbolt,** (501-620-4475, www.ambergriscaye.com/thunderbolt) connects San Pedro and Corozal Town. Daily – though at times service may be less than daily -- it leaves Corozal from the municipal (Reunion) pier at 7 a.m. and San Pedro at 3 p.m. for the 1½- to 2-hour trip. Fare is US$25 one-way, US$45 round-trip. On demand the boat stops at Sarteneja.

What to See and Do in Corozal

Ho hum, Corozal Town has few must-see attractions. It's more of a place just to visit, wander around the main plaza or waterfront, have a soft drink or beer and enjoy the Latin-Caribbean ambiance. Outside of Corozal Town, if you have the time and hemorrhoids for it, you really must drive up the Sarteneja peninsula to experience Belize off-the-beaten track. Also, go for a swim in Four Mile Lagoon or a take a boat or fishing trip in the beautiful Bay of Chetumal.

Corozal House of Culture. 1st Avenue, 501-422-0071, www.nichbelize.org. You'll recognize this place, in a landmark building over 100 years old, by its clock tower and new red roof. In the waterfront park, between 2nd Street South and the bay, the museum has, among other interesting artifacts, hand-blown rum bottles, a traditional Maya thatch hut and displays from the lighthouse that once stood on this site. It also presents rotating art and history displays. After renovation, it reopened in early 2012 and is now operated by the National Institute of Culture and History (NICH). Admission US$5.

Gabriel Hoare Market. This market, which replaced the old one by the bay, is in a two-story concrete building on 6th Avenue near the center of town. The first level has numerous fruit and vegetable stalls, with good seasonal selections of local items such as papaya, mangos, watermelon, citrus, bananas, onions, potatoes, peppers, ginger and beans. Upstairs are several inexpensive restaurants for a quick breakfast or lunch, along with some shops selling clothing and other items. There also are stands beside the main market building.

Corozal Town Hall. Stop by on weekdays for a look at the mural by Manuel Villamar Reyes. It depicts the region's history. Nearby, in the center of town, are the ruins of Fort Barley, built to thwart attacks by Maya Indians.

Maya Sites
Cerros

Cerro Maya (sometimes referred to as Cerros) was an important jade and obsidian trading center during the Late Pre-Classic Period, with its heyday being from 400 BC to 100 CE. The site apparently suffered an economic decline and was mostly abandoned in the Early Pre-Classic period after 250 CE, although there were residents there until around 1300 CE.

This site is on 53 acres on a hill beside the Bay of Chetumal. Cerros was first studied by the amateur archeologist Thomas Gann in the early 1900s. It was surveyed and excavated by David Freidel of Southern Methodist University in the 1970s. More recently a group of archeologists including Debra Walker, Kathryn Reese-Taylor and Beverly Mitchum Chiarulli brought to light several new structures including a ball court and a major monument.

Three main structures have been excavated, along with plazas and ball courts. One structure rises about 65 feet. The site is of special interest because of its location overlooking the Bay of Chetumal. Its waterfront location is reminiscent of the better-known Tulum site in the Yucatán.

A pedestrian and auto ferry across the New River has cut travel time by car to Cerros. Drive to Copper Bank village and turn left, following signs. A faster way is by boat from Corozal Town. Expect to pay around US$20 and up per person for someone with a skiff to take you and your party to Cerros, about 15 minutes away.

Admission: Daily 8-5, US$5.

Santa Rita

The Santa Rita archeological site is thought to be a small remnant of the Maya city of Chetumal, or Chactemal, an important Maya center since it controlled trade routes along the coast and into what is now Mexico and Guatemala. This center was occupied by the Maya from at least 2000 BC to the 16th century CE.

Thomas Gann worked here around the turn of the 20th century. Systematic excavations were by Diane and Arlen Chase from 1979 to 1985.

Only a small area has been excavated, and it is thought that much of the ancient city of Chetumal is now covered by the town of Corozal. One large Post-Classic structure with several chambers is excavated and open to visitors.

Santa Rita is located on a small hill at the northwest edge of Corozal Town, near the Coca-Cola plant. Follow the Santa Rita Road toward the Mexican border. About ½ mile from Corozal, bear to the right at the statue. Then, in a few hundred yards, take the first road to the left and then go about 2/10ths of a mile to the site.

Currently Santa Rita is closed, though you can walk around it. There are plans to develop the site for visitors and even weddings. Admission free.

Corozal Lodging

Almond Tree Hotel Resort. 425 Bayshore Dr., South End, 501-628-9224; www.almondtreeresort.com. This small inn is a fine upscale choice at reasonable rates. Set directly on the bay at the South End of town, Almond Tree has a fresh water pool. There are eight rooms/suites. Rates range from US$98 and $119 double, plus tax. There is air conditioning in rooms, cable TV, laundry services, bikes and wireless access throughout most of the premises.

George Hardie's Las Vegas Hotel & Casino. Mile 91.5 George

Price Highway, Corozal Free Zone. 501-423-7000; www.lvbelize.com. Located in the Corozal Free Zone area at the Belize-Mexico border, this is the newest and best hotel in the casino area. The main hotel is 106 rooms with a large pool, bar and fitness room. It opened in late 2015. Also here is the smaller, older Las Vegas Gardens Hotel. Rates around US$115-$150 double, plus tax. The hotel is a part of the 54,000 sq. ft. casino, the largest in the region.

Serenity Sands Bed & Breakfast. Mile 3, Consejo Road (P.O. Box 88, Corozal Town), 501-669-2394; www.serenitysands.com. Serenity Sands B&B is serenely hidden away off the Consejo Road north of Corozal Town. On the second floor of a large modern concrete home, there are four tastefully decorated rooms with private balconies, Belizean art and locally made hardwood furniture. Although not directly on the water, Serenity has a private beach on the bay a few hundred feet away. Rates are an excellent value for the high quality you enjoy, from US$90 to $95 in high season, US$80 to $85 off-season, plus tax. Full breakfasts, mostly organic, are included. Best visited with a rental car. Recommended.

Tony's Inn. South End, Corozal Town, 501-422-2055; www.tonysinn.com. A longtime favorite of travelers to Corozal, Tony's has 24 motel-like rooms with tile floors, cable TV and A/C. Many of the rooms recently have been renovated and upgraded, and rates for these have gone up. The breezy bayside palapa restaurant, Y Not Grill, is one of the most pleasant places to eat in Corozal. Rates: Upgraded rooms, US$120 double January-April, US$100 rest of the year; standard rooms US$80 in-season, US$70 off-season. All rates plus tax.

Copa Banana Guesthouse. 409 Bay Shore Drive., South End, (P.O. Box 26, Corozal Town), 501-422-0284; www.copabanana.bz. Whether you're just passing through or in town shopping for property around Corozal, you couldn't do much better than this guesthouse. There are five rooms/suites in two guesthouses. All have air-conditioning and wi-fi. There's a pool. The rates are affordable, you can cook meals in a common kitchen, complete with dishware, stove, coffeemaker, microwave and fridge. Rates: US$60 to $70 double, plus tax, with reduced rates for stays of at least 10 days. Complimentary bikes for rides into town from the South End. Currently, this property is for sale.

Las Palmas. 123 5th Ave., Corozal Town; 501-422-0196; www.laspalmashotelbelize.com. This was formerly the budget-level

Nestor's Hotel. It has was renovated and rebuilt, moving the whole property somewhat upmarket. The 27 rooms, with A/C, microwave, small fridge and wi-fi, go for about US$60 to $80 a night, double, plus tax. Las Palmas is currently for sale.

Sea Breeze Hotel. 19 1st Avenue, 501-422-3051; www.theseabreezehotel.com. The Sea Breeze is a good budget choice in Corozal. In 2015, the owner moved the inn to a new location about 150 feet from where it had been since 2008. There are now only three rooms that share two baths. Economy rooms are US$25, and the premium room is US$30 (US$40 with A/C) plus 9% tax. Sea Breeze has a boat that will take you across the bay to the Cerros ruins for US$20.

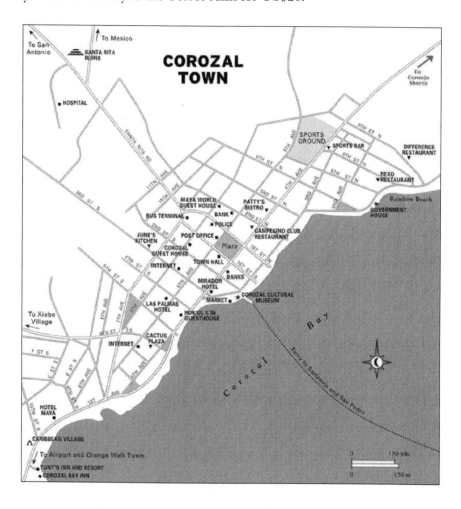

Dining in Corozal Town

Price ranges shown are for typical meals for one (usually dinner), not including tip, tax or alcoholic drinks. Price ranges:

Inexpensive: Under US$7

Moderate: US$8-$19

Expensive: US$20-$39

Very Expensive: Over US$40

Restaurants here are listed alphabetically.

Corozo Blue. South End, Corozal Town, 501-422-0090. In a beautifully redone stone building on the bay, this is a good spot for drinks and wood-fired pizza. Moderate.

June's Kitchen. Third Street South, Corozal Town, 501-422-2559. Miss June's Kitchen is the total favorite of many locals for its flavorful Belizean food. Breakfast is great, and there are specials for lunch every day, such as ribs, conch soup or a boil-up. Open for breakfast and lunch daily. Inexpensive to Moderate.

Patty's Bistro. 2nd Street North, Corozal Town, 501-402-0174. You can eat your fill of fried chicken, pork chops, stew chicken, conch soup and other local dishes for very modest prices. It moved in 2009 to 2nd Street North. Inexpensive to Moderate.

Venky's. 5th Avenue, across from the Immigration office, Corozal Town, 501-402-0536. For takeout curries and other Indian food at modest prices, Venky's is the place. Inexpensive to Moderate.

Y Not Grill. Tony's Inn on the South End, Corozal Town. Y Not is Tony's spelled backwards, get it? The best fajitas in Belize, good conch fritters, too, in a pleasant, breezy bayside setting. A little more expensive than most other eateries in Corozal. Moderate.

Other favorites in Corozal include **Scottie's Crocodile Cove** and **RD's Diner. Wood House Bistro serves** Chinese food. Also, check out the **Buccaneer Palapa** and **Smuggler's Den** in the Consejo area.

Rural Corozal District
COPPER BANK/CERROS AREA

Getting Here from Corozal Town: You can drive from Corozal Town, crossing the New River on the hand-pulled ferry. To get to the ferry from Corozal, take the Goldson Highway south toward Orange Walk Town and watch for ferry sign. Turn left and follow this unpaved road for 2½ miles to the ferry landing. At a T-intersection, turn left for Copper Bank. The trip to Copper Bank takes about a half hour, but longer after heavy rains, as the dirt road can become very bad. As you enter Copper Bank, watch for signs directing you to Cerros Maya.

You can also hire a boat in Corozal to take you across the bay. Rates vary but can be as low as US$20 one-way.

Where to Stay

Cerros Beach Resort. Near Cerros Maya site on north side of Cerros peninsula; entering Copper Bank village, watch for signs to Cerros Beach Resort; 501-623-9763 or 518-872-3052 U.S. number; www.cerrosbeachresort.com. This is a laid-back, off-the-grid option for good food and simple lodging on Corozal Bay, near the Cerros ruins. For overnight stays, four small solar-powered cabañas go for US$60 year-round. Cerros Beach Resorts offers complimentary kayaks, bikes, snorkeling gear, fishing poles and wi-fi. There's cable TV in the lounge.

ORCHID BAY

Where to Stay

Crimson Orchid Inn. 59 Pescadores Park, Orchid Bay, Chunox, 501-669-5076; www.thecrimsonorchidinn.com. Opened in late 2012, the Crimson Orchid Inn is located in the heart of the Orchid Bay development. Those checking out Orchid Bay for a lot or home stay here while visiting the property, but it's also open to the public. Stephen and Laurene Honeybill, who were in the theatre and entertainment in Britain, are the innkeepers. The B&B-style inn has nine rooms, with rack rates of US$100 to $200 in-season and US$80 to $150 off-season, plus 9% tax. Casitas at Orchid Bay also are offered for overnight guests, at US$95 to $175 plus tax, depending on the unit and the time of year. Crimson Orchid Inn guests can eat at the restaurant at Orchid Bay, Tradewinds *(see below)*.

Dining at Orchid Bay

Tradewinds Restaurant. Orchid Bay, 501-650-1925. Although most of the diners here are part of the "captive audience" of residents, visitors and would-be buyers at Orchid Bay, the food is pretty good, and the beer is cold. The menu is a combination of bar food, seafood and Belizean dishes. The clientele seems friendly and happy to be here. Moderate to Expensive.

SARTENEJA

This small Mestizo and Creole community enjoys waterside setting that makes it one of the most relaxed and appealing in all of Belize. It's one of the few places where you can see the sunset over the water. Lobster fishing and pineapple farming are the town's two main industries, although tourism is creeping in, and Sarteneja is also known for building wooden boats. Most residents speak Spanish as a first language, but many also speak English. Real estate investors are beginning to discover Sarteneja.

How to Get There: Driving to Sarteneja from Corozal Town takes about 1½ hours via the New River ferry and a second ferry across the mouth of Laguna Seca. The road is unpaved and can be very muddy after heavy rains. On the way here you'll pass several developments, including Orchid Bay. You also can drive to Sarteneja from Orange Walk Town, a trip of about 40 miles and 1½ hours. There are several buses a day, except Sunday, from Belize City via Orange Walk Town.

The daily water taxi, Thunderbolt, between Corozal Town and San Pedro, will drop you at Sarteneja on request.

Lodging in Sarteneja

Backpackers Paradise. Bandera Road, Sarteneja, 501-403-205; www.bluegreenbelize.org. This is basically a hostel. Rates are US$11 double for a small cabaña with share outside bathrooms or US$3.25 per person for camping. A "honeymoon cabaña" with private bath is US$19 double. The cabañas are barely large enough for a double bed, lacking chairs, closet and frills. A common kitchen is available for those who want to cook their own meals. Free wi-fi. Nathalie's Restaurant on-site serves inexpensive dishes including French crepes, at low prices. There's also a common kitchen for those who want to do their own cooking.

Fernando's Seaside Guesthouse. 62 North Front Street, Sarteneja, 501-423-2085. This is one of Sarteneja's first lodging spots, and it still enjoys a great location, on Front Street across the street from the water. Rooms are clean and have A/C and TV, but only the two at the front have views of the water. The owners live on the first floor. Rates around US$50 double, plus tax.

Oasis Guest House. Verde Street, Sarteneja. This centrally located guesthouse in Sarteneja, about a block back from the water, has two pleasant rooms for around US$50 double.

The **Sarteneja Homestay Program** (501-634-8032, email sartenejahomestay@gmail.com) can provide accommodations in local homes for around US$25 per person, including meals.

Our long-time favorite, **Candelie's Seaside Cabañas**. North Front Street, Sarteneja, on the seafront at the west end of the village, 501-423-2005, as of this writing doesn't seem to be open, but perhaps it will reopen. Candelie's has two charming cottages by the sea -- Wood Stork and Brown Pelican. When open, they rented for around US$60 double.

Dining in Sarteneja

Liz's Fast Food. 501-665-5998. Liz's is a snack shack two blocks back from the water, in the center of town near the old Catholic church. It's super cheap, with three small tacos or empanadas for US$1 – very tasty! Usually open for breakfast, lunch and dinner daily. Inexpensive.

Pablito's. No phone. Open for lunch and dinner daily. Also known as Estrella del Mar, serves cheap local food, notably fresh seafood, at a few tables under a thatch palapa. Open for lunch and dinner daily. Inexpensive.

Ritchie's Place. Front Street, 501-668-1531. Ritchie's has been around for a good while, serving fried seafood and other dishes. Owner Ritchie Cruz will also arrange fishing trips. Inexpensive to Moderate.

Entrance to Nahil Mayab restaurant in Orange Walk Town

CHECKING OUT ORANGE WALK

Your first introduction to Orange Walk District likely will be the sugar cane fields — and concomitant hulking sugar cane trucks — near Orange Walk Town on the Goldson Highway. Orange Walk Town itself is a somewhat scruffy, bustling place with more of a Mexican than Belizean ambiance, having not a great deal of interest for the visitor. There's a formal plaza, and the town hall is called the Palacio Municipal. The businesses and houses along the main drag — Queen Victoria Avenue or the Belize-Corozal Road — have barred windows, and some of the hotels and bars are in fact brothels.

The real Orange Walk is the big, wide and lightly populated area to the west of Orange Walk Town, up against the Guatemala border. Here you'll find large tracts of public and private land, teeming with deer, oscellated turkey, toucans and all manner of other wildlife. A handful of remote jungle lodges offers you the chance to see crocodiles, howler monkeys and even the illusive jaguar. Maya sites, discovered and undiscovered, are everywhere, including one of the most impressive and beautifully situated ones in the region, Lamanai.

Mennonites are a potent agricultural and economic force in Orange Walk, especially in the Shipyard area. Farmland and a rural acre or two would be the appeal for expats in this part of Belize.

Getting There: By car via the Goldson Highway, Orange Walk Town is about 55 miles north of Belize City and 35 miles south of Corozal Town. From Belize City or Corozal Town to Orange Walk Town, several bus lines offer frequent bus service — every hour or so — on the Philip Goldson Highway. There is charter air service to Orange Walk Town on Tropic Air.

To Lamanai: By road from Orange Walk Town, take the all-weather road west to Yo Creek, then southwest to August Pine Ridge and San Felipe, bearing left (southeast) at San Felipe to Indian Church Village near the Lamanai ruins, a total distance of about 36 miles from Orange Walk. Alternatively, you can go from near Orange Walk Town through the village of Guinea Grass to Shipyard. Figure about 3 hours by car from Belize City. There's limited non-daily bus service to Indian Church from Orange Walk. A more scenic option is a boat trip up the New River to the New River Lagoon, about 1 1/2 hours and around US$45 per person. If you are staying at Lamanai Outpost, the hotel will arrange your transportation. If not, boat trips can be arranged at the New River bridge or in Orange Walk Town.

To Gallon Jug/Chan Chich: You follow the same route as to Lamanai, but at San Felipe you turn right and go west to Blue Creek Village, a Mennonite settlement. The Mennonites have paved part of the road here. From Blue Creek, it's about 35 miles to Gallon Jug. Figure about 4 hours by car from Belize City. Charter flights are available from Belize City to Gallon Jug's modern little airstrip.

What to See and Do in Orange Walk

In Orange Walk Town, the **Banquitas House of Culture** (Main Street, 501-322-0517, www.nichbelize.org) has displays on the Mestizo history of Orange Walk area, the sugar industry and archeology. Open 9-6 Monday-Friday, free.

Created with the help of British naturalist Gerald Durrell, **the Río Bravo Conservation & Management Area** covers 260,000 acres in rural Orange Walk District west of Orange Walk Town. The three-hour drive from Orange Walk Town takes you through wild lands where you may encounter a troupe of spider monkeys, wildcats, flocks of oscellated turkeys, a dense shower of butterflies—almost anything but a lot of other vehicles. Managed by Belize City–based **Programme for Belize** (www.pfbelize.org), a not-for-profit organization whose mission is the wise use and conservation of Belize's natural resources, the Río Bravo Conservation Area contains some 400 species of birds, 70 species of mammals, and 200 types of trees. About one-half of Río Bravo is managed as a nature reserve, and the rest is managed to generate income, from forestry and other activities, including tourism.

Maya Sites

Within the reserve's borders are more than 60 Mayan site, many still unexplored. The most important is **La Milpa.** At its height between ad 400 and 830, La Milpa was home to almost 50,000 people. The suburbs of this city spread out some 3 miles from the city centre, and the entire city encompassed some 30 square miles in area. So far, archaeologists have discovered at least 20 large courtyards and 19 stelae.

Visiting Río Bravo, like the other areas of rural northwestern Orange Walk, is best done in a four-wheel-drive vehicle. You must make arrangements to visit in advance with Programme for Belize, as the entire Río Bravo conservation area is managed by this private, nonprofit organization, and the main road through its lands is gated.

You also need advance reservations to stay at La Milpa Field Station *(see below)*. Staying overnight or longer at this field station is the best way to see Río Bravo, but you can visit it briefly on a day trip. Another field station at Hill Bank, primarily serves as a research base for sustainable forest management but visitors with an interest in forest research can be accommodated in two cabañas and a dorm that sleeps six. Contact Programme for Belize for information.

Guides and information are available at La Milpa Field Station. Chan Chich Lodge, Lamanai Outpost Lodge, and other hotels also can arrange visits with guides to La Milpa and the Río Bravo Conservation & Management Area.

La Milpa Field Station. Programme for Belize, 1 Eyre Street, Belize City, 501-227-5616; www.pfbelize.org. About 3 miles rom La Milpa Mayan site, this field station is a combination of summer camp and lodge. Stay in rustic thatch cabañas with private bath or in a dorm. Since you're in a remote area, you'll take all your meals, generally simple Belizean-style dishes such as rice and beans with stew chicken or pork, at the field station. Hiking trails are maintained around the lodge, and guides are available to take you to La Milpa and other Mayan sites. In spring and summer you can visit archaeological teams working at La Milpa. All-inclusive rates with meals and tours are around US$150 per person in the dorm and US$180 per person, double occupancy in cabañas.

Blue Creek

The Blue Creek Mennonite settlement gives you a fascinating glimpse into one aspect of Mennonite culture in Belize. Progressives dominate here, so you will see vehicles and diesel tractors. The village manages its owns affairs, including paving streets. A gas station (closed Sunday) is on the hill just past the village, near Hillside Bed & Breakfast. If you're driving, definitely fuel up here. (Don't confuse the Blue Creek in Orange Walk District with the Blue Creek in Toledo.)

Hillside Bed & Breakfast. P.O. Box 2, Blue Creek Village, 501-323-0155. Mennonites John and Judy Klassen opened this small B&B at the edge of Blue Creek settlement. It has five motel-like rooms on a hill overlooking Blue Creek village, with two larger thatch cabañas nearby, down steep wood stairs. Kitchen facilities available, and breakfast is included in the moderate rates of around US$60.

Lamanai

With its stunning setting on the New River Lagoon and many excavated ruins, Lamanai is the top Maya site in Orange Walk District. Hundreds of structures have been identified in a 2-square-mile area by archeologist David Prendergast of the Royal Ontario Museum and others. Lamanai is believed to have been continuously occupied from around 1,500 B.C. to the 19th century C.E., longer than any other Maya site in the region. There are four main temples to see, a residential area and a reproduction of a Lord Smoking Shell stela. The High Temple, at 100 feet, is the tallest known Pre-Classic temple in the Maya world. Admission: Daily 8 to 5, US$10. Due to day trips from cruise ships, Lamanai can get quite busy. There's a nice visitor center and local people sell souvenirs and snacks. Most tour operators in Belize City, Ambergris Caye, Caye Caulker, Orange Walk Town and even Corozal Town can arrange trips day trips to Lamanai, or you can take a boat up the New River from Orange Walk Town (around US$45 round-trip.)

Orange Walk District Lodging
Chan Chich Lodge. Gallon Jug, 501- 223-4419 or 877-279-5726 in U.S./Canada; www.chanchich.com. Very simply, this is one of the classic jungle lodges of the world. It was developed by the late Barry Bowen, a fifth-generation Belizean whose family has the Coca-Cola bottling franchise in Belize and brews Belikin beer, among many other endeavors.

The lodge literally is built in the middle of a Maya site – the mounds around the lodge are unexcavated Maya buildings and temples. Chan Chich, in a setting of incredible beauty, is in a 130,000-acre private nature reserve. Nearby is the large working Gallon Jug farm.

The trip here by car from Orange Walk Town is an incredible experience. If you don't have a rental car, the lodge offers road transfers from the international airport near Belize City for US$299 for two people, US$50 each for additional persons. The drive takes you through deep bush, including the 262,000 acres of Programme for Belize lands next door, and around every curve you might encounter anything but another vehicle — deer, a quash, a snake sliding across the road, one of Belize's cats, a flock of oscellated turkeys, a dense shower of butterflies. Closer to the lodge, which is on a quarter million acres of private land, you'll spy the neatly fenced fields of Bowen's 2,500-acre Gallon Jug farm, which raises cattle, corn, soybeans, cacao and coffee. Gallon Jug is the only place in Belize that produces coffee in any commercial amount. The lodge, across a suspension bridge at the end of a short paved road, enjoys an astounding setting. It was built literally on top of a Maya plaza. Around the lodge are tall, unexcavated mounds.

If you want to get here more quickly, you can come by charter plane. The lodge will assist you in arranging the charter.

Chan Chich has 12 standard and superior thatch-roof cabañas, comfortable rather than luxurious, each with two queen beds, 24-hour electricity (but not air-conditioning), bath with hot and cold water shower, and a wrap-around verandah. There also is a two-bedroom villa with A/C. Meals are served in a large thatch cabaña, which also houses a gift shop, and the bar is next door — guests congregate there for a social hour before dinner. A lovely swimming pool, located at the edge of the jungle, is screened to keep out bugs. Wi-fi is available only around the main lodge building, not in the cabañas.

Around the lodge grounds is a series of cut and raked trails, ideal for wildlife spotting and birding. You can enjoy the jungle setting without having to wrestle snakes and briars. Will you see a jaguar? There's a better chance here than at most other places in Belize. The lodge has been averaging about one to two jaguar sighting a week. Even if you don't see the elusive big cat, you'll definitely see plenty of other wildlife including howler monkeys, whether you walk the trails on your own or go on one of the nature tours offered by the lodge. Guides at Chan Chich are very knowledgeable, and you should take at least one guided nature tour while at the lodge. Guided tours around the lodge are US$12 to $20 per person, if you are not on the Discovery Package *(see below)*. Birding is terrific here, with more than 350 species identified; often 40% or more of guests are birders. Canoeing, horseback riding, birdwatching and nature tours, and trips to Maya sites are available.

Rates: Double rooms, with breakfast, are US$350 to $420 Nov. 1-Apr. 30, US$260 to $305 the rest of the year. The villa (for two people) is US$625 in-season, US$495 off-season; additional adults in the villa are US$220 each. A "Discovery Package," which includes all meals, Belikin beer, Cokes and most tours, is an additional US$119 per person per day (children 5-11 are US$69). Rates are plus the usual 9% hotel tax and 12.5% GST on meals but do not include a service charge. Chan Chich's approach, which we like, is to tip what you feel is fair (tips are divided among all staff) and only once, at the end of your stay. Sometimes rates in summer are steeply discounted.

Lamanai Outpost Lodge. Indian Church Village, 954-636-1107 or 877-222-3549 in the U.S., or 501- 225-2441; www.lamanai.com. Lamanai Outpost is another extraordinary jungle lodge. One of the reasons it's so special is the setting. Built by the late Colin Howells, a pioneering legend in hospitality circles in Belize, Lamanai Outpost perches on a low hillside with a view of the beautiful New River Lagoon. The lodge has 20 rooms in thatch cabañas set among hillside gardens. Lamanai Outpost Lodge is closely involved with archeological and nature study programs. On one visit here, my family enjoyed meeting grad students from the University of Texas who were doing crocodile research in the New River Lagoon. We went along on a night trip to catch crocs (fortunately, that night they didn't catch any). Kids love Lamanai, as there always seem to be monkeys, parrots and other creatures around. Next to the open-air dining room, in what was the former restaurant, is a bar and lounge, The Digger's Roost, with archaeological memorabilia and a full-size reproduction of a Lamanai stela showing Lord Smoking Shell. A dock extends 130 feet into the lagoon and is good place for stargazing and swimming — just keep an eye out for Ol' Mister Croc. Birding is superb in this area, with at least 375 species identified nearby. The Lamanai ruins and archeological reserve are within walking distance. Indian Church village is also within walking distance, and near the village are the ruins of two Spanish churches. Package rates include lodging, meals and tours and are not cheap. They are around US$500 a night per person. Room only rates are more affordable.

Orange Walk Town Lodging

Few tourists linger long in Orange Walk Town, and most hotels cater to visiting Belizeans and Mexicans.

El Gran Mestizo Riverside Cabins. Naranhal Street, Orange Walk Town, 501-322-2290: www.elgranmestizo.com. Associated with the Hotel de la Fuente, the relatively new El Gran Mestizo is now the top lodging choice in Orange Walk Town. It has six pleasant cabins with handcrafted furniture, air-conditioning, cable TV and wi-fi. El Gran Mestizo is on the New River, conveniently located but a bit away from the bustle of the town centre. Premium cabins on the river are US$130 a night; standard cabins are US$80 to $110, plus tax.

Hotel de la Fuente. 14 Main Street, Orange Walk Town, 501-322-2290; www.hoteldelafuente.com. Orlando de la Fuente and his wife run this affordable, clean and centrally located addition to the limited hotel scene in Orange Walk Town. The low rates (around US$35 to $85 plus tax) put it among the best values in Northern Belize. All 23 rooms and suites have air conditioning and wi-fi, and suites have kitchenettes.

St. Christopher's. 10 Main Street, Orange Walk Town, 501-322-2420. This well-established hotel on the New River has comfortable rooms, some air-conditioned. Rates for doubles with A/C and wi-fi are about US$55 plus tax.

Dining in Orange Walk Town

Price ranges shown are for typical meals for one (usually dinner), not including tip, tax or alcoholic drinks. Price ranges;

Inexpensive: Under US$7

Moderate: US$8-$19

Expensive: US$20-$39

Very Expensive: Over US$40

Restaurants here are listed alphabetically.

El Establo. Belize-Corozal Road, 501-322-0094. Located at the northern outskirts of Orange Walk Town near where the bypass meets the main highway, El Establo is well established, comfortable, friendly and good. We especially love the escabeche. Lunch and dinner daily. Moderate.

Maracas Bar & Grill. Naranhal Street, Orange Walk Town, 501-600-9143. Located beside the New River at El Gran Mestizo Riverside Cabins, Maracas is one of the top spots to eat in Northern Belize. Try the shrimp, conch or lobster ceviche, fajitas, grilled fish or chaya empanadas. Open for lunch and dinner. Moderate.

Mi Cocina Sabor. Belize-Corozal Road, Orange Walk Town, 501-322-3482. This restaurant on the south end of the main road through Orange Walk Town has Mexican and Belizean-American dishes, good drinks, big-screen TVs and a friendly, well-trained waitstaff. Chef Victor Ramirez does a very good job with dishes that are better presented and more interesting than the average in this area. Open for lunch and dinner. Closed Tuesday. Moderate.

Nahil Mayab. Corner of Santa Ana and Guadalupe Streets, Orange Walk Town, 501-322-0831. Lovely and not overdone Maya-themed decor, good service and the best ceviche we've had in years, only a few U.S. dollars for a serving of shrimp and conch ceviche, beautifully presented and big enough for two. There's air-conditioned dining inside and a lovely outdoor patio. Moderate.

The half dozen small stalls and restaurants in **Central Park** (aka Cairns Fort) serve garnaches, tacos, empanadas, burgers, waffles and other breakfast, lunch and snack dishes for amazingly low prices. Open daily until around dark. Inexpensive.

Partially excavated Maya site at Pook's Hill

CHECKING OUT CAYO DISTRICT

How to Get There

San Ignacio is about 67 miles, or about 1 3/4 to 2 hours by car, west of Belize City, and the Guatemala border is another 9 miles west. Belmopan City is about 45 miles west of Belize City.

The George Price Highway (formerly Western Highway) is a paved two-lane road from Belize City to Belmopan and then on to San Ignacio. It continues (as the Benque Highway) to Benque Viejo Town and the Guatemala border. After rain parts of the road can be extremely slick, and in most places there are no shoulders, so accidents are common.

Several bus lines run from Belize City to Belmopan and San Ignacio, with frequent, inexpensive service (US$4 to $5) from Belize City. The buses run from the main terminal (the old Novelo's terminal) in Belize City. If coming from the international airport, you'll have to take a taxi into town (US$25) or lug your bags by foot or take a taxi, if available, about 2 miles to the Philip Goldson Highway, where you can catch a bus into Belize City (US$1) and connect with a San Ignacio bus at Novelo's.

In addition, several operators have shuttle vans running from the airports and water taxi places in Belize City to San Ignacio. Fare is about US$40 to $75 per person one-way. You need to book ahead. Here are some of the shuttle services. William's Shuttle, run by a longtime local expat in Cayo, is probably the most recommended. Rates to Belmopan are usually lower.

William's Shuttle Belize (www.williamsshuttlebelize.com)
Discounted Belize Shuttles and Tours (www.discountedbelizeshuttlesandtours.com)
Belize Shuttles and Transfers (www.belizeshuttlesandtransfers.com)
Belize Transportation Services (www.belizeshuttleservices.sanignaciotown.com)
Mayan Heart World (www.mayanheartworld.net)
PACZ Tours (www.pacztours.net)

Most hotels and lodges around San Ignacio and in the Mountain Pine Ridge also will provide transport for US$120 to $180 for up to four persons.

Guatemalan transportation services **Linea Dorado** and **Fuente del Norte** run daily from the Belize City Marine Terminal near the Swing Bridge to Flores, Guatemala, near Tikal, for around US$25. These busses are not supposed to pick up or drop off passengers in Belize (except in Belize City), but usually you can get off at the Belize-Guatemala border, or even in San Ignacio.

Finally, some taxis at the international airport will drive you to San Ignacio. Bargain, but expect to pay around US$100-$125 for up to four people.

Flights to Belmopan and San Ignacio: Tropic Air (www.tropicair.com) has three daily flights from the international airport near Belize City to Belmopan and to Maya Flats between San Ignacio and Benque Viejo. Cost one way to Belmopan is US$90 and to San Ignacio/Benque US$91.

Getting Around the Mountain Pine Ridge: To explore the Mountain Pine Ridge on your own, you must have a car, as there is no bus service. Two roads lead to the Mountain Pine Ridge reserve. The first, the Pine Ridge Road (also known as the Chiquibul Road) turns off the George

Price Highway at Georgeville, at about Mile 63. This road, unpaved and very rough in places, depending on when it has rained and when it was last scraped, runs past the Barton Creek area, large farms and the Slate Creek preserve, leading to the entrance of the Mountain Pine Ridge reserve. It's about 10 miles from Georgeville to the reserve gate, where you must stop and register with the guard, who will take your name, vehicle information and destination, but there is no entrance fee.

The other route to the Pine Ridge is the Cristo Rey Road, which turns off the George Price Highway at about Mile 68 1/2, at Santa Elena just before you enter San Ignacio. The mostly unpaved road runs through Cristo Rey and San Antonio villages. It is about 12 1/2 miles by this route to the junction with the Pine Ridge Road, and then another 1 1/2 miles to the reserve gate, the same gate you would reach from Georgeville.

From the Pine Ridge gate, you continue on an unpaved road. At some points the roadbed is sandy, and at others red clay. If you are going to Hidden Valley Inn or Hidden Valley Falls, about 4 miles into the reserve you turn left (watch for a sign) and go a few miles to the lodge or falls. If, instead of turning, you go on, you'll soon see the Pine Ridge Lodge, on the right, a little more than 4 miles past the entrance gate. About 1/2 mile farther, there's a turn to the right to Blancaneaux Lodge; Five Sisters Lodge is a little farther on the same spur road. If you continue on the "main road" rather than turning on the spur road to Blancaneaux and Gaia Lodge, you will pass near the Rio On, a popular swimming area, and the Rio Frio cave. At about 14 miles into the reserve, you'll reach Douglas De Silva (formerly called Augustine), a tiny collection of small white frame houses with tin roofs. Turn left here and you'll be on your way to Caracol. Ten miles from Douglas De Silva, you cross the Macal River and are in the Chiquibul wilderness. Caracol is about 50 miles from the reserve entrance gate.

Note that due to occasional bandit attacks in the Mountain Pine Ridge, you are asked not to go on your own to Caracol. You are supposed to go in a convoy guarded by Belize Defence Forces troops. Check locally to see if this plan is still in effect and for times to meet up with the convoy. At the time of this writing it was 9:30 a.m. in Augustine village. You can drive alone to the four lodges in the Pine Ridge, but not all the way to Caracol.

Keep in mind that all of the roads in this region are logging roads. After heavy rains, the clay sections in particular can become extremely slick and difficult to negotiate, even with a four-wheel drive vehicle. If you do not have your own vehicle, you can take a taxi from San Ignacio to the lodges in the Pine Ridge (perhaps US$75-$100 for up to four or five people). A Mesh bus makes trips daily except Sunday from San Ignacio to Cristo Rey and San Antonio villages (about US$1.50, locally for exact schedule). It gets within about 1½ miles of the Mountain Pine Ridge entrance gate. The lodges in the Pine Ridge also provide transfers from Belize City to the Pine Ridge (about US $150 to $200 per party, one-way). Hotel packages usually include transfers from Belize City. You also take a charter flight to Blancaneaux's airstrip.

What to See and Do in Cayo

This part of Cayo offers some of the best caving in Central America. **Actun Tunichil Muknal** near Teakettle village is a must-see. A full-day guided tour from San Ignacio is around US$100-$125, including transport, a guide –you cannot go into this cave without a licensed, trained guide and lunch. Many other caves are in the region, including **Barton Creek Cave** off the Chiquibul Road – it is best viewed by canoe. **Chechem Ha** cave is on private property about 25 minutes from San Ignacio, and **Flour Camp Cave** is another popular cave. **Rio Frio** is an open cave in the Mountain Pine Ridge. **St. Herman's Cave** is off the Hummingbird Highway near the inland Blue Hole.

There also excellent hiking, mountain biking, birding, cave tubing, canoeing and horseback riding. There are important Maya sites, including **Caracol, Cahal Pech, El Pilar** and **Xunantunich**.

There are government-sponsored **Houses of Culture** in San Ignacio/Santa Elena (7 King Street, San Ignacio, 501-824-0783) and Benque Viejo (64 Joseph Street, 501-823-2697, both www.nichbelize.org). The **Belize Botanic Gardens** (www.belizebotanic.org, open daily, admission US$15 for self-guided tour and US$30 for guided tour) at duPlooy's Lodge are the largest gardens in Belize, and well worth visiting. **Green Hills Butterfly Farm** (Mile 8, Chiquibul Road, 501-834-4017, www.greenhills.net, open daily, admission US$10) is the most interesting butterfly operation in Belize. There is also a small butterfly center at Chaa Creek Lodge.

For zipline enthusiasts, **Calico Jack's zipline** is at Seven Mile/Progresso off the Chiquibul Road toward the Mountain Pine Ridge, and **Jaguar Paw zipline** is at Cave's Branch near Belmopan.

There's even a small golf course, the nine-hold **Roaring River Golf Course** near Belmopan off Mile 50½ of the George Price Highway. You can play all day for US$25. Rental clubs available. Watch out for the crocs in the water traps.

Also near Belmopan – actually in Belize District, not Cayo – but an easy stop when traveling between San Ignacio/Belmopan and Belize City-is the wonderful **Belize Zoo** (Mile 29, George Price Highway, 501-822-8000, www.belizezoo.org). It's fairly small, on 29 acres, but it has 125 of Belize's native mammals and many of its birds and reptiles, all in natural settings. Absolutely worth seeing anytime you're in Belize. Open daily 8:30 to 5, admission US$15 adults, US$3 children.

Near Belmopan, too, is the **Hummingbird Highway.** This is Belize's most scenic road. You'll take this road when going to Dangriga, Hopkins, Placencia or Punta Gorda. Along the way, don't miss stopping and taking a swim in the inland Blue Hole (**St. Herman's Blue Hole National Park,** open daily 8 to 4:30, admission US$4.) While you're there, also visit St. Herman's Cave. A little farther south is **Five Blues Lake National Park** (Mile 32, Hummingbird Highway, admission US$5), where there are small Maya sites as well as a lake. The lake mysteriously drained to almost nothing in 2006, but strangely filled back up in 2010.

In Belmopan City, of course, are many Belize government buildings as well as a number of embassies, including the US$50 million U.S. Embassy complex.

About a half an hour southeast from San Ignacio is the **Mountain Pine Ridge** reserve, which covers more than 100,000 acres. Visitors here are surprised by what they find. Instead of low-lying, bug-infested tropical vistas, they find hills and low mountains with few mosquitoes and temperatures that can dip into the 40s and 50s F. in winter. Instead of lush Tarzan-style jungle, in some parts of the region they find pine woods, sparse grass and red clay mindful of the Southern Appalachians. Many of the Mountain Pines (also known as Honduras Pines) in this area have been killed by the Southern Pine Beetle, but the pines are coming back.

Except for a small settlement at Augustine/Douglas de Silva, groups of workers living at the area's handful of lodges and some remote squatter settlements occupied by illegal immigrants from Guatemala, few people live in the Mountain Pine Ridge. Much of the land is government property, and some is owned, mostly in large tracts, by foreign interests or wealthy Belizeans. The roads in the region are former logging roads, most hardly better than dirt tracks. Controlled logging continues, and the area is also the site of occasional Belize Defence Force or U.S. Army training exercises. In the dry season, usually March to late May or early June, the area sees higher temperatures (though still cooler than in most of the rest of inland Belize), and forest fires are a threat.

Also in this area is **Noj Koxx Meen Elijio Panti National Park** (www.epnp.org), a 13,000-acre park named after the fame Guatemalan natural healer who died at age 103 in 1997. There is as yet little good access or development of this park for visitors.

Beyond the Mountain Pine Ridge is **Chiquibul,** a great wilderness area and forest reserve. It is home to Caracol, the largest and most important Maya site in Belize. Once into the Chiquibul, the vegetation turns to broadleaf rainforest, more like the jungle you've seen in the movies. It is beautiful country, with isolated waterfalls where you can slip in for a skinny dip, incredible cave systems, unpolluted streams and blue skies.

San Ignacio has many tour operators that can take to Maya sites and other attractions in Cayo. These include PACZ Tours, Yute Expeditions, River Rat, Belizean Sun Tours, Paradise Expeditions and others. You'll typically pay about US$80 to $90 per person for a tour, including lunch.

It's not really a visitor destination, but especially if you're thinking seriously of living in Belize, you must visit **Spanish Lookout.** This is a progressive Mennonite community just north of San Ignacio. It's the farming center of Belize, producing most of the country's chickens, eggs, cheese and truck crops. It's also where you can look at and buy Mennonite prefab houses. There are a number of large (for Belize) stores such as Westrac auto parts, Reimer's Feeds and Farmer's Trading Centre, places where you can buy hardware, building supplies, auto parts, tires and other necessities at good prices. There are three gas stations, a couple of mediocre restaurants but no hotels. It's also worth seeing what hard work and self-sufficiency can do.

An offbeat attraction west of San Ignacio is **Poustinia Land Art Park** (www.poustinialandart.org), a former 100-acre cattle ranch that is now home to a collection of about three dozen outdoor sculptures and installations. Poustinia was established by an architect in Belmopan.

Admission requires an appointment and costs US$10. Call the Benque House of Culture at 501-823-2697 for information on how to visit.

Maya Sites

Caracol (www.caracol.org), Spanish for "snail," perhaps named for the many snail shells found on the site, is located on the Vaca Plateau in the Chiquibul Forest Preserve at about 1,600 feet elevation. It was one of the most important Maya political and population centers of the Classic Period. At its height it covered more than 75 square miles in area and had a population of nearly 200,000, more than twice the population of present-day metropolitan Belize City, and some 36,000 structures. It rivaled Tikal in size and power and in the middle of the 6th century CE it fought wars with that mighty city-state. At one point Caracol's rulers conquered Tikal, at least for a time.

Archeologists Diane and Arlen Chase of the University of Central Florida have been working at Caracol for many years, along with other archeologists. Still, only a small percentage of the buildings have been excavated. **Caana** is the centerpiece. At 136 feet, this temple is still the tallest human-built structure in all of Belize. You can climb Caana and view much of Caracol, which has been partly cleared of vegetation and undergrowth.

Tour operators in San Ignacio and at various lodges in Cayo will take you to Caracol for around US$100 to $125 per person including transport, lunch, guide and admission fee. You can drive yourself, but at most times, due to the ongoing risk of bandits in the area from Guatemala, drivers go in convoys accompanied by Belize Defence Force soldiers. Check locally for the time when you meet up with the BDF at Douglas de Silva. Currently it is at 9:30 a.m. It is about a 50-mile, two to three-hour drive, depending on road conditions, from San Ignacio. Roads to Caracol are being improved, but in the rainy season especially it can be slow going. Gas up before you go as there are no gas stations along the way. Caracol has a good visitor center, and the site is open daily from around 8 to 5. Admission US$15. If not with a group, you can hire a guide at the site.

Xunantunich ("Stone Woman" from the Yucatec and Mopan Maya languages and pronounced shoo-NAN-ta-nitch) is 8 miles west of San Ignacio, just off the Benque Road/George Price Highway. It is on a hill overlooking the Mopan River. It was settled around 400 BC and

347

abandoned around 1000 CE. At its height, some as many as 10,000 people lived here. While it's not a huge site, it's popular because it's easy to get to from San Ignacio by bus (BZ$1.50), taxi (around US$10) or car. You cross the river on a hand-pulled pedestrian and car ferry, free but it's nice to tip the hard-working operator, and then go up a hill to the informative new visitor center. El Castillo is the most prominent building at Xunantunich and is only one foot shorter than Caana at Lamanai. From the top, there are amazing views into Guatemala. Open daily during daylight hours. Admission US$10. Licensed guides (not necessary but can add to the value of your visit) charge around US$20 for a small group. If you choose to go on a tour from San Ignacio, you'll pay US$45 to $50 per person, including transportation from downtown San Ignacio, guide, entrance fee and a snack.

El Pilar, about 7 miles north from Bullet Tree Falls on the Guatemala border, provides a quiet experience for the few visitors. It is also an excellent birding site. There are two groupings of temple mounds, ball courts and courtyards. The excavations here so far are minor, and the site is overgrown with vegetation. Before going, visit Be Pukte Cultural Center in Bullet Tree Falls. Admission is US$10. If you're not driving, you can probably get a taxi for around US$25 to $30. Only a few tour companies visit El Pilar.

Cahal Pech, ("Place of the Ticks" although you probably won't be bothered by any) located on a high hill just west of San Ignacio, near the Cahal Pech Village hotel. Cahal Pech was re-discovered in the 1950s, but archeological work didn't begin in earnest until 1988, when a team from San Diego State, along with Belizean archeology expert Dr. Jaime Awe, found almost three dozen structures on a three-acre site. Excavation is on going. This isn't nearly as impressive as Caracol or Xunantunich, but it's easy to get to and has an informative visitor center (501-824-4236.) Cahal Pech is open 8 to 5 daily. Admission is US$5. Until you're in good shape, we recommend you drive or take a taxi up the steep hill to Cahal Pech.

Belmopan Lodging

The lodging choices in Belmopan proper are small motels and hotels, geared more toward the needs of government bureaucrats and others on government business than of tourists. Jungle lodges and other more interesting lodging choices are located outside of Belmopan along the

George Price and Hummingbird highways. Lodging listed alphabetically.

Bull Frog Inn. 25 Half Moon Avenue (P.O. Box 28, Belmopan City), 501-822-2111; www.bullfroginn.com. This will remind you of a small mom 'n pop motel in the U.S. or Canada. The 25 rooms have air-conditioning, cable TV and wi-fi and are clean and comfortable enough, though your bed may not be quite as new as you'd like. Rates, geared to business people and government officials who make up 70% of the guests here, are US$98 double, plus tax, year-round. There's an open-air restaurant at the motel.

Hibiscus Hotel. Hibiscus Plaza, Melhado Parade, Belmopan City, 501-633-5323; www.hibiscusbelize.com. This six-room hotel is one of Belmopan's better values, and it's next door to a good restaurant, Corker's (under the same family ownership). Rooms have king or twin beds, A/C, cable TV and mini-fridges. Room rates are US$60 plus tax. You can feel good about staying here, as some of the profits go to **Belize Bird Rescue** (www.belize-birdrescue.com), which saves parrots and other birds. Choose this for honest value.

Inn at Twin Palms. Mile 54, Hummingbird Highway, Belmopan City, 501-822-0231. A few years ago, this small six-room inn was named one of the best of its kind in the world by a major social media site. That's a little hard to understand, as although this is a good place, it's hardly a world leader. It does having a swimming pool. Rates are US$115-$125 double, plus tax.

KenMar's Bed & Breakfast. 22-24 Halfmoon Avenue, Belmopan City, 501-822-0118; www.kenmar.bz. This attractive guesthouse, located near the Bull Frog Inn, has 10 spotless, air-conditioned rooms, with mini-fridges and cable TV. There's also a deluxe suite. US$85 to $125, plus tax.

El Rey Hotel. 23 Moho Street, Belmopan City, 501-822-3428, www.elreyhotel.com. A budget spot in Belmopan for more than two decades, a change in management in 2012 upgraded it some. The new expat managers have ambitious plans to build a national lodging brand. Well, maybe it will happen. Rates here start at around US$30 plus tax for budget rooms with fans but go up to nearly three times that figure for a junior suite with A/C.

Yim Saan Hotel & Restaurant. 4253 Hummingbird Highway, Belmopan City; 501-822-1356; www.yimsaan-hotel.com. This Chinese-owned property is among the nicer lodgings in Belmopan. Rooms are modern and clean, with A/C, wi-fi and cable TV. There's a Chinese restaurant on the first floor. Rates around US55 to $85 double, plus tax.

Belmopan Area Jungle Lodges
Banana Bank Lodge. Off Mile 49, George Price Highway (P.O.
Box 48, Belmopan City), 501-832-2020; www.bananabank.com.
Directions: From George Price Highway, turn north at Mile 49 and cross
bridge over Belize River. Follow gravel road 3 miles until you see Banana
Bank sign. Turn right and follow dirt road 2 miles. You're guaranteed to see
a jaguar at this lodge. A spotted jaguar called Tika lived here for 26 years
and after her death was replaced by Tika 2. The Belize government has
granted permission for the lodge to have the jaguar. John Carr, who in his
youth was a real Montana cowboy and rodeo star, in 1973 with a partner
bought Banana Bank, then a 4,000-acre ranch with 1,500 head of cattle. At
one time the ranch was headquarters for Belize Estates, one of the large
companies that in colonial days logged huge tracts of land granted them by
the Crown. John Carr and his wife, Carolyn, have lived on the ranch since
1977, one of a small group of pioneering American expats who adopted
Belize as their home. Carolyn is a noted artist. Her paintings of Belize street
scenes and wild creatures have been widely exhibited, and her work has
appeared on the cover the Belize telephone book twice, most recently in
2009. She has a studio at the lodge. Our favorite is her painting titled
"Jimmy Hines," which shows the old market in Belize City where fishermen
are cleaning lobster, snapper and jimmy hines, the local name for a type of
sea bass or grouper.

Anyway, back to the lodge. It's a family-oriented spot, a great place for
kids. Daughter Leisa now helps run the lodge. The lodge has five cabañas,
with bay leaf thatch, on a bank above the Belize River. The cabañas are
spacious, with curving internal walls and 24-hour electricity, but no air-
conditioning. Rooms are also available in the Gallery, Chateau Brio and
Chalet building. Some rooms have air-conditioned. You can hear howler
monkeys calling, and besides Tika 2, on the grounds of the lodge are
toucans, parrots and a spider monkey named Simon. (Note that some
wildlife rescue organizations and other groups in Belize strongly oppose the
practice of keeping wild animals and birds in captivity, even with
government permission.) The food is filling and tasty, served family-style.
Banana Bank is especially good for those who like to ride, as the lodge keeps
about 100 horses. The horses are mixed breeds, mostly quarter horses.

There's a large stable, a round pen to hone your riding skills and a larger arena. New in 2006 was a swimming pool, with a bar and dining area added in 2009-2010. Free wi-fi at the pool. Rates: US$50 to $175 double, plus 9% tax, breakfast included. Lunch is US$10 and dinner, US$15. Meal rates are plus 12.5% GST tax. Meals are well prepared and served family style. Note that there is something of a Christian atmosphere here, with prayers sometimes offered at meals. The lodge also has many packages, which include tours, all meals and horseback riding. Transfers from the international airport near Belize City are US$120 one-way for one to four persons.

Belize Jungle Dome. Off Mile 47, George Price Highway, Belmopan City, 501-822- 2124; www.belizejungledome.com. Directions: From George Price Highway, turn north at Mile 49 and cross bridge over Belize River. Follow gravel road 3 miles until you see Banana Bank sign. Turn right and follow dirt road 2 miles. The suites and rooms here have tile floors, lots of windows, air-conditioning and an uncluttered look. You can check your email at the wireless hotspot by the swimming pool, take a yoga or pilates class or eat an organic meal (breakfast US$12, lunch $17, dinner US$22) on the terrace. Rates: US$95 to $165 in-season, double; US$85 to $135 off-season, all plus tax. For large groups, a three-bedroom house is available. This property is currently for sale.

Ian Andersons's Caves Branch Adventure Co. & Jungle Lodge. Hummingbird Highway (P.O. Box 356), Belmopan City), 501-610-3451 or toll-free 866-357-2698 from U.S./Canada; www.cavesbranch.com. Directions: About 14 miles from Belmopan at Mile 41½ of the Hummingbird Highway (mile markers on the Hummingbird from Belmopan run backwards, starting at Mile 55 at the George Price Highway), turn left and follow a dirt road less than a mile to the lodge grounds.

Set in a large chunk of private land on the Caves Branch river, this is one of Belize's premier jungle lodges for travelers who like to do things outdoors. Ian Anderson, a Canadian, and his teams run strenuous caving, hiking and river trips, and they do a top-flight job. They call them adventure trips, not sightseeing. In short, this is not a place for couch potatoes. More than a dozen adventure tours are offered, open to non-guests as well as guests. Each Caves Branch guide has been trained in first aid and in cave and wilderness rescue. However, the lodge is going more upscale, with a new swimming pool, botanical garden and tony treehouse suites. The treehouses are operated by Viva, which also runs La Beliza Resort on North Ambergris Caye, Jaguar Reef and Almond Beach in Hopkins and other properties.

Rates: The new hillside, split level treehouse suites are the most upmarket, at US$386 to $506 year-round. The jungle suites are also fairly luxe, with a master bedroom with king-size bed, inside bathroom with hot and cold shower and toilet, wicker-furnished living room with pull out bed, at US$251 double. Jungle bungalows with queen beds are US$211 double. Jungle cabañas are more basic, with outside washroom facilities, for US$147 double. Rates are plus hotel tax. Buffet meals are delicious and healthful, though not bargain-priced, at US$14 for breakfast, US$16 for lunch, US$26 for dinner. Meals plus 12.5% GST. Caves Branch also has a variety of adventure and tour packages, including meals, lodging and trips. Note that in late spring the river that runs by the lodge may be completely dry.

Pook's Hill. Off Mile 52 1/2, Teakettle Village (P.O. Box 14, Belmopan City); 501-820-2017; www.pookshillbelize.com. Directions: Turn south off the Western Hwy. at Mile 52 1/2 at Teakettle village. Go about 4 miles on a dirt road, then turn right and go another 1½ miles to the lodge (the route is well-signed.) How about a remote lodge in deep jungle, next to a river, near Actun Tunichil Muknal and on the site of a Maya plaza, run by an engaging international staff where meals and drinks are by lantern-light and you're isolated from the cares of civilization? That pretty much describes Pook's Hill, a collection of thatched, Maya-style cabañas on 300 acres next to Tapir Mountain Reserve and the Roaring River. There is a partially excavated Maya site at Pook's Hill. Hiking, tubing and river swimming in the Roaring River and excellent birding are available. Actun Tunichil Muknal tours from the lodge are US$110 per person, plus 12.5% GST. Cabaña rates US$200 to $300 in high season, US$160 to $240 June to November, all plus 9% tax. Meals, served buffet-style with a common table sure to get everyone talking, are tasty and filling -- US$8 breakfast, $12 lunch and $20 dinner, plus 12.5% tax. Transfers for up to four persons from the international airport near Belize City are US$125, and US$50 from the Belmopan airstrip, plus 12.5% tax. Pook's Hill, by the way, is named after Rudyard Kipling's Puck of Pook's Hill. The lodge is for sale.

Sleeping Giant Rainforest Lodge. Mile 36, Hummingbird Highway; www.vivabelize.com. Part of the Viva Belize group that includes La Beliza Resort on North Ambergris Caye and Jaguar Reef and Almond Beach in Hopkins, plus the treehouses at Ian Anderson's Caves Branch, Sleeping Giant is one of the newer jungle lodges in Cayo. It's at the edge of the Sibun Forest Reserve on the Sibun River, which is swimmable, but there is also a swimming pool and hot tub. Most of the accommodations are in very attractive casitas with stone, stucco, tile and thatch, and ceiling skylights. They're air-conditioned but don't have TV. Avoid rooms in the main lodge near the bar and restaurant, due to noise. Rates in the rooms start at US$120 off-season, and in the casitas at US$180 (rates plus tax and service) and go up to near $500 in-season.

Dining in Belmopan

Price ranges shown are for typical meals for one (usually dinner), not including tip, tax or alcoholic drinks. Price ranges:

Inexpensive: Under US$7

Moderate: US$8-$19

Expensive: US$20-$39

Very Expensive: Over US$40

Restaurants here are listed alphabetically.

Caladium. Near Market Square, Belmopan City, 501-822-2754. Caladium is an old-school Belizean-owned restaurant serves good breakfasts and Belizean favorites such as stew chicken, plus burgers and even steaks. Air-conditioned, and it has a bar. Often busy. Open daily for breakfast, lunch and dinner. Closed Sunday. Inexpensive to Moderate.

Cheers. Mile 31, George Price Highway, 501-822-8014. This roadside restaurant (it also has some cabañas for overnight) is not in Belmopan City or even in Cayo District but is on the way, not far from the Belize Zoo. It's a good stopping point for a Belikin and a beefburger or some Belizean food. Inexpensive to Moderate.

Corker's Restaurant and Wine Bar. Hibiscus Plaza, corner of Constitution and Melhado Parade, Belmopan City, 501-822-0400. This is our favorite place to stop for a meal and a drink in Belmopan. It's on the second floor of Hibiscus Plaza and next door to the Hibiscus Hotel (owned by members of the same family.) The menu has a huge number of choices, from around a dozen kinds of salads and more than 15 varieties of beef and chicken burgers to fish and chips to ribs and steaks and several Italian pasta dishes. The combo platters, while not cheap – some are over US$30 – are huge. Drinks are good pours and not overpriced. Local rums are most US$2.50 and Jack Daniels is under US$4. Open for lunch and dinner. Closed Sunday. Moderate to Very Expensive.

Everest Indian Restaurant. Belmopan City, 501-662-2109. Located behind the fire station, near the market and bus station, in a small, unprepossessing shack, the relatively new Everest serves wonderful Indian and Nepalese food. The couple who own it are friendly and work hard to please. Try the vegetarian platter, but there are chicken and other non-veg dishes as well. It's all well prepared and delicious, not to mention being a good value. Inexpensive to Moderate.

Miriam's Sunrise. Near Court House Plaza, Belmopan City. This local spot is good for breakfast or a Belizean lunch. Open daily for breakfast and lunch. Inexpensive.

San Ignacio Santa Elena Area Lodging

These hotels and guesthouses are listed in rough order of cost.

Ka'ana Boutique Resort and Spa. Mile 69¼, George Price Highway (P.O. Box 263, San Ignacio), 501-824-3350, 305-735-2553 in U.S.; www.kaanabelize.com. Ka'ana is your most upscale non-jungle lodge option in or near San Ignacio. It has a wine cellar, bar, spacious deluxe rooms outfitted with extras like iPod docks and espresso machines and flat-screen TVs, plus one- and two-bedroom villas with private plunge pools. Rates are US$285 for standard rooms in a main house, US$450 for large suites to $1,200 a night for the two-bedroom villas, higher at Christmas. Rates plus tax and service. The main infinity swimming pool with waterfall uses a saltwater filtration system. La Ceiba restaurant, while attractive, is expensive.

San Ignacio Resort Hotel. 18 Buena Vista Street (P.O. Box 33, San Ignacio), 501-824-2125; www.sanignaciobelize.com. The San Ignacio Resort Hotel is the closest thing to an international-style hotel in San Ignacio Town. But, in Belize, that can mean anything, and in this case it means a green iguana project out back, with 14 acres of bush. The location is convenient on a low hill on the west side of town. The redone rooms are comfortable, the pool relaxing, the Running W Steakhouse & Restaurant satisfying, the new lounge bar a good place to grab a cool one and the management and staff accommodating. Unfortunately, rates are on the high side. Rates: US$191 to $400 in-season, US$172 to $360 off-season, plus 9% hotel tax and 10% service. A branch of the Princess Casino adjoins the hotel.

Cahal Pech Village Resort. Cahal Pech Road, 1 mile west of town off George Price Highway, San Ignacio, 501-824-3740; www.cahalpech.com. This resort is set on a high, steep hill at the western edge of San Ignacio, near the Cahal Pech Maya site. It is very popular and often full, due to the relatively moderate rates and scenic views over the valley. Ever expanding, the property now has 53 rooms, suites and cabañas. The more recent additions are new hillside cottages and a two-level swimming pool, guarded by a giant statue of a pteryldactl. The restaurant breakfasts (US$9 plus 12.5% tax plus tip) are okay. Year-round rates are US$103 to $140 double, with four- to six-person cabañas US$140 to $163, all plus 9% tax and 10% service charge.

Aguada Hotel & Restaurant. Aguada Street, Santa Elena, 501-804-3609; www.aguadabelize.com. Across the George Price Highway from La Loma Luz hospital, this motel is a real find. You can stay here in a clean, modern room or small suite with air-conditioning for around US$47-$79 double year-round, plus 9% tax and 6% service. The 18 rooms — some were added on the second floor and in a new building in the back — are not overly large, but there is a swimming pool. The café is a friendly, casual place serving Belizean and American dishes at around US$5 to $10 for a full meal.

Western Guest House. 54 Burns Avenue, San Ignacio. Located above a hardware store, this inexpensive six-room guesthouse has large, clean rooms with private baths and wi-fi. There's a common kitchen. In-season rates around US$60 plus tax.

Casa Blanca Guest House. 10 Burns Avenue, San Ignacio, 501-824-2080; www.casablancaguesthouse.com. While it's in the center of busy San Ignacio, this small guesthouse, winner of the Belize Tourism Board's "best small hotel award" a few years ago, is quiet and a great choice if you want to save money. The eight rooms, with white walls trimmed in mahogany and locally made wood furniture, are a step above typical budget lodging. More-expensive rooms have air-conditioning. You can prepare snacks or full meals in the shared kitchen. Casa Blanca is often fully booked. Rates: US$30 to $70, plus tax.

Hi-Et Guest House. West Street, San Ignacio, 501-824-2828. This 10-room guesthouse may be your best option starting in the cheapie segment. Five of the rooms, in the owner's big home, cost only US$12.50 with share baths, no hot water, but they're clean. We'd go for the rooms with private baths in an adjoining building, at US$25. There's a common room with fridge and free wi-fi. No air-conditioning. Other ultra-budget options are **Tropicool Hotel** (30A Burns Avenue) and **J & R's Guest House** (26 Far West Street).

Benque Viejo/Succotz Area Lodging and Dining

Trek Stop. Mile 71½ George Price Highway (Benque Road), 501-823-2265; www.thetrekstop.com. This collection of little wood cottages near the Xunantunich ruins and Succotz village, across the highway from the river, is a good budget choice, although prices have gone up some recently. Rates are US$24 to $60 double for cabins. There's also Don Tino's Guesthouse, a dorm like guesthouse with shared baths for US$37.50 double. Camping is US$7 per person. All rates plus 9% tax. There's a little restaurant on site and a small butterfly farm, plus a disc golf course.

Benny's Kitchen. 139 Belize Street, San José Succotz Village, across Benque Road from ferry to Xunantunich, 501-823-2541. This little open-air restaurant near Xunantunich is a local find. Lots of local Maya, Creole and Mestizo dishes, including pibil (Mayan pork), chilimole (chicken with mole sauce) and escabeche (onion soup with chicken) and of course stew chicken with rice and beans. Low prices and large portions. Open daily for breakfast, lunch and dinner. Inexpensive to moderate.

Jungle Lodges on the Macal River

Most of Cayo's jungle lodges are on either the Macal or Mopan rivers. In general, the lodges on the Macal are more upmarket. With some exceptions don't expect to be in a "movie jungle" or rainforest. Most lodges share their locations with cattle ranches or citrus farms and second-growth bush, though the jungle is seldom far away. List in rough order of cost.

The Lodge at Chaa Creek. Chial Road (P.O. Box 53, San Ignacio), 501-824-2037; www.chaacreek.com. Directions: From San Ignacio, go 4 3/4 miles west on Benque Road. (George Price Highway) and turn left on Chial Road (look for signs to Chaa Creek, duPlooy's and Black Rock lodges). Follow signs on this unpaved road, past Maya Flats airstrip, 3 1/2 miles to Chaa Creek. Mick and Lucy Fleming started Chaa Creek in 1980 when tourists were almost unknown in Cayo. Over the years, they've expanded, improved and fine-tuned their operation until it has become one of the best run, most-professional operations in all of Central America. Everything works here: The grounds, comprising a total of 365 acres on the Macal River, are beautifully planted and maintained. A gorgeous swimming pool was added in 2009. The 23 large rooms and suites are mostly in thatch cottages, and all have high-quality furnishings set off with Guatemalan wall hangings and bedspreads, the perfect marriage of comfort and exoticism. The honeymoon Treetop Suites, Garden Suites, Orchid Villa, Spa Villa, Macal Cottage and Sky Room offer more privacy and extra room. Staffers are friendly, not fawning, and move quickly to solve any problem. There's electricity, plenty of hot water and cold beer, and, if you like, Chaa Creek will sell you a good cigar to enjoy after dinner with your cognac. There's a fully equipped, modern spa, arguably the best in Belize, offering everything from aromatherapy to seaweed wraps, and a conference and meeting center. You won't run out of things to do here, either. You can visit the Chaa Creek Natural History Centre and Blue Morpho Butterfly Breeding Centre, tour the Rainforest Medicine Trail, visit a Maya-style cacao plantation and other farming projects, go horseback riding or canoeing, or take one of the many top-notch tours offered by Chaa Creek Expeditions. Chaa Creek helped reintroduce howler monkeys to the Macal River Valley. Birding is excellent, with some 250 species spotted on the grounds. Chaa Creek has won a number of environmental and other awards. For all this, you pay a premium price. Rates: Rooms are US$360 to $350 double in-season, and suites US$415 to $680 year-round. Rates include breakfast if staying in the cottages; otherwise, breakfast is US$10. All lodging rates are plus 9% tax and 12% service. A delicious dinner is US$36 plus 12.5% tax. Packages are available. Transfers from the international airport are US$150 plus 12.5% GST one-way for one to four persons. For those who want the Chaa Creek experience at a Walmart price (US$130 double including breakfast and dinner, plus 9% hotel tax and 12% service), the Macal River Camp has 10 small "cabinettes" on platforms and very good Belizean-style meals. Both the lodge and river camp are highly recommended.

Mystic River Resort. Mile 6, Cristo Rey Road, San Antonio Village; 501-834-4100, 335-510-0675 in U.S.; www.mysticriverbelize.com. This jungle lodge helps raise the bar on dining and stylish luxury on the

Macal. Mystic River has six cottages, with views of the river from covered porches, stone fireplaces, king beds and designer furnishings. The lodge is mostly on solar power, and there is no air-conditioning or TVs. At the lodge's restaurant, La Ranita (Little Frog), in a high-ceiling thatch palapa set about 100 feet above the river, you'll enjoy good Belizean and international dishes while you take in the views and sounds of the jungle up close and personal. Full American or Belizean breakfasts are US$14 tax included. Dinner entrees are around US$15 to $20, and appetizers are US$10 to $15. The lodge is involved in making artisanal cheeses. The Jasmine Spa is now open. Rates for one- and two-bedrooms suites are US$275 to $500, plus tax and service. Transfers from the international airport near Belize City are US$160 one-way for up to four persons. Helicopter transfers by Astrum start at US$1,700 one-way for up to four persons. Recommended.

duPlooy's Lodge. 10 miles from San Ignacio, Cayo, 501-824-3101 or 512-243-5285 in the U.S.; www.duplooys.com. Directions: From San Ignacio, go 4 3/4 miles west on Benque Road (George Price Highway) and turn left on Chial Road (look for signs to Chaa Creek, duPlooy's and Black Rock lodges). Follow signs on this unpaved road past Maya Flats airstrip about 4 miles to duPlooy's. Since it opened in the late 1980s, duPlooy's has been seen by some to play second fiddle to its Macal River neighbor, Chaa Creek. But that's unfair, because duPlooy's has its own style — a little more casual, a little more oriented to birders and tree-huggers and nature lovers. On part of the lodge's grounds about 10 miles from San Ignacio, Judy and the late Ken duPlooy created something very special: the 45-acre **Belize Botanic Gardens** (www.belizebotanic.org), with plantings of some 2,500 trees from all over Belize and Central America. An orchid house, with some 120 species of orchids from all over Belize, is also in the gardens. For most guests, the focus of the lodge is the remarkable deck, which rambles 200 feet off from the bar. From vantage points on the long walkway beside the Macal River, you're sure to see a variety of birds, iguanas and other wildlife. Bring your camera and binoculars. About 300 species of birds have been identified within 5 miles of the lodge. In accommodations, duPlooy's offers something for anyone, with bungalows, suites rooms and a large house with 10 beds. In-season rates are around US$190 to $315 and are plus 9% hotel tax and 10% service. Room rates are discounted in the off-season. Regardless of lodging, a full meal plan is extra – US$65 a day per person including tax and service. Note that duPlooy's does not serve beef, due to what the owners consider is rainforest deforestation associated with cattle ranching, but it does serve pork, chicken and seafood, along with vegetarian dishes. The lodge also has a good selection of tours to Cayo and Petén sites. Package plans including meals, transfers from Belize City and tours are available. duPlooy's is selling some of its lodge units as residences.

Table Rock Lodge. Cristo Rey Rd., San Antonio Village; 501-672-4040; www.tablerockbelize.com. This small ecolodge, owned by an American couple, has already made a big name for itself, rating highly on TripAdvisor.com and other sites and winning awards from the Belize Tourism Board. The lodge has only a handful of thatch cottages, all with tile floors and four-poster beds, plus one house. It is part of a small working farm, perched just above the Macal River. You can explore winding pathways and cut trails down to the river, or visit with the donkeys, Napoleon and Josephine. Rates for cottages are US$175 to $225 double in-season, US$130-$170 May-October, plus 9% tax and 10% service. The Shamrock Bluff House is US$300 year-round, or US$1,500 a week, plus tax and service. Meals here are excellent. A meal package including breakfast and dinner is US$32 per person plus 10% service and 12.5% tax. Riverside camping also is available for around US$30 plus tax and service, including tent, set up and break down and firewood. Transfers from the international airport are US$140 one-way. Highly recommended.

Black Rock Lodge. Above Macal River off Chial Road, 501-834-4038; www.blackrocklodge.com. Black Rock enjoys a stunning location overlooking the Macal River. It's also one of the most isolated lodges in the area, at the end of a long, mostly dirt road that winds for miles through citrus groves, teak plantations and farms off the graveled Chial Road. There are 14 cottages, including the premium river view suites with marble floors and decks. Rates US$110 to $215 in-season and US$90 to $195 off-season, not including hotel taxes or meals. Breakfast and lunch are US$12 each and a four-course dinner is US$22. Even if you have a car, you're unlikely to go anywhere else for meals, due to the distance involved, and the lodge's transfer to San Ignacio is US$40 one-way, plus 12.5% tax, for one to four persons. The lodge offers a wide selection of trips and tours.

Crystal Paradise. Crysto Rey Village (P.O. Box 126, San Ignacio, Cayo), 501-824-2772. Directions: From San Ignacio, take the Cristo Rey Rd. about 4 miles to Crystal Paradise. This is one of the few lodges in Cayo owned and operated by native-born Belizeans, in this case by the Tut family (pronounced Toot). Many of the numerous Tut family pitch in and help at the lodge, which is located near the village of Cristo Rey on the Macal River. The lodge has 17 rooms and unit with private bath with hot and cold water, ceiling fan and 24-hour electricity. The Tuts offer horseback riding (US$35 per person for a half day), mountain bikes to rent and a variety of tours. Rates from around US$100 a day.

Lodges on the Mopan River

Clarissa Falls Resort. Mile 70, George Price Highway/Benque Road), 501-833-3116; www.clarissafalls.com. Friendly owner Chena Galvez has spent her life on a cattle ranch here, 5½ miles west of San Ignacio, on a rolling 800-acre expanse of grassy, hilly pasture and bush. The family has built pleasant though very simple thatch cabañas. Rates US$75 double plus tax for a cabaña. If you're on a tight budget, there's camping at US$7.50 per person. A large family cabaña is perhaps overpriced at US$175. You can swim or tube on the river – just try not to think about that the river comes from Guatemala where it is used for all sorts of purposes, including sewerage -- go horseback riding or take one of the tours that the lodge can arrange. The little restaurant serves tasty Creole and Mestizo dishes at moderate prices.

Parrot Nest Lodge. Bullet Tree Falls, 501-660-6336; www.parrot-nest.com. Set on shady grounds on the Mopan River, Parrot Nest has five cottages and two treehouses for around US$50 to $65 plus tax.

Vanilla Hills Lodge. Guana Belly Drive, off Bullet Tree Falls Road, 501-634-0011; www.vanilla-hills.com. This little lodge, between San Ignacio and Bullet Tree Falls, about a US$8 cab ride from San Ignacio, has become popular because of its affordable rates and comfortable accommodations. Rates for the three cottages are US$90 to $110 year-round, double, plus 9% tax. Food is freshly prepared from local markets and the lodge's own greenhouse and chickens.

Camping/RV Campgrounds

Cayo has more camping options than any other area of Belize. Here is a sampling. For other places that allow camping, ask locally. A number of the hotels and lodges in the area will permit overnight camping or RV parking.

Clarissa Falls. Mile 70½ George Price Highway/Benque Road. (P.O. Box 44, San Ignacio), 501-833-3116; www.clarissafalls.com. This popular Belizean-owned cabaña colony on the Mopan River (see above) also allows camping, at US7.50 per person. RVs and trailers permitted, too.

Inglewood Camping Grounds. Mile 68 1/4, George Price Highway, 501-824-3555; www.inglewoodcampinggrounds.com. A newer, more complete camping option with water and electric hook-ups and a dump station is on the Price Highway/Benque Road just west of San Ignacio. Inglewood offers tent camping with hot and cold showers and hook-ups for RVs. US$15 to $20 for tent camping space, US$30 for RV camping with water, plus US$0.40 per kilowatt for electricity. Hot showers and sanitary dumping, no charge.

River Park Inn. 13 Branch Mouth Road, San Ignacio, 501-824-2116; www.riverparkinnbelize.com. This place, a short distance from San Ignacio on the Mopan River, has tent and RV camping, plus cabins for rent.

Smith's Family Farm. 13 Branch Mouth Road, San Ignacio, 501-604-2227. Camping here is US$7.50 per-person. Little cabins are US$25.

Mountain Pine Ridge Lodging

Blancaneaux Lodge. Mountain Pine Ridge (P.O. Box B, Central Farm, Cayo); 501-824-4912 or 866-356-5881 in the U.S. and Canada; www.thefamilycoppolaresorts.com/w/blancaneaux-lodge. Directions: From San Ignacio, go 12½ miles via the Christo Rey Road to the entrance to the Mountain Pine Ridge reserve or go by way of the Pine Ridge/Chiquibul Road from Georgeville, then 4½ miles (watch for sign) and turn on dirt road. Go approximately 1/2 mile to the lodge. You also can fly here via a charter, as the lodge has an airstrip.

Francis Ford Coppola ought to win a sixth Oscar for his incredible lodge, to add to the collection he won for the *Godfather* movies and other parts of his oeuvre. Coppola has said Belize reminds him of the verdant jungles of the Philippines, where he filmed *Apocalypse Now*, the movie that best caught the crazed atmosphere of the Vietnam war. In 1981, he bought an abandoned lodge, spent a fortune on fixing it up and reopened it in 1993. Mexican architect Manolo Mestre created the jungle chic look, and Francis and Eleanor Coppola themselves chose the Mexican and Guatemalan furnishings for the villas and cabañas.

The result is simply one of the most extraordinary lodges in the world. It seems impossible, but Blancaneaux looks better and better each time we visit, even considering the loss of a number of pine trees due to Southern Pine Beetle blight. The grounds are beautifully maintained, with native flowers accenting pathways, grass areas are manicured. On our last several stopovers, we stayed in a villa, where we dreamed about selling that screenplay to Hollywood. A villa has two huge bedrooms. They look even larger than they are, because the thatch roofs soar more than two stories high. There's a screen deck area with views of the Privaisson River. The tiled Japanese-style baths are large and special soaps and lotions are complimentary. Between the two bedrooms is a great room with kitchen and an unscreened deck (mosquitoes are only rarely a problem in the Pine Ridge.) Note that getting about Blancaneaux's hilly grounds requires climbing many steps up and down.

The regular cabañas, though less spacious and luxurious than a villa or luxury cabaña, are pleasant for a couple. They're also less of a burden on your credit card, at US$289 to $699 double, as opposed to US$469 to US$1,029 for the luxury cabaña with plunge pool or the two-bedroom villa, all depending on the time of year and number of people. Mr. Coppola's personal villa is US$759 to $1,319. The Enchanted Cottage ($699 to $1,800) sits on a hill away from the main lodge grounds. The cottage has a private pool, a bedroom with king bed and fireplace, a kitchen with wine cooler, espresso machine and heated slate floor, and a bath house with Japanese tub and steam room. Wow! Who can afford the rates these lodges in the Pine Ridge are charging now?! All rates are plus 9% hotel tax and 10% service. Included is a continental breakfast. During the season and at holidays there's a two- to four-night minimum stay.

The lodge has 24-hour electricity provided by a hydroelectric plant. Staffers can enjoy satellite TV in their rooms, but nothing so pedestrian is available in the guest lodging. The dining room in the main lodge building is comfortably upscale. The Italian and other dishes in the restaurant are excellent, if a little pricey, and gradually a wider variety of choices has been added, a boon to those staying for more than a few days. You can even get real espresso and pizza from a wood-burning pizza oven. Most of the fruits and vegetables served are grown in the lodge's organic gardens. Wines from the Niebaum-Coppola Estate Winery in Napa Valley are available.

When you're in the bar, just off the lobby, note the slate bar top carved by the Garcia sisters, and the ceiling fan, which was used in *Apocalypse Now*. A restaurant serving Guatemalan food is at the far end of the new pool, where the croquet pitch used to be. In the winter, the fireplace in the bar adds a cozy touch when nights drop into the low 50s. The hotel and restaurant service is excellent. Many tours are available. Coppola also operates the Turtle Inn in Placencia and La Lancha near Tikal in Guatemala.

Gaia Riverlodge. Mountain Pine Ridge (P.O. Box 173, San Ignacio, Cayo), 501-834-4024; www.gaiariverlodge.com. Formerly Five Sisters Lodge, Gaia Riverlodge is now owned by the same folks who operate Matachica on North Ambergris. It has 16 upgraded mountain, garden and riverview cabañas situated above Five Sisters Falls not far from Blancaneaux Lodge. There's a riverside villa, too. It's 360 steps down – and up – if you go to the falls, but there is a tram. Rates range from around US$200 to $400, plus tax. There are Matachica-Gaia jungle and beach packages, of course. Gaia Riverlodge has been honored by the BTB as one of the top hotels in Belize.

Hidden Valley Inn. Mountain Pine Ridge (P.O. Box 170, Belmopan), 877-773-1774 or 501-822-3320; www.hiddenvalleyinn.com. Directions: From San Ignacio, go 12½ miles on Cristo Rey Road to the entrance to the Mountain Pine Ridge reserve, (or go by way of the Pine Ridge/Chiquibul Road from Georgeville), then 4 miles (watch for sign to Hidden Valley Falls and Inn) and turn left on dirt road to the lodge. You can also fly to Hidden Valley – a three-seater plane charters for US$340 one-way from Belize City and US$490 from San Pedro. With its 7,000 acres of surrounding property, private waterfalls and great birding, Hidden Valley Inn always has had the potential to be one of the best lodges in Belize. Now, with ownership by the well-to-do Roe family of Belize City, who also are involved in the SunBreeze and SunBreeze Suites in San Pedro and the Biltmore in Belize City and who have many other interests in Belize, and new management, Hidden Valley is moving back to top form. The 12 private cottages, each with a bedroom (queens or two doubles), living room and tiled bath, are not your traditional thatch but marl daub with zinc roofs. They've been spruced up, and two are billed as deluxe units. All have salt tile floors and comfortable furnishings, and the fireplaces come in handy in the winter.

There's a beautiful swimming pool and a hot tub, in a grand setting by the side of the main lodge building. The lodge also has a spa. On recent visits, we had several delicious meals in the comfortable lodge dining room. It's wonderful to wake up early in the invigorating air of the Pine Ridge and walk some of the trails around the lodge. We're told there are 90 miles of trails, several leading to waterfalls that are open only to Hidden Valley guests. Honeymooners or even old married folks can reserve Butterfly Falls or other falls for your own private day at a waterfall, complete with champagne. You can also walk through a small coffee finca — the lodge grows and roasts its own coffee. Yes, many of the pines in this area have succumbed to the beetle infestation, but they are quickly regenerating. Many already 20 feet tall. The birding is actually better than ever here, as it's now much easier to spot the little feathered friends. A sizable percentage of Hidden Valley Inn guests are birders, who want to add to their life lists rare birds such as the Orange-breasted Falcon, King Vulture and Keel-billed Motmot.

Rates at Hidden Valley: For room only, US$350 to $455 double November to April, US$265-$370 rest of year (higher rates during Christmas), plus 9% hotel tax and 10% service. Rooms and all meals are US$490 to $605 per day double in-season, and US$420 to $530 off-season. Transfers for up to four from Belize City are US$190, or US$110 from San Ignacio, plus 12.5% tax. Packages are available, and the hotel offers many tours and trips.

Dining in San Ignacio

Price ranges shown are for typical meals for one (usually dinner), not including tip, tax or alcoholic drinks. Price ranges:

Inexpensive: Under US$7
Moderate: US$8-$19
Expensive: US$20-$39
Very Expensive: Over US$40

Restaurants here are listed alphabetically.

If you're staying at a jungle lodge, you'll probably take most of your meals there. Chaa Creek, Blancaneaux, Hidden Valley Inn, duPlooy's, Caves Branch, Table Rock and other lodges have excellent, if pricey, meals. San Ignacio is the center for dining in Cayo, with a host of small, generally inexpensive restaurants.

Erva's. 4 Far West Street, San Ignacio, 501-824-2821. A favorite for simple Belizean Mestizo food, rum punch and also pizzas. Inexpensive to Moderate.

Fuego Bar & Grill. Cayo Welcome Center, San Ignacio, 501-824-3663. Located next to the Cayo Welcome Center, Fuego has an upscale atmosphere, and it also has outdoor seating. It's a fun place for drinks and Caribbean-Belizean food. Service can be hit-and-miss. Open for lunch and dinner. Expensive.

Guava Limb Café. 75 Burns Avenue, San Ignacio, 501-824-4837. Opened by Chaa Creek Lodge, Guava Limb is now widely considered the best restaurant in San Ignacio. Its menu changes frequently, with a variety of creatively presented international dishes from seafood stew to pepper rubbed steak to beer-battered fish with cassava Lyonnaise. Excellent breakfasts, and it's a good place to drink, too. Excellent service and a charming atmosphere. Open for breakfast, lunch and dinner Monday to Saturday and brunch/lunch and dinner on Sunday (though off-season it may be closed on Sunday and Monday). Expensive.

Hode's Place Bar & Grill. Savannah Road, San Ignacio, across from soccer stadium, 501-804-2522. With a large shaded patio and swings and slides for the kids at the back, plus an ice cream stand, Hode's has good food in large portions and at modest prices. It has long been popular for its traditional menu, cold beers, karaoke and billiards. Outdoor seating at the edge of an orange grove. Inexpensive to Moderate.

Ko-Ox Han-Nah. 5 Burns Avenue, 501-824-3014. Formerly Hannah's (the new name in the Maya language means "Let's go eat"), this is probably San Ignacio's most popular restaurant, and deservedly so. It's not fancy—you eat on simple tables in a room opening on busy Burns Avenue—but the food is moderately priced and well prepared. In addition to beans-and-rice dishes, Hannah's serves salads, sandwiches and East Indian curries. Open for breakfast, lunch and dinner daily. Moderate.

Mr. Greedy's Pizzeria. 34 Burns Avenue, San Ignacio, across from Venus Hotel, 501-804-4688. Good pizza in Cayo. A large cheese pizza is US$14. In the afternoons, a cheap happy hour draws a crowd. Breakfast, lunch and dinner daily. Free wi-fi, too.

Pop's. West Street, San Ignacio. This is where to go for the best breakfasts in Cayo. Try the chaya scrambled eggs, fry jacks and freshly squeezed juice. Open daily for breakfast until about 1 p.m. Inexpensive to Moderate.

Sanny's Grill. East 23rd Street, San Ignacio, 501-824-2988. Heading west of San Ignacio, look for sign on the Benque Road just beyond UNO station. On a good night, this is one of the best restaurants in Cayo. Sanny's restaurant transforms Belizean basics, like chicken or pork chops, beyond standard fare. Eat in the casual dining room or out on the covered deck. Open for dinner only. Moderate to Expensive.

Serendib. 27 Burns Avenue, San Ignacio, 501-824-2302. This was Belize's only Sri Lankan restaurant, but it has changed owners. You can still get authentic curries, plus burgers and such. On busy Burns Avenue, with access from the Cayo Welcome Center. Indoor and outdoor seating. Closed Sunday. Moderate.

Local buses serve parts of the Southern Zone

CHECKING OUT HOPKINS AND DANGRIGA

Getting There

Dangriga is connected with the north by the Hummingbird Highway and by the Coastal Highway, which is also known as the Manatee Highway. Running south from Dangriga to Punta Gorda, a distance of about 100 miles, is the Southern Highway. Once this was widely considered the worst "main" road in Belize, with cars and big trucks raising thick clouds of dust in dry weather and bogging down in the mud in wet.

Things have improved a lot. The Southern Highway is now completely paved and one of the best roads in the country. **James Bus Line** (www.jamesbusline.com) buses connect Dangriga with Belize City (US$8). Dangriga has an airstrip, with regular service on **Maya Island Air** (www.mayaislandair.com) and **Tropic Air** (www.tropicair.com) from Belize City. One-way fares from the international airport are around US$92, and from municipal about US$61. There also are shuttle services from Belize

City, San Ignacio and elsewhere that will take you in a van to Dangriga or Hopkins. *See the section below on Checking Out Placencia for more information on shuttles.*

The road into Dangriga Town is completely paved. The access road to Hopkins from the Southern Highway also is now paved, and that to Sittee River is paved as well (though the paving ends around Sittee village before you get to Hopkins).

You'll probably get wet, you'll probably get eaten up by mosquitoes, but you'll get to experience the "real jungle" at **Cockscomb Basin Wildlife Sanctuary**. This preserve covers nearly 150 square miles of broadleaf rainforest. Much of it has been selectively logged for mahogany and other valuable trees, and some of it was affected by hurricanes, but to the novice bushwalker the rainforest canopy, up to 130 feet high, and the exotic plants and trees are nothing at all like back home. Parts of the preserve get up to 180 inches of rain a year, and the preserve includes the two highest peaks in Belize, Doyle's Delight at 3,688 feet and Victoria Peak at 3,675 feet.

Cockscomb has the most extensive trail network of any park in Belize. Trails at the preserve vary from short self-guided hikes near the visitor center to a 17-mile multi-day trek to Victoria Peak, only for the physically fit and best done with a local guide during the dry season. While it's unlikely that you will see one of the 200 or so jaguars in the preserve, you may well see tracks or scat, as the jaguars do frequent the trails and entrance road at night. If you hike long enough, however, you will run into quite a few other wild creatures. The preserve is home to some 300 species of birds, along with all five types of Belize's wild cats, black howler monkeys, peccaries and snakes of all types and biting abilities. The best time to see wildlife is at the start of the rainy season, usually mid-June to early August, although with luck you will see wild creatures anytime you are in the preserve. Animals are most active on cooler, cloudy days.

Mayflower Bocawina is a smaller park, but perhaps more interesting to the casual visitor than Cockscomb, as it has several beautiful waterfalls and some Maya sites.

Dangriga, with a population of around 9,000, is the largest town in Belize south of Belize City. Until the 1980s it was known as Stann Creek, when it was renamed Dangriga, meaning "sweet waters" in the Garifuna language. Dangriga, like Orange Walk Town, is not at all a visitor destination, though it is a useful jumping off spot for some of the central and southern cayes. Physically, it slightly resembles the older sections of Belize City, although it is much smaller.

What to See and Do in Dangriga and Hopkins

Few visitors stay for long in Dangriga In many ways that's a shame, because Dangriga is home to a unique culture, the Garifuna. It is also home to a number of nationally and internationally known painters and drum makers. The town, scruffy at first look, is actually quite photogenic.

One interesting attraction in Dangriga is the **Gulisi Garifuna Museum** (George Price Drive, 501-669-0539, open 10 to 5 Monday-Friday and 8 to noon Saturday, admission US$5). It has excellent displays on Garifuna culture, art and history.

Another must-see near Dangriga is the **Marie Sharp's Factory** (Melinda Road, off Stann Creek Valley Road, 501-532-2087, www.mariesharps-bz.com.) It's open 9-4 Monday-Friday. You can usually take a brief tour, or at least a look, at the small factory that produces the famous hot sauce and other condiments. You can also buy all the Marie Sharp's products at a shop there. Marie Sharp herself is often there. There is another Marie Sharp's store in Dangriga (near Stann Creek Bridge, 501-522-2370, open 8-5 Monday-Friday.

Dangriga is also something of an art center, with **Pen Cayetano's Studio Gallery** (3 Aranda Crescent, Dangriga, 501-628-6807, www.cayetano.de). Cayetano himself now spends most of his time in Germany.) **Austin Rodriquez's drum workshop** is here, too Artist Benjamin Nicholas and doll-maker Mercy Sabal also do their work in Dangriga. Pen Cayetano painted an impressive mural for the Dangriga Town Hall in 2012.

The biggest event of the year here is **Garifuna Settlement Day,** celebrated on November 19 and the days around that date. There's a reenactment of the Garingu landing in British Honduras, along with drumming concerts, dancing, music concerts, art exhibits and more.

Dangriga is also a **jumping off point** for many offshore cayes, including Southwater Caye, Tobacco Caye, Cocoplum Caye, Fantasy Caye and Thatch Caye, all with accommodations or resorts. It's also a good place for departures to the wonders and the several resorts on Glover's Reef Atoll.

A little farther south, the **village of Hopkins** offers Garifuna culture is an easier-to-absorb form, and of course the beaches, restaurants, dive resorts and small guesthouses are draws here. Hopkins bills itself as being midway between the reef and the rainforest. You can go diving one day, and the next tour the jungles of **Cockscomb Basin Wildlife Sanctuary** and **Mayflower Bocawina National Park.**

Cockscomb, often called the Jaguar Preserve, consists of more than 150 square miles of pure nature. As many as 200 jaguars are believed to be in and around the sanctuary. There also are other cats including margay, ocelot, puma and jaguarondi, along with tapirs, howler monkeys, deer, crocodiles and many species of birds. Take the entrance road to Cockscomb at Maya Centre, where a women's co-operative sells Maya and other local crafts. There's also a small private museum here, Maya Centre Maya Museum (admission US$7.50). Sanctuary admission is US$5. If you don't have your own transport, you can hire a taxi at Maya Centre for around US$15. Near the visitor center at the sanctuary is a campground (US$10 per person per night) and rustic cabins from around US$20 to $55. Reservations can be made through the **Belize Audubon Society** (www.belizeaudubon.org.) Bring your own food and water.

Mayflower Bocawina National Park (admission US$5) comprises about 7,000 acres. In the park are five waterfalls and a small Maya site. Getting to the waterfalls requires a fairly strenuous hike. Also in the park is a jungle lodge, **Bocawina Rainforest Resort and Adventures,** (501-670-8019, www.mamanootsbocawina.com) formerly Mama Noots Eco-Lodge. Bocawina Rainforest Resort has a variety of accommodations, from rooms to suites to cottages, for US$120 to $225 in-season and US$99 to 185 off-season. Rates plus 9% hotel tax and 9% service. There's also a restaurant and bar at the resort and what is billed as the longest zipline in Belize. The 2½-mile zipline costs around US$65 plus 12.5% GST for daytime tours and US$75 plus tax for a night zip.

Dangriga Lodging
Pelican Beach Resort. Scotchman Town, on the sea near the airstrip, 501-522-2044; www.pelicanbeachbelize.com. The rambling white wood-frame main building at Pelican Beach, reportedly once a dance hall, always reminds us of boarding houses of our youth in Florida; others say it reminds them of old hotels on the coast of Maine. Inside, though, it's vintage Belize, with simple wood paneling and furniture that wasn't selected

by any interior designer. There are about a dozen rooms in the main building and others in a separate structure. All rooms have fans, and some have air conditioning. In any event, this is the best hotel in Dangriga. It's on the water at the north edge of town, and there's a beach area and a breeze-swept pier. Some people swim here, but it's not exactly Cane Garden Beach in the British Virgin Islands. The Coconuts Grill & Bar is quite good, if a bit expensive (US$18 to $35 for dinner). Originally opened in 1971, Pelican Beach is operated by Tony and Therese Rath. Therese's family, the Bowmans, was prominent in colonial days, and she is prominent today in Belize's conservation organizations. Tony, a noted photographer, is among Belize's internet entrepreneurs, running the Belize by Naturalight web sites and doing web design for many Belize businesses. Rates: Doubles range from around US$135-$147 double in-season (mid-November thru mid-May) and US$106 to $105off-season. Prices are plus 9% hotel tax and 8.5% service. Packages are available. Pelican Beach is associated with the delightful Pelican Beach cottages on Southwater Caye.

Chaleanor Hotel. 35 Magoon Street, 501-522-2587; e-mail chaleanor@btl.net. This is a decent budget/low moderate choice in Dangriga. It's well run and a good value. The 18 rooms in this tall, three-story hotel are larger than at many budget hotels, and all have private baths. Some rooms with TV and air-conditioning. Rates around US$22 to $75, plus tax. Another budget spot nearby is the recently upgraded, 16-room **Pal's Guesthouse** (868 Magoon Street, 501-660-1282) with rooms from around US$45 to $60.

Hopkins Lodging

A seaside Garifuna village of about 1,400 people living in unpretentious frame houses, Hopkins was first settled in1942 after a hurricane devastated New Town, a Garifuna community just north of present-day Hopkins. The village gets its name from Frederick Charles Hopkins, a Catholic bishop of the early part of the 20th century. Hopkins was itself leveled by Hurricane Hattie in 1961. The village only got electricity and telephones in the mid-1990s. If "poor but proud" fits anywhere, it fits here. Villagers have gotten by on subsistence fishing and farming, and some are now earning cash money from tourism. You'll find most folks friendly. Many are eager to share their thoughts with visitors, and it's safe to walk around the village most anytime. The beach is nice, though many coco palms have died. Just south of Hopkins is the Sittee Point and False Sittee Point area, where hotel and real estate development are taking off. Many lots have been sold to expats looking for their little piece of the Caribbean, though only a few homes have so far been built.

You may have heard about the ferocious sand flies in this area, and, yes, they can be pretty bad. At other times, they're hardly to be noticed. Sorry, but we're not able to predict exactly when they are at their worst. The hotels here do their best to control the little devils, without resorting to hydrogen bombs, but at times the sandflies can be a pain in the neck, and also the foot, leg and everywhere else. An oily lotion such as baby oil and a bug spray with DEET helps.

Hamanasi. Sittee Point, Stann Creek District, 844-235-4930 or 877-552-3483 in U.S./Canada; www.hamanasi.com. Opened in 2000, Americans Dana and David Krauskopf quickly made Hamanasi one of the top beach and dive resorts in southern Belize. It has been named "Hotel of the Year" by the Belize Tourism Board and gets high ratings on TripAdvisor.com and other social media sites. On about 22 acres with 400 feet of beach frontage, the resort is south of Hopkins village. The restaurant and lobby are attractive, graced with local art, the grounds well kept and the pool, with a "zero effect," one of the nicest in Belize. There are several types of accommodations — 10 rooms and two suites in beachfront buildings and five deluxe and eight regular "tree houses" (actually just units raised on stilts and set in the trees in the back). All the accommodations are attractive, though we like the beachfront suites best. Hamanasi's dive operation provides full diving services. Hamanasi has three dive boats, including a big 45-footer with three 200-horsepower Suzuki outboard engines. A two-tank dive on the southern barrier reef is US$115 and a three-tank, full-day dive trip to Turneffe Atoll is US$185, and to Glover's Atoll US$195. A half-day reef snorkeling trip is US$75. Prices don't include dive or snorkel equipment rental. The resort also offers inland trips. Tours to Cockscomb are US$75. Room rates are way up there: US$398 to $690 in high season (Christmas and mid-February until Easter), US$333 to $608 in shoulder season and US$251 to $462 in low season (early June to mid-December, excepting U.S. Thanksgiving). Rates plus 9% hotel tax and 8% service charge. Continental breakfast included in room rates. The hotel's restaurant is very good, if very expensive, with a fixed-price dinner at US$50. There are usually minimum-stay requirements of three to five days, depending on the season.

Packages are available: Three-night packages including a beachfront standard room, meals, taxes and service fees, air and ground transfers from Belize City and one tour (such as a half-day dive trip or tour of Cockscomb) start at US$1,161 per person in high season, based on double occupancy, a little lower the rest of the year. A top end high-season seven-night package in a beachfront suite is US$3,091 per person.

Jaguar Reef Lodge & Spa. Sittee Point, Stann Creek District, 501-523-7365, or 866-910-7373 in the U.S. and Canada; www.jaguarreef.com. Jaguar Reef is now jointly operated with Almond Beach next door. These two Hopkins properties are part of the Viva Belize group that also includes La Beliza on North Ambergris, Sleeping Giant Lodge on the Hummingbird Highway and the treehouses at Ian Anderson's Caves Branch Lodge. The resort has many different types of accommodations. The attractive main lodge building houses the beachfront restaurant, bar, gift shop and front desk. The beach here is very nice. Jaguar Reef runs a variety of tours, both on land and sea. Rates for cottage rooms start at around US$130 off-season and go up to over twice that in-season. Rates are plus 19% for tax and service. Packages and specials are available. The Viva website is confusing and really hypes the discounts – call and see what they tell you.

Belizean Dreams. Hopkins, 501-523-7272 or 800-456-7150; www.belizeandreams.com. This condo colony just north of Jaguar Reef is among the most upscale accommodation choices on the Southern Coast. All villas have the same floor plans and furnishings, but some are directly on the beach, and the others have sea views. The units can be reserved as a complete three-bedroom villa, or choose a single bedroom or two-bedroom suite. The bedrooms have vaulted ceilings with exposed beams and four-poster king beds. Rates: US$295 to $675 in high season, US$225 to $575 in summer. Rates include taxes and service. All-inclusive packages available.

Beaches and Dreams Seafront Inn and Barracuda Bar & Grill. Sittee Point, 501-523-7259; www.beachesanddreams.com. Owners Tony and Angela Marsico traded running a restaurant in Alaska for operating a beachside inn and restaurant in Belize. They spruced up the inn's two octagonal cottages, each with two units with vaulted ceilings and rattan furniture, totally redid the main building, adding a couple of rooms, plus a treehouse that sleeps up to five. They also turned the restaurant into one of the better eateries on the southern coast. Rates US$125 to $215 in-season, US$99 to $169 mid-April to mid-November, plus 9% hotel tax and 9% service fee. The property is currently for sale.

Jungle Jeanie by the Sea. Hopkins, 501-533-7047; www.junglejeanie.com. These cabañas are on a nicely shaded stretch of beach a little south of Hopkins village. Founders "Jungle Jeanie" Barkman and husband, John, Canadians who lived in Belize for years, made this into one of the nicest little moderate range beach resorts in southern Belize. Rates for cabañas are US$60 to$120 double, plus hotel tax. Jeanie is now putting an emphasis on yoga here.

Hopkins Inn. Hopkins (P.O. Box 121, Dangriga), 501-665-0411; www.hopkinsinn.com. Attractive cottages on the beach, with full bath, fridge, fan and private verandah with sea views. The Hopkins Inn is well run by Greg and Rita Duke, who are knowledgeable about the area. Rates US$59 to $109 double, including continental breakfast, plus tax. German spoken.

Tipple Tree Beya Inn. Hopkins, 501-533-7006; www.tippletree.com. If you're looking for an affordable simple little place on the beach, this is a great choice. The hotel is popular, so reserve in advance. Beachside room and cabin rates range from US$40 to $98 double, plus tax. There's also a two-bedroom apartment with air-conditioning sleeping up to four person for US$175. All rates plus 9% tax. German spoken.

Dining in Hopkins

Price ranges shown are for typical meals for one (usually dinner), not including tip, tax or alcoholic drinks. Price ranges:

Inexpensive: Under US$7
Moderate: US$8-$19
Expensive: US$20-$39
Very Expensive: Over US$40
Restaurants here are listed alphabetically.

Restaurants at the larger resorts, including **Hamanasi** and **Jaguar Reef,** are attractive if expensive, but you don't need to limit yourself just to hotel dining. There are several excellent chefs and cooks in Hopkins, and a number of new eateries have opened in the past couple of years.

Barracuda Bar and Grill. South of Hopkins village at Sittee Point, 501-523-7259. A part of Beaches and Dreams inn, this waterfront restaurant has a long-time reputation for tasty seafood and interesting takes on Belizean dishes, along with good pizza. Closed Monday. Expensive.

Chef Rob's, Parrot's Cove Lodge, south of Hopkins village at Sittee Point, 501-670-0445. For upscale dining, Chef Rob Pronk's place is the number one restaurant in Hopkins and one of the best in southern Belize. Nice seaside setting at Parrot's Cove Lodge. Chef Rob also does Love on the Rocks, his cook-your-own concept where you grill your seafood or meat on 700-degree lava slabs. Open for dinner Tuesday-Saturday. Expensive.

Driftwood Beach Bar and Pizza Shack. Beachfront at north end of village, 501-667-4872. Popular seaside place for drinks and wood-fired pizza. Open for lunch and dinner. Closed Wednesday. Moderate to Expensive.

Gecko's. 101 North Road, north Hopkins, 501-629-5411. Laidback spot a really good meal. Check the blackboard for what's cooking -- dishes like jerk chicken, a huge pork chop and fish tacos. Open for lunch and dinner. Closed Sunday and sometimes Tuesday. Moderate to Expensive.

Innie's. Main Street, Hopkins, 501-503-7333. Not as cheap as it used to be, but it still serves authentic local Garifuna dishes, such as *hudut* (fish in a coconut broth with plantains) and seafood at moderate prices. Open daily for breakfast, lunch and dinner. Moderate.

Loggerheads Pub & Grill, Sittee Village Road, south of Hopkins, 501-667-4872. This second-story bar and grill is the best place in the area for a beefburger or seafood sandwich and a cold beer. Moderate.

Thongs Café. Main Street, 501-662-0110. This European-owned café is popular for morning coffee and breakfast – it's open 8-2 Wednesday-Sunday. Inexpensive to Moderate.

Dining in Dangriga

Your best option in Dangriga is the **Coconuts Grill** restaurant (Expensive) at **Pelican Beach Hotel.** It has a nice setting with a sea view. For something more local, try the **Riverside Café** (Inexpensive), a good choice for breakfast, or **King's Burger** (Inexpensive), which does have good beefburgers along with standard Belizean dishes such as stew chicken.

CHECKING OUT PLACENCIA

Getting There
By Car

From Belize City (the Goldson International Airport) to Placencia village by road is a trip of about 140 miles, via the George Price Highway, Hummingbird Highway, Southern Highway and Placencia Road. All these roads are paved and in good to excellent condition. However, with speed bumps and road conditions, it will take you at least three hours non-stop and likely a little longer. It is shorter by about 30 miles to take the Coastal Highway (aka Manatee Highway) from the village of Democracia on the George Price Highway to near the start of the Southern Highway, but as the Coastal Highway is unpaved it is usually smarter, and certainly more scenic, to go via the Hummingbird.

From the intersection of the Hummingbird Highway (also known at this point as the Stann Creek Valley Highway) and the Southern Highway, it is about 22 miles to the turn-off to Placencia. The left turn is well marked.

Then, from the Southern Highway, it is about 9 miles to near Riversdale, the elbow point at which you may begin to see the blue Caribbean to your left. From here, it is another 16 miles or so to the south end of Placencia village.

Glory be! Paving of the road to Placencia is completed, and it is now one of the best roads in Belize, although in some sections you have to watch out for jumbo speed bumps or "speed humps."

Air

Maya Island Air (www.mayaislandair.com) and **Tropic Air** (www.tropicair.com) each have seven or eight flights daily from Belize City. Fares from the international airport are about US$133 one-way and from the municipal airport, about US$112.

Bus

As of early 2016 **James Bus Line, Ritchie's, G-Line** and **Williams** are the bus lines licensed to go to the Southern Zone from Belize City. Several other bus lines operate from Dangriga south to Punta Gorda. This could change.

Ritchie's Bus Service (501-523-3806, www.ritchiesbusservice.com). is the only bus line that offers one-line – that is, no change of bus line -- service from Belize City (the Novelo's station) to Placencia. Ritchie's has only one departure a day to Placencia from Belize City, currently at 3:30 p.m. It is regular service, not express, with scheduled stops at Belmopan and Dangriga plus pick-ups en route on demand. Cost from Belize City is US$10.

James Bus Line (7 King Street, Punta Gorda, 501-664-2185, www.jamesbusline.com) is the largest and best (all things being relative) of the lines and has the most daily service to the south. As of early 2016, James has 10 daily departures (nine on Sunday) from Belize City's Novelo's bus terminal to Punta Gorda, beginning at 5:30 a.m. (this express bus doesn't operate on Sunday), with the last departure at 3:45 p.m. Although these buses don't go to Placencia, they do make a stop in Independence, across the lagoon from Placencia. The cost from Belize City to Independence is about US$8. From Independence/Mango Creek you can take the little pedestrian water ferry, the *Hokey Pokey* (501-622-3213, www.aguallos.com/hokeypokey) across the lagoon to Placencia. This boat has nine daily crossings (eight on Sunday) from Independence to Placencia, starting at 6:30 a.m. and the last at 5:30 p.m. (4:30 p.m. on Sunday). Cost is US$5 per person one-way. G-Line, RDS and A-Jays bus lines also offer service from Dangriga to Independence.

Otherwise, you can take James or another bus line from Belize City, Belmopan or San Ignacio, or by flagging down a bus anywhere on those routes, to Dangriga and change to a Ritchie's bus there. Ritchie's at present has at four departures daily, currently at 11 a.m. and 2, 4:30 and 6:15 p.m., from Dangriga direct to Placencia village. Cost from Dangriga to Placencia is US$5. As always, schedules and prices are subject to frequent change. Service may be reduced seasonally and on some holidays.

Shuttles

Several shuttle services will take you between Belize City or San Ignacio, or elsewhere, and Placencia. Tour companies such as PACZ Tours in San Ignacio also provide shuttle services. Rates vary depending on several factors including the number in the party, whether it is a private shuttle or a group shuttle and whether you go on a pre-arranged pick-up schedule or on a custom schedule. Expect to pay about US$50 to $125 per person between Belize City and Placencia and around US$40 to $110 between San Ignacio and Placencia. Check with the services and compare prices and schedules:

Discounted Belize Shuttles and Tours (www.discountedbelizeshuttlesandtours.com)

William's Shuttle Belize (www.williamsshuttlebelize.com)

Belize Shuttles and Transfers (www.belizeshuttlesandtransfers.com)

Mayan Heart World (www.mayanheartworld.net)

PACZ Tours (www.pacztours.net)

What to See and Do in Placencia

Some of the same destinations that you can reach from Hopkins and Dangriga are also possible from Placencia, especially now as the paved Placencia Road makes it easier and faster to get back to the Southern Highway. You can drive yourself or take a tour to **Cockscomb Basin Wildlife Sanctuary** and **Mayflower Bocawina National Park** (see above in the Dangriga/Hopkins section for information.) Daytrips to

Hopkins, Dangriga and also Monkey River village are also possible. Another destination closer to Placencia than to other places in the area is **Red Bank** village, known for its Scarlet Macaws, especially from January to March, when the annatto fruit that the Macaws feed on are ripe.

You can also make day trips to the **Lubaantun** and **Nim Li Punit** Maya sites near Punta Gorda. *For more information, see the Punta Gorda/Toledo section of this book.*

A main reason to come to Placencia is for activities on the water, primarily fishing, diving and snorkeling. There are plenty of tour operators and dive shops on the peninsula that will take you snorkeling or diving on the Belize Barrier Reef, about 20 miles out, or on patch reefs, sometimes called the inner reef, closer in around **Laughing Bird Caye National Park** (www.laughingbird.org), about 11 miles from Placencia village, or at other marine locations such as the **Silk Cayes** or **Southwater Caye Marine Reserve.** Dive operators also make trips to **Glover's Reef,** about a two-hour boat trip away.

Among the better-known dive shops on the peninsula are **Seahorse Dive Shop** (near pier in Placencia village, 501-523-3166, www.belizescuba.com) and **Splash Dive Center** (Chabil Mar Villas, 501-523-3080, www.splashbelize.com). **Ocean Motion** (in the village, on the sidewalk near the pier, 501-523-3363, www.oceanmotionplacencia.com) arranges snorkeling trips and also does land tours. Several of the larger hotels, including Turtle Inn and Inn at Robert's Grove have their own dive operations. You'll pay around US$85 a person for a Laughing Bird snorkel trip and around US$130 for a two-tank dive; to Southwater Caye snorkeling is around US$90 to $100, and diving US$150-$180. A full day of snorkeling at Glover's Reef runs around US$100 per person. Dive trips to Glover's Reef are around US$180 to $220 depending on the number of dives. Equipment rental is extra.

If you want to see fish without getting wet, **Sea n' Belize's glass bottom boat** (based at Inn at Robert's Grove Marina, 501-610-1012) is a very nice way to do it. The boat has a mahogany interior and 24 square feet of glass for viewing underwater. A half-day trip is around US$80 per person.

One of the more unusual marine attractions near Placencia are **whale sharks.** These gentle giants – they are sharks, but they eat only plankton and other small things, not humans – show up at Gladden Spit and elsewhere in late spring and early summer. The whale shark is the largest fish on earth, although it is smaller than some whales, which of course are mammals. You're mostly likely to see a whale shark about three days before and after a full moon during the months of March, April, May and June. But spawning dates vary from year to year, so sighting dates may change, and there are no guarantees, especially since whale sharks are mostly night feeders. Dive and snorkel shops in Placencia often book up well in advance for the limited number of available spaces.

Sport fishing is big here. Bonefish and permit are the main targets for fly anglers on the flats inside the barrier reef. Add tarpon and you've got a "grand slam." Bones, permit and tarpon can be caught year-round off Placencia. A day of fly-fishing on nearby flats costs around US$300 to $400 for two persons including boat, guide and lunch and refreshments. You'll need a Belize saltwater fishing license (US$10 a day or $25 a week). Ideally you should bring your own equipment and flies. According to local guides, flies should be unweighted and tied on a #6 hook. The best colors are orange, white, brown and pink.

Spin casting and trolling trips, using live bat or artificial lures, inside and around the barrier reef also are an option. Fishing for jacks and king fish is usually good. You'll pay about the same for a trolling/spin casting trip as for a fly fishing trip, around US$300-$400 for two persons, including boat, guide and refreshments.

Destinations Belize, run by former U.S. attorney Mary Toy (www.destinationsbelize.com) is a good source of information on fishing around Placencia and also on tours.

Day sailing on a catamaran (check with **Daytripper Catamaran Charters**, 501-666-3117, www.daytripperbelize.com), **canoeing or kayaking** in the lagoon on the back side of the peninsula or **paddlesports** are other recreational options.

The Moorings, (844-573-7936, www.themoorings.com), based at Laru Beya's marina, **charters monohull sailboats and catamarans,** starting at around US$4,000 a week. Bareboat charters must stay inside the barrier reef. A licensed captain is required for visiting the barrier reef or going to the atolls.

Believe it or not, there's a bowling alley on the Placencia peninsula – **Jaguar Lanes and Jungle Bar** (501-601-4434) in Maya Beach.

To get to know Placencia village, take a stroll on the narrow concrete **sidewalk** that runs for more than a mile north-south through the village. Along the sidewalk there are little gift shops, a few eateries and bars and access to small guesthouses. The sidewalk is a lot quieter than the main road (Placencia Road) through the village, which is often gridlocked with vehicles.

The jam-up may get worse when the new **Norwegian Cruise Lines Port** gets up to full speed in late winter 2016 on **Harvest Caye.** NCL ships carrying 2,400 to more 4,500 people will dock here, mostly skipping Belize City. The US$100 million cruise port has been controversial. Many local people on the Placencia peninsula strongly opposed cruise tourism. Construction has been delayed several times.

Easter weekend in Placencia is always busy, as is the Placencia Lobsterfest the third week of June.

Placencia Peninsula Lodging

You have a choice to make about where to stay on the Placencia peninsula. You have to decide whether you want to stay in Placencia village, the main "population center" for the area, or north of the village. Placencia village is a Creole village at the southern tip of the peninsula. It's a bit funky, and nearly all of the lodging choices here are in the budget or moderate categories, but it is the focus for restaurants and what shopping there is.

By contrast, the area north of Placencia village has most of the peninsula's upmarket resorts. It's less jammed up, and the beaches are generally prettier. If you're a budget traveler, or if you don't have a car (and don't want to bike or take a taxi back and forth between your hotel and the village) you may want to stay in or near Placencia village. If you decide you want something more upscale and with fewer people around, then your decision becomes: Where north of Placencia village do you want to stay?

There are two "addresses" north of Placencia village: Seine Bight, a Garifuna village about 5 miles north of Placencia village, and Maya Beach, about 7 miles north of Placencia village. Maya Beach isn't a village but a small collection of houses and hotels. Another collection of houses and hotels, most very expensive, is farther north, between Maya Beach and Riversdale, the elbow point where the Placencia Road from the Southern Highway comes near the Caribbean Sea and turns south down the peninsula.

A primary consideration is how far north of the "action" in Placencia village you want to be. Unless you have a car, you're at the mercy of your hotel shuttle, if there is one, taxis (which cost as much as US$20 one-way to go between Placencia village and the north end of Maya Beach). Some hotels do offer guests the complimentary use of bicycles, which is another option for getting back and forth, though not a very good one after dark. On the peninsula, you can also rent a golf cart, a car or a scooter.

There are many other options for lodging on the peninsula than just the ones listed here. For information on other place, visit the Belize Tourist Industry Association's Placencia site, www.placencia.com, or the Belize Tourism Board's site, www.travelbelize.org.

Properties listed here are arranged roughly by cost, from highest to lowest.

Turtle Inn. Placencia, 501-523-3150 or 800-746-3743 in U.S./Canada; www.thefamilycoppolaresorts.com/w/turtle-inn. The original Turtle Inn was a fixture for many years in Placencia, when the late Skip White ran it as an inexpensive barefoot beach spot. It was bought by Francis Ford Coppola and reopened as Blancaneaux's Turtle Inn. Not long after the purchase a nasty lady named Iris paid a visit to Placencia in October 2001, and Turtle Inn was virtually blown away. After a complete rebuild, Turtle Inn reopened in early 2003. It has since grown to a total of 25 units, all located just a short drive (or a long hike) north of Placencia village.

Our experience staying at Turtle Inn has been somewhat mixed. On one stay, we had a two-bedroom sea front villa, and you couldn't ask for anything nicer or more stylish. The villas and some of the single cabañas sit just feet from the sea, so the gentle lap-lap of the Caribbean soothes you, and the prevailing offshore breeze keeps you cool. There is no air-conditioning, so on a calm summer day it can get pretty warm. Our villa was a pure delight: The bay-thatch ceiling soars high, there's a wide screened porch across the front and the main living area has comfy seating and a fridge. The two bathrooms are in the Japanese-style, with both showers and tiled square tubs (there also are outdoor garden showers, which are more fun than you'd think.) The villas and cabañas at Turtle Inn are Balinese in inspiration, with wonderful art and furnishing. Even the doors were picked out personally in Indonesia by Mr. Coppola and his wife.

However, on another stay we had a cabaña at the back of the resort, away from the breeze and with no view of the sea. It was hot! The cabaña, especially the bath, also needed some TLC. Your mileage may vary.

In any case, you'll be happy with the resort's grounds. The pools include a large turtle-shaped, zero-effect pool between the restaurant and the attractive sandy beach, and another infinity pool in the triangular shape of the Coppola Resorts logo. There's also a private pool at Mr. Coppola's personal Pavilion villa. The beach here is pretty good for Belize, but not as good as the beaches farther north on the peninsula at Maya Beach. Turtle Inn has a small marina on the lagoon side, and one lodging unit is on that side.

The main restaurant at Turtle Inn is Mare, open to the breeze with a thatch roof, bar and a tropical atmosphere. It features Italian and seafood dishes. Like Blancaneaux, Turtle Inn has a wood-burning pizza oven and serves excellent wines from the Niebaum-Coppola winery. Prices aren't cheap. There are two other dining options for dinner, the Gauguin Grill and Auntie Luba's, which purports to serve Belizean food, along with the delightful Laughing Fish beach bar. We found the food, drink, service, amenities and staff responsiveness all very accommodating. At the prices you pay here, you would expect them to be.

Rates at Turtle Inn range up into the stratospheric category. Cabañas not on the water are US$319 to $829 double, depending on the time of year. Seafront cabañas are US$529 to $1,019. Two-bedroom villas and the three cottages/bungalows are US$649 to $1,469 double. Coppola's Pavilion, Sofia's Cottage, Ramon's Lagoon Bungalow and the Starfish Cottage range from US$859 to $4,519, with occupancy of up to eight persons in some cases. Rates are plus 9% hotel tax and 10% service. From January through April there is a three- to four-night minimum stay, seven-day minimum at Christmas. Off-season, May 1 to mid-December, provides the lowest rates. A continental breakfast of fresh-baked breads and fruits is included in the room rate.

Chabil Mar Villas. Placencia, 501-523-3606 or 866-417-2377 in U.S./Canada; www.chabilmarvillas.com. This gated condotel resort, a 10-minute stroll on the beach from the north end of Placencia village, is one of the most upscale places to stay on the peninsula. Chabil Mar means "beautiful sea" in the Kekchi Maya language, and the sea and 400 feet of beach here are indeed beautiful. The 19 one- and two-bedroom deluxe villas and one suite are tastefully designed and luxuriously furnished, down to wine corkscrews and service for eight. They have stylish features such as marble floors, original art and four-poster king beds. Every comfort is at hand, from wi-fi to cable TV to DVD players to washers and dryers in each unit. There's a private pier with al fresco dining and a beach bar, plus two infinity swimming pools. Room-only rates are around US$375 to $525 double per night, depending on the time of year and the unit, plus 9% tax and 10% service. A four-night package that includes air transfer from Belize City, lodging, all meals, one full-day snorkeling tour and two other tours, use of golf cart for two days, all taxes and service (but not drinks) is US$1,631 to $2,023 per person in summer, based on double occupancy, and US$1,762 to US$2,226 in winter, higher during peak holidays. You'll need to call or email to reserve your villas, as Chabil Mar doesn't have online booking.

Inn at Robert's Grove. Seine Bight, 501-523-3565; www.robertsgrove.com. This large property on 22 acres just south of Seine Bight, originally opened in 1997, raising the standard on what visitors to this part of Belize could expect in a beach resort. It was developed by New Yorkers Risa Frackman and Robert Frackman. When they owned it, it was our favorite place to stay on the Placencia peninsula, but all things change. They sold it and now only visit occasionally. It's still a good lodging choice, but somehow, at least for us, it's not the same.

Inn at Robert's Grove has a big variety of lodging choices, from standard rooms to one- to three-bedroom seafront suites to new lagoon-side one- to four-bedroom villas. Some of the units are available for sale as condos. Our favorites always have the deluxe one- and two-bedroom seafront suites. They have a large, strikingly decorated living room — a happy mélange of Mexican tile, Guatemalan fabrics and African art nicely put together by Risa Frackman — with cable TV, veranda with a sea view, bedrooms with king-size bed with a luxuriously firm new U.S.-made mattress and jumbo bathroom, with big, tiled combination bath and shower. However, the marina/lagoon-side villas are the newest accommodations at the resort, developed by the new owner.

The resort has three swimming pools, a fitness room, private pier and small sailboats, kayaks, canoes, windsurfers, bikes and other equipment for guest use. The main restaurant, Seaside, has sea views. A casual restaurant on the lagoon side, Habanero Mexican Café at the marina and near the dive shop, and a Belizean-style spot, Sweet Mama's, located where the tennis courts used to be, are open at times. There's a small bakery and deli, a tour desk, PADI dive center and a sandy beach where you can actually swim. In-season, rates are from US$195 for a double in standard garden view rooms to $655 for three-bedroom seafront suites, while the marina villas are US$395 to $910 depending on the number of bedrooms and number of people (maximum occupancy in the four-bedroom villas is eight persons). Off-season, rates range from US$170 to $695, again depending on the size and location of the accommodation and the number of people. All rates plus 9% tax and 10% service. Robert's Grove also all-inclusive lodging, meal and drinks packages at a private island, either the lovely Ranguana Caye, which has a nice beach and good snorkeling, and to tiny Robert's Caye. Weekly package rates start at US$1,903 in-season and US$1,608 off-season.

Laru Beya. Placencia Road, Seine Bight, 501-523-3476 or 800-890-8010 in U.S./Canada; www.larubeya.com. This upscale resort on a nice beach just south of Seine Bight village, next door to Inn at Robert's Grove, offers deluxe seaside accommodations at somewhat lower rates than the competition. It has a good restaurant, the Quarterdeck, and bar on-site. In-season rates for seafront rooms US$170, seafront suites, US250 to $390 (a three-bedroom seafront penthouse is US$520); off-season rooms US$140, suites US$180 to $300 (penthouse US$400). Rates plus 9% hotel tax and 10% service. Complimentary use of sea kayaks, small sailboats, bikes and wi-fi. There's a fresh-water infinity pool and a small mini-golf course.

Maine Stay. Seine Bight, 207-512-2381 in the U.S.; www.traversbelize.com. This is a good spot for families to stay for a week or longer. Cabaña suites have a pair of wooden cabañas, connected by a covered breezeway and deck, with two bedrooms and two baths. Both have kitchen, washer and dryer and wi-fi. There's 400 feet of beach and a 100-foot pier. Rates in-season (November–May) for four persons is US$1,895 per week and US$1,295 off-season, plus tax (no service charge). Owners, from Maine of course, live across the street. It can be booked through Vacation Rentals By Owner (www.vrbo.com).

Maya Beach Hotel and Bistro. Maya Beach, 501-533-8040; www.mayabeachhotel.com. Before ending up here, owners John and Ellen Lee (he's Australian, she's American) traveled and worked in 20 countries. They must have figured out what travelers like, because their little hotel is a classic beachy inn and their seaside Bistro *(see below)* is one of the best restaurants in Belize. A swimming pool is beside the restaurant, steps from a lovely stretch of beach. In addition to the five simple but pleasant and reasonably priced hotel rooms with views of False Caye and the sea, the hotel rents seven apartments and houses nearby. Hotel room rates: US$109 to $159 in-season, US$104 to $139 off-season. Rates plus 9% tax and 10% service charge. Highly recommended.

Barnacle Bill's. Maya Beach, 501-523-8110; www.barnaclebills-belize.com. American owners Barnacle Bill (known as the wit of Maya Beach) and Adriane Taylor have two one-bedroom Mennonite cottages about 60 feet from the beach. The bungalows are on stilts, cooled by fans and sea breezes, and each has a full kitchen with fridge, microwave, two-burner stove and cooking utensils. They'll sleep up to three. The bedroom has a queen bed, and there's a sofa sleeper in the living/dining area. For groceries, a small market is not far away, and there are several restaurants and bars nearby. Doubles are US$115 Nov.-May, US$100 rest of year, plus hotel tax. Minimum-stay five nights, seven at Christmas.

Tradewinds. Placencia village, 501-523-3122. If you want a beachfront cottage but don't want to pay the higher prices north of the village, Tradewinds is a pretty good bet. The nine pastel-colored cabins right on the beach at the south end of Placencia village are cute as a bug's ear. They're not large, and could stand some maintenance and improvements but at about US$75 to $100, they're a decent value. Fridges, fans and two double beds are standard. The beach sand here is a little rough on your naked feet.

Seaspray. Placencia village. 501-523-3148; www.seasprayhotel.com. This oldie goldie (it was the first hotel in Placencia, opened in 1964) has seaside and non-seaside rooms, plus one cabaña on the beach, located in the heart of the village. Not fancy, but okay if you're not too picky. Fans, no A/C, cable TV and small fridges. Some rooms with kitchenettes. Rates US$27 to $70 in-season, plus tax.

Deb & Dave's Last Resort. North end of Placencia village, 501-523-3207. Budget travelers will enjoy one of the four rooms with shared baths at Deb & Dave's. It's in a shaded area of the village but not on the water. Fans, no A/C, free wi-fi. The owners are helpful and knowledgeable. Rates around US$25 plus tax.

Lydia's Guest House. Placencia village; tel. 501-523-3117; e-mail lydias@btl.net. This is a top backpacker's choice in the village. It offers eight basic but clean rooms, with fans, shared bath, shared kitchen, refrigerators and, on the second floor of the wood-frame house, a veranda with hammocks. Rates around US$25 double plus tax.

Dining in Placencia

Mare at **Turtle Inn** and **Quarterdeck** at **Laru Beya**, both in the Expensive/Very Expensive category, are worthy hotel restaurants. In addition, try the following local places, listed alphabetically.

Price ranges shown are for typical meals for one (usually dinner), not including tip, tax or alcoholic drinks. Price ranges:

Inexpensive: Under US$7

Moderate: US$8-$19

Expensive: US$20-$39

Very Expensive: Over US$40

Brewed Awakenings. Placencia Road, Placencia village, 501-668-1715. Popular place to get your latte or other fresh-brewed coffee. Open from 6:30 a.m. to 5 p.m. Closed Sunday, Inexpensive. For fresh-baked goodies to go with your coffee, look for signs to **John the Bakerman's** house in the village.

Dawn's Grill 'n Go. Placencia Road, Placencia village, 501-602-9302. This little spot by the main road cooks up tasty Belizean and American food. The fried chicken is excellent. Open for breakfast, lunch and dinner. Closed Sunday. Moderate.

De Tatch. Laidback and tropical, De Tatch is popular for its beer and simple but pretty good food. In the village at the Sea Spray Hotel. Inexpensive to Moderate.

La Dolce Vita. Placencia Road in Placencia village, 501-523-3115. Located upstairs next to Wallen's grocery, La Dolce Vita is our long-time fave for good Italian in Placencia. The chef-owner makes his own pasta, sauces and breads. Moderate to Expensive.

Maya Beach Hotel Bistro. Maya Beach, 501-520-8040. The restaurant at this small inn is probably the best restaurant in Southern Belize and one of the top three or four in the country. The seaside setting is wonderful, service is very friendly and virtually anything you order you will love. The Bistro has a selection of small plates and appetizers including fish cakes, a shrimp corn dog and honey-coconut ribs, along with regular entrees, creatively presented, such as cocoa-dusted pork chop on risotto, prosciutto-wrapped grouper and lobster grilled cheese. The Bistro bakes its own breads, cinnamon rolls (huge) and other pastries. Highly, highly recommended. Open daily for breakfast, lunch and dinner. Reservations for dinner suggested. Moderate to Very Expensive.

Rumfish y Vino. Placencia village, 501-523-3293. Run by expat New Yorkers, in a breezy second-story location in Placencia village, Rumfish y Vino is a good spot to have drinks and interesting food. Try the lionfish sashimi or blackened lionfish (great way to help get rid of this alien intruder that is messing the Caribbean ecosystem), lobster pizza or one of the ceviches. Nice selection of wines. Lunch and dinner daily. Expensive.

Tiger Beach Club. Seine Bight, 501-628-1250. This is *the* spot for authentic Indian food in southern Belize. The chef, from Mumbai, works his wonders with naan, samosas and curries in an open kitchen in the middle of the restaurant. Tiger Beach Club is open to the breezes. Closed Tuesday. Expensive.

Secret Garden. Placencia village, 501-523-3617. Pleasant spot to have dinner in a garden patio setting. The menu has been revamped, offering Argentinian steak, seafood gumbo, pasta and other dishes. Open for dinner. Closed Sunday. Moderate to Expensive.

Tranquilo. Placencia Caye, 501-620-7763. Hop on a free shuttle boat at the Placencia pier for a short ride to this new restaurant on Placencia Caye. Open for dinner daily except Tuesday. The setting is marvelous and the food, mostly seafood dishes, is pretty good. In-season, reservations suggested. Moderate to Expensive.

Tutti-Frutti. Placencia Road, Placencia village. Great place for amazingly delicious and authentic Italian gelati in a variety of tropical fruit and other flavors. Highly, highly recommended! Inexpensive.

Other places for inexpensive local food in Placencia village include **Omar's, The Shak** and **BJ's Bellyful.**

Where to Party
Barefoot Beach Bar (it relocated to the beach in Placencia village) is a very popular spot to drink and eat. There's often live music, and you can dance your heart out. Next door, also on the Belize, is another party place, **Tipsy Tuna.** Rum drinks are just BZ$3 at happy hour. **Yoli's** on a pier at the south tip of the peninsula has the most tropical setting in the village to

sip your Belikins. Good food, too. **Pickled Parrot,** in the middle of the village, is under new ownership. Come here for the beer, drinks and TV. **Street Feet Lounge** is an indoor nightclub in the village, under the same ownership as Barefoot Beach Bar. DJs play, you drink and dance. When visiting bars and clubs in Placencia village at night, keep in mind that there aren't a lot of streetlights. It's dark out there!

Rio Grande in Toledo District

CHECKING OUT PUNTA GORDA

Getting There

Via the Southern Highway, Punta Gorda is about 100 miles by car from the junction with the Hummingbird/Stann Creek Valley Highway near Dangriga. Since the Southern Highway is now fully paved, if you push it a little you can make the trip in about two hours. Add up to three hours if leaving from Belize City, and two hours from San Ignacio, depending on your route and driving habits.

By bus from Belize City -- **James Line** (www.jamesbuslines.com) is your best choice -- figure about six hours minimum. Besides regular buses, James has two daily express buses that are a little faster. Fare from the Novelo's bus station in Belize City to PG is around US$6.

Both **Tropic Air** (www.tropicair.com) and **Maya Island Air** (www.mayaislandair.com) each have about four or five flights a day from Belize City to PG. From the international airport to Punta Gorda, the fare is around US$175 one-way and from municipal, US$148.

Shuttle service by van is also available to Punta Gorda. See the Placencia section for information on shuttles. A shuttle from Belize City to PG will be at least US$200 for up to two or three people.

One of these days soon, the San Antonio Road to the Guatemala border will be completely finished and a new border crossing opened, connecting Belize's Far South with the Pan American Highway. That will change the dynamics in Toledo, not just in tourism but also in other areas such as retailing and agriculture.

Moving on from PG, there is regularly scheduled pedestrian water taxi service between PG and Puerto Barrios, Guatemala. Currently, there are four boats daily to Puerto Barrios – Requena's, Tek-Dat, Pichilingo and Sharkboy -- at 9:30 a.m. and 1, 2 and 4 p.m. respectively. The trip takes about an hour and the one-way fare is US$20 to $25. There's one boat daily to Livingston, Guatemala, Memos, at 1 p.m. Fare depends on the number of people going.

What to Do and See in PG and Toledo

The Deep South of Belize offers a lot to do on land and sea. It's too bad that so few visitors make it here. Unfortunately, prices for tours tend to be high, due to lack of volume and the distances involved.

Punta Gorda Town has an attractive waterfront location. However, there are no real beaches in or near PG. The town, with its mix of Garifuna, Creole, Maya, Guatemalans and quite a few expat Americans, is generally safe. There's not much to see or do in town, except for a few small shops along Front Street and elsewhere in town. At Central Park is a large clock tower and a market with lots of shops selling used clothing and other miscellaneous junque. **Fajina Women's Group Craft Center** (Front Street near the pier) is a small co-op selling Maya crafts.

Cacao growing is big business (but with a lot of small cacao farmers) in Toledo. The Toledo Cacao Growers Association (www.tcgabelize.com) has some 600 members. Most grow their cacao organically and bring it to a central facility for processing. A small chocolate factory (**Cotton Tree Chocolate Shop**, 2 Front Street, 501-621-8772, www.cottontreechocolate.com) is in PG. Other chocolate making operations include the **Ixcacaco May Belizean Chocolate** (San Felipe village, 501-742-4050, www.ixcacaomayabelizechocolate.com).

Near Mafredi village is the **Maya House of Cacao** (San Antonio Road, 501-722-2992, open daily 8-5), which opened in late 2015. It has exhibits on cacao, chocolate making and a gift shop.

The **Chocolate Festival** (www.chocolatefestivalofbelize.com), held the third week in May) is a growing annual event held downtown and in other venues in Toledo.

PG has a couple of Garifuna drumming schools, including Ray Mcdonald's **Warasa Drum School** (501-632-7701, www.warasadrumschool.com) and **Maroon Creole Drum School** (501-632-7841) run by noted drummer and drum-maker Emmeth Young. Mr. Young's drums are sold at the Driftwood Café at 9 Front Street in PG.

In rural Toledo, you'll see true rainforests, lush and green, Maya villages that are little changed from 1,000 years ago and several interesting Maya sites, including Lubaantun and Nim Li Punit. You can also hike in the national parks and forest reserves and go caving.

While you're here you must visit the rural areas where there are a number of Mayan villages, both Mopan and Kekchi. **San Pedro Columbia** and **San Antonio,** a Kekchi village, are two of the largest. San Pedro Columbia is home to **Eladio Pop's Cacao Trail.** Mr. Pop will take you on a tour of his cacao farm and demonstrate how the ancient Maya made chocolate.

Other interesting villages are **Blue Creek** (Kekchi and Mopan), home to **Blue Creek Cave.** You'll need a guide to explore the cave, although you can swim a few hundred feet into the cave on your own. The **Tumul K'in Center of Learning** (501-608-1070, www.tumukinbelize.org), dedicated to preserving Maya heritage and practices, is also in Blue Creek. **International Zoological Expeditions** (IZE, 501-532-2404, www.izebelize.com), which runs educational and research programs in several parts of Belize, has a small lodge and research station at Blue Creek with a couple of treehouse cabins and a dorm. Rates for lodging, meals and a couple of tours are around US$115 per person per night.

At **Santa Cruz** village is **Río Blanco National Park,** a small (105-acre) park with a waterfall, small lake and a cave. Near **San Miguel village** is **Tiger Cave.**

Near **Big Falls** village is the **Living Maya Experience** (501-627-7408), which provides visitors with an immersion experience in Kekchi Maya culture, including farming, making tortillas and basket weaving. You visit two Maya families.

Not associated with the Living Maya Experience but in the same area is a zip line operated by **Big Falls Extreme Adventures** (www.bigfallsextremeadventures.com). Doing the zip line costs US$40 per person. A half-day combination zip line, river tubing and Lubaantun tour is US$110.

Near **Golden Stream** village about 30 miles north of PG is the **Belize Spice Farm & Botanical Gardens** (501-732-4014, www.belizespicefarm.com). This farm, owned by an American couple of East Indian descent, is one of the largest vanilla and black pepper farms in Belize. Tours are in a trailer behind a tractor. They cost US$10 per person.

Ya'axché Ranger Program (www.yaaxche.org) allows you to experience a day with a ranger in the rainforest. You'll call with a Ya'axché ranger as he travels around trying to find illegal hunting. You might track a jaguar or tapir. The program starts at Golden Stream Field Center. There's no fixed charge, but a donation to Ya'axché of US$35 to $50 is requested.

Payne's Creek National Park, north of PG, covers more than 37,000 acres of mixed saltwater, freshwater and savannah land habitat. It has manatees, yellow-headed parrots, howler monkeys and all five species of Belize's wild cats including jaguars. It is administered by the Belize Forestry Service and the Toledo Institute for Development and Environment (TIDE).

Barranco is a Garifuna fishing village of about 600 people near the Sarstoon-Temash National Park. It was the home of Andy Palacio and a number of other well-known musicians and artists. There is a dügü, a Garifuna temple, here along with the **Barranco House of Culture.** A TIDE tour of Barranco is around US$100 for two people.

For a more complete immersion in Maya life, consider a **homestay** or **guesthouse stay** in a Maya village. Several different programs are available in Toledo.

One is the **Toledo Ecotourism Association** (TEA) program (501-633-9954, www.teabelize.org. TEA offers stays in guesthouses (not individual homes) in five villages: Laguna, San Antonio, Santa Elena, San Jose and San Miguel starting at US$28 per person. A one-day, one-night program including guesthouse stay, three meals and various activities is US$100 per person. TEA also offers farm, village, cave, chocolate making and other day tours, most from about US$10 to $30 per person.

Another is the **Aguacate Belize Homestay Program** (501-633-9954, www.aguacatebelize.com). Stays in a Maya home in Aguacate village, a Kekchi community, are around US$8 per person per night, with meals US$3.50 per meal, plus a one-time US$5 registration fee. Keep in mind you will stay in a Maya thatch home with dirt floor that will not have electricity or running water. You'll sleep in a hammock, bathe in a creek and eat simple meals of tortillas, beans and eggs that the family eats.

Maya Sites

Nim Li Punit, near Indian Creek village off Mile 75 of the Southern Highway, 501-665-5126, open 8 to 5 daily, admission US$5, is a late Classic period site noted for its stelae. More than 25 large stelae have been found at the site. Some of the stelae and other artifacts are on display at the informative visitor center. Nim Li Punit is on a hilltop with good views of the surrounding rainforest. Maya women and children from Indian Creek set up tables near the exit area, selling their Maya crafts.

Lubaantun, near San Pedro Columbia village off the San Antonio road, is a late Classic period site. The site is open daily from 8 to 5. Admission is US$5. There is a visitor center. Lubaantun was at its peak from around 730 to 900 CE. The site has 18 plazas. From the tallest structure in the plaza, about 50 feet high, you can see the sea. Lubaantun was first rediscovered in 1875 and has been excavated by a number of different archeologists, including F.A. Mitchell-Hedges, Thomas Gann and Norman Hammond. The so-called "Crystal Skull" allegedly was discovered here in 1924 by Anna Mitchell-Hedges, the daughter of F.A. Mitchell-Hedges. In fact, F.A. likely bought the skull at an auction in London in 1943. Tests suggest the skull is of modern origin.

Pusilhá and **Uxbenka** are two other Maya sites in Toledo. Neither is much excavated Both are difficult to visit except on a tour (around US$100 for two people).

Maya Villages and Offshore Cayes

Getting to the Maya villages areas is easiest done with your own transportation, but you can also go on a tour or take a bus. A bunch of local buses leave from the clock tower area to go to various Maya villages and to Barranco in Toledo. Usually there is just one or two buses a day to each village. Ask locally for current schedules, or look in the local tourist newspaper, *The Toledo Howler.*

Off the coast of Toledo are some of Belize's most pristine cayes and excellent diving, snorkeling and fishing.

Closest to PG are the **Snakes Cayes** in the **Port Honduras Marine Reserve.** These cayes offer good snorkeling, diving and swimming about a 30-minute boat ride from town. There are **East, South, West and Middle Snake** cayes. The best beach is on West Snake Caye. South Snake Caye has abundant sea life on view for snorkelers and divers. East Snake Caye has a lighthouse. Middle Snake Caye is for researchers only, off limits to regular visitors. There is a US$5 per person per day reserve fee for visiting Port Honduras Reserve.

Farther out are the **Sapodilla Cayes** in the **Sapodilla Cayes Marine Reserve.** It's about a 90-minute boat ride from PG, and when the weather is bad it's a rough ride. Hunting Caye and Lime Caye both have good swimming and snorkeling, and you can overnight at either one. On **Lime Caye** is Garbutt's Fishing Lodge (501-73209979, www.garbuttsfishinglodge.com) offers several packages for US$350 to $700 per person including transportation, lodging, meals, snorkeling, fishing and park fees. (This marine reserve has a US$10 per person per day reserve fee.) **Hunting Caye** is the site of one of the University of Belize's small satellite campuses, and it sometimes rents out its basic rooms for visitors (around US$40 per person). The Belize Coast Guard is also stationed here. Camping on the island is US$5 per person.

Reef Conservation International (501-702-0229, www.reefci.com) has a combination research operation and dive lodge on Tom Owens Caye. Rates for divers are around US$1,200 per week per person for divers and US$900 for non-divers.

There are about a dozen registered and licensed tour operators in Toledo, including the ones below. They can arrange land and marine tours. The larger lodging properties also run tours. Full-day land tours range from about US$100 to $150 per person. These tours include guide, transportation from PG and lunch. Full-day snorkel and swimming tours to the Snake Cayes cost around US$250 for two persons on a private tour. If you can join a group, the rate may be lower.

Garbutt's Marine, Joe Taylor Creek, Punta Gorda, 501-722-0070, www.garbuttsfishinglodge.com.

PG Tours, 501-629-4266, Punta Gorda, www.pgtours.com.
TIDE Tours, Mile 1, San Antonio Road, 501-722-2129,
www.tidebelize.org.
Toledo Cave & Adventure, 501-604-2124, Sun Creek,
www.tcatours.com.

For more information on tours and about the Toledo area in general, visit the Belize Tourism Industry Association (BTIA) office on Main Street, 501-722-2531. Pick up a copy of *The Toledo Howler* tabloid, published several times a year.

Punta Gorda Lodging

Lodging in the PG area is listed roughly by cost, from high to low.

Belcampo Lodge. Wilson Road, 5 miles north of PG, 800-299-9940 in U.S. and Canada; www.belcampobz.com. Formerly the fishing lodge known as El Pescador PG, and then Machaca Hill, Belcampo Lodge now focuses on more traditional jungle lodge activities, such as trips and tours in the Laughing Falcon Reserve, an 12,000-acre private nature reserve. The owner has taken the lodge far upscale, redoing the main lodge and adding a gorgeous spa. Rates with meals are among the highest of any lodge in Belize. The lodge is set on a steep hill, called Big Hill for the farm that was originally here, on 470 acres above the Rio Grande. A small tram takes guests down to the boats docked on the river at the base of the hill. It's really cool! Up top, on a clear day, you have views of the Gulf of Honduras, with Guatemala and Honduras in the distance. Troops of howler monkeys come by frequently. After a day exploring the Toledo rain forest, dive into the pool, then dine on fish and fresh vegetables from the lodge's organic garden. The 16 renovated cottage suites have vaulted ceilings, tile floors and air-conditioning. Room rates start at US$380 to $455 per night, plus tax and 10% service. An eight-night package including lodging, all meals, air transfers from Belize City, taxes, service and several tours and activities is a whopping US$4,320 per person based on double occupancy.

Cotton Tree Lodge. San Felipe village; 501-670-0557 or U.S. number 212-529-8622; www.cottontreelodge.com. Named after the silk cotton tree, aka kapok or ceiba, a giant example of which stands near the main lodge building, Cotton Tree Lodge sits on 100 acres beside the Moho River about 15 miles from Punta Gorda. Cotton Tree accommodations include rooms, one- and two-bedroom cabañas and even a river cabaña anchored in the middle of the Moho River. The lodge has raised wooden walkways; in the summer rainy season the Moho sometimes floods, and at times the lodge grounds become a shallow pond. Good meals are served in a huge thatch palapa. Room rates US$196-$350 double in-season are US$162 to $306 off-season. All-inclusive rates that include all meals and daily guided tour are US$459 to $614. All rates are plus 9% tax and 12% service.

Lodge at Big Falls. Big Falls (P.O. Box 103, Punta Gorda), 501-732-4444; www.thelodgeatbigfalls. This lodge, on about 30 acres on the banks of the Rio Grande River near the village of Big Falls, is an attractive option for birders, nature lovers and outdoor lovers. The owners are Rob and Marta Hirons. They've done a good job developing the lodge property. The accommodations are what most visitors are looking for in a lodge — there are thatch cabañas, but nice ones, with tile floors and private baths. In addition, the lodge has three newer cabins with air-conditioning. There's a swimming pool, but you can also swim in the Rio Grande. The main lodge building has a restaurant and library. Current rates: High season (November to May), US$206 to $225 double; May to October, US$161 to $181 double. Rates are plus 9% tax and are higher Christmas/New Years. Breakfast is an additional US$14, packed lunch US$12 and dinner US$40 per person, plus 12.5% tax.

Tranquility Lodge. Just off the Southern Highway on San Felipe Road, Jacintoville, 501-677-9921; www.tranquility-lodge.com. This lodge has gone through several changes of ownership over the last 10 or 15 years. It has rooms, thatch cabañas and a restaurant on about 20 acres on the Jacinto River. Rates are US$125 to $145 double, in season and US$105 to $125 off-season, all plus 9%tax and 10% service charge.

The Farm Inn. San Antonio-Santa Cruz Road, Toledo, 501-732-4781; www.thefarminnbelize.com. The Farm Inn is a small lodge on 52 acres just off the newly paved San Antonio Road. The managers are from South Africa. The Farm Inn has three rooms in a two-story building near a small creek, plus two other rooms closer to the lodge office. All rooms have private baths and fans, no air-conditioning (power at the lodge is solar). Rates are US$107 to $162 double year-round, including tax and breakfast. The restaurant serves Belizean and South African dishes, with many items from the lodge's own garden. Guinea fowl and other creatures scamper around the grounds.

Coral House Inn. 151 Main Street, (P.O. Box 43, Punta Gorda), 501-722-2878; www.coralhouseinn.net. Americans Rick and Darla Mallory bought and renovated a 1938 colonial-era house and turned it into one of the coolest guesthouses in Belize. You'll recognize it by the coral color and the vintage red and white VW van parked in front. There's a small swimming pool and use of bikes is complimentary. Nearby are Confederate graves in a cemetery, a legacy of the Confederate immigration to Toledo after the U.S. Civil War. The five guest rooms and one suite --US$96 to $108 double year-round, plus tax -- have tile floors, good beds, air-conditioning and free wi-fi. Highly recommended.

Blue Belize Guest House. 139 Front Street, Punta Gorda, 501-722-2678; www.bluebelize.com. This pleasant, well-located guesthouse is owned by marine biologist Rachel Graham, though last we heard Dr. Graham was in San Pedro. You can do your own thing in one of the five attractive self-catering flats, with kitchenettes, large bedrooms and verandas with hammocks. The guesthouse is set on a bluff overlooking the water, within a short stroll of everything in town. A continental breakfast is included. Bikes are complimentary. Rates US$75 to $135 plus 9% tax.

Hickatee Cottages Lodge. Mile 1.5, Ex-Servicemen Road, Punta Gorda, 501-662-4475; www.hickatee.com. This charming and down-to-earth lodge on 20 acres just south of Punta Gorda was created by a British couple, Ian and Kate Morton. It opened in late 2005 and quickly became one of the best little inns in Belize. Sadly, however, as of this writing reportedly it is for sale, and it's unclear what changes may occur. The Caribbean-style cottages, with zinc roofs and private porches, are nestled in lush foliage. Rates for the six rooms are an affordable US$65 to $130 double, including continental breakfast. There's a small but well-stocked bar with free wi-fi. On certain days, the lodge offers guests free visits to Fallen Stones butterfly farms. A hickatee, by the way, is a river turtle, *Dermatemys mawii*. Highly recommended.

Tate's Guest House. 34 José Maria Nuñez Street, Punta Gorda, 501-722-0147. Run by William Tate, a long-time post office worker in PG, and his family, this guesthouse on a quiet residential street is a good value. The rooms are clean, and the atmosphere friendly. There's a small common kitchen with refrigerator and microwave for guest use. Rates around US$20 to $45.

Nature's Way Guesthouse. 65 Front Street, Punta Gorda, 501-702-2119; e-mail natureswayguesthouse@hotmail.com. This rambling, funky old guesthouse/hostel appeals to the hippy backpacker in us. Run by long-time expat Chet Schmidt, it has a nice location, on the water toward the south end of town. Guests here are often well traveled, with stories to tell. There are nine basic rooms, three with private baths. At these prices — at around US$19-$25 — don't expect a Hampton Inn.

Dining in Toledo

In addition to the restaurants listed below, **Belcampo Lodge** (Expensive to Very Expensive) has an excellent restaurant, open to the public by reservation. **The Farm Inn** restaurant, (Moderate) serves an unusual combination of Belizean and African dishes. The South African dishes are cooked in a three-legged cast iron pot.

Price ranges shown are for typical meals for one (usually dinner), not including tip, tax or alcoholic drinks. Price ranges:

Inexpensive: Under US$7

Moderate: US$8-$19

Expensive: US$20-$39

Very Expensive: Over US$40

Restaurants are listed alphabetically.

Asha's Culture Kitchen. 80 Front Street, Punta Gorda, 501-632-8025. This is usually our first stop for dinner in PG. For one thing, the setting is great: Asha's is in a wooden building over the water, with a windy deck with views of the sea. For another, its serves tasty seafood and other Creole dishes in large portions at modest prices. It's one of the few restaurants in town that draws a crowd – as the evening wears on, the availability of the day's dishes are checked off on a chalkboard. Open for dinner daily except Tuesday. Inexpensive to Moderate.

Coleman's Café. Big Falls village, near the rice mill, 501-720-2017. This restaurant in Big Falls village serves simple but tasty Belizean dishes such as stew chicken with beans and rice. Sit at tables with under a covered patio, open to the breezes, and enjoy real Belizean hospitality. Inexpensive to Moderate.

Gomier's Restaurant and Soy Centre. 5 Alejandro Vernon Street, Punta Gorda, 501-722-2929. This restaurant opens only if the St. Lucia-born owner, Ignatius "Gomier" Longville, feels like cooking. If open

Gomier's does excellent vegetarian meals, from organic ingredients mostly grown by the owner. Closed Sunday and some other days. Inexpensive to Moderate.

Grace's. Main Street, Punta Gorda, 501-702-2414. This long-established local place is especially good for breakfast. Open for breakfast, lunch and dinner daily. Inexpensive to Moderate.

Mangrove Inn at Casa Bonita. Front Street in Cattle Landing area, Punta Gorda, 501-722-2270. The cook and co-owner of this little restaurant, Iconie Williams, formerly operated one of PG's best eateries, also called Mangrove Inn, and she reopened it here in the B&B in her home. Iconie cooks different dishes every evening, but you'll usually have a choice of seafood (snapper, snook, or shrimp) or hearty fare like roasted chicken. Open daily for dinner only. Inexpensive to Moderate.

Marian's Bayview. 76 Front Street, Punta Gorda, 501-722-0129. Here you choose from a couple of dishes owner Marian prepares for the day, perhaps local fish or an East Indian dish. The restaurant is on the third floor of a concrete building, with views of the water. It has bare light bulbs and rough cement floors, but you come here for the food, not the atmosphere. Open daily for lunch and dinner. Inexpensive to Moderate.

Snack Shack. Main Street, Punta Gorda, at Belize Telemedia Ltd. parking lot, 501-702-0020. This is PG's version of fast food − build-your-own burritos, freshly made flavored tortillas, pancakes, fruit smoothies and such. Try the papaya shake. Open Monday-Saturday for breakfast and lunch. Inexpensive.

Where to Party in PG

There's not much action after dark in PG. You can get a cold one and a snack at **Waluca's Bar & Grill** across from the water a little north of the main part of town or at **D'Thatch** on Front Street.

"Hello, how are you today?"

QUESTIONS & ANSWERS ON BELIZE

Here are some of the questions on living, working and buying property in Belize folks have posed to me, together with my answers. Names of the people who posed the questions have been expunged to protect the innocent. Other Q&As are on my website at www.belizefirst.com.

Q. Since my wife and I have a very limited income, do you think that it's possible to retire to the Cayo District on a $2000 a month total budget? We would be looking to rent a 3-bedroom property with air conditioning, as I'm extremely sensitive to heat.

A. Living on US$2,000 a month in Cayo with air conditioning, yes, I think that's possible, though having to rent takes a big chunk of your income. Your biggest expense will be the home rental itself, including possibly having to put in some appliances and furnishings, and depending on what you want and expect it may take awhile to find a three bedroom with A/C. Electricity will probably be your next biggest expense. As a rule of thumb, electricity is about twice as expensive in Belize as the average in the U.S., and most homes are not well insulated, if at all. Except for very top end properties, it's not usual to have central air. If the house is properly built with roof overhangs and situated for cross-ventilation, many people fairly quickly acclimate to not having A/C or perhaps only using A/C in the hotter months such as April and May. And many just air-condition only certain rooms, such as bedrooms, if they have A/C at all. Although there are window A/C units, a lot of places have built-in wall units, splits -- long, narrow units that fit high up on the wall -- that are controlled by a "zapper." You've probably seen these. They seem to work better, plus there's less chance of someone breaking in by removing the window unit. They are something of a pain, and expensive, to retrofit if they weren't originally installed. The units aren't cheap and you have to punch through the wall, maybe add 220/230 electric service for larger units, etc. That could be an issue with rental property.

Q. After 24 years as an architect, I've had enough of the daily retrace and associated struggles. I was fortunate enough to work in Mauritius for 4 years and just realized again that living in the tropics and close to the sea is where I need to be. I simply love the sea and have been a keen fisherman my entire life. We looked at a few possibilities and Belize and Panama stood out. We are however leaning more towards Belize as a viable option. The plan is that my wife and son will move to Belize and settle there until I can join them in a year or two on a permanent basis. I want my son to start a business for me in the meantime. The idea is to have a kayak fishing charter and maybe a small eco-lodge...only a few rooms. I'm keen on the South and love the idea of forest and sea combination...maybe incorporate some hiking trails etc. Anyway, I suppose my question would be twofold:

1) Would it be possible for my wife and son to start a small (one-man) business...say only 3-4 kayaks to start with, and what is the legal implications...or do they have to live in the country for a year before they can start any type of business, and

2) Is there a large enough market for this type of enterprise?

The plan is that I save enough to purchase a few acres and build a couple of log cabins and then rely in income from the charter and lodge to sustain my family.

A. There are several parts to your question. Let me try to answer them as best I can. First, there is no residency or other requirement to buy land or other real estate in Belize. Anyone can buy any property in Belize, except in a few rare circumstances where land, say on an island, has been reserved for members of a certain village or community.

However, there are a couple of kinks you'll have to deal with. One is that to start a business you (or another member of your family) will have to obtain a self-employment work permit. Usually that is not a problem if you are investing money in land or a business and have plans to start a business that will employ Belizeans. But if you want to start the business fairly soon someone in your family will have to apply for the work permit, and there is a fee.

After one year of residence in Belize, you (or members of your family) can apply for permanent residency, and PR status allows you to work for pay in Belize and to operate a business without any special permit, except the usual business permits that are required of anyone. It might take as long as another year, a good deal of paperwork and visits to Belmopan to get approval for PR.

But there's another kink as well. That is that there are a few jobs in Belize that are reserved only for Belizean citizens. One of those happens to be tour guide, and that category includes fishing guides. A way around that is that non-Belizeans can own a tour company, but the company would have to employ Belizeans who are qualified and licensed as tour guides as the actual guides. That doesn't mean you can't own an eco-lodge with kayaks for rent or for the free use of guests, but again the people actually guiding tours or guiding fishing trips must be Belizeans with the proper tour guide certification. (There are courses and tests administered by the Belize Tourism Board/Ministry of Tourism.)

As to the broader question of the viability of a small lodge and tour guide business, that's much tougher to answer. Basically, it depends on things like your location (beach, lagoon and riverfront), your marketing and promotion, and your skills as a business owner and manager. In the south, the two main areas for this kind of business are the Placencia peninsula and Hopkins/Sittee River. But both have a lot of establish competition. There are other areas in the south with less competition, such as Monkey River, the Dangriga area, Punta Negra and the Punta Gorda area, along with some offshore islands, but there are various disadvantages to these such as accessibility issues and much smaller number of visitors.

I would certainly advise you to spend as much time in that part of Belize as you can before making a decision to buy property, talk to as many guides and hotel owners as you can. Good luck and best wishes on whatever you decide to do.

Q. Is Belize a place where a 36-year-old Californian (with no kids who's tired of the rat race) could move and live permanently? Are there any decent jobs...even at any of the resorts? Is it safe?

A. I guess the answer is: Possibly. Belize is a small, developing country, with high unemployment especially in rural areas, a population of only around 360,000 and the economy of a small town of 30,000 or 40,000 people in the U.S. Pay scales are much lower than in the U.S., roughly one-sixth to one-fourth of those in the U.S. for similar jobs. To work in Belize you need a work permit, and, unless self-employed or hired by a Belize company that cannot fill the position with a Belizean, you also need official residency status, which requires you to live in Belize for a full year, leaving for no more than 14 days. The Belize government encourages immigration by people who have money to invest and who can create jobs for Belizeans; it makes it more difficult for others. Having said all that, there are Americans who have come to Belize and have found work fairly easily, mainly in the hotel industry or in real estate sales. And quite a few Americans have come to Belize and started businesses with some success.

Q. My wife and I are both 55 and would like to retire but work in Belize. She is a teacher. I am in management. Are there any opportunities? Do I need to start a business, i.e. refrigeration repair or like type? Most importantly, my wife is a diabetic. How is the available care? My thoughts are to settle in the Dangriga area.

A. Under the Qualified Retired Persons program, which offers some tax and other incentives for retiring in Belize, you cannot work for pay in Belize (although you can have income from businesses outside Belize and from investments in Belize.) To work in Belize, you would need a work permit, either a regular one if working for someone else, or a self-employed work permit if you run your own business. You would also need regular residency, which in some cases requires that you live in Belize for a year before applying. While expats in Belize can and do find work, jobs other than those in tourism are fairly scarce and pay is much lower than in the U.S. More than 100,000 Belizeans have left Belize, mostly going to the U.S. to find better paying jobs. Teaching jobs are pretty hard to find in Belize, as there are many Belizeans who are qualified. Pay is low, often under US$1,000 a month for a high school teacher. Your best bet probably would be to start a business in Belize, one that employs Belizeans. The government encourages that kind of investment. Belize has a mixed public and private medical system. Care is inexpensive but certainly is not up to the standards of the U.S. or Canada. There is a regional hospital in Dangriga. I don't know the specifics about diabetes care in Dangriga, but since there are many few diabetics in Belize there is local care. However, don't expect the high-quality, evidence-based medicine that you find in the U.S. or Canada.

Q. Recently, I saw an advertisement in a magazine offering Belize passports. Is this real or a scam of some kind? I am a Canadian with a valid Canadian passport, presently living and working at Nigeria in the offshore exploration business.

A. The Belize Economic Citizenship ("buy-a-passport") program was controversial and was discontinued as of January 2002. The ad you saw is a scam.

Q. I have just finished reading your one of your books on living in Belize. My wife and I have made the decision to move to Corozal Town area. I do have a couple of questions that I am having a hard time getting a definitive answer to. The first question is how do my wife and I enter the country as tourists and bring in our personal belongings (we intend to apply for a self-employment work permit after we are in the country). The second question is how do we get government departments to return e-mails about these inquiries. Thanks for your help with our questions and congratulations on a job well done with your book.

A. Thank you for buying my book. I appreciate it! As to your questions, the letter of the law is that you will not be able to bring in your household goods and such without paying import duties and taxes on them. Of course as a visitor you can bring in items for personal use and can bring in a vehicle for temporary use (it will be entered on your passport). As to government officials not answering your questions, welcome to Belize! You will find that as a non-voter, non-Belizean you will often run into this problem, especially if you are working via e-mail or even by phone. In person, things work a little more smoothly. One of the points I make in my books is that expats are not so much at the bottom of the social ladder as beside it — government officials (there are exceptions, of course) are much more responsive to their political constituencies. In Belize, I am afraid, you are a "nobody" at least until you become an official resident or a citizen. In the meantime, I'd suggest you telephone government offices, or better yet, visit in person. It's easier to ignore e-mail than a persistent, but polite, voice on the phone or in person. If you are investing in Belize, you may get a more attentive hearing, but that depends in part on how much you are investing and how you "work" with the government officials. Those who decide to enter Belize under the Qualified Retired Persons Program generally find that the Belize Tourism Board, which administers that program, is more responsive. Of course, retired persons under this program cannot work.

Q. I have been researching Belize with the intent of relocating there. I have been interested by properties having some type of fruit or nut plantations. I would like to know if I owned one of these properties could I benefit from the sale of the fruit? Can one make enough money to live without having to get a job? What about raising geese or chickens? Could they be sold to a market? Is this line of thinking feasible or am I wasting my time?

A. Of course there are many sides to the issue, but there's no reason why one couldn't make a sort of living from small farming operations, truck gardening, fruit and such. Certainly there are Mennonites and others who do. You have to keep in mind that the Belize market is small and spread out, so export operations, for cacao, citrus or for high-value niche products such as herbs or organic produce, are often more feasible than selling to domestic markets. However, it may also be possible to generate good income from well-run truck farming, raising fowl or livestock, especially if you can serve a specialty market such as local tourist hotels and restaurants. I recommend that you spend as much time in Belize as possible, talking to other farm and ranch owners to see the special problems faced in Belize. Remember, Belize is a sub-tropical area with a lot of bugs that love to feast on tender plants and fruits. Farming in Belize is not easy!

Q. Like probably everybody who contacts you, I am thinking about relocating to Belize. I am 53. I have built up a pretty decent nest egg. Not decent enough to retire yet in the USA, but possibly in Belize if what I am thinking about is realistic. Two questions:

1) Why do you suggest keeping most of one's money out of Belize - is there really significant risk of one of the major banks defaulting, or somehow stealing depositor funds?

2) If I came to Belize, as a tourist, opened a bank account, purchased a CD at the same bank, would the interest on that CD be taxable?

The big picture is I am mulling the possibility of permanently relocating to Belize. I would purchase a very large CD, and live off of the interest. I would work towards becoming a permanent resident, not via the QRP because I have been self employed all my working life and have no pension and can't start collecting social security for another 12 years. So the CD interest would be my sole income. Would that income be taxable? Based on the general approach I have laid out, would I be able to attain the non-QRP permanent residency? I hope I have clearly described what I am thinking about.

A. On the safety of Belize banks, I think most people would say that the chance of a Belize-based bank going bankrupt, defaulting on payments to depositors or otherwise losing the money of its customers is quite low. Banks in Belize are small, typically with assets of less than a few hundred million U.S. dollars (about the size of a small hometown bank or savings bank in the U.S.), but they generally are conservative and well capitalized. However, you should know that there is no deposit insurance in Belize, so all your money on deposit is 100% at risk, however slight the risk may be. In addition, there is also the risk of a devaluation of the Belize dollar -- that risk, again while slight is probably higher than the risk of bank default or bankruptcy. Belize has a high external debt relative to GDP, and government finances are not in good shape. If the Belize dollar were devalued, say by 25%, then the value of your nest egg would also be reduced by 25% when measured in a hard currency such as the U.S. dollar or euro.

I guess it comes down to what level of risk you are willing to accept on your life savings in return for what will probably be a significantly higher interest rate on savings and CDs in Belize as compared with the U.S. Personally, I would be reluctant to keep a large proportion of my nest egg in a local Belize bank, or a small bank in any country that does not offer some kind of deposit protection.

As to taxes on interest and dividends, this is a fairly complicated question and I do not have the expertise to provide tax or investment advice. You should consult a competent tax attorney, CPS or investment adviser. However, in general, there are several different situations that may apply:

One is if you are officially a resident of another country, not Belize. In that case, you can open an "offshore" account in Belize, whether through the establishment of an International Business Company or simply by opening a savings or time deposit account with the international division of a Belize bank. This account could be in U.S. dollars, euros or many other currencies. In this case, you would not pay Belize income tax on your savings. However, you may be and probably are subject to tax on the interest in the U.S. assuming you are a U.S. citizen.

As a Belize permanent resident or Belize citizen, you are subject to Belize income taxes on all income derived in Belize, including interest income. However, there is an exclusion on the first BZ$20,000 in income -- that is not taxable. Income derived outside Belize is not taxable in Belize.

In general, without knowing anything about your personal situation, I would say you would have a good chance of getting permanent residency in Belize, assuming you pass the health exam, background check, etc. As you may know, this requires living in Belize for one year, at which time you can apply for residency. Approval can take up to a year, sometimes even longer. Among several other things, you have to demonstrate that you have adequate financial resources, and your savings in the U.S. or Belize would likely satisfy that requirement. Good luck.

Q. I have a few questions about some "logistics" of living in Belize: What is veterinary availability like in Belize? (Based on government website, it appears it is possible to bring small domestic pets.) I gather there are not a lot of bookstores and/or newsstands in Belize. How's the library? I hesitate to ask this for fear of sounding snooty, but might as well: What does Belize offer in the way of the arts? How easy/difficult is it to get things to Belize.... like mail order items, etc. on an occasional basis (I'm not talking about huge stuff that requires a container.)

A. There are vets in Belize City, Corozal Town, San Pedro, Cayo and elsewhere. Expats with dogs or cats don't seem to have trouble getting care for their animals, although most of the 20 or so vets in Belize concentrate their practices on large farm animals. Some pets don't adapt well to the hot, humid Belize climate, however, and may suffer from diseases they pick up from stray animals. But it seems to me that most expats in Belize do have a dog, and generally they report no big problems. Yes, it's simple to bring pets into Belize. *See detailed information on bringing in your pets elsewhere in this book, in the section Mechanics of Moving to Belize.* Right, there are not a lot of bookstores in Belize. There are small bookshops in Belize City, San Pedro and San Ignacio, but the inventory is limited at best. There are public libraries in all towns. Don't expect the New York Public Library but at least you can find some reading matter. If fine arts — opera, dance, symphony, theater, galleries — are a priority, Belize is not for you. There are only two movie theaters in the entire country, on North Ambergris and the Ramada

Princess Hotel & Casino in Belize City. There was a tiny one in downtown San Ignacio. Some talented artists are working in Belize, and several galleries in Belize City and San Pedro have interesting work. There are a couple of dance troupes. Belize is a lot like a small town in the U.S. There aren't a lot of public venues for the arts, but artists, writers and musicians find each other and there are small groups that support the arts and hold meetings and such. As to ordering items from abroad, yes you can do that. There are companies such as MyUS.com that provide you with a U.S. mailing address. You can order from companies such as Amazon or Best Buy and ship to your MyUS.com mailing address. MyUS.com will consolidate your purchases and forward on to Belize via FedEx, DHL Express or UPS. But it's quite expensive. You will have to pay import duty on a lot of items, which can be substantial, and shipping charges (especially for heavy items like books) are high.

Q. We are moving to Belize and want to buy a car when we get there. I'm 55 years old and qualify as a retired person. Are there used cars for sale in Belize? What are the price ranges for say a ten-year-old car or truck? Could one buy a Volkswagen in Mexico, say in Chetumal or Cancún, and drive it into Belize? Or would it be better to buy it in Miami and ship it to Belize?

A: Yes, there are used cars for sale in Belize, mostly at dealerships in Belmopan and Belize City, though some are by private owners. It's possible you could find a good deal, but in general the relatively small market for used cars and lack of competition mean that prices are usually higher, 10 to 20% higher, than in the highly competitive U.S. market, and the selection is much smaller. Also, many used cars in Belize have had a hard life, due to the bad roads. In some cases flooded or wrecked cars are brought into Belize and resold there without disclosure of their past history. If possible, get the Vehicle Identification Number (VIN) and check its history online. There are no laws to protect consumers if you get a lemon. Under the Qualified Retired Persons Incentive Act, any car you bring into Belize (including one you buy from Mexico) is supposed to be three years old or less. If it is older, in theory (and probably in practice) you will have to pay duty on it. Duty varies by number of cylinders, type of vehicle and the value of the car, but with duty and tax figure 65 to 80% of book value. Pick-up trucks (not SUVs) are taxed at a lower rate, a little over 20% including GST. Overall, if you are going to be in Belize long-term under the QRP I think you would be better off bringing in an almost new vehicle from the U.S., even with the cost of shipping from Miami or wherever, you'll likely come out ahead. There's a glut of quality used cars now in the U.S., prices are low and selection is huge. As a Qualified Retired Person, your vehicle would be entered duty-free.

Q. I am a builder in Arizona with many years in commercial and residential development and interested in relocating to Belize. What is the demand for a person with my expertise in Belize?

A. There is certainly demand for qualified builders in Belize. That said, whether you can successfully enter the market or not is another matter. As in many places, well-established local firms dominate the market. Mennonite builders in particular are in demand. Further, you face competition from many individual builders and contractors, most of whom work for rates that are much lower than you are probably accustomed. You also face a number of obstacles in terms of getting residency and work permits. Working, and specifically building, in Belize is quite different from the U.S. The materials are different, the way people do things are different, there are shortages of many materials and of skilled or semi-skilled workers in some cases. Theft and shrinkage is a problem, and many expat business people have problems dealing with local politicians and ways of doing things. Keep hammering away!

Q. Are there ophthalmologists (medical eye doctors) or optometrists (nonmedical practitioners) in Belize? How many of each and where are they located? How many people are thought to be retired in Belize?

A: There are ophthalmologists and optometrists in Belize, mostly located in Belize City but some have offices elsewhere including San Pedro. I do not know the exact number, but there are at least five ophthalmologists in practice in Belize City alone, and several opticians and optometrists. The ophthalmologists offer the usual range of services including cataract surgery, intraocular lens implant, radial keratomy, etc. There also are a number of eye surgeons and other eye specialists across the border in Chetumal and Mérida, Mexico.

I am not sure if you are asking about how many expats are retired or otherwise living in Belize, but if so the answer is, no one knows for certain. The latest Belize Census showed that about 47 million foreign-born people live in Belize, around 15% of the population reported in 2010, but that includes large numbers of immigrants from other Central American countries, including Guatemala, El Salvador and Honduras, along with immigrants from China and elsewhere in Asia.

My estimate is that the number of expats in Belize from the U.S., Canada and Europe, number fewer than 5,000, but many people from these areas have bought property in Belize but do not live in Belize year-round, or who live in rental property for a few months in the winter, so their number is not usually included in official reports.

Q. I saw an ad for a house in Corozal for $25K looks too good to be true. Just wondering if you knew of it or another cheap place. I have a limited trust fund income. Do you know of any communities that I could live at on say $1000/month? I would not want to buy at first. Have had some big personal problems here (like anybody cares about a divorced guy) and need someplace with a supportive environment.

A. You can live in Corozal Town or Cayo or Toledo for US$1000 a month, or less, but that would be a basic kind of lifestyle. Rental houses start at under US$250 a month for something Belizean and basic but you'd probably pay more in the range of US$350 and can go up a long way from there. Belizeans are among the friendliest folks you'll ever meet. But don't move to Belize to escape your problems. They have a pesky tendency to follow you.

Q. I am a citizen of Houston, Texas, and I'm thinking of possibly moving to Belize in the future because I'm afraid that the laws on identification are going to start to chafe me pretty soon because of the so-called "war on terrorism" here. I'm as hurt by the attack on us as much as anybody but there's a limit to what I'm going to be able to take in the name of increased national security. My concerns about Belize may seem unreasonable, but I believe you'll see that they are also typically Texan. First on my mind are the regulations on firearms. Here in Texas we're free to own guns and we don't even have to put up with those stupid 3-day waiting periods for handguns as I hear they do in Florida. We're also allowed to carry concealed handguns provided we take tests and get a license from the state of Texas. Businesses can prohibit them on their premises by posting a sign. So I'm curious about whether it's legal to own a gun in Belize, whether they have registration or licenses or whether you can just own one. And if the situation is so bad that people aren't allowed to protect themselves, even in rural areas what the penalty might be for illegally possessing firearms. Contrariwise, what might be the easiest way to bring my gun or guns with me to

Belize?

A. Gun laws in Belize are much more restrictive than in Texas, especially since now any Texan who has a legal pistol can carry it in a holster almost anywhere, just like in the old Wild West days. Tourists and nonresidents in Belize may not import or possess guns at all. Citizens and official residents with a need for them – farmers in rural areas, for example — may own guns legally if they obtain a license from the government and pay a fee. However, gun permits are getting more difficult to obtain. Even the possession of a single 22 rifle or shotgun shell without a license can land you jail. In Belize, it is also illegal to own bulletproof vests.

Q. Are there any chiropractors in Belize? In your opinion is there a need for more?

A. Yes, there are chiropractors in Belize City, San Pedro and Placencia and one or two elsewhere. Local bush doctors with chiropractic skills are called "bonesetters" in Belize. Belize is a country with around 360,000 people and with per-capita GDP only about one-tenth that of the U.S. Thus, total demand for chiropractic services in all of Belize is probably no more than in an American town of 40,000 people.

Q. If I have $5,000 in my pocket, a college degree, scuba diving certification, how hard would it be for me to come to Belize and get a job?

A. Fairly difficult. The unemployment rate in Belize is higher than that in the U.S. Pay scales vary, but in general are one-fourth that in the U.S. To work in Belize you have to have a work permit, which is not easy to get and costs US$1,500 a year for most positions. Non-Belizeans are not allowed to take certain jobs, such as tour guides (generally, scuba or snorkel guides are considered tour guides.) Since 2002, it has been illegal for an employer to hire or employ a worker without a Belize Social Security card. It's not impossible to find work in Belize, and quite a number of expats have done it successfully, but it won't be easy, and you probably won't make much money.

Q. I am writing to inquire about a business venture I am considering in San Pedro. I spent some time in San Pedro recently and saw an opportunity to start a business that would not compete with the locals, at least it appeared so to me, and would like to get your input. I will be taking a huge risk to leave my current job and start new at 41, but I feel it could be the opportunity of a lifetime, as well as assist some Belizeans in fulfilling their dreams as well. I am considering opening a tattoo shop in San Pedro and know that I could employ Belizeans to work there as well. What do you think of this idea? Am I way off track? I have investigated the business side and am aware of all the licensing, etc., that I will need. I don't want to overload you with information on my research. So, can you share your thoughts on this idea with me? I would really appreciate it.

A: You would just as well ask the Man in the Moon his opinion on a tattoo parlor in San Pedro, as I know absolutely nothing about the tattoo business and in general don't understand the appeal of tattoos. I have no idea whether it would work in San Pedro. I would only be able to make two comments: One, over the years I have noticed that expats opening a business in Belize have a tougher time than they think they will. Almost everything takes longer and is more expensive and more difficult to execute than they had anticipated. My advice is always to take the revenue figures in your pro forma and cut them by half and then double your expense figures, and you may have a good idea of what your business in Belize will actually do. Two, if you are going to open a business in Belize, I think San Pedro is the place to do it, at least for the next five years or ten years. Tourism is fairly healthy in San Pedro. It is more or less year-round rather than being highly seasonal as in some other areas, and there is enough money running through the economy that a well-run business can get a piece of it.

Q. Does Belize use the metric system?

A. As with the English language, refugees from the U.S. will not have to learn a new measurement system in Belize. The metric system, regardless of its merits, hasn't made much of an inroad in Belize. Distance is measured in miles, feet, yards and inches. (However, some rental cars may have odometers in kilometers.) Road signs say 55 mph. Liquids are measured in quarts and ounces, not liters. You buy gasoline by the U.S. gallon. And speaking of inroads, yes, you drive on the right in Belize, despite its British heritage. Electrical current and outlets in Belize are the same as in the U.S. and Canada.

Q. What time is it in Belize?

A. Belize Time. No, seriously, local time is the same as U.S. Central Standard Time. Belize does not observe Daylight Savings Time.

Q. What job opportunities are there in Belize in the hospitality industry?

A. Most hotels in Belize are small and owner-operated. The largest property in the country has only about 160 rooms, and most have fewer than 20, so opportunities for management level work are somewhat limited. In the restaurant and bar field, it is almost impossible for a non-Belizean to get a work permit, unless you are investing in business and operating it. Having said that, there are always opportunities for hardworking people who have a variety of skills and experience in operating in developing countries. If you are interested in working in Belize, I'd suggest you e-mail your resume to the larger properties and also come to Belize and try to meet as many resort and hotel owners as you can.

Q. My wife and I are just over 50 years old, and we are looking to retire in Belize. We are wondering what kind of job opportunities there are in Belize. I am a pilot and my wife is in computer technology. Can Belize use our skills? Who would we contact?

A. While your skills are in some demand in Belize, whether you can find work there or not depends on a variety of factors — your willingness to work for a fraction of U.S. salaries, whether you can get a work permit and whether you are willing to spend some time in the country to explore opportunities, among others. It is highly unlikely that you can find work without being in the country. There are two small airlines in Belize — Maya Island Air and Tropic Air, plus several charter operators. Computer work is limited, but a few larger companies such as Belize Telecommunications Ltd. do have a need for those with computer skills. Since you are over 45, you likely qualify for the incentives available under the Qualified Retired Persons Incentive Act. However, residents under that program cannot work for pay in Belize; you would need to get regular residency.

Q. I was recently in Belize and looked at a piece of property for sale in a "development" about 8 miles east of San Ignacio. It was an absolutely beautiful lot of around 5 acres on top of a mountain with an incredible 200-degree view of the surrounding countryside. The owner will provide electricity but there is no water. It's one of the most beautiful properties and view I have ever seen. There are 8 lots for sale, all between 3 and 5 acres, costing between US$40,000 to $70,000. The lot I'm considering is US$60,000. The owner will finance at 10% down for 10 years at 10%. My question is do you think that this price range is considered extravagant in Belize for *this type of property? Or is that about right for this area?*

A. I'm not an expert on real estate. I would think, though, that the prices being asked for the property you are considering are more than the average in Cayo, even for prime property. US$2,000 to $4,000 an acre is considered fairly pricey for accessible land in small tracts in Cayo, and the tracts you are talking about are in the range of US$10,000 an acre. It is unlikely you could sell the land for anything like the price you are paying. Or you might sell it but it could take 30 years. It's one thing to buy land in Belize. It's another thing to sell it. However, all real estate is unique, and if you love the property and don't expect it to sell it at a profit anytime soon, then who is to tell you that you shouldn't buy it?

Q. I have read much of your writings about Belize, over the years. My wife and I purchased property on Ambergris caye two years ago. Last year we paid our property taxes while we were in San Pedro for vacation. This year we will not be down in the country (we live in Florida). My question to you is can I send my tax payment to San Pedro (we got our bill last week) and pay with a personal check from my Bank of America account? Thank you for your help.

A. Property taxes in Belize are normally due on April 1. If not paid by the end of April there is a 1% per month late charge. You can pay property taxes at one of about eight Department of Lands and Surveys offices. Most of the tax records in Belize are now on computer. You can pay by check or wire transfer. Your Bank of America check should be okay and should be sent to San Pedro Town Council, P.O. Box 54, Barrier Reef Drive, San Pedro Town, Ambergris Caye, Belize, Central America. If you decide to make a wire transfer you could check with the Town Council on details of how to do it. The number is 501-226-2198 and email sptb@btl.net.

Q. While traveling around the country, should we rent a car, take a bus, fly or hire a taxi?

A. Each has advantages and disadvantages. With a rental car, you go when and where you want, including remote areas that don't have air or bus service or to sites that would otherwise require an expensive guided tour. However, auto rental costs are high, and gas is near US$5 a gallon. Buses provide a true local experience and fares are dirt cheap, but buses mainly run on the major roads and stop frequently to pick up and drop off passengers. Buses take up to twice as long as a private car. Flying is the fastest way to get around the country; service is frequent on most routes, and the views from low altitudes are often dramatic. The downside? Fares—especially if you're traveling with a family—can add up, and not all destinations have service. In some cases, transfers by taxi can be an option, although taxis generally are quite expensive. For most long-distance trips, there are no set fares, so the rate is a matter of negotiation and can vary considerably, depending on your bargaining skills. Drivers may also ask a little more if there are three or four going together, rather than just one or two. Expect to pay around US$1.50 a mile for longer trips in Belize.

Magnificent ruins of Tikal are only 1½ hours from Cayo

APPENDIX A: RECOMMENDED READING

Many of these books are available from Amazon.com, either as new books or through their used-book sellers system. Many are also available as ebooks for Kindle (Amazon), Nook (Barnes & Noble), iPad (Apple) or other formats. Also, try ABE (www.abebooks.com) for out-of-print books. In the case of books published by Cubola, a Belize publishing company, visit www.cubola.com. Note that the publication dates given are usually those for the original edition, except in the case of travel guidebooks, where the most recent edition publication date is provided.

Archaeology

Awe, Jaime. *Maya Cities, Sacred Caves*, Cubola Productions, 2005, 104 pp. A guide to 10 noted Maya sites in Belize, by the director of Belize's Institute of Archaeology.

Coe, Michael D. *The Maya*, Thames and Hudson, 7th ed., 2005, 224 pp. Originally published in 1993, this is the best general introduction to the subject.

Coe, William R. *Tikal, A Handbook of the Ancient Maya Ruins,* University Museum at the University of Pennsylvania, 1967. Useful when touring Tikal.

Ferguson, William M. and Adams, R.E.W. Mesoamerica's Ancient Cities: Aerial Views of Pre-Columbian Ruins in Mexico, Guatemala, Belize and Honduras, University Press of Colorado, rev. ed., 2000, 272 pp.

Foster, Byron, Ed. *Warlords and Maize Men, A Guide to the Maya Sites of Belize,* Cubola Productions, Belize, 1992, 82 pp. The first popular guide focused entirely on Maya sites in Belize, by the late Dr. Foster (he was murdered at his farm in western Belize.) Maps, color photos.

Garber, James F., ed. The Ancient Maya of the Belize Valley: Half a Century of Archeological Research, University of Florida Press, 2003, 448 pp.

Guderjan, Thomas H. *Ancient Maya Traders of Ambergris Caye,* Cubola Productions, 1993, 40 pp.

-- The Nature of an Ancient Maya City: Resources, Interaction, and Power at Blue Creek, Belize, University of Alabama Press, 2007, 244 pp.

Hammond, Norman, Ed. *Cuello: An Early Maya Community in Belize,* Cambridge University Press, 1991 (hardcover), 2009 (paper). 284 pp.

Harrison, Peter D. Pulltrouser Swamp: Ancient Maya Habitat, Agriculture and Settlement, University of Utah Press, 2000, 294 pp.

Henderson, John S. *The World of the Ancient Maya,* Cornell University Press, 1981, 271 pp.

Kelly, Joyce. *An Archaeological Guide to Northern Central America: Belize, Guatemala, Honduras, and El Salvador,* University of Oklahoma Press, rev. ed. 1996, 352 pp. Includes coverage of many smaller sites. Photographs by Jerry Kelly.

McMillon, Bill. *The Archeology Handbook: A Field Manual and Resource Guide,* Wiley, 1991, 259 pp. Not specific to Belize, but provides the amateur archeologist or volunteer with information on excavation techniques, tools, methods, etc.

Montgomery, John. Tikal: An Illustrated History of the Ancient Maya Capital, Hippocrene Books, 2001, 275 pp.

Sharer, Robert and Traxler, Loa. *The Ancient Maya,* Stanford University Press, 6th ed. 2005, 931 pp. A classic in the field, this is the most comprehensive work on the Maya.

Thompson, J. Eric S. The Maya of Belize: Historical Chapters Since

Columbus, Cubola Productions.

Boating

Calder, Nigel. *The Cruising Guide to the Northwest Caribbean*, McGraw-Hill, 2nd ed., 1991, 272 pp. Navigational and anchorage information on the Caribbean Coast of Mexico, Belize, Guatemala and Honduras. Unfortunately this has not been recently updated.

Copeland, Liza. *Comfortable Cruising Around North and Central America*, Romany Enterprises, 2001, 312 pp. Several chapters on cruising the Caribbean Coast of Central America, including Belize.

Rauscher, Freya. *Cruising Guide to Belize and Mexico's Caribbean Coast*, Windmill Hill Books, 3rd ed., 2007, 312 pp. with 117 charts and 185 photos. Comprehensive cruising guide, the best available to this region, from Isla Mujeres in Mexico to the Rio Dulce in Guatemala. Includes large charts of Belize's coast and Mexico's Caribbean Coast.

NOAA-28004 *Nautical Chart of Caribbean Sea, Northwest Part*, 1:1300,000 scale, undated. Includes Belize.

Waterproof Chart # 4, Caribbean and Gulf of Mexico.

Cookbooks

Aponte-Jolly, Minvera (ed.), *Aaah ... Belizean Rum Recipes*, Cubola Productions, 2003, 152 pp. If you like more than a rum and tonic or a rum and Coke.

Arvigo, Rosita, *Food of the Gods, Vegetarian Cooking in Belize*, Cubola Productions, 2010, 158 pp. Guide to Belizean vegetarian cooking by the noted natural healer who moved to Cayo.

Burns, E. L. What's Cooking in the Belizean Kitchen, Angelus Press, 74 pp.

de Langan, Tracey Brown. *Mmmm ... a Taste of Belizean Cooking*, Cubola Productions, 2003, 142 pp. Chefs from leading Belizean restaurants contributed to this cookbook.

Nord, Alice, Martinez, Myrna and Shrine, Kaaren. *Cooking Belize*, self-published, c. 1995, 126 pp.

Belize Hospital Auxiliary Cookbook, Angelus Press, 126 pp.

Belizeous Cuisine, Delicious Belizean Recipes, by Los Angeles Belizean Educational Network (LABEN), 1997, 102 pp.

To Catch a Cook, by South Ambergris Caye Neighborhood Watch, self published, 2009

Silly Bug & Bittle Recipes, Crooked Tree Village Creative Women's Group, self-published, 100 pp.

U Toucan Cook Belize Cookbook, self-published, 126 pp.

Fiction, Drama and Poetry

Auxillou, Ray. *Blue Hole,* self-published, date unknown, 479 pp. A collection of tales about mercenaries, drug runners and adventure. Other books in the same vein by Auxillou include *Belize Secret Service, Belize Connection* and *The Belize Vortex.*

Crone, Andrew. *Chameleon War,* Booksurge Publishing, 2008, 244 pp. You'll want to wash your hands after you read this garbage.

Coxe, George Harmon. *With Intent to Kill,* Knopf, 1964, 180 pp. Action/adventure.

Edgell, Zee. *Beka Lamb,* Heinemann, 1982, 192 pp. Classic novel about ordinary life in British Honduras.

— *In Times Like These,* Heinemann, 320 pp. English-educated Belizean returns home.

— *The Festival of San Joaquin,* Heinemann, 1997, 155 pp. Explores domestic violence in Belize.

Ellis, Zoila. *On Heroes, Lizards and Passion, Seven Belizean Short Stories,* Cubola Productions, 1994, 130 pp. "White Christmas an' Pink Jungle" is one of seven deliciously Belizean stories, from a distinguished Belizean/Garifuna writer.

Esquivel, Cathy. *Under the Shade,* Angelus Press, 192 pp. Tales of the drug trade.

Godfrey, Glenn D. *The Sinners' Bossanova,* Cubola Books, 1987, 269 pp. Action/adventure.

Hagerthy, Tim, and Parham, Mary Gomoz, Eds. *If Di Pin Neva Bin, Folktales and Legends of Belize,* Cubola Productions, 128 pp.

Hernandez, Felicia. *Those Ridiculous Years,* 64 pp. Short stories about Garifuna life.

Heusner, Karla. *Food for Thought, Chronicles of Belize,* Cubola Productions, 2004, 207 pp. Collection of weekly newspaper columns by a Belizean journalist who now lives in the U.S.

Koerner, Nancy R. *Belize Survivor: Darker Side of Paradise,* NK Marketing, 2007, 300 pp. A novel, based on a true story, of a young woman who comes to Belize, lives in the bush and gets more than she bargained for.

Lindo, Louis. *Tales of the Belizean Woods*, Cubola Productions, 82 pp. Short stories set in backabush Belize.

McKay, Claudia. *Twist of Lime, A Lynn Evans Mystery*, New Victoria Publishers, 1997, 188 pp. Mystery featuring lesbian newspaper reporter on Maya dig in Belize.

Miller, Carlos Ledson. *Belize, A Novel*, Xlibris Corp., 1999, 402 pp. Fast-paced saga of father and sons over four decades, beginning with Hurricane Hattie in 1961.

Miller, Harold R. *The Belize File*, Taylor-Dth Publishing, 2008, 372 pp. An ex-DEA agent turned private eye is hired to find a friend's daughter, missing on her honeymoon in Belize.

Mueller, William Behr. *Operation Belize*, CreateSpace, 2008, 358 pp. The U.S. Secretary of State is kidnapped in Belize, and American Special Forces attempt a rescue.

Patrick, William. *The Five Lost Days*, Pearhouse Press, 2008, 336 pp. A documentary filmmaker travels to the Maya Mountains of Belize to get footage of a Maya healer.

Phillips, Michael, Ed. *Of Words, an Anthology of Belizean Poetry*, Cubola Productions, 1997, 104 pp. A collection of poems by more than three dozen Belizean poets.

-- *Ping Wing Juk Me, Six Belizean Plays*, Cubola Productions, 2004, 120 pp. A collection of plays by George Gabb, Carol Fonseca Galvez, Evan X. Hyde, Glady Stuart, Shirley Warde and Colville Young.

-- *Snapshots of Belize, an Anthology of Belizean Short Fiction*, Cubola Productions, 2004, 122 pp. A collection of short stories by seven Belizean writers.

Rimmer, Stephen. The Way to Go: Four Men & Three Women Sailing from Florida to Cozumel & Belize – A Story of Sex, Lust & Drug Trafficking, with a New Kind of Morality about Sinning of All Kinds!, IUniverse, 2000, 428 pp. This novel is an example of the downside of the new print-on-demand technology.

Ruiz Puga, David Nicolas. *Old Benque*, Cubola Productions, 160 pp. Short stories in Spanish.

Stray, P.J. *The Danger on Lighthouse Reef*, Silver Burdett Press, 1997, 144 pp. Children's mystery story.

Theroux, Paul. *The Mosquito Coast*, Houghton-Mifflin, 1982. Obsessed

American drags his family to Central America. Actually set in Honduras, not Belize, but the movie of the same name was filmed in Belize.

Vasquez, Ian. *In the Heat,* St. Martin's Minotaur, 2008, 245 pp. Caribbean Noir mystery set in Belize City and Cayo, by a talented new Belizean writer who now lives in Florida. *In the Heat* in 2009 won the Shamus Award for best first novel from the Private Eye Writers of America.

-- *Lonesome Point,* Minotaur Books, St. Martin's Press, 2009, 263 pp. Vasquez's second novel is set in Florida, with flashbacks to Belize.

Westlake, Donald. *High Adventure,* Mysterious Press, 1985. Dope, dummies and deliverance in Belize, by popular adventure writer.

Wilentz, Gay. *Memories, Dreams and Nightmares, Vol. 1, a Short Story Anthology by Belizean Women Writers,* Cubola Productions, 2004, 164 pp. Collection of stories by 13 Belizean female writers.

-- Memories, Dreams and Nightmares, Vol. 2, a Short Story Anthology by Belizean Women Writers, Cubola Productions, 2005, 124 pp. The second volume.

Young, Colville. *Pataki Full,* Cubola Productions, 120 pp. Collection of short stories by noted Belizean writer and scholar.

ZooDoc. *War Star Rising: Legend of Toucan Moon,* Star Publish, 2008, 216 pp. Young adult novel about a Maya princess at Xunantunich who speaks out against human sacrifice.

Guidebooks/Travel Guides

Brown, Joshua Samuel, *Lonely Planet Belize,* 5th ed., Lonely Planet Guides, 2013, 320 pp. An improvement over previous LP Belize guides.

Eltringham, Peter. *Belize, The Rough Guide,* Rough Guides, 2014, 400 pp. Thoroughly researched guide by knowledgeable writer who spent many years in Belize and Guatemala. Peter Eltringham passed away in 2008. Updated by various Rough Guide authors.

Girma, Lebawit Lily, *Moon Belize,* Moon Handbooks, 2015, 424 pp. Good, up-to-date guide that builds on the work of Joshua Berman, who formerly did the *Moon Belize* guides.

Glassman, Paul. *Belize Guide,* Open Road Publishing, 12th ed. 2006, 295 pp. Glassman was a pioneering guidebook author to destinations in Central America, including Costa Rica, Nicaragua and Belize. A Kindle edition was released in 2012.

Greenspan, Eliot. *Frommer's Belize,* Wiley Publishing, 2011, 352 pp.

Useful guide though now dated.

Harvard Student Agencies, *Let's Go Guatemala & Belize: The Student Travel Guide*, Let's Go, 2009, 304 pp. Budget-oriented guide researched by intrepid Harvard students. Now out-of-date, however.

Insight Guides Belize, Insight Guides, 5th. ed., 2015, 341 pp. Unmatched photos and good general background on the country; weak on hotels and restaurants.

Jones-Burgess, Kate, *Explorer's Guide Belize*, Explorer's Great Destinations, Countryman Press, 2010, 368 pp. One of our very favorite guides ever written to Belize – too bad it hasn't been updated and reprinted.

King, Emory. *Driver's Guide to Beautiful Belize*, Tropical Books, 2007, 40 pp. Mile-by-mile guide to most roads in Belize. Not updated since Emory King's death and currently out of print.

Lougheed, Vivien. *Adventure Guide to Belize*, Hunter Publishing, 6th edition, 2006, 555 pp. Tons of good information by the author of *Central America by Chickenbus*.

-- *Belize Pocket Adventures*, Pocket Adventures, 2009, 316 pp. Shorter version of Lougheed's early book for Hunter Publishing. Also available in a Kindle edition.

Mahler, Richard. *Adventures in Nature Belize*, Avalon, 1999, 362 pp. A guidebook that focuses on nature travel in Belize. This was a good idea that was canned by Avalon. Someone should do the concept again, as this guide is now badly out-of-date.

Middleton, Ned. *Diving Belize*, Aqua Quest Diving, 1998, 128 pp. Better than Lonely Planet's dive guide though an update is needed.

Morris, Charlie. *Open Road's the Best of Belize*, Open Road, 2nd. ed. 2009, 256 pp. Guidebook series claims to cut to the chase and give only what's best at the destinations.

Rock, Tim. *Lonely Planet Diving & Snorkeling Belize*, 4th. edition, Lonely Planet, 2007, 144 pp. Improved from earlier editions, but overlooks some dive and snorkel sites.

Sluder, Lan. *Fodor's Belize*, Fodor's Travel/Random House, 2014, 355 pp. Lan Sluder has been doing the Fodor's guides to Belize, with coverage of parts of Guatemala, for nearly 20 years. Sluder did the first and all subsequent *Fodor's Belize* guidebooks and before that did the Belize portion of *Fodor's Belize and Guatemala*.

—*All the Best in Belize: Belize Locations, Maya Sites, Attractions, Hotel,*

Restaurants, Roads and More Rates A+ to F, Equator, 2016, 300 pp. The author uses his quarter century of experience in Belize to review and rate the best and worst in Belize from A+ to F (extraordinary to failing).

— *Belize Islands Guide,* Equator, 2010, also available as an ebook (2016) and on Kindle, 204 pp. Guide to Ambergris Caye, Caye Caulker and all the islands of Belize.

— *San Pedro Cool, Guide to Ambergris Caye, Belize,* Equator, 2002, updated as an ebook in 2009, 201 pp. Comprehensive guide to Ambergris Caye, with short section on Caye Caulker and other islands.

— *Belize Book of Lists 2000,* Equator, 1999, 112 pp. Lists the 5 to 10 best in each category — jungle lodges, seaside resort hotels, beaches, etc.

— *Belize First Guide to Mainland Belize,* Equator, 2000, 288 pp. Focuses on the mainland of Belize.

— *Best Belize Hotels and Restaurants,* Equator, 2016, 156 pp. This ebook reviews and rates the best hotels and restaurants in Belize.

History and Culture

Balboni, Barbara. *Taking Stock: Belize at 25 Years of Independence,* Cubola Productions, 2007, 343 pp. Noted Belizeans take a look at what Belize has achieved in its first 25 years of independence.

Barry, Tom with Vernon, Dylan. *Inside Belize,* Resource Center Press, 2nd. ed., 1995, 181 pp. Useful but now somewhat dated overview of history, politics, media, education, economy and the environment.

Bolland, O. Nigel, *Colonialism and Resistance in Belize, Essays in Historical Sociology,* Cubola Productions, 2003, 228 pp. Examines colonialism in the country over three centuries.

Bulmer-Thomas, Barbara, and Bulmer-Thomas, Victor, *The Economic History of Belize,* Cubola Productions, 2012, 214 pp. An economic history of Belize from the 17th century to after independence.

Burdon, Sir John Alder (ed.). *Archives of British Honduras* (3 vols.), Sifton Praed, 1931-35. This controversial history of British Honduras by Sir John Burdon, a governor of the colony, helped create and perpetuate myths about British colonialism and "benign" slavery in Belize that continued to influence historians for decades.

Burnworth, Joe. *No Safe Harbor: The Tragedy of the Dive Ship Wave Dancer,* Emmis Books, 2005, 256 pp. The story of the 21 people who died on the Wave Dancer live-aboard in Hurricane Iris in October 2001.

Cayetano, E. Roy. *The People's Garifuna Dictionary,* Angelus Press, 82 pp. Work in progress —a dictionary of the Garifuna language.

Cayetano, Sebastian. Garifuna History, Language & Culture of Belize, Central America & the Caribbean, Angelus Press, 170 pp.

Crosbie, Paul, editor-in-chief; Herrera, Yvette; Manzanares, Myrna; Woods, Silvana; Crosbie, Cynthia; and Decker, Ken, eds. *Kriol-Inglish Dikshineri English-Kriol Dictionary,* Belize Kriol Project, 2007, 465 pp. First comprehensive dictionary to the Belize Kriol language.

Dobson, Narda. *A History of Belize,* Longman Caribbean, 1973, 362 pp. History from Early Maya period to 1970.

Foster, Byron. *The Baymen's Legacy,* Cubola Productions, 2nd. ed., 1992, 83 pp. A history of Belize City.

— *Heart Drum,* Cubola Productions, 60 pp. A look at dagu and other aspects of Garifuna life.

Henderson, Peta. *Rising Up: Life Stories of Belizean Women,* Sister Vision Press, 1998, 302 pp.

Kane, William and Stanton, John. A Jesuit in Belize: The Life and Adventures of Father Buck Stanton in Nineteenth Century Central America, CreateSpace, 2008, 422 pp.

King, Emory. *Diary of St. George's Caye,* Tropical Books, 32 pp.

— *The Great Story of Belize,* Volume 1, Tropical Books, 1999, 53 pp. The first in what was to be a four-volume set, this volume covers the history of Belize from 1511 when the first Europeans arrive until 1798, when the Baymen won the battle of St. George's Caye.

— *The Great Story of Belize,* Volume 2, Tropical Books, 1999, 87 pp. Volume 2 tells the history of Belize from 1800 to 1850, the period which shaped Belize's history for generations to come.

— 1798 *The Road to Glory,* Tropical Books, 1991, 348 pp. Fictionalized and somewhat glorified account of the Battle of St. George Caye.

Koop, Gerhard S. *Pioneer Years In Belize,* Angelus Press, 144 pp. History of the Mennonites in Mexico and Belize.

Leslie, Robert, Ed. *A History of Belize: Nation in the Making,* Cubola Productions, rev. ed., 1995, 125 pp. First published in 1983, this history of Belize is written for Belize schoolchildren.

McClaurin, Irma. *Women of Belize: Gender and Change in Central America,* Rutgers University Press, 1996, 232 pp. Three women describe their experiences in Belize.

Merrill, Tim. *Guyana and Belize Country Studies*, Federal Research Division, Library of Congress, 2nd. ed.,1993, 408 pp. One in the Area Handbook series sponsored by the U.S. Army; nevertheless, the historical, cultural and economic information is first rate.

Peedle, Ian. *Belize, A Guide to the People, Politics and Culture*, Interlink Books, 1999, 100 pp. Tries to cover everything in a small volume, and fails.

Setzekorn, William David. *Belize, Formerly British Honduras*, Ohio University Press, 1981, 300 pp. A profile of Belize's folklore, history, culture, economics and geography.

Shoman, Assad. *Thirteen Chapters of a History of Belize*, Angelus Press, 1994, 4th. printing 2000, 297 pp. Somewhat left-wing interpretation of Belize history, by a prominent Belizean intellectual and politician.

Simmons, Donald C. Jr. *Confederate Settlements in British Honduras*, McFarland & Co., 2001, 176 pp. Discusses ex-Confederates who settled in Belize after the U.S. Civil War.

Smith, Godfrey P., *George Price: A Life Revealed*, Ian Randle Publishers, 2011, 358 pp. Godfrey Smith is an attorney and PUP politician, so this is not exactly an unbiased biography of the "father of Belize," but it is well written and goes a long way to explain why the late George Price was so beloved in Belize.

Sutherland, Anne. *The Making of Belize, Globalization in the Margins*, Bergin & Garvey, 1998, 202 pp. An American university professor with long family ties to Belize looks at "postmodern" Belize.

Thomson, P. A. B. *Belize, A Concise History*, MacMillan Caribbean, 2005, 192 pp.

Twigg, Arthur. *Understanding Belize: A Historical Guide*, Harbour, 2006, 240 pp. Arthur Twigg is the editor of a Canadian book magazine.

Waddell, D.A.G. *British Honduras, A Historical and Contemporary Survey*, Greenwood Press, 1961, reprinted 1981, 151 pp. An academic history.

Wilk, Richard R. Household Ecology: Economic Change and Domestic Life Among the Kekchi Maya in Belize, Northern Illinois University Press, 1997, 280 pp.

Young, Colville. *Creole Proverbs of Belize*, Cubola Productions, 44 pp.

Maya Atlas: The Struggle to Preserve Maya Land in Southern Belize, compiled by the Maya People of Southern Belize, Toledo Maya Cultural Council, 1997.

Living in Belize

Day-Wilson, Victoria *Moon Living Abroad in Belize*, Avalon Travel Publishing, 2012, 328 pp. It is what it is.

Dhillon, Bob, and Langan, Fred, *Business and Retirement Guide to Belize: The Last Virgin Paradise*, Dundurn, 2011, 128 pp. Short book, short on illustrations, maps and information.

Gallo, Roger. *Escape from America*, Manhattan Loft Publishing, 1997, 352 pp. Devoted to living/retiring abroad. Includes chapters on Belize. Roger Gallo later established the EscapeArtist.com website, based in Panama where he lived.

Golson, Barry and Golson, Thia. *Retirement Without Borders*, Scribner's, 2008, 432 pp. Looks at retirement options in a number of countries around the world. Lan Sluder contributed the chapter on Belize.

Gray, Bill and Gray, Claire (pseudonyms). *Belize Retirement Guide*, Preview Publishing, 4th ed., 1999, 140 pp. Guide to "living in a tropical paradise for $450 a month." Somehow, we kinda doubt it.

Koerner, Nancy R., *Belize Survivor: The Darker Side of Paradise*, NKD Marketing, 2007, 300 pp. Personal memoir of being abused in a relationship in Belize. Not so much about Belize as about the author.

King, Emory. *"Hey, Dad, This Is Belize,"* Tropical Books, Belize, 4th printing, 114 pp. Collection of vignettes about Belize and Belizeans. Originally appeared in the Belize Times and other publications.

— *How to Visit, Invest or Retire in Belize,* Tropical Books, 1989, 32 pp. Early booklet on the subject.

— *"I Spent It All In Belize,"* Tropical Books, 194 pp. More sketches of Belizean life. Emory King was a genius at picking book titles.

Marsh, Sonia, *Freeways to Flip-Flops, A Family's Year of Gutsy Living on a Tropical Island,* Gutsy Publications, 2012, 328 pp. A breezy memoir of a family moving from Southern California to Belize and trying to make a life on Ambergris Caye. It wasn't long before the author picked up and left.

Peham, Helga. *Escaping the Rat Race – Freedom in Paradise,* World Audience, 2007, 344 pp. A series of interviews with expats and others in Belize, by a woman who lived in Corozal. Also available in a Kindle edition.

Roebuck, G., *Moving to Belize, Not for Me!* CreateSpace, 2014, 102 pp. Thin little book. Everyone is entitled to an opinion.

Salisbury, Christina and Salisbury, Kirby. *Treehouse Perspectives: Living High on Little,* Mill City Press, 2009, 324 pp. Memoir of a couple's 36 years living in a treehouse in Toledo.

Sluder, Lan. *Living Abroad in Belize,* Avalon, 2005, 367 pp. Comprehensive guide to living, retiring, working, and investing in Belize.

— *Adapter Kit: Belize,* Avalon, 2001, 261 pp. The predecessor edition of *Living Abroad in Belize.* Still in the libraries of many expats and hotel owners in Belize.

-- *Easy Belize: How to Live, Retire, Work and Invest in Belize, the English Speaking, Frost Free Paradise on the Caribbean Coast,* Equator, originally published in 2010, fully revised and expanded 2016, 282 pp. This is the new edition of the best-selling book and ebook on living or retiring in Belize. Available from Amazon.com as a paperback and in a Kindle edition.

-- *Island Living in Belize,* Equator, 2010, 201 pp. This revised edition of the eBook focuses on retiring, living and investing on Ambergris Caye, Caye Caulker and other islands in Belize. Available as a paperback and in a Kindle edition.

Memoirs

Conroy, Richard Timothy. *Our Man in Belize,* St. Martin's, 1997, 324 pp. Fascinating, highly readable memoir of life in former British Honduras in the late 1950s and early 60s. We love this book!

DeMarks, Dean Fortune. *The Tourist: Who's Too Dangerous for Belize,* BookSurge Publishing, 2009, 354 pp. Semi-literate account of why Belize is such a terrible place, by a would-be Placencia real estate developer who was deported from the country.

Fry, Joan. *How to Cook a Tapir: A Memoir of Belize,* University of Nebraska Press, 2009, 294 pp. Fascinating recollections of a young American woman's experiences in Toledo in the early 1960s.

King, Emory. *The Little World of Danny Vasquez,* Tropical Books, 1989, 134 pp. Emory King's presentation of his father-in-law's memoirs.

Natural History

Ames, Oakes and Correll, Donovan Stewart. *Orchids of Guatemala and Belize,* Dover Publications, 1985, 779 pp. with 204 black-and-white illustrations. Republication of Chicago Natural History Museum 1953 field guide and 1965 supplement. Exhaustive, covering 527 species.

Arvigo, Rosita and Balick, Michael. *Rainforest Remedies, One Hundred Healing Herbs of Belize,* Lotus Press, 1993, 221 pp. Guide to traditional Mayan/Belizean herbal remedies.

Arvigo, Rosita with Epstein, Nadine and Yaquinto, Marilyn. *Sastun, My Apprenticeship with a Maya Healer,* HarperSanFrancisco, 1994,190 pp. Story of Arvigo's time with Don Elijio Panti.

Arvigo, Rosita with Epstein, Nadine. Rainforest Home Remedies: The Maya Way to Heal Your Body and Replenish Your Soul, HarperOne, 2001, 240 pp.

Barcott, Bruce. *The Last Flight of the Scarlet Macaw: One Woman's Fight to Save the World's Most Beautiful Bird,* Random House, 2008 hard cover, 2009 paper, 336 pp. Remarkable, gripping story of Sharon Matola's fight against the Chalillo dam.

Beletsky, Les. *Travellers' Wildlife Guide, Belize and Northern Guatemala,* Travellers' Wildlife Guides, 2010, 477 pp. Lavishly color-illustrated guide, oriented to the amateur, to the most commonly spotted mammals, birds, amphibians, reptiles, fish and corals.

Belize Bird Guide, Rainforest Productions, 2012. A 14-page laminated pamphlet to help you identify common birds in Belize.

Campbell, Jonathan A. *Amphibians and Reptiles of Northern Guatemala, the Yucatán, and Belize,* University of Oklahoma Press, 1998, 380 pp., with 176 color photographs. The best guide to herpetofauna of the region.

Emmons, Katherine. Cockscomb Basin Wildlife Sanctuary: Its History, Flora and Fauna for Visitors, Teachers and Scientists, Community Conservation Consultants, 1996. Definitive on the subject.

Frenz, Bert, *A Birders Guide to Belize,* American Birding Association, 2012, 374 pp. The newest and one of the most useful books on birding in Belize. It has a detailed guide to the locations where you're likely to see specific birds. However, for bird identification you'll need Lee Jones' *Birds of Belize (see below).*

Greenfield, David W. and Thomerson, Jamie E. *Fishes of the Continental Waters of Belize,* University Press of Florida, 1997, 311 pp. Comprehensive guide, with black-and-white illustrations.

Edwards, Ernest Preston, illustrated by Butler, E.M. *A Field Guide to the Birds of Mexico and Adjacent Areas: Belize, Guatemala, and El Salvador,* University of Texas Press, 1998, 288 pp. This is used by many local guides in Belize.

Harris, Kate. *Trees of Belize,* self-published, 2009, 120 pp. Handy guide to common and notable trees of Belize, with color photos of most of them.

Horwich, Robert H. *A Belizean Rain Forest,* Orang-utan Press, 1990, 420 pp. A look at the Community Baboon Sanctuary and the northern forests of Belize.

Jones, H. Lee and Gardner, Dana. *Birds of Belize,* University of Texas Press, 2004, 445 pp. The gold standard of Belize bird books. A must for any birder traveling to Belize.

Keesmaat, Irene, *A Rainbow of Colors, A Guide to the Flowers of Belize,* Cubola, 2011, 30 pp. Short booklet on some popular flowers of Belize.

Koeppel, Dan, *Banana, The Fate of the Fruit That Changed the World,* Hudson Street Press, 2008, 281 pp. Fascinating story of how the banana became the most popular fruit in the world. Sections of this book are on banana production in British Honduras/Belize.

LaBastille, A. *Birds of the Mayas,* West of the Winds Publications, 1993.

Lee, Julian. A Field Guide to the Amphibians and Reptiles of the Maya World: The Lowlands of Mexico, Northern Guatemala and Belize, Cornell University Press, 2000, 488 pp.

Matola, Sharon. *Birds of Belize, A Field Handbook,* Belize Zoo, 28 pp.

Meyer, John R. and Foster, Carol Farneti. *A Guide to the Frogs and Toads of Belize,* Krieger Publishing, 1996.

Miller, Carolyn M. and Miller, Bruce W. *Exploring the Tropical Forest at Chan Chich Lodge Belize,* Wildlife Conservation Society, 2nd. ed., 1994, 51 pp.

Peterson, Roger Tory and Chalif, Edward L. *A Field Guide to Mexican Birds: Mexico, Guatemala, Belize, El Salvador,* Peterson Field Guides/Houghton-Mifflin, 1999. The birder's pal, though it lacks Spanish names of birds.

Rabinowitz, Alan. *Jaguar,* Arbor House, 1986, 368 pp. Fascinating story of effort to establish the Cockscomb Preserve.

Reichling, Steven B. *Tarantulas of Belize,* Krieger Publishing Co., 2003, 148 pp. Everything you ever wanted to know about tarantulas in Belize.

Sayers, Brendan, and Adams, Brett, *A Guide to the Orchids of Belize,* Cubola, 2009, 152 pp. Not as thorough as some orchid guides but certainly sufficient for the layperson.

Stafford, Peter J. and Meyer, John R. *A Guide to the Reptiles of Belize,* Academic Press, 1999, 356 pp.

Stevens, Kate. *Jungle Walk.* Birds and animals of Belize, with many illustrations

Woods, R.L., Reid, S.T. and Reid, A.M. *The Field Guide to Ambergris*

Caye. Near exhaustive study of the island and surrounding sea.

Wright, Charles. *Land in British Honduras: A Report of the British Honduras Land Use Survey Team,* Her Majesty's Stationery Office, 1959, 327 pp. What began as a soils survey by Toledo resident Charles Wright became a detailed analysis of farming practices and land use in mid-twentieth century British Honduras.

Snakes of Belize, Belize Audubon Society, 55 pp. Short guide to the snakes you probably won't see in Belize.

Tales of Travel

Canby, Peter. *Heart of the Sky, Travels Among the Maya,* HarperCollins, 1992, 368 pp. Modern classic on the modern Maya.

Chaplin, Gordon. *The Fever Coast Log,* Simon & Schuster, 1992, 229 pp. Couple sets sail aboard the Lord Jim to sail the Caribbean Coast. You know it's all going to end badly.

Faber, Carol and Perlow, Paula. *2 Jamericans Travel to San Pedro, Belize,* Trafford Publishing, 2006, 136 pp. Little book on the experiences of two women vacationing in San Pedro.

Davis, Richard Harding. *Three Gringos in Venezuela and Central America,* Harper & Brothers, 1896. Early travelogue begins in British Honduras.

Heistand, Emily. The Very Rich Hours: Travel in Orkney, Belize, the Everglades and Greece, Beacon Press, 1992, 236 pp.

Janson, Thor. Belize, *Land of the Free by the Carib Sea,* Bowen & Bowen, 2000, 96 pp. Published in Belize, this book has wonderful photos of the country and the people.

Huxley, Aldous. *Beyond the Mexique Bay,* Greenwood, 1975. First published in 1934, this book by the author of *Brave New World* holds the record for the most-quoted comment on British Honduras: "... if the world had any ends, British Honduras would surely be one of them."

Pride, Nigel. *A Butterfly Sings to Pacaya,* Constable. A 1970s trip through Mexico, Belize and Guatemala.

Roberts, Orlando W. *Voyages and Excursions on the East Coast and in the Interior of Central America,* University of Florida Press, reprint 1965 (originally published in 1827).

Sluder, Lan, *Rambles Around Belize,* 2005-2012. Short ebooks, published annually, on travels around Belize.

Stratman, Steve. *Belize to Guatemala: a nine-day adventure guide,* The Artful

Nomad Company, 2006, 60 pp. The author narrates a short trip from Caye Caulker via San Ignacio to Flores and Tikal, Guatemala.

Straughan, Robert P. *Adventure in Belize,* A.S. Barnes & Co., 1975, 215 pp. Explorations in Belize, by a pet store and tropical fish store owner.

Stephens, John L. *Incidents of Travel in Central America, Chiapas and Yucatan,* Harper and Brothers, 1841. The great classic of early Central American travel books.

Wright, Ronald. *Time Among the Maya: Travels in Belize, Guatemala and Mexico,* Grove Press, 2000, 464 pages. Travel diary in impressionistic style.

Maps and Atlases

Ambergris Caye Belize Dive Map & Reef Creatures Guide, Franko Maps, 2011. Laminated fish card.

Atlas of Belize, Cubola Productions, 20th ed., 1995, 32 pp. with 11 maps and 80 photographs. Prepared for use in schools.

Belize Atolls Dive Map & Reef Creatures Guide, Franko Maps, 2013. A small map of the atolls is on one side and an identification guide to fishes around the atolls is on the other. Laminated. Useful aid for divers and snorkelers.

Belize National Geographic Adventure Map, National Geographic Maps, 2009. Helpful, but with some errors.

Belize Traveller's Map, ITMB, 2005. The best general road map of Belize, although it is now somewhat out of date. Scale 1:250,000.

British Ordnance Survey, Topographical Map of Belize, 1991. Two sheets, with maps of Belize City and towns on reverse. 1:250,000-scale. Out of print.

British Ordnance Survey, Area Topographical Maps, 1970s-1990s. Country is divided into 44 sections, each 1:50,000-scale. Out of print.

Insight Fleximap Belize, American Map, 2003. Sturdy and water-resistant but not fully up-to-date.

Laminated Belize Map, Borsch, 2012. German cartography company produced this handy, durable map. Scale 1:500,000. Would have been nice if the scale were a little larger. In English, Spanish, French and Italian.

Wall Map of Belize, Cubola Productions. This large 36 x 58 inch color map of Belize is suitable for hanging on your wall. Scale is 1:250,000.

APPENDIX B: BELIZE ATTORNEYS

The following list of attorneys practicing in Belize was provided by the U.S. Embassy in Belize. Neither the Embassy nor the author assumes any responsibility for the professional ability of the individuals or firms listed here. Names are listed alphabetically, and the order in which they appear has no other significance. The information in the list on professional credentials, areas of expertise and language ability are provided directly by the lawyers. You may receive additional information about the individuals by contacting the Belize Bar Association at 501-227-2785.

ARGUELLES, EMIL of ARGUELLES & COMPANY LLC, 35 New Road, Belize. Born July 4, 1972, Belize. Graduated from Marquette University, B.A.; U.W.I., LL.B.; Norman Manley Law School, C.L.E. Trust & Estate Practitioner (TEP). Admitted to Belize Bar in 1998. Appointed Speaker of House of Representatives in 2008. Corresponds in English. Corporate, Tax, Intellectual Property, Real Estate and General Practice. Can provide translator/reporter/ stenographer/notary. Will take cases outside Belize City. Office Phone: 501-223-0088, 223-0858. Fax: 223-6403. Cell Phone: 610-2961. Email: info@belizelawyer.com/ Website: www.belizelawyer.com. Personal Email: belizelawyer@hotmail.com

ARNOLD, ELLIS R. LL.B. (Hons) CLE 52 Albert Street, Belize City, Belize. Graduated from the Norman Manley Law School, C.L.E.; University of the West Indies LL.B. in 1977. Admitted to Belize Bar in 1983. Corresponds in English. General Practice and criminal matters. Notary Public. Will take cases outside of Belize City. Office phone 501-227-0810; 227-1106; Fax: 227-1119; Cell: 610-1276 E-mail: ellisarnold@hotmail.com

BARROW, DYLAN, of the LAW OFFICES OF RAYMOND H. BARROW, 121 Albert Street, Belize City, Belize. Born January 24, 1950, Belize. Graduated from U.W.I. C.L.E. Admitted to Belize Bar in 1985. Corresponds in English. General Practice and Criminal Matters. Can provide translator / reporter / stenographer / notary. Office Phone: 501-227-2912. Fax: 227-1270.

BRADLEY, JR., LEO, 90A New Road, Belize City, Belize. Born December 31, 1967, Belize. Graduated from St. Thomas University, B.A. U.W.I., LLB. Norman Manley Law School, C.L.E. Admitted to Belize Bar in 1998. Corresponds in English and Spanish. General Practice and Criminal Matters. Can provide translator / reporter / stenographer / notary. Office Phone: 501-223-3014

CHEBAT, MICHELLE of SHOMAN, CHEBAT, & ASSOC., 53 Barrack Road, Belize City, Belize. Born January 27, 1964, Belize City, Belize. Graduated from U.W.I., C.L.E. Admitted to Belize Bar in 1988. Corresponds in English and Spanish. General Practice with specialty in commercial / corporate / offshore. Can provide translator / reporter / stenographer / notary. Will take cases outside Belize City. Office Phone: 223-4160 / 223-4161 Fax: 223-4222. Email: attorney@btl.net www.shomanchebat.com

COURTENAY, S.C., DEREK of W. H. COURTENAY & CO., 1876 Hutson Street, Belize City, Belize. Corresponds in English and Spanish. Commercial and General Practice. Can provide notary. Office Phone: 501-223-5701; 224-4248. Fax: 223-9962. Email: derek@courtenaylaw.com

COURTENAY, S.C., DENISE of W. H. COURTENAY & CO., 1876 Hutson Street, Belize City, Belize. Corresponds in English and Spanish. Commercial and General Practice. Can provide notary. Office Phone: 501-223-5701; 224-4248. Fax: 223-9962. Email: denise@courtenaylaw.com

COURTENAY, JEREMY of W. H. COURTENAY & CO., 1876 Hutson Street, Belize City, Belize. Corresponds in English. Commercial and General Practice. Office Phone: 501-223-5701; 224-4248. Fax: 223-9962. Email: jeremy@courtenaylaw.com

RETREAGE, VANESSA of W. H. COURTENAY & CO., 1876 Hutson Street, Belize City, Belize. Corresponds in English. Commercial and General Practice. Office Phone: 223-5701; 224-4248. Fax: 223-9962. Email: vanessa@courtenaylaw.com

LINDO, DEAN R. of LINDO'S LAW FIRM, 7 Church Street, (P.O. Box 558, Belize City, Belize. Born September 4, 1932, Belize. Graduated from Wesley College. NYU, BSc and LL.M. University of Durham, England, LL.B. (Hons.). Gray's Inn. Admitted to the Belize Bar in 1964. Corresponds in English and Spanish. General Practice. Can Provide translator / reporter / stenographer / notary. Will take cases outside Belize City. Office Phone: (501) 227-7388 Fax: (501) 2275168 Home Phone: 224-4217 Email: linlaw@btl.net

LUMOR, FRED of MUSA & BALDERAMOS, 3750 University Blvd Edem Place, P.O. Box 2577, Belize City, Belize. Born November 17, 1952, Ghana. Graduated from Rivers State in Nigeria, LL.B. (Hons.) Ministry of Justice 4.5 years. Corresponds in English. General Practice. Can provide translator / reporter / stenographer / notary. Will take cases outside Belize City. Office Phone: 501-223-6024 Fax: 501-223-6001. Email: flumor_co@yahoo.com

MARIN, MAGALI G. , 99 Albert Street, P.O. Box 617, Belize City, Belize. Born November 18, 1971, Belize City. Graduated from University of Oklahoma, B.A. U.W.I., LL.B. Norman Manley Law School, C.L.E. Admitted to the Belize Bar in 1997. Corresponds in English and Spanish. General Practice. Can provide translator / reporter / stenographer / notary. Will take cases outside Belize City. Office Phone: 501-227-5280 Fax: 501-227-5278. Email: attorneys@barrowandwilliams.com Website: www.barrowandwilliams.com

MARSHALLECK, E. ANDREW of BARROW & COMPANY, 23 Regent Street, Belize City, Belize. Born July 23, 1969, Kingston, Jamaica. Graduated from Regis College, BA. U.W.I., LL.B. Norman Manley Law School, C.L.E. Admitted to Belize Bar in 1996. Corresponds in English. General Practice. Can provide translator / reporter / stenographer / notary. Will take cases outside Belize City. Office Phone: 223-5900/ 223-5903/ 22-35908 Fax: 223-5913 Email barrowco@btl.net

MOORE, ANTOINETTE of the LAW OFFICES OF ANTOINETTE MOORE, Cassian Nunez Street, Dangriga Town, Stann

Creek District. Born June 3, 1955, Brooklyn, New York. Graduated from Lawrence University, B.A. Loyola University of Chicago, J.D. Norman Manley Law School, C.L.E. Admitted to Belize Bar in 1996. Temporary member of Belize Supreme Court. Corresponds in English and some Spanish. General Practice and Criminal Matters. Can provide translator, reporter, stenographer and notary. Will take cases outside Belize City. Office Phone: 522-2457 Fax: 522-2457 Email: moorelaw@btl.net

MUSA-POTT, SAMIRA Suite 308 Marina Towers, Newtown Barracks Belize City, Belize. Born April 29, 1971, Belize City, Belize. Graduated from Florida Int'l University, B.A. U.W.I., LL.B. Norman Manley Law School, C.L.E. Admitted to Belize Bar in 1996. Corresponds in English and some Spanish. General Practice. Can provide translator / reporter / stenographer / notary. Will take cases outside Belize City. Office Phone: (501) 223-2238 35924 Fax: (501) 223-2360 Email: smusapott@btl.net

SABIDO, OSCAR A. of OSCAR A. SABIDO & CO., #5 New Road, Belize City, Belize. Born January 7, 1949, San Ignacio Town. Graduated from U.W.I., LL.B. Norman Manley Law School, C.L.E. Admitted to Belize Bar in 1979. Corresponds in English and fluent Spanish. General Practice and Criminal Matters. Can provide translator / reporter / stenographer / notary. Will take cases outside Belize City. Office Phone: 223-5803 Fax: 223-5839. Home Phone: 227-2901 Email: oasabido@btl.net

SOOKNANDAN, LUTCHMAN of SOOKNANDAN'S LAW FIRM, 3 Barrack Road, Belize City, Belize. Born March 21, 1948, Guyana. Graduated from U.W.I., LL.B., C.L.E. Admitted to Belize Bar in 1986. Corresponds in English. General Practice and Criminal Matters. Office Phone: 223-2469. Home phone: 223-2625 Fax: 223-5164 Email: lsooknan@btl.net

TWIST, OSWALD H. of the BELIZE LEGAL AID CENTER, 16 Bishop Street, Belize City, Belize. Born June 9, 1959, Belize. Graduated from U.W.I., LL.B. Norman Manley Law School, C.L.E. Admitted to Belize Bar in 1996. Corresponds in English. General Practice and Criminal Matters. Can provide translator / reporter / stenographer / notary. Office

Phone/Fax: 227-5781 BELMOPAN OFFICE: Phone: 822-1475 Fax: 822-1476 Home Phone: 802-3471

WILLIAMS, RODWELL of BARROW & WILLIAMS, 99 Albert Street, Belize City, Belize. Born September 29, 1956, Belize City, Belize. Graduated with B.A., LL.B., C.L.E. Admitted to Belize Bar in 1985. Corresponds in English. General Practice. Can provide translator / reporter / stenographer / notary. Will take cases outside Belize City. Office Phone: 227-5280. Fax: 227-5278 Email: attorneys@barrowandwilliams.com Website: www.barrowandwilliams.com

YOUNG, MICHAEL CLARENCE EDWARD of YOUNG'S LAW FIRM, 28 Regent Street, Belize City, Belize. Born January 7, 1955, Southhampton, England. Graduated from U.W.I., LL.B. Norman Manley Law School, (Hons) C.L.E. Admitted to Belize Bar in 1977. Solicitor of the Supreme Court of Belize. Corresponds in English. General Practice. Office Phone: 227-7406 / 72408 / 72544 Fax: 227-5157 Home Phone: 223-2519 Email: services@younglaw.bz Website: www.younglaw.bz

LOIS YOUNG BARROW & COMPANY 120 A New Road, PO Box 565, Belize City, Belize Tel: 501-223-5924 Email loisblaw@btl.net

APPENDIX C: BEST BELIZE WEBSITES

Here are some of our favorite web sites about Belize:

Destination and General Websites

www.ambergriscaye.com Impressive site with massive amount of material about Ambergris Caye. Good links to other sites, including most hotels, dive shops, real estate firms and other businesses on the island. Active message board.

www.sanpedrosun.com News about Ambergris Caye by its leading weekly newspaper

www.corozal.com Pretty good information about Corozal District, provided by students of Corozal Community College. A sister site, www.corozal.bz, has business listings and information.

www.hopkinsbelize.com Information on Hopkins village.

www.placencia.com Good tourist information on the Placencia peninsula from the BTIA.

www.destinationsbelize.com All kinds of news and information about Placencia.

www.cayecaulkervacation.com Official site of BTIA in Caulker.

www.puntagordabelize.com The official web site of the town of Punta Gorda.

www.belmopanbelize.com Information on Belize's capital city.

www.belizefirst.com On-line magazine about Belize (Lan Sluder, editor and publisher) with dozens of articles on travel, life and retirement in Belize.

www.belize.gov.bz Official site of the Government of Belize – not always up-to-date, unfortunately.

www.belizeinvest.org.bz Site of Beltraide, which is charged with attracting business investment to Belize.

www.belizenet.com Well-done site on Belize travel and other information, by folks who provide a lot of web design services in Belize. Associated with an active message board, Belize Forums at www.belizeforum.com.

www.channel5belize.com This Belize City TV station provides the most definitive and reliable source of news on Belize. The weekday evening news broadcast is provided in transcript form and also in video.

www.7newsbelize.com Another good Belize City TV station with transcripts of the evening news broadcasts.

www.belizenews.com This site has links to most newspapers, TV and radio stations, magazines and other media in Belize.

www.stonetreerecords.com Stonetree has been making Belize music since 1995.

www.cubola.com Site of publisher of books and maps on Belize.

www.travelbelize.org Recently revised version of the official site of the Belize Tourism Board, with tons of information on hotels and sightseeing.

www.fodors.com Some guidebooks authored or co-authored by Lan Sluder, including *Fodor's Belize, Fodor's The Carolinas and Georgia,* and the new *InFocus Great Smoky Mountains National Park* are published by this Random House division, and parts of these books are available on-line.

www.belizeembassy.gov Official site of the U.S. Embassy in Belize.

www.expatexchange.com This site has a fairly active forum section on moving to and living in Belize.

www.internationalliving.com This for-profit company runs articles regularly and sells reports on Belize. There's a lot of useful information, but it is laced with commercial plugs. Don't believe everything you read here.

Best Belize Blogs

http://belizebus.wordpress.com Excellent site with up-to-date information on bus, water taxi, air and other transportation options in Belize.

www.tacogirl.com Perhaps the best of all the personal blogs about Belize. Covers the country although mostly focused on Ambergris Caye, where the author lives.

http://winjama.blogspot.com Run by a man who moved to Corozal, this very helpful blog focuses on living in Belize.

http://tropicat.wordpress.com This blog is about living in the Belize bush.

http://bubbasbirdblog.blogspot.com Elbert Greer's blog on birding in Belize.

http://exploringbelizecontinues.blogspot.com Adventures of two expat women in San Pedro.

http://barnaclesbelize.blogspot.com Great Belize photos on this blog by Barnacle Bill Taylor in Maya Beach.

http://latitudesbelize.blogspot.com Put together by the owners of Changes in Latitudes B&B in San Pedro.

http://moonracerfarmbelize.blogspot.com A young couple with a small lodge in Cayo near the Mountain Pine Ridge blog on living and running a hotel in Belize.

www.caribbean-colors.blogspot.com Lee Vanderwalker, who divides her time between Caye Caulker and Chetumal, Mexico, blogs about her life and art.

Appendix D: Belize Census Key Facts

Summarized from Statistical Institute of Belize Reports on the Belize Census of 2010, the latest full Census of Belize. Some but not all Census results are updated annually or even more frequently

Population
- Belize's population is 312,971, up 30.2% from 2000
- 55% rural, 45% urban
- Median average age 22
- Average household size 3.9 persons
- 102 males for every 100 females
- 35.6% of the Belize population is age 14 or younger
- 55.8% of the Belize population is age 24 or younger

Largest Population Centers
Towns & Cities
1. Belize City 53,532
2. San Ignacio/Santa Elena 16,977
3. Belmopan City 13,654
4. Orange Walk Town 13,400
5. San Pedro 11,510
6. Corozal Town 9,871
7. Dangriga 9,096
8. Benque Viejo 5,824
9. Punta Gorda 5,205

Districts
1. Belize District 89,247
2. Cayo District 73,202
3. Orange Walk District 45,419
4. Corozal District 40,324
5. Stann Creek District 32,166
6. Toledo District 30,538

- San Pedro was the fastest-growing urban area in Belize, with the population increasing 156% since 2000

• Cayo District was the fastest-growing district, with population increasing 39% since 2000, followed by Belize District with a 34% increase

Belizean Ethnicity
• Belize's population is:
50% Mestizo
21% Creole
10% Maya
   6% Mixed Race
   4.5% Garifuna
   3.6% Mennonite
   2.1% East Indian
   1% White/Caucasian
   0.9% Asian

MARITAL AND FAMILY RELATIONSHIPS

• 33.1% of those 15 and over are married and living with spouse, 23.3% have a common law relationship, 6% are in a visiting partner relationship and 37.3% are not in a union
• 65.8% of children 18 and under are living with both parents
• 22.6% of children 18 and under are living with mother only and 2.5% with father only

FOREIGN BORN POPULATION

• Almost 15% of the population is foreign born, of which about 4 in 10 are from Guatemala and 3 in 10 are from El Salvador or Honduras
• 3,279 Belize residents or about 1% of the total Belize population (not of the foreign born) were born in the U.S. (almost double the number in 2000) and 1,567 or 0.5% in China and 667 in Canada

EDUCATION

• 87,991 Belizeans are enrolled in formal education of which 70% are in primary school and 19% in high school, and over 8% are in some type of tertiary program

RELIGION

• 40% Catholic

- 8.5% Pentecostal
- 5.5% Seventh Day Adventist
- 4.6% Anglican
- 3.8% Mennonite
- 3.6% Baptist
- 2.9% Methodist
- 2.8% Nazarene
- 1.7% Jehovah's Witness
- 10.2% Other
- 15.6% None

LABOUR FORCE

- 131,000 Belizeans are in the labour force
- About 30,000 Belizeans of the labour force, or about 23%, do not have a job (exact definition of this "unemployment rate" was not provided)
- Of those working 57% work for a private company, 25% are self-employed and 15% work for the government
- Women in the labour force are twice as likely as men not to have a job – 33.1% for women versus 16.7% for men

HOUSING

- Belize has 75,848 dwelling units, an increase of 46% since 2000
- 82% of dwelling units are houses, as opposed to apartments or condos
- 64.1% of Belizeans own their own dwelling, while 33% rent
- Of those who own, almost 79% do not have a mortgage
- 50% of dwelling units have concrete walls and 80% have sheet metal roofs
- 11% of dwellings do not have kitchens in the building
- About 83% of households cook with butane, while 15% cook with wood or charcoal and only 1% with electricity
- 48% of Belizean households have municipal garbage collection, while 27% burn garbage and 11% take it to a dump
- 85% of households have running water
- 51% of households use bottled water as their main source of drinking water
- About 65% of Belizean dwellings have flush toilets, while 31% use a

pit latrine (outhouse) and 3% have no toilet facilities
* Of those with flush toilets, 80% have septic tanks while 20% are on municipal sewage systems
* 83% of households have electricity from BEL, while 9% use kerosene lamps or candles, 4% have a drop from a neighbor, 2% have generators and 1% use solar
* Of Belizean dwellings 83% have stoves, 66% have refrigerators, 65% have washing machines, 42% have microwaves and 8% have air-conditioning; 62% have showers or tubs

COMMUNICATIONS
Of Belizean households ...
* 76% have a cell phone
* 75% have TV
* 75% have radio
* 50% have DVD player
* 26% have computer

INTERNET USAGE
* About 23% of Belizeans age 5 or over have used the internet in the past 3 months

AUTOMOBILES
* 33.7% of Belizeans have a private motor vehicle

CRIME
Households reporting being victims of crime (time frame not given):

Robbery	41.6%
Burglary	33.7%
Assault	11.8%
Shooting	2.4%
Murder/Manslaughter	2.2%
Domestic violence	2.2%
Sexual assault	1.3%

APPENDIX E: BELIZE NATIONAL PARKS

Around 40% of Belize's land is protected in government-owned national parks, monuments and reserves. There are also some quasi-official privately managed reserves. Here are some of them:

Actun Tunichil Muknal National Monument, Cayo District

Bacalar Chico National Park and Marine Reserve, Ambergris Caye, Belize District

Billy Barquedier Park, Stann Creek District

Bladen Reserve, Toledo District

Blue Hole National Monument, Lighthouse Reef Atoll, off Belize District

Burden Canal Reserve, Belize District

Chiquibul Forest Reserve, Cayo District

Chiquibul National Park, Cayo District

Cockscomb Basin Wildlife Preserve, Stann Creek District

Columbia River Forest Reserve, Toledo District

Community Baboon Sanctuary, Bermudian Landing, Belize District

Corozal Bay Reserve, Corozal District

Crooked Tree Wildlife Sanctuary, Crooked Tree, Belize District

Deep River Forest Reserve, Toledo District

Elijio Panti National Park, Cayo District

Five Blues Lakes National Park, Hummingbird Highway, Cayo District

Fresh Water Creek Forest Reserve, Corozal and Orange Walk Districts

Gales Point Wildlife Sanctuary, Belize District

Glovers Reef Marine Reserve, Glovers Atoll, off Stann Creek District

Gladden Spit and Silk Cayes Marine Reserve, off Stann Creek District

Guanacaste National Park, Belmopan, Cayo District

Half Moon Caye Natural Monument, Lighthouse Reef Atoll, off Belize District

Hol Chan Marine Reserve, off Ambergris Caye, Belize District

Honey Camp, Orange Walk and Corozal District

Laughing Bird Caye National Park, off Placencia, Stann Creek District

Manatee Preserve, Belize District

Mango Creek Forest Reserve, Stann Creek District

Mayflower Bocawina National Park, Stann Creek District

Mountain Pine Ridge Reserve, Cayo District

Paynes Creek, Toledo District

Port Honduras Marine Reserve, off Toledo District

Rio Bravo Conservation and Management Area (Programme for Belize), Orange Walk District

Sapodilla Cayes Marine Reserve, off Toledo District

Sarstoon-Temash, Toledo District

Shipstern Nature Reserve, Corozal District

Sibun River Forest Reserve, Cayo District

Sittee River Forest Reserve, Stann Creek District

Southwater Caye Marine Reserve, off southern Belize, Stann Creek District

Spanish Creek Reserve, Belize and Orange Walk Districts

St. Herman's Blue Hole National Park, Hummingbird Highway, Cayo District

Swallow Caye Reserve, Belize District

Tapir Mountain Nature Reserve, Belmopan Area, Cayo District

Victoria Peak National Monument, Stann Creek District

APPENDIX F: ARCHEOLOGICAL SITES

Most of these archeological sites are Maya sites, but several are from the British colonial period.

Altun Ha, Belize District
Barton Creek, Cayo District
Cahal Pech, Cayo District
Caracol, Cayo District
Cerros Maya, Corozal District
El Pilar, Cayo District
Lamanai, Orange Walk District
Lubaantun, Toledo District
Marco Gonzalez, Ambergris Caye, Belize District
Nim Li Punit, Toledo District
Nohoch Che'en (Caves Branch), Cayo District
Santa Rita, Corozal District
Serpon Sugar Mill, Stann Creek District
Slate Creek Preserve, Cayo District
Xunantunich, Cayo District
Yarborough Cemetery, Belize City, Belize District

ABOUT LAN SLUDER

Lan Sluder is an old Belize hand, having been reporting on and writing about Belize since 1991. The author of more than a dozen books and ebooks on Belize, Sluder has helped many people plan the adventure of a lifetime in this fascinating little English-speaking country on the Caribbean Coast of Central America.

Among Lan Sluder's Belize books, besides *Easy Belize,* are *Fodor's Belize, Living Abroad in Belize, Adapter Kit: Belize, San Pedro Cool, Belize Islands Guide, Belize Book of Lists* and *Belize First Guide to Mainland Belize.* Sluder is also founder, editor and publisher of *Belize First Magazine* – a web edition is at www.belizefirst.com.

In addition to his books on Belize, Sluder has authored several books on Asheville and the North Carolina mountains, including *Amazing Asheville, Asheville Relocation, Retirement and Visitor Guide* and *Moving to the Mountains*. He wrote *Frommer's Best Beach Vacations: Carolinas and Georgia, Fodor's InFocus Great Smoky Mountains National Park* and co-authored *Fodor's The Carolinas & Georgia*. His Asheville website is www.amazingasheville.net. In addition, he has written books on the game of bridge, *Play Bridge Today,* and a book on vintage Rolls-Royce and Bentley motorcars, *Buy a Classic Rolls-Royce or Bentley*. His forthcoming books include *All the Best in Belize, Higher Ed Cookbook* and *25 Great Private Eyes in Books, Movies and TV: Their Dives, Digs, Drives and Drinks*.

A former business newspaper editor and reporter in New Orleans, where he won a number of Press Club awards, Sluder has contributed articles on travel, retirement and business subjects to media around the world, including *The New York Times, Chicago Tribune, Miami Herald, Where to Retire,* Canada's *Globe and Mail, Bangkok Post, The Tico Times, Newsday,* TravelChannel.com and *Caribbean Travel & Life*.

Sluder was educated at Duke University and in the U.S. Army in Vietnam. When not in Belize or traveling elsewhere, Sluder lives on a mountain farm near Asheville, N.C., with wife Sheila M. Lambert, an attorney.

The opinions in this book are those of Lan Sluder. Questions, complaints and rants to Lan Sluder can be sent to him at lansluder@gmail.com. Although every effort was made to ensure that the information in this work was correct at press time, things change. We will attempt to correct any errors as soon as possible and disclaim any liability for loss or damage caused by omissions or errors.

Rose Lambert-Sluder, who shot most of the photos for this book, has traveled extensively in North, Central and South America, Europe, Eastern Europe and Turkey. She graduated with highest honors from the University of North Carolina at Chapel Hill and now is a Graduate Teaching Fellow and a graduate student in the Master of Fine Arts program in fiction at the University of Oregon at Eugene.

INDEX